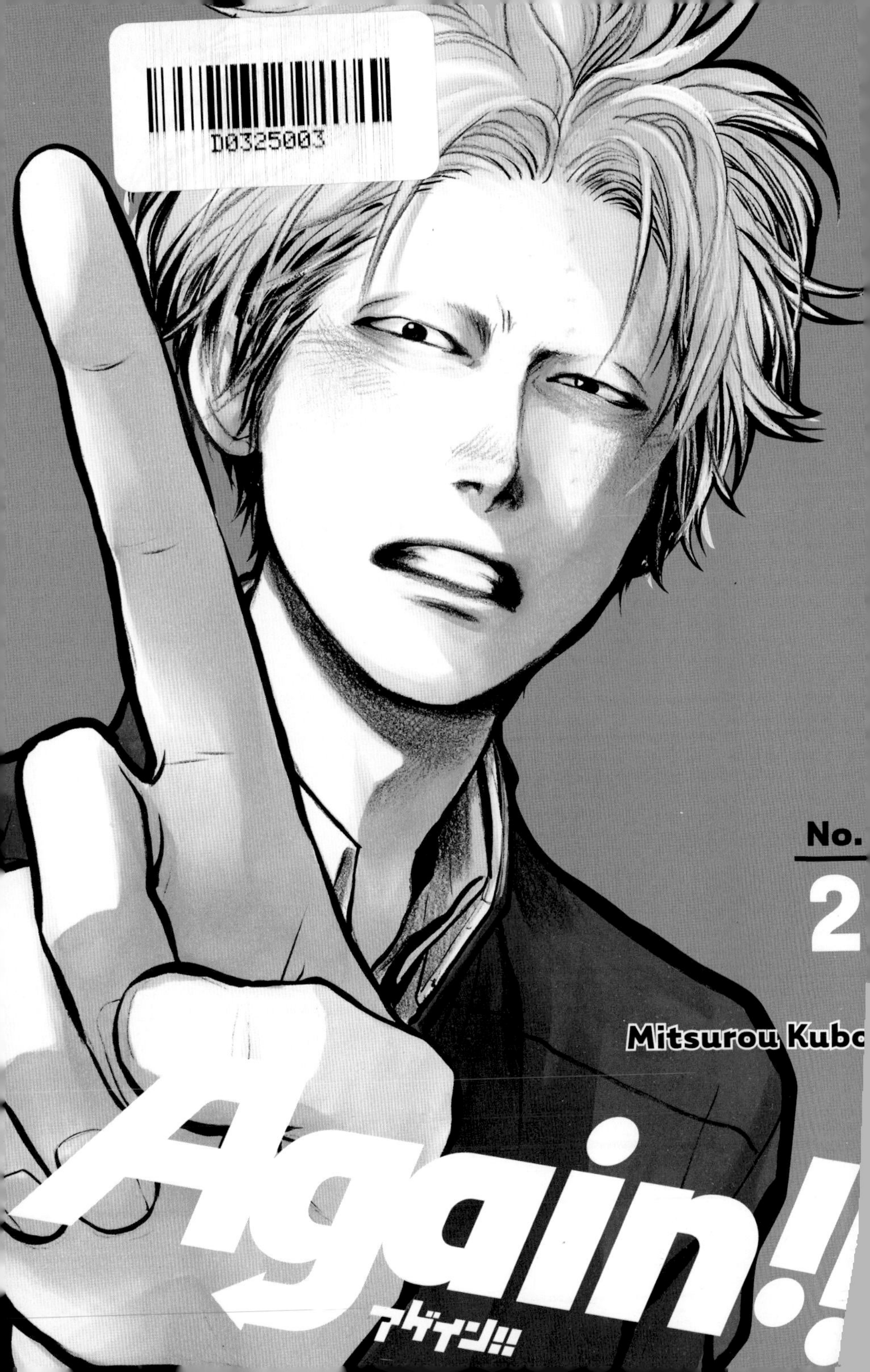
D0325003
No.
2
Mitsurou Kubo
Again!!
アゲイン!!

c o n t e n t s

Chapter 10   Hugging Hazard   003

Chapter 11   The Road to the Third-Years   021

Chapter 12   Everybody Yell Now!   043

Chapter 13   The Day Before The Big Day   061

Chapter 14   All Night Party!   077

Chapter 15   Screw It!   095

Chapter 16   Raw Feelings   113

Chapter 17   Cheer!!!   131

Chapter 18   The Girl Who Didn't Want To Leap Through Time   151

Chapter 19   Destined For Defeat   169

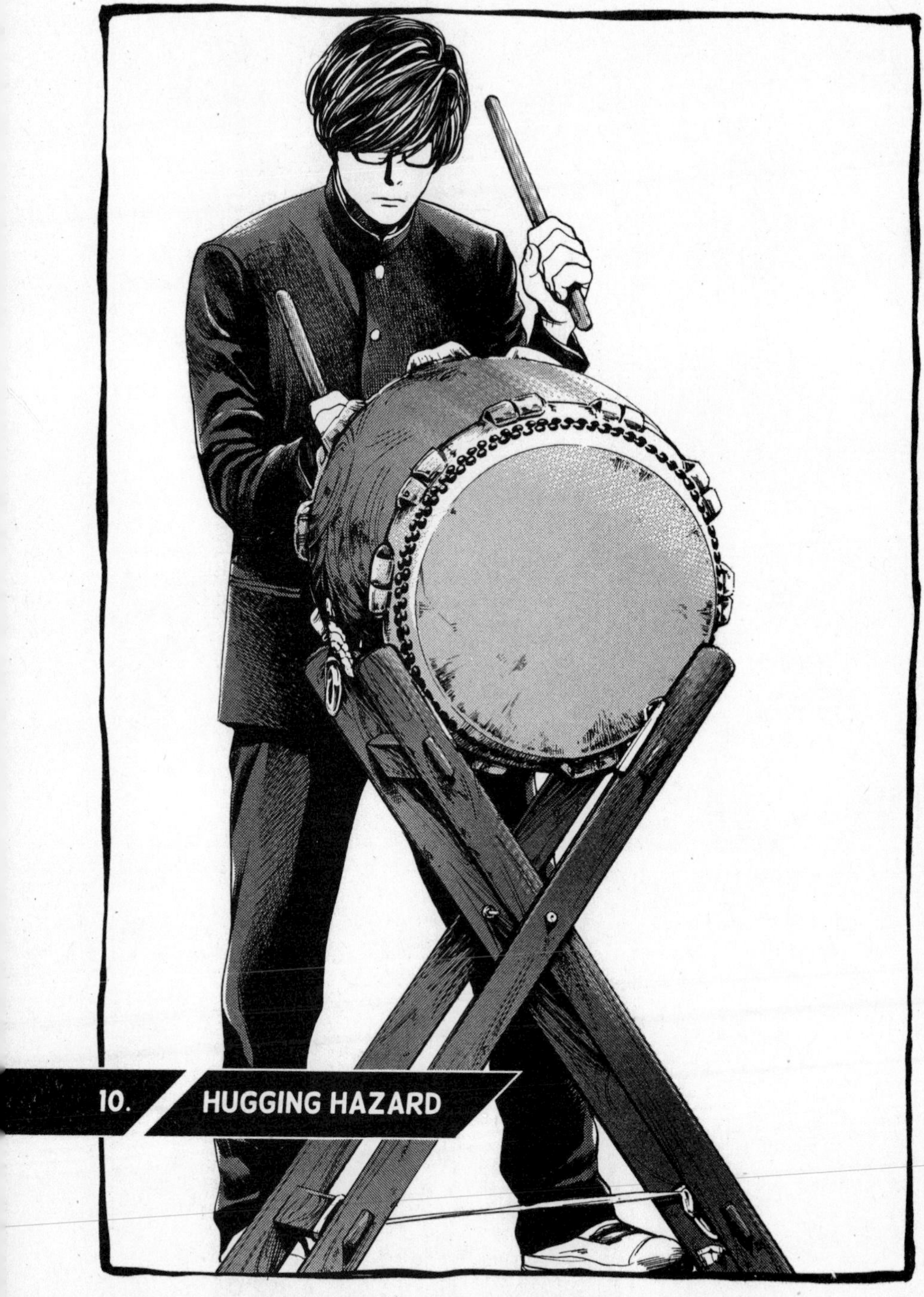

10. HUGGING HAZARD

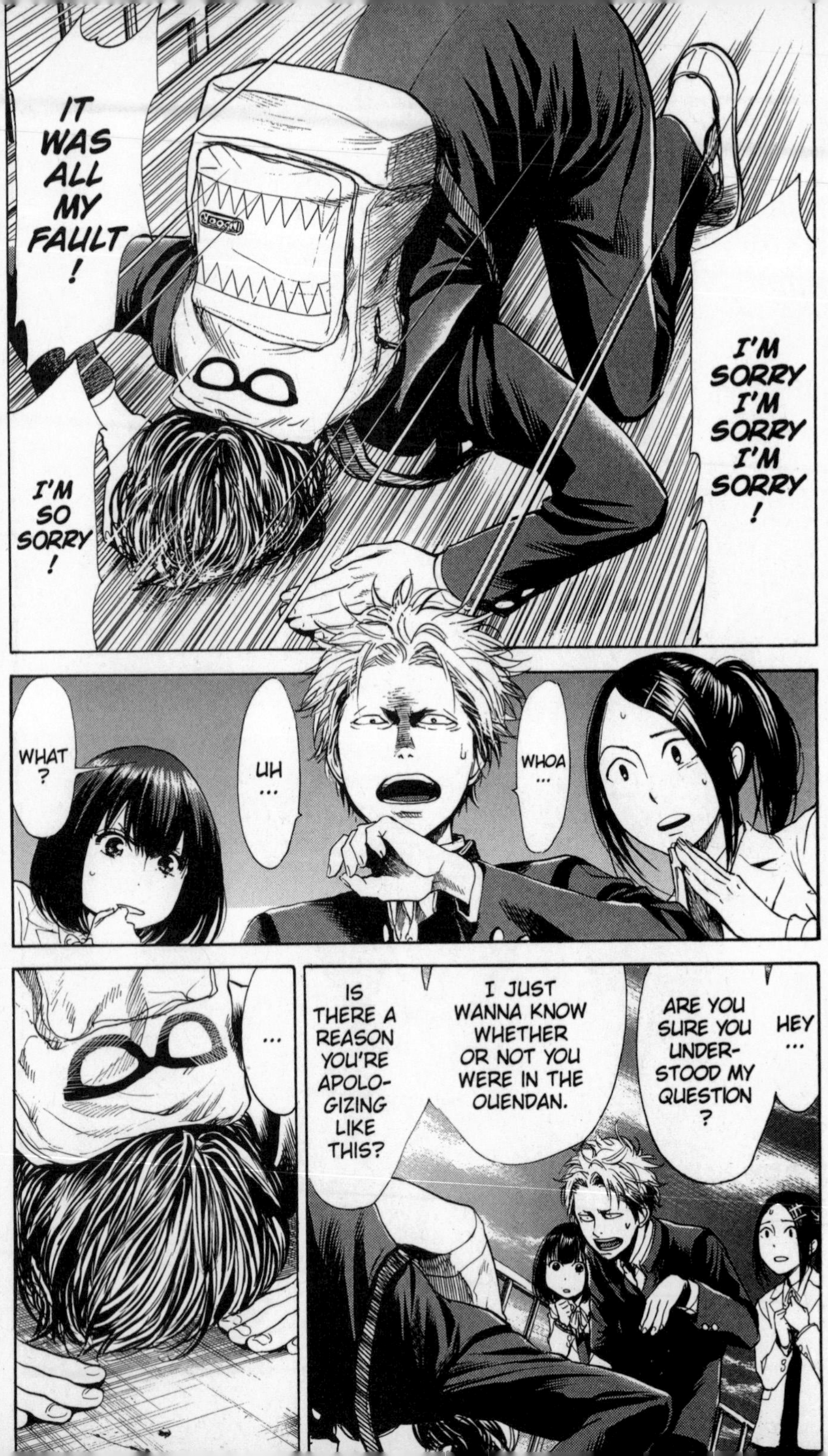
I'M SORRY I'M SORRY I'M SORRY !
IT WAS ALL MY FAULT !
I'M SO SORRY !
WHOA ...
UH ...
WHAT ?
HEY ...
ARE YOU SURE YOU UNDERSTOOD MY QUESTION ?
I JUST WANNA KNOW WHETHER OR NOT YOU WERE IN THE OUENDAN.
IS THERE A REASON YOU'RE APOLOGIZING LIKE THIS?
...

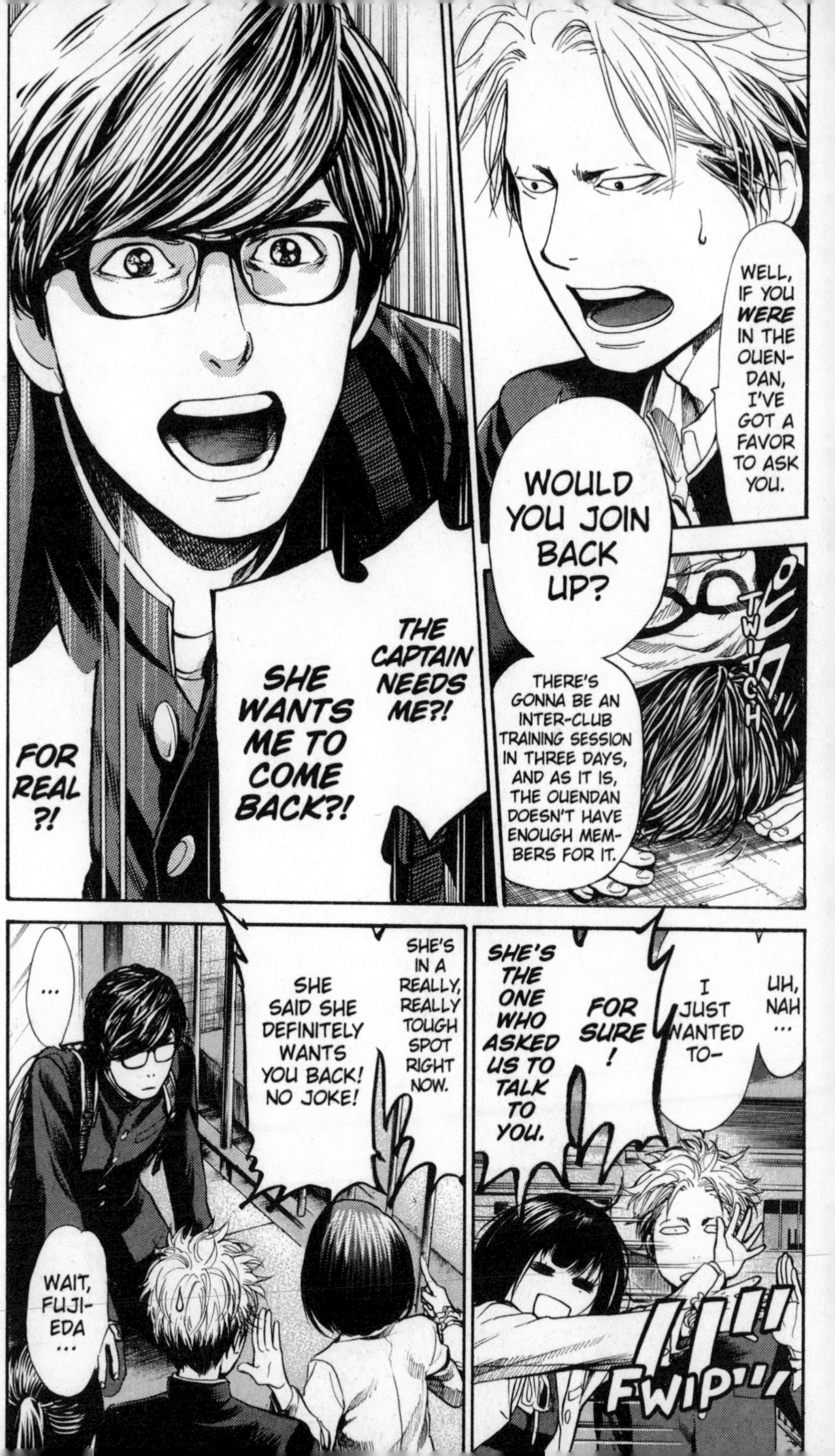
WELL, IF YOU *WERE* IN THE OUEN-DAN, I'VE GOT A FAVOR TO ASK YOU.
WOULD YOU JOIN BACK UP?
THERE'S GONNA BE AN INTER-CLUB TRAINING SESSION IN THREE DAYS, AND AS IT IS, THE OUENDAN DOESN'T HAVE ENOUGH MEM-BERS FOR IT.
TWITCH
THE CAPTAIN NEEDS ME?!
SHE WANTS ME TO COME BACK?!
FOR REAL?!
UH, NAH...
I JUST WANTED TO–
FOR SURE!
SHE'S THE ONE WHO ASKED US TO TALK TO YOU.
FWIP
SHE'S IN A REALLY, REALLY TOUGH SPOT RIGHT NOW.
SHE SAID SHE DEFINITELY WANTS YOU BACK! NO JOKE!
...
WAIT, FUJI-EDA...

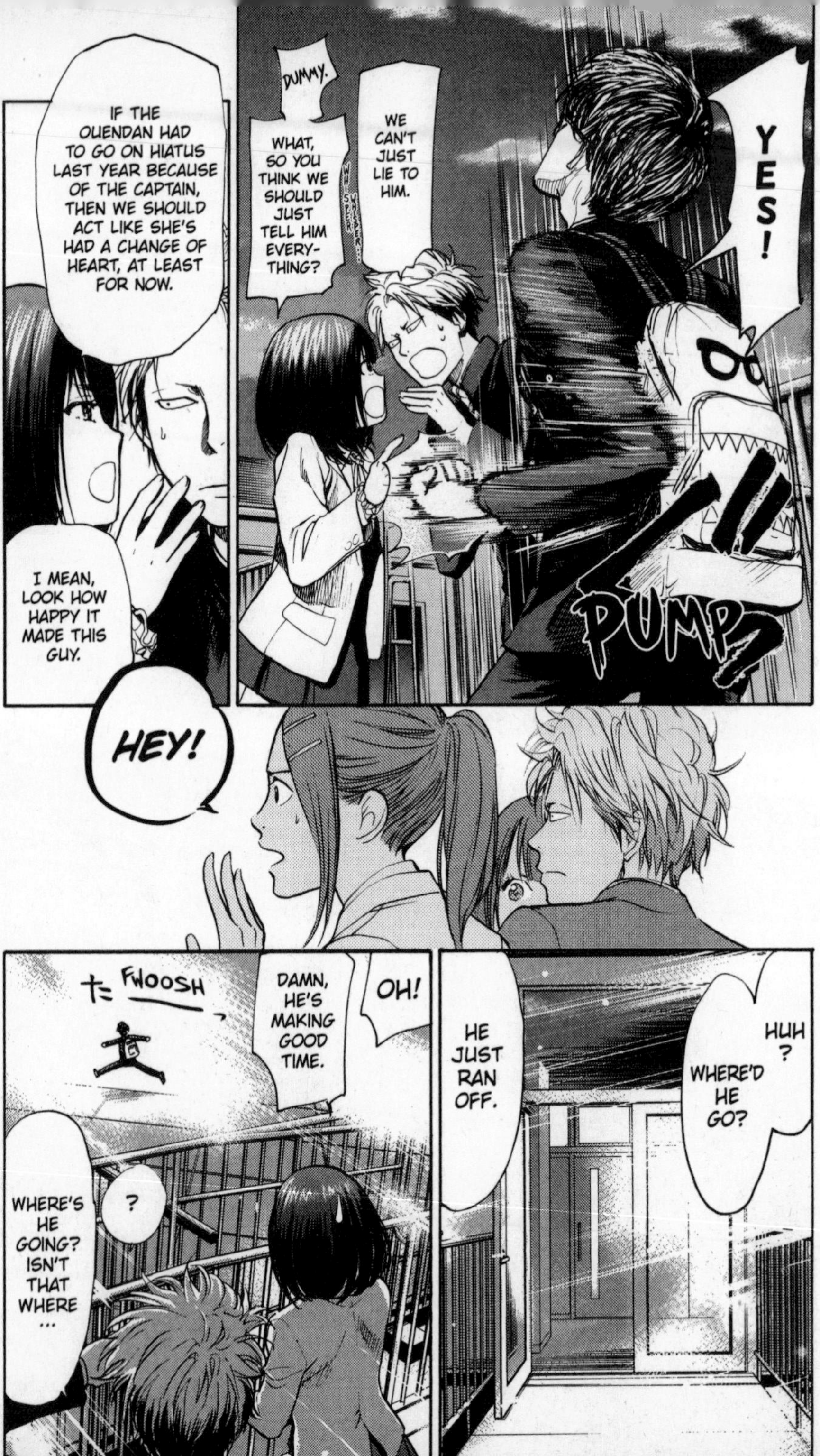
YES!
DUMMY.
WE CAN'T JUST LIE TO HIM.
WHAT, SO YOU THINK WE SHOULD JUST TELL HIM EVERYTHING?
PUMP
IF THE OUENDAN HAD TO GO ON HIATUS LAST YEAR BECAUSE OF THE CAPTAIN, THEN WE SHOULD ACT LIKE SHE'S HAD A CHANGE OF HEART, AT LEAST FOR NOW.
I MEAN, LOOK HOW HAPPY IT MADE THIS GUY.
HEY!
HUH? WHERE'D HE GO?
HE JUST RAN OFF.
OH!
DAMN, HE'S MAKING GOOD TIME.
FWOOSH
?
WHERE'S HE GOING? ISN'T THAT WHERE ...

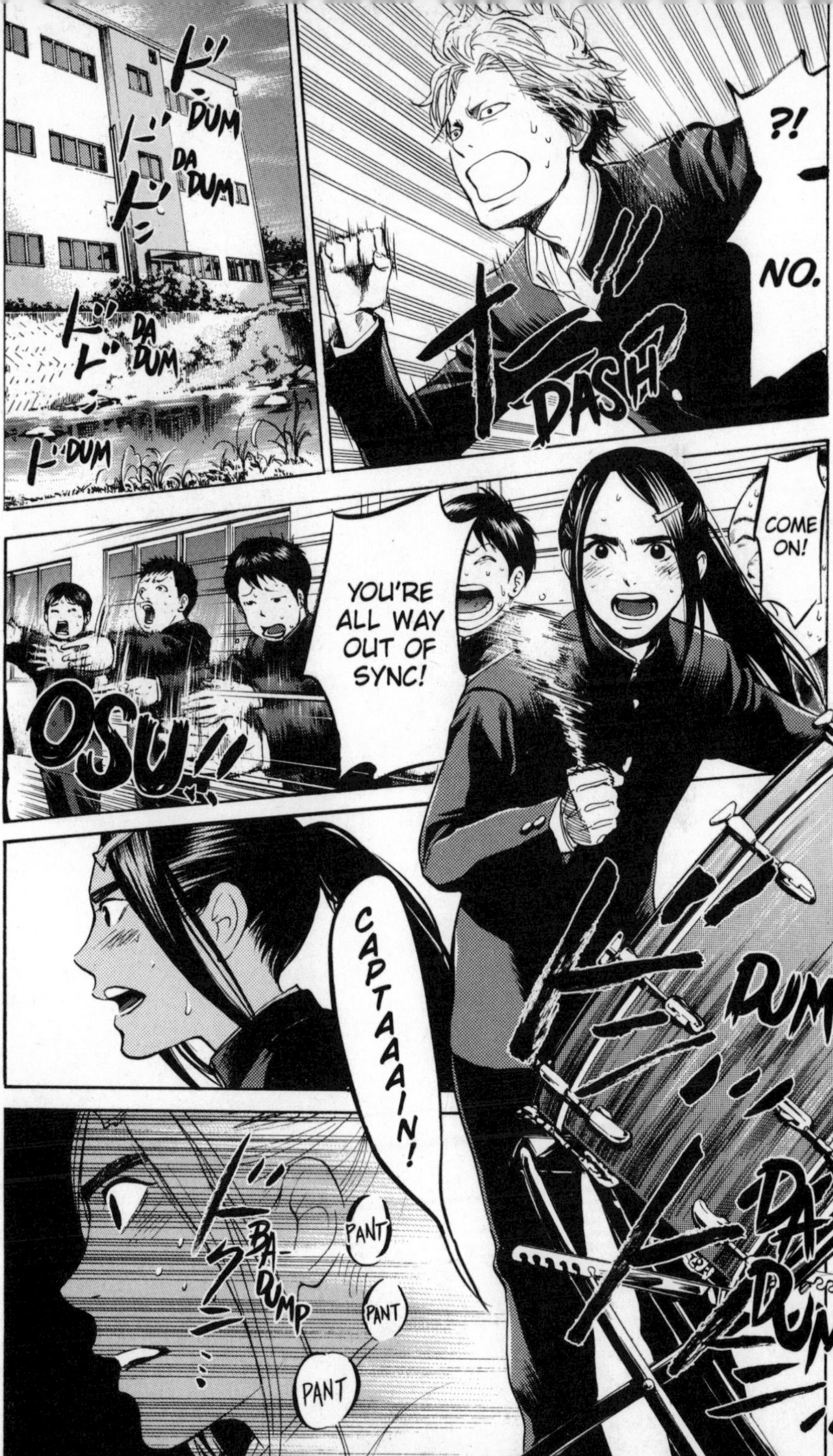
?!
NO.
DASH.
DUM
DA DUM
DA DUM
DUM
COME ON!
YOU'RE ALL WAY OUT OF SYNC!
OSU!!
DUM
DA DUM
CAPTAAAAIN!
BA DUMP
PANT
PANT
PANT

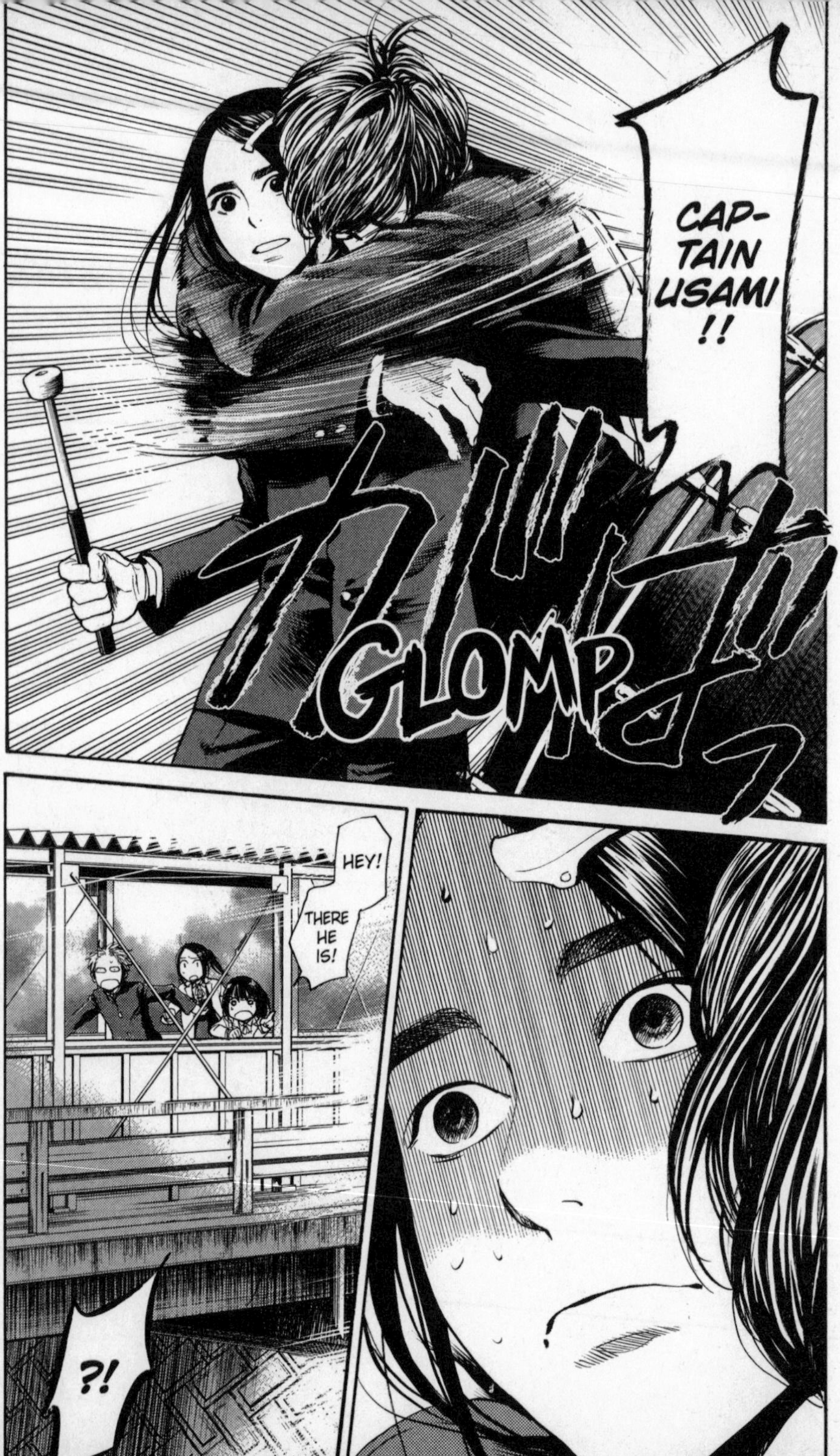

CAP-TAIN USAMI!!
GLOMP
HEY!
THERE HE IS!
?!

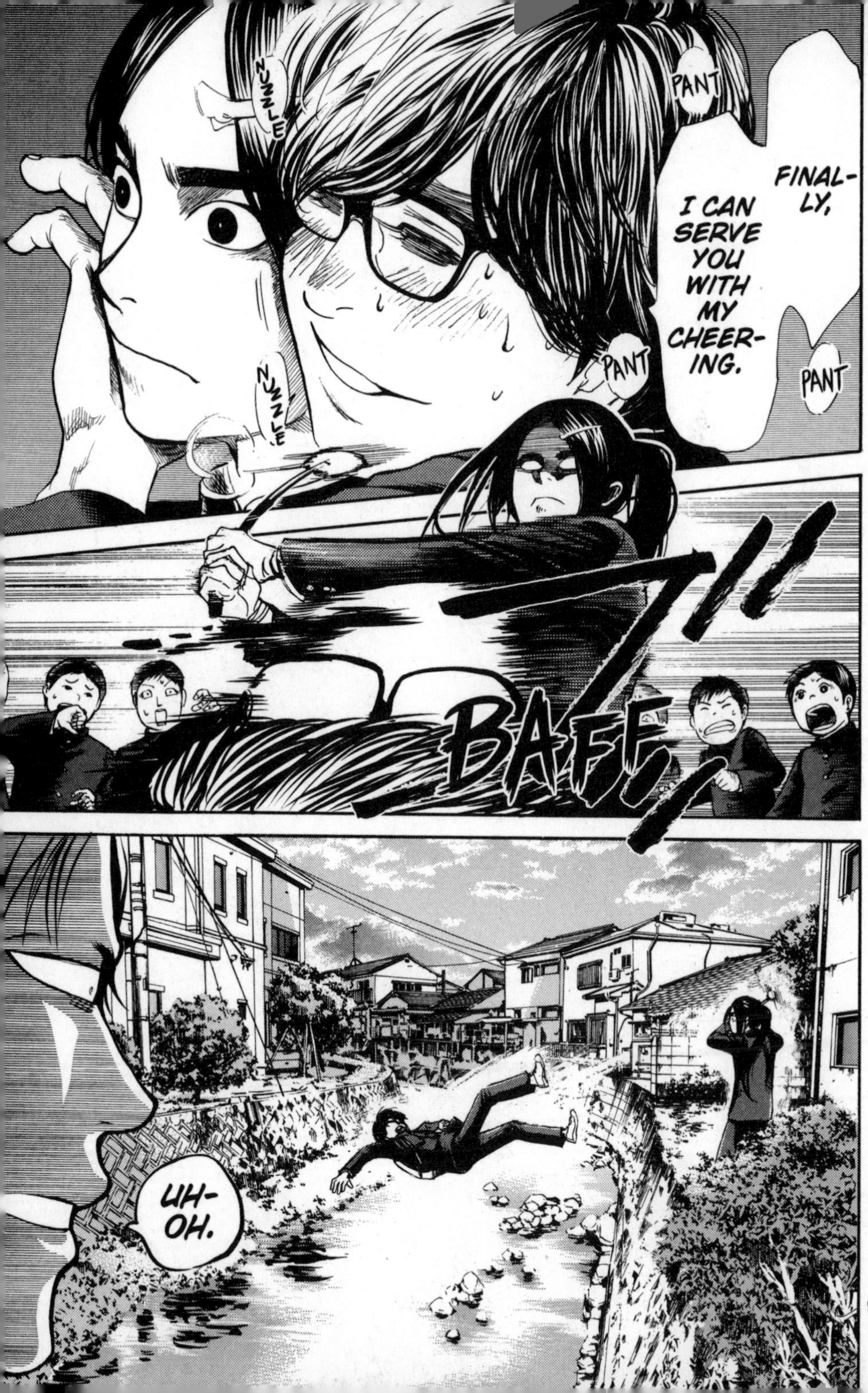
PANT
FINAL-LY, I CAN SERVE YOU WITH MY CHEER-ING.
PANT
PANT
NUZZLE
NUZZLE
BAFF
UH-OH.

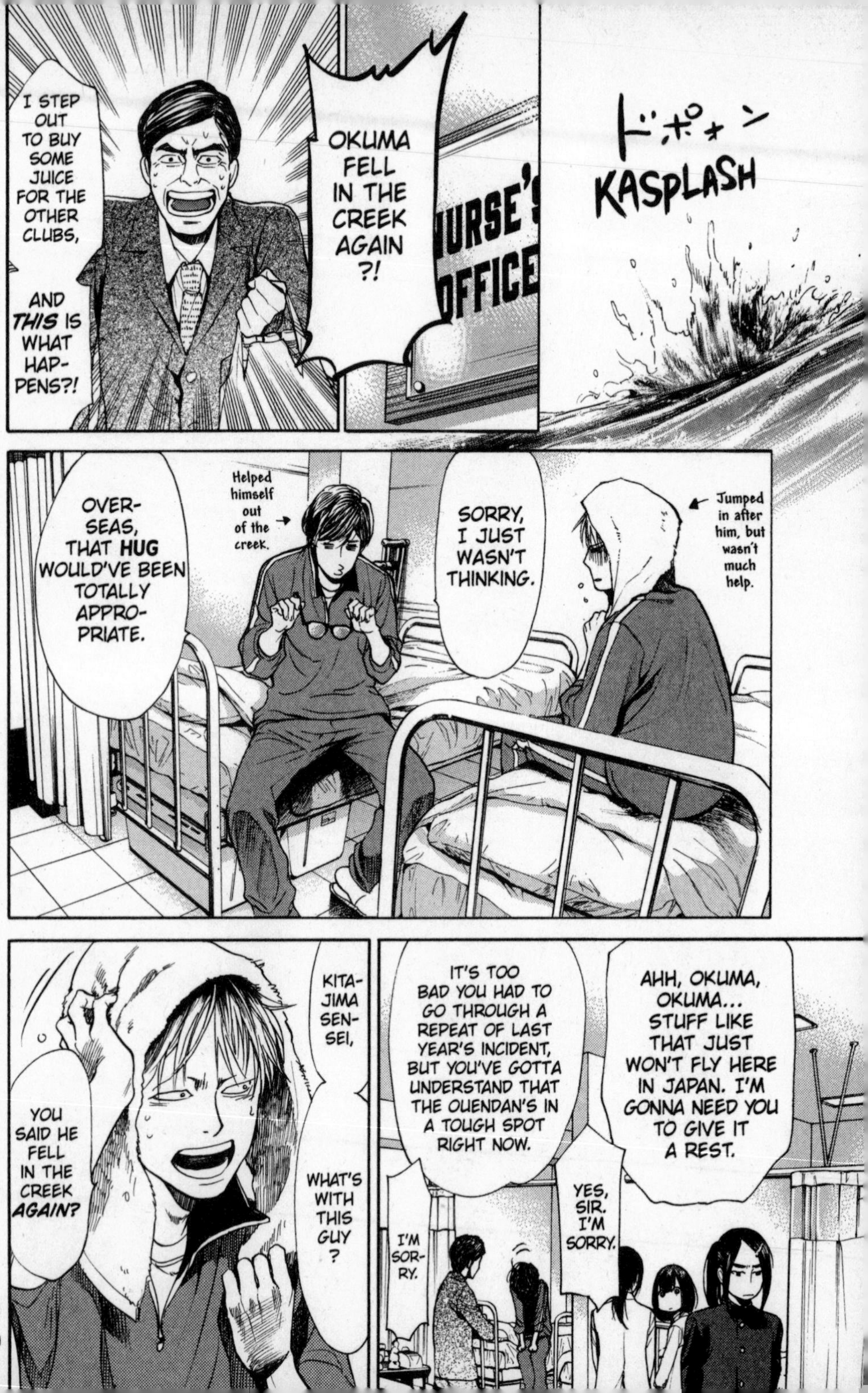

ドポォン
KASPLASH
NURSE'S OFFICE
OKUMA FELL IN THE CREEK AGAIN?!
I STEP OUT TO BUY SOME JUICE FOR THE OTHER CLUBS,
AND ***THIS*** IS WHAT HAP-PENS?!
Jumped in after him, but wasn't much help.
SORRY, I JUST WASN'T THINKING.
Helped himself out of the creek.
OVER-SEAS, THAT **HUG** WOULD'VE BEEN TOTALLY APPRO-PRIATE.
AHH, OKUMA, OKUMA... STUFF LIKE THAT JUST WON'T FLY HERE IN JAPAN. I'M GONNA NEED YOU TO GIVE IT A REST.
IT'S TOO BAD YOU HAD TO GO THROUGH A REPEAT OF LAST YEAR'S INCIDENT, BUT YOU'VE GOTTA UNDERSTAND THAT THE OUENDAN'S IN A TOUGH SPOT RIGHT NOW.
YES, SIR. I'M SORRY.
I'M SOR-RY.
KITA-JIMA SEN-SEI,
WHAT'S WITH THIS GUY?
YOU SAID HE FELL IN THE CREEK ***AGAIN?***

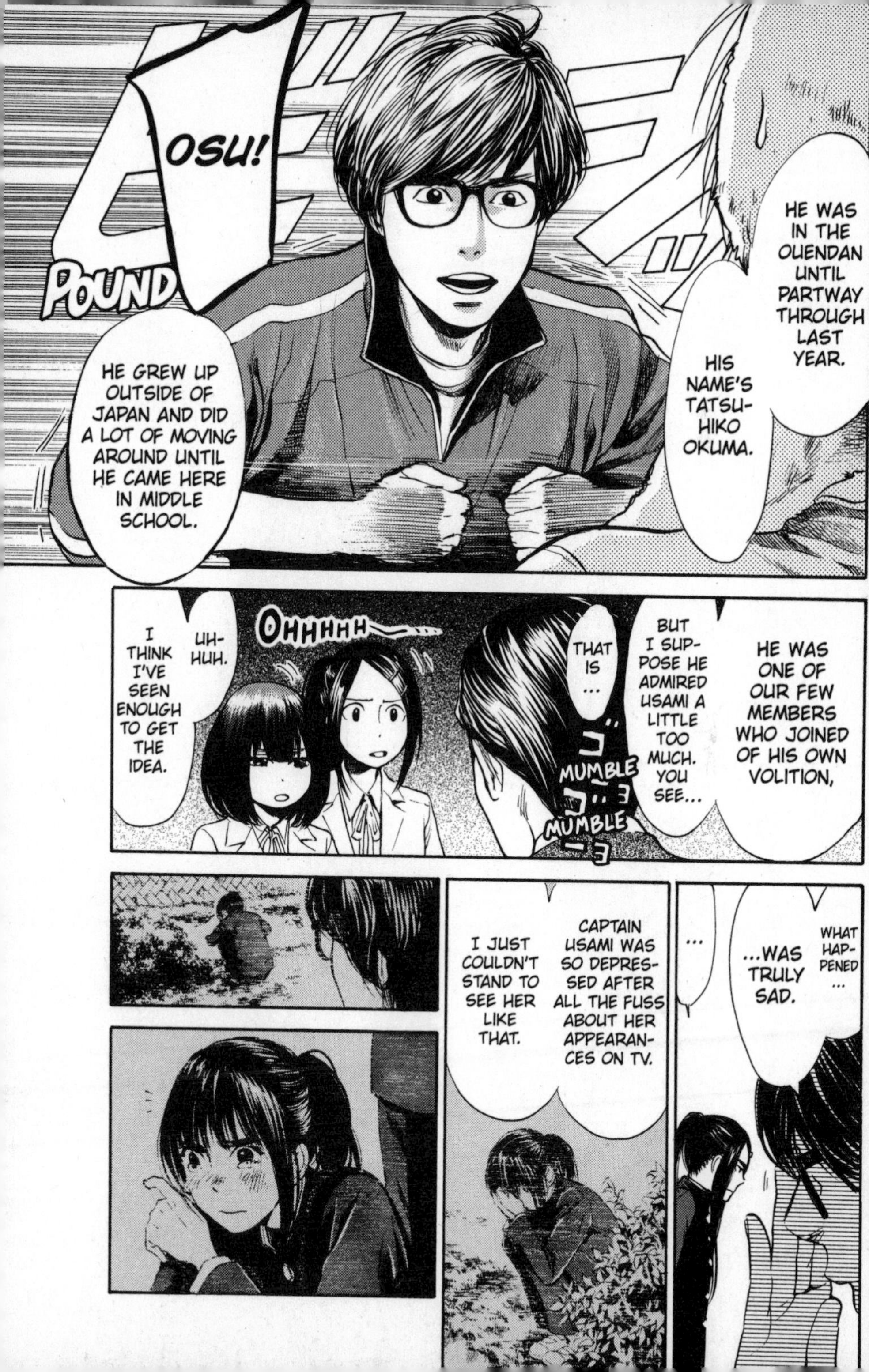
HE WAS IN THE OUENDAN UNTIL PARTWAY THROUGH LAST YEAR.
HIS NAME'S TATSU-HIKO OKUMA.
OSU!
POUND
HE GREW UP OUTSIDE OF JAPAN AND DID A LOT OF MOVING AROUND UNTIL HE CAME HERE IN MIDDLE SCHOOL.
HE WAS ONE OF OUR FEW MEMBERS WHO JOINED OF HIS OWN VOLITION,
BUT I SUPPOSE HE ADMIRED USAMI A LITTLE TOO MUCH. YOU SEE...
THAT IS ...
MUMBLE
MUMBLE
OHHHHH
UH-HUH.
I THINK I'VE SEEN ENOUGH TO GET THE IDEA.
WHAT HAPPENED ...
...WAS TRULY SAD.
...
CAPTAIN USAMI WAS SO DEPRESSED AFTER ALL THE FUSS ABOUT HER APPEARANCES ON TV.
I JUST COULDN'T STAND TO SEE HER LIKE THAT.

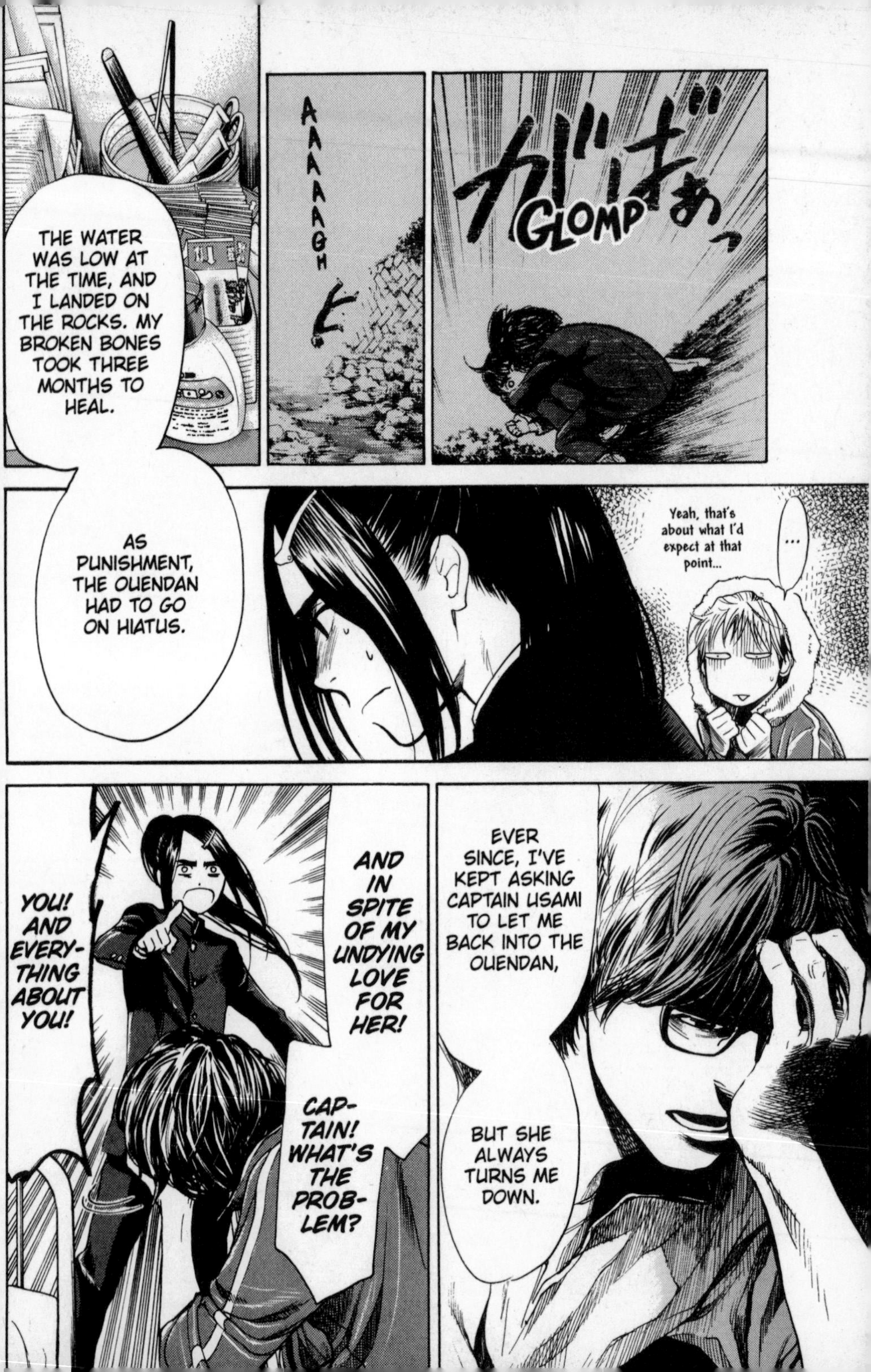
GLOMP
AAAAAAGH
THE WATER WAS LOW AT THE TIME, AND I LANDED ON THE ROCKS. MY BROKEN BONES TOOK THREE MONTHS TO HEAL.
AS PUNISHMENT, THE OUENDAN HAD TO GO ON HIATUS.
...
Yeah, that's about what I'd expect at that point...
EVER SINCE, I'VE KEPT ASKING CAPTAIN USAMI TO LET ME BACK INTO THE OUENDAN,
BUT SHE ALWAYS TURNS ME DOWN.
AND IN SPITE OF MY UNDYING LOVE FOR HER!
CAPTAIN! WHAT'S THE PROBLEM?
YOU! AND EVERYTHING ABOUT YOU!

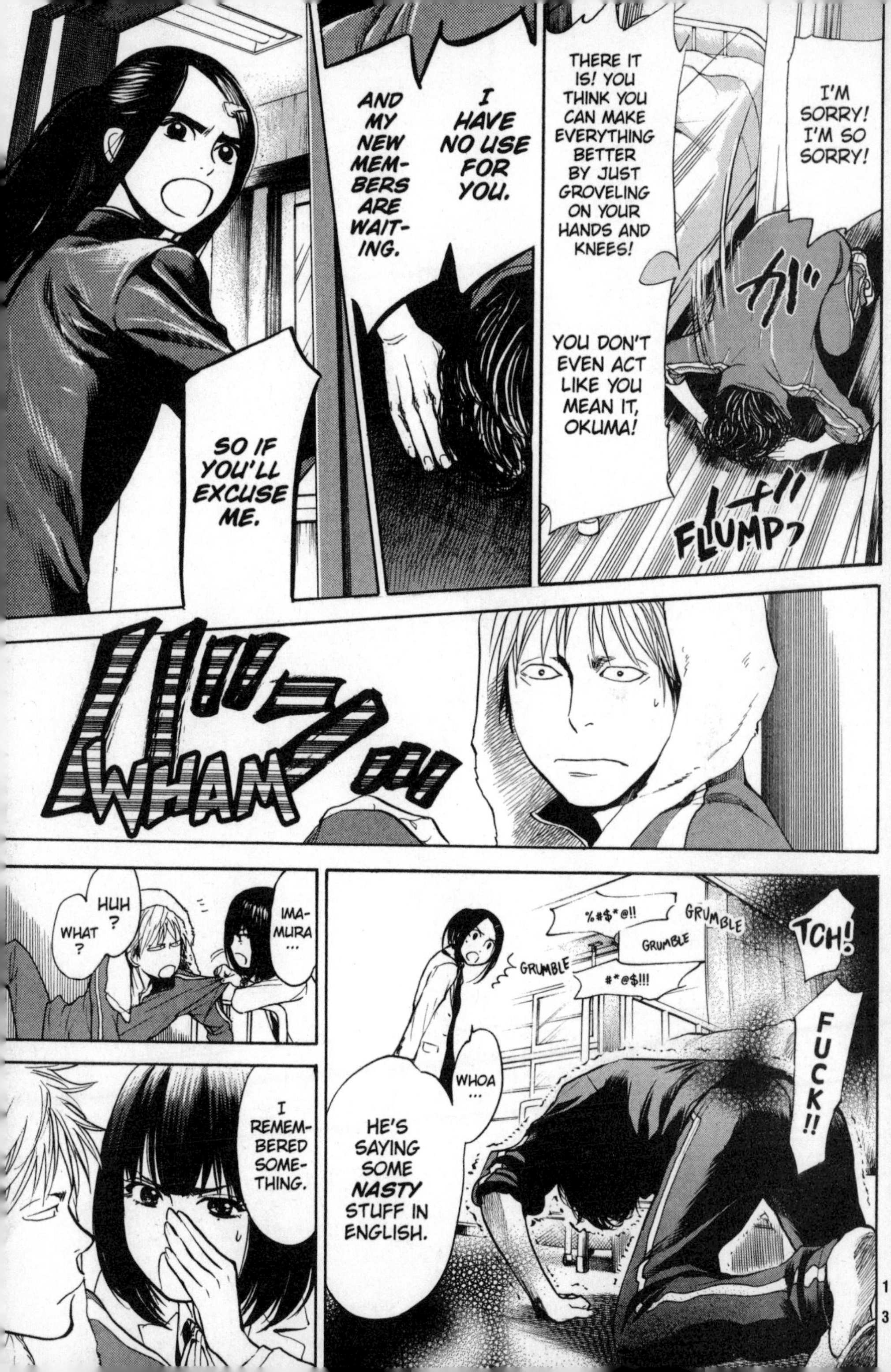

I'M SORRY! I'M SO SORRY!
THERE IT IS! YOU THINK YOU CAN MAKE EVERYTHING BETTER BY JUST GROVELING ON YOUR HANDS AND KNEES!
YOU DON'T EVEN ACT LIKE YOU MEAN IT, OKUMA!
FLUMP
I HAVE NO USE FOR YOU.
AND MY NEW MEMBERS ARE WAIT-ING.
SO IF YOU'LL EXCUSE ME.
WHAM!!
TCH!
%#$*@!!
GRUMBLE
GRUMBLE
GRUMBLE
#*@$!!!
FUCK!!
IMA-MURA...
HUH?
WHAT?
WHOA...
HE'S SAYING SOME NASTY STUFF IN ENGLISH.
I REMEM-BERED SOME-THING.

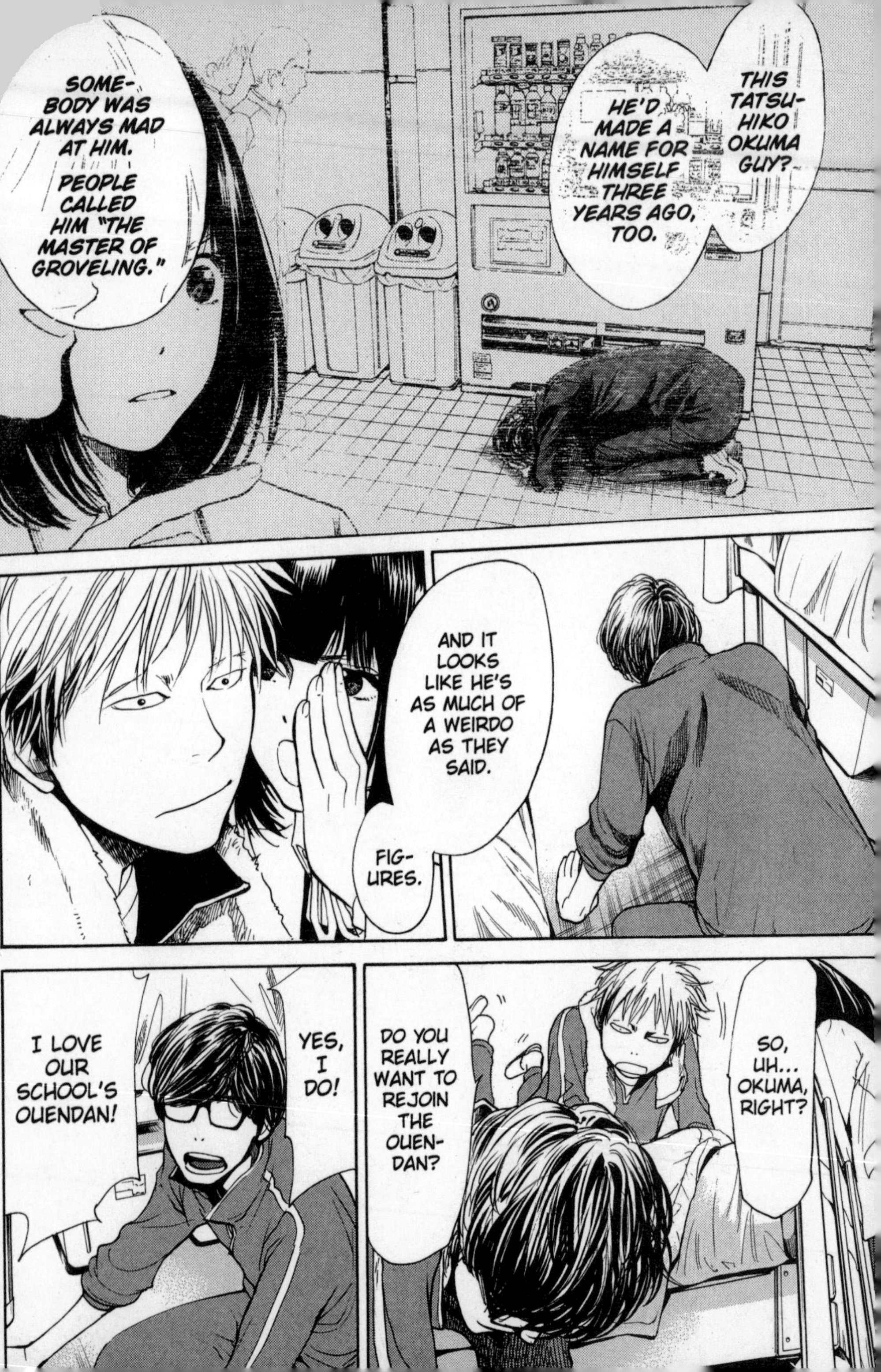
THIS TATSUHIKO OKUMA GUY?
HE'D MADE A NAME FOR HIMSELF THREE YEARS AGO, TOO.
SOMEBODY WAS ALWAYS MAD AT HIM.
PEOPLE CALLED HIM "THE MASTER OF GROVELING."
AND IT LOOKS LIKE HE'S AS MUCH OF A WEIRDO AS THEY SAID.
FIGURES.
SO, UH... OKUMA, RIGHT?
DO YOU REALLY WANT TO REJOIN THE OUENDAN?
YES, I DO!
I LOVE OUR SCHOOL'S OUENDAN!

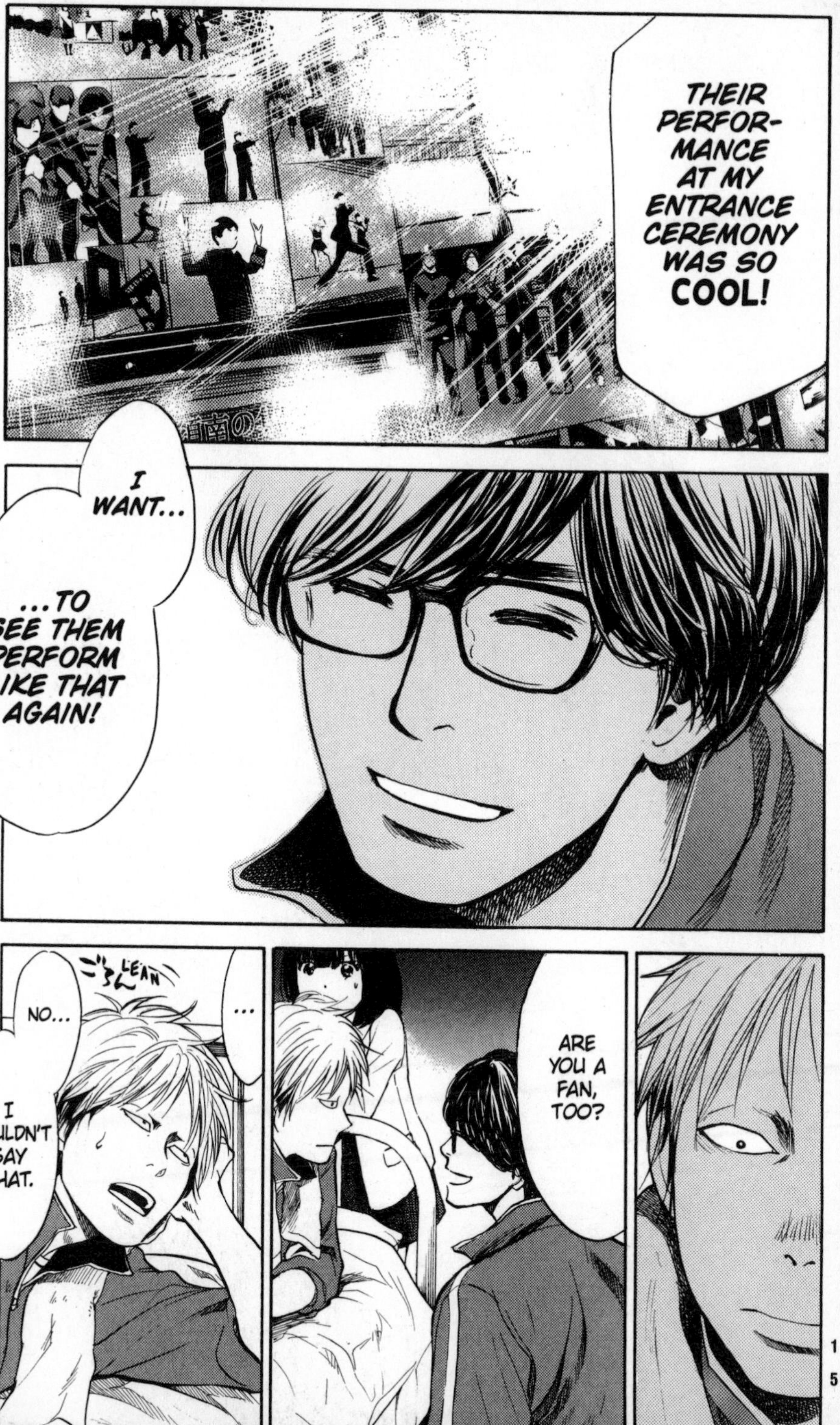
THEIR PERFORMANCE AT MY ENTRANCE CEREMONY WAS SO COOL!
I WANT...
...TO SEE THEM PERFORM LIKE THAT AGAIN!
ARE YOU A FAN, TOO?
...
ごろん LEAN
NO...
I WOULDN'T SAY THAT.

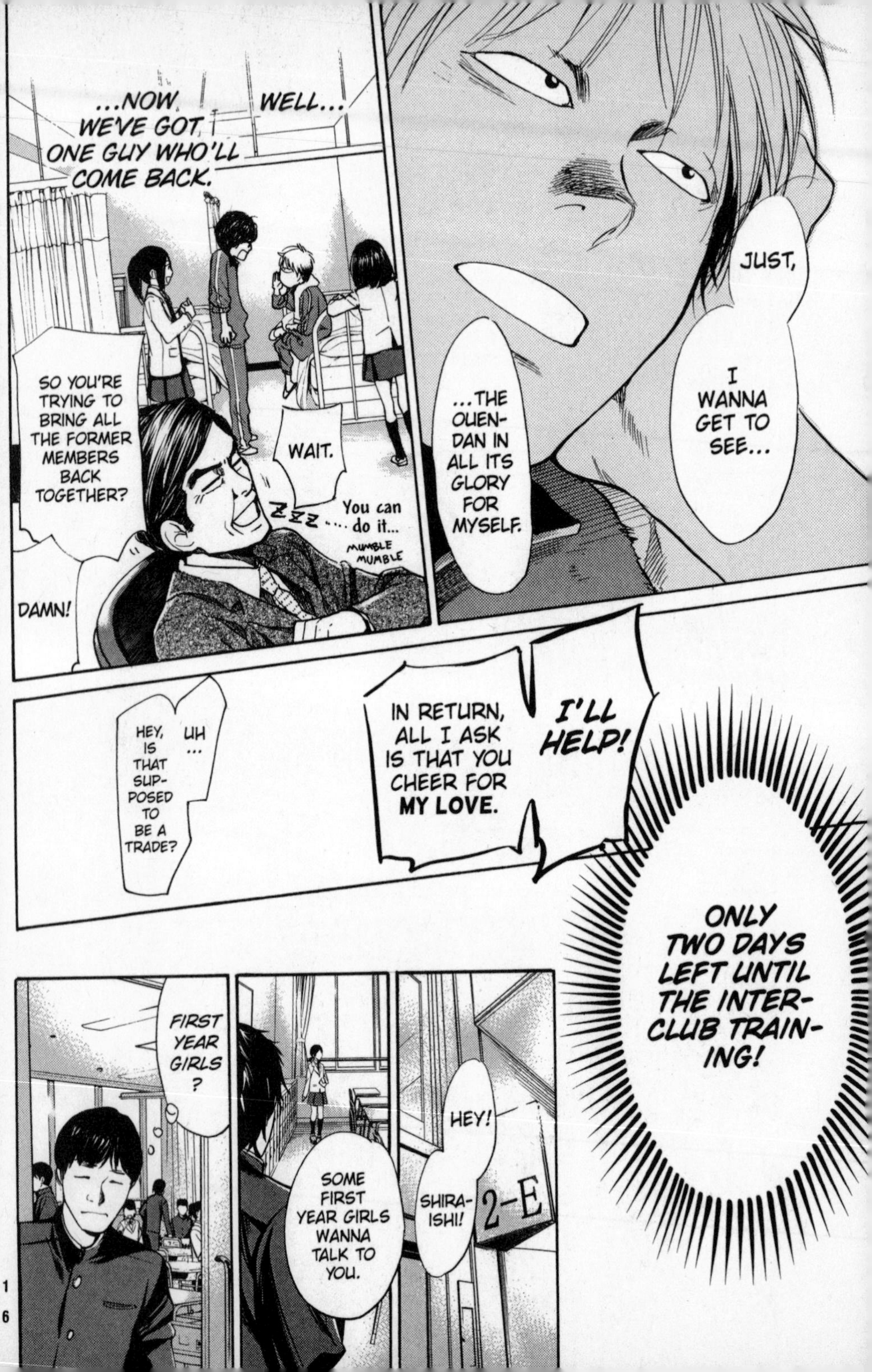
JUST,
I WANNA GET TO SEE...
...THE OUEN-DAN IN ALL ITS GLORY FOR MYSELF.
WELL...
...NOW WE'VE GOT ONE GUY WHO'LL COME BACK.
SO YOU'RE TRYING TO BRING ALL THE FORMER MEMBERS BACK TOGETHER?
WAIT.
ZZZ ... You can do it... MUMBLE MUMBLE
DAMN!
I'LL HELP!
IN RETURN, ALL I ASK IS THAT YOU CHEER FOR **MY LOVE**.
UH ...
HEY, IS THAT SUP-POSED TO BE A TRADE?
ONLY TWO DAYS LEFT UNTIL THE INTER-CLUB TRAIN-ING!
2-E
HEY!
SHIRA-ISHI!
SOME FIRST YEAR GIRLS WANNA TALK TO YOU.
FIRST YEAR GIRLS?

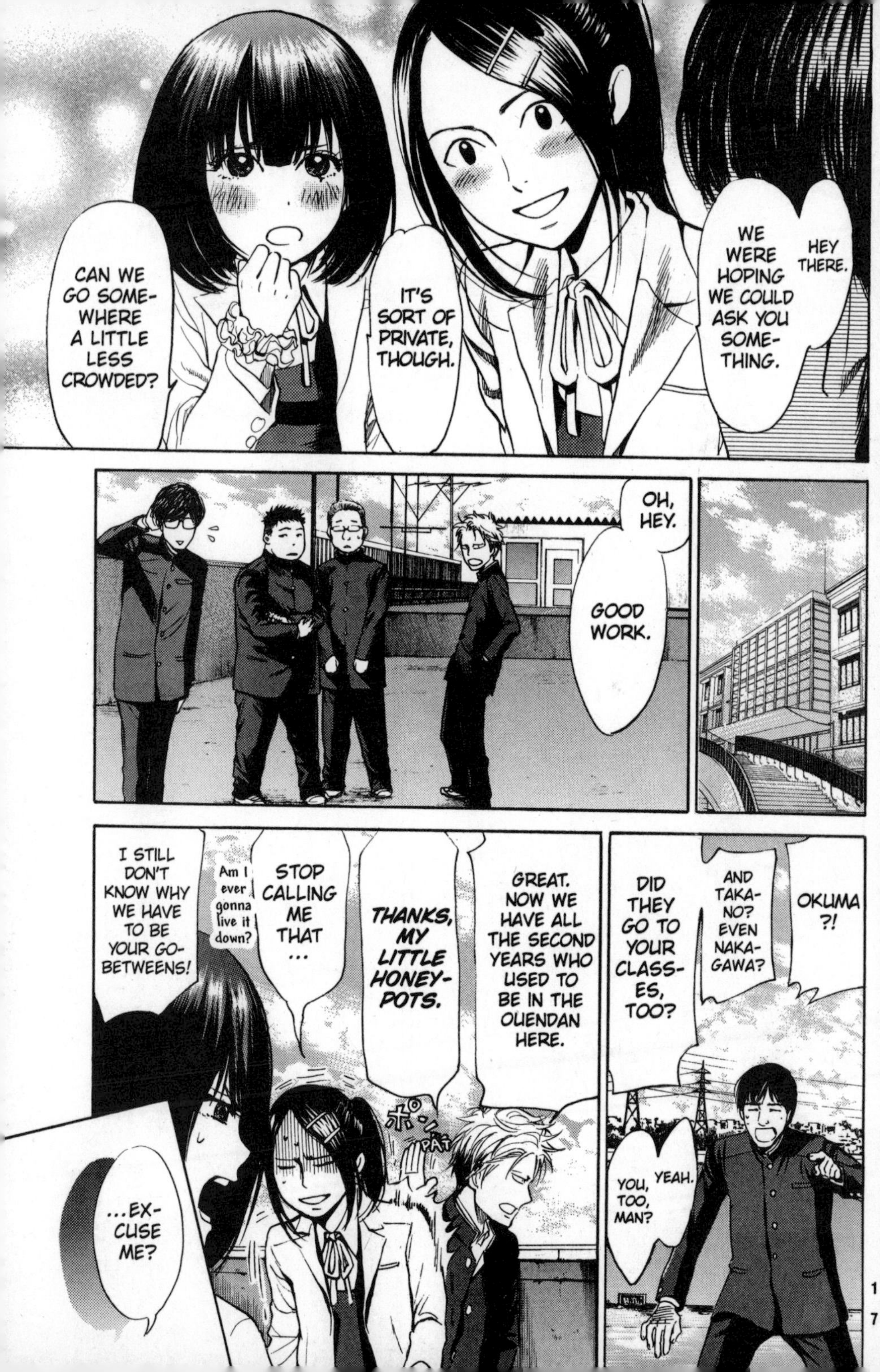
HEY THERE.
WE WERE HOPING WE COULD ASK YOU SOMETHING.
IT'S SORT OF PRIVATE, THOUGH.
CAN WE GO SOMEWHERE A LITTLE LESS CROWDED?
OH, HEY.
GOOD WORK.
OKUMA?!
AND TAKANO? EVEN NAKAGAWA?
DID THEY GO TO YOUR CLASSES, TOO?
YEAH.
YOU, TOO, MAN?
GREAT. NOW WE HAVE ALL THE SECOND YEARS WHO USED TO BE IN THE OUENDAN HERE.
THANKS, MY LITTLE HONEY-POTS.
PAT
STOP CALLING ME THAT...
Am I ever gonna live it down?
I STILL DON'T KNOW WHY WE HAVE TO BE YOUR GO-BETWEENS!
...EXCUSE ME?

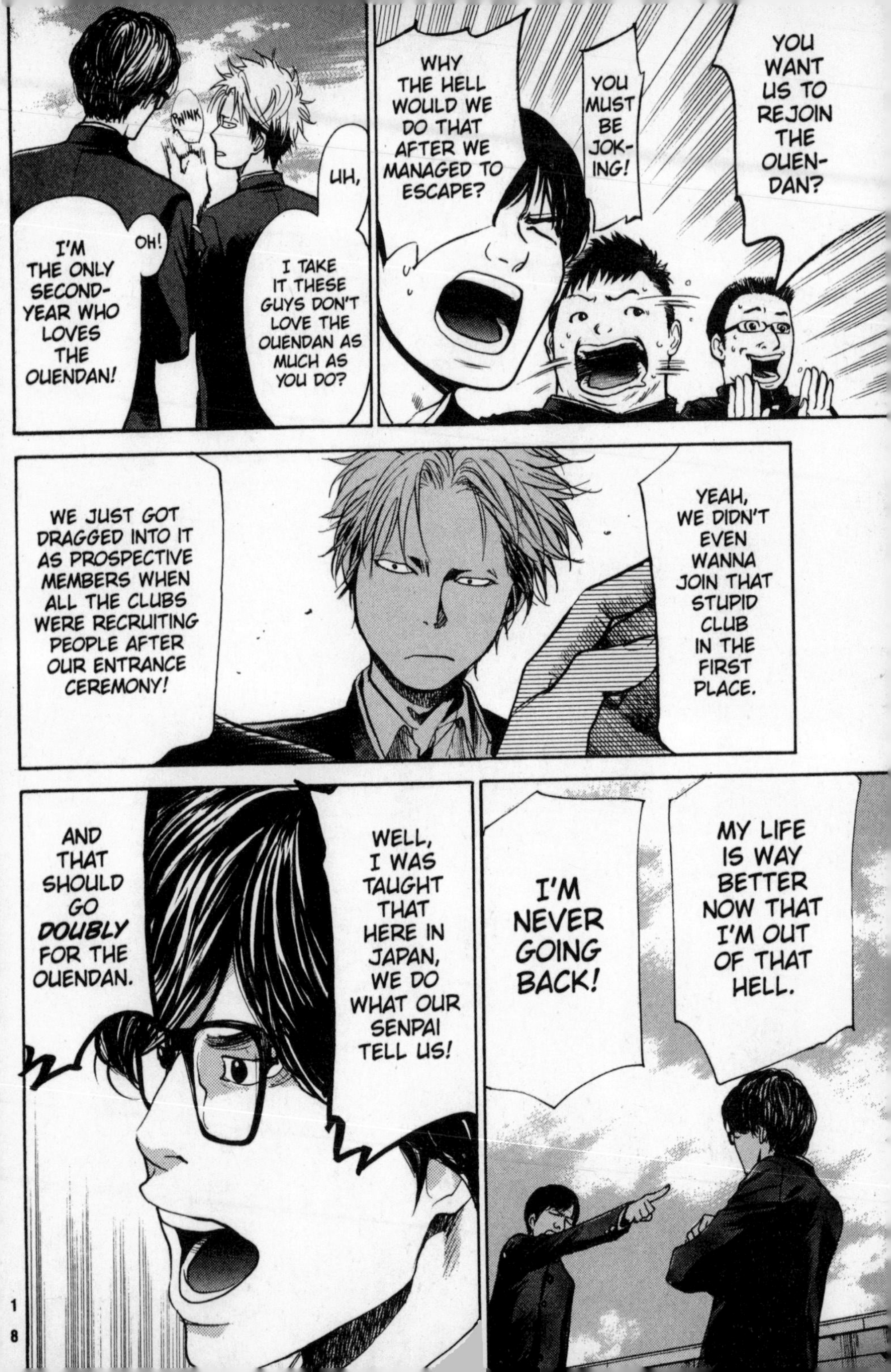
YOU WANT US TO REJOIN THE OUENDAN?
YOU MUST BE JOKING!
WHY THE HELL WOULD WE DO THAT AFTER WE MANAGED TO ESCAPE?
UH,
I TAKE IT THESE GUYS DON'T LOVE THE OUENDAN AS MUCH AS YOU DO?
PWINK
OH!
I'M THE ONLY SECOND-YEAR WHO LOVES THE OUENDAN!
YEAH, WE DIDN'T EVEN WANNA JOIN THAT STUPID CLUB IN THE FIRST PLACE.
WE JUST GOT DRAGGED INTO IT AS PROSPECTIVE MEMBERS WHEN ALL THE CLUBS WERE RECRUITING PEOPLE AFTER OUR ENTRANCE CEREMONY!
MY LIFE IS WAY BETTER NOW THAT I'M OUT OF THAT HELL.
I'M NEVER GOING BACK!
WELL, I WAS TAUGHT THAT HERE IN JAPAN, WE DO WHAT OUR SENPAI TELL US!
AND THAT SHOULD GO *DOUBLY* FOR THE OUENDAN.

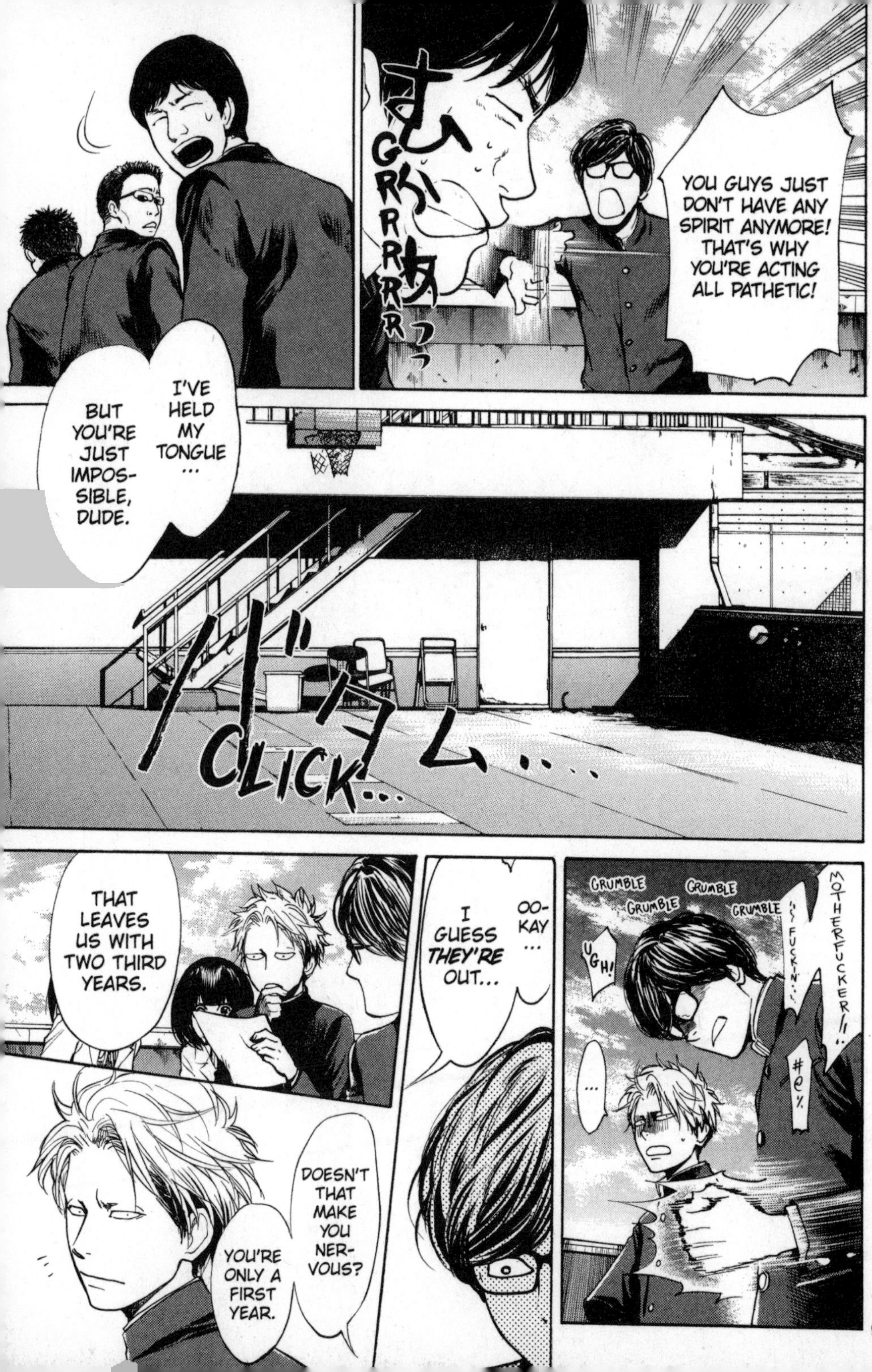
YOU GUYS JUST DON'T HAVE ANY SPIRIT ANYMORE! THAT'S WHY YOU'RE ACTING ALL PATHETIC!
GRRRRRR
I'VE HELD MY TONGUE...
BUT YOU'RE JUST IMPOSSIBLE, DUDE.
CLICK...
MOTHERFUCKER!!
FUCKIN'...
GRUMBLE GRUMBLE GRUMBLE GRUMBLE
UGH!
...
OO-KAY...
I GUESS THEY'RE OUT...
THAT LEAVES US WITH TWO THIRD YEARS.
DOESN'T THAT MAKE YOU NERVOUS?
YOU'RE ONLY A FIRST YEAR.

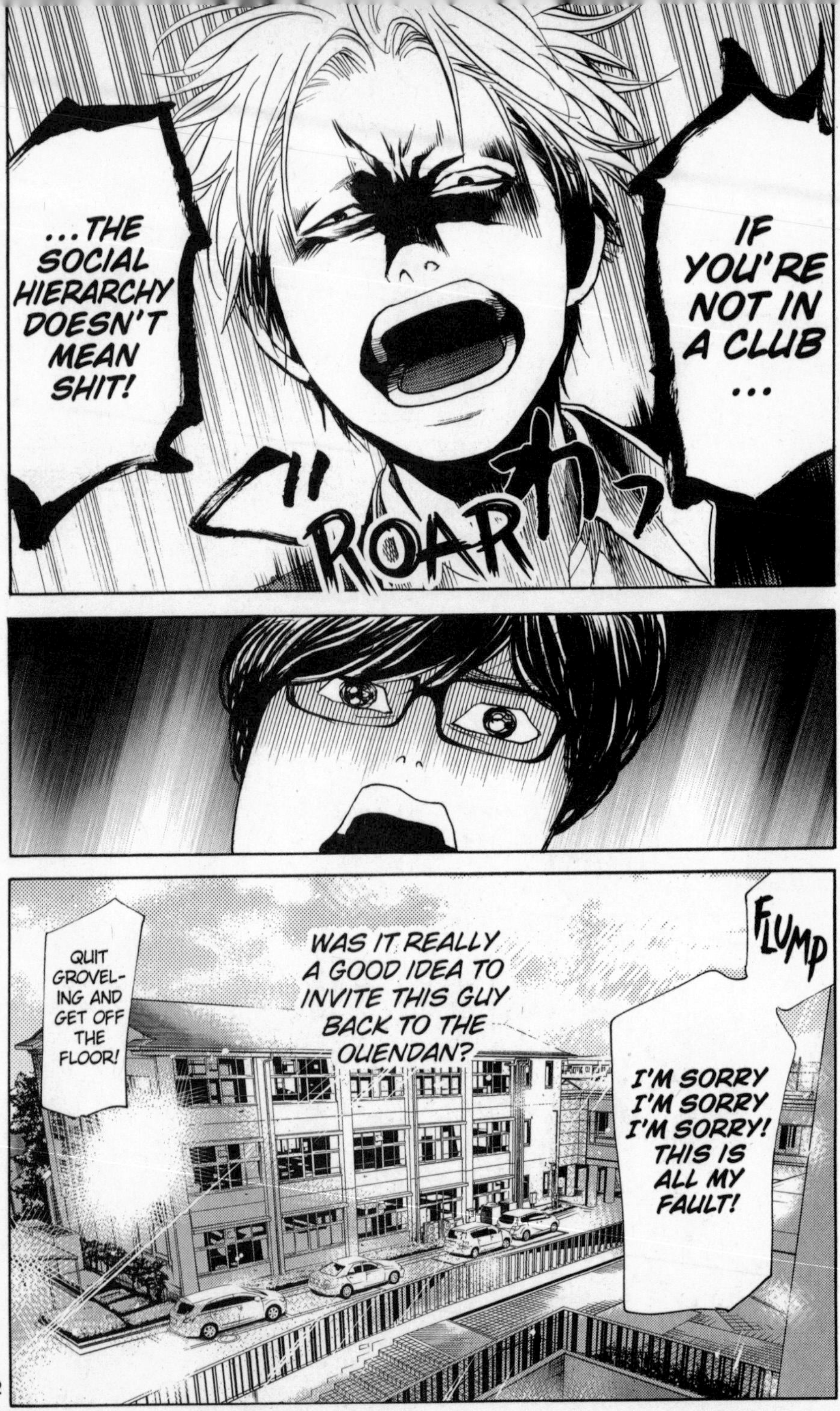
IF YOU'RE NOT IN A CLUB ...
...THE SOCIAL HIERARCHY DOESN'T MEAN SHIT!
ROAR
FLUMP
I'M SORRY I'M SORRY I'M SORRY! THIS IS ALL MY FAULT!
WAS IT REALLY A GOOD IDEA TO INVITE THIS GUY BACK TO THE OUENDAN?
QUIT GROVEL-ING AND GET OFF THE FLOOR!

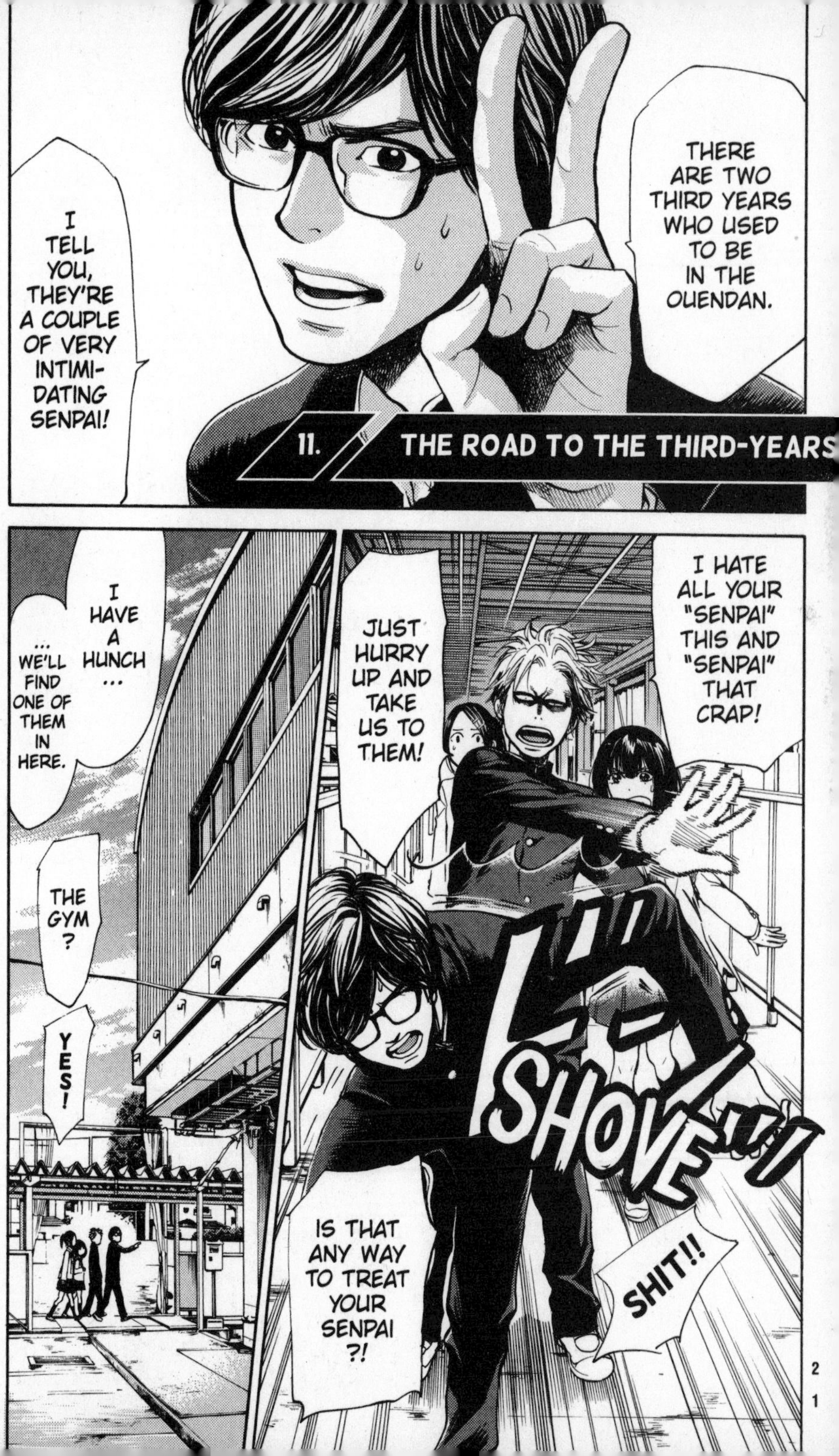
THERE ARE TWO THIRD YEARS WHO USED TO BE IN THE OUENDAN.
I TELL YOU, THEY'RE A COUPLE OF VERY INTIMI-DATING SENPAI!
11. THE ROAD TO THE THIRD-YEARS
I HATE ALL YOUR "SENPAI" THIS AND "SENPAI" THAT CRAP!
JUST HURRY UP AND TAKE US TO THEM!
SHOVE!!!
SHIT!!
IS THAT ANY WAY TO TREAT YOUR SENPAI?!
I HAVE A HUNCH...
...WE'LL FIND ONE OF THEM IN HERE.
THE GYM?
YES!

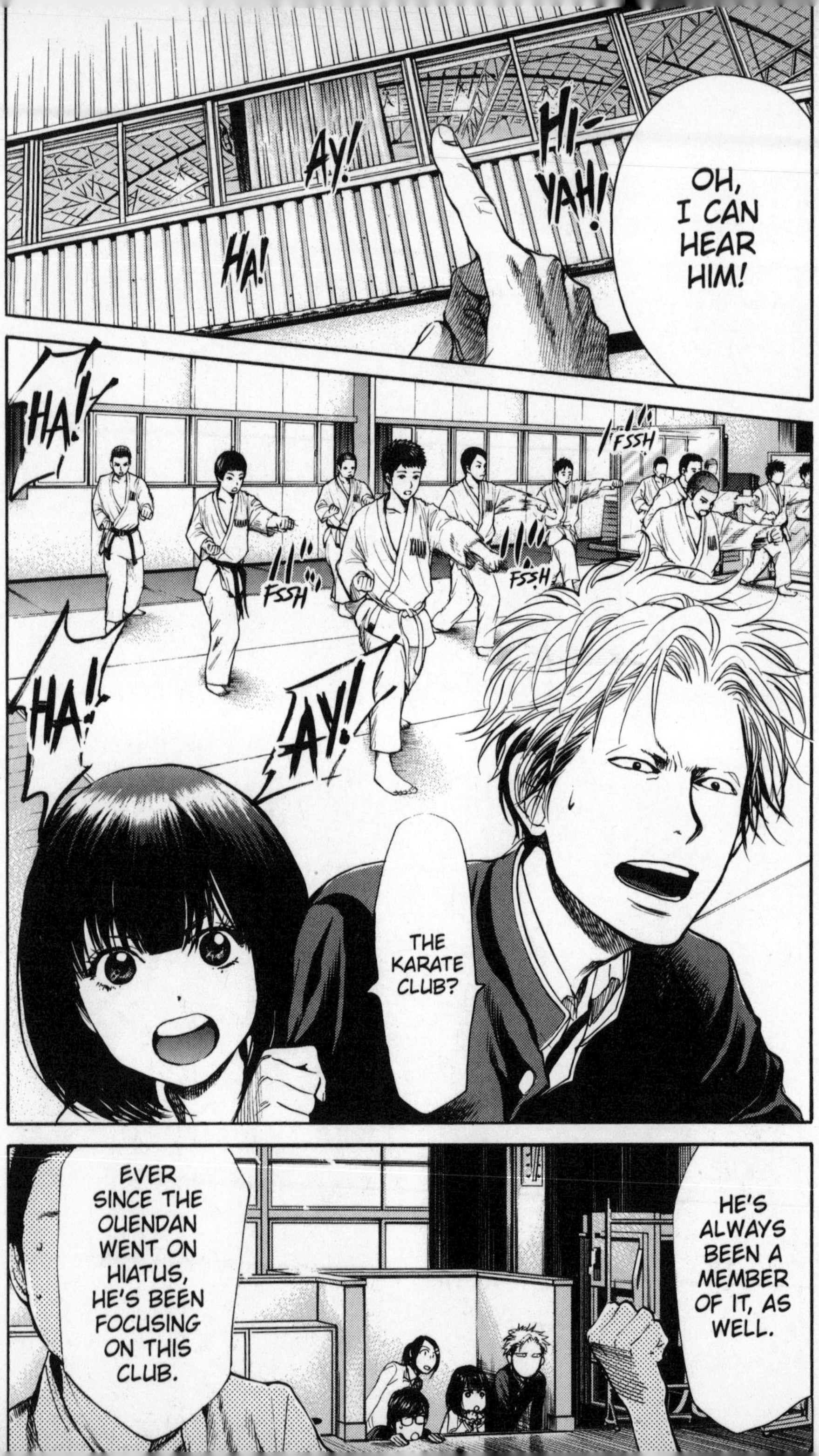
OH, I CAN HEAR HIM!
HI-YAH!
AY!
HA!
FSSH
FSSH
HA!
FSSH
THE KARATE CLUB?
AY!
HA!
HE'S ALWAYS BEEN A MEMBER OF IT, AS WELL.
EVER SINCE THE OUENDAN WENT ON HIATUS, HE'S BEEN FOCUSING ON THIS CLUB.

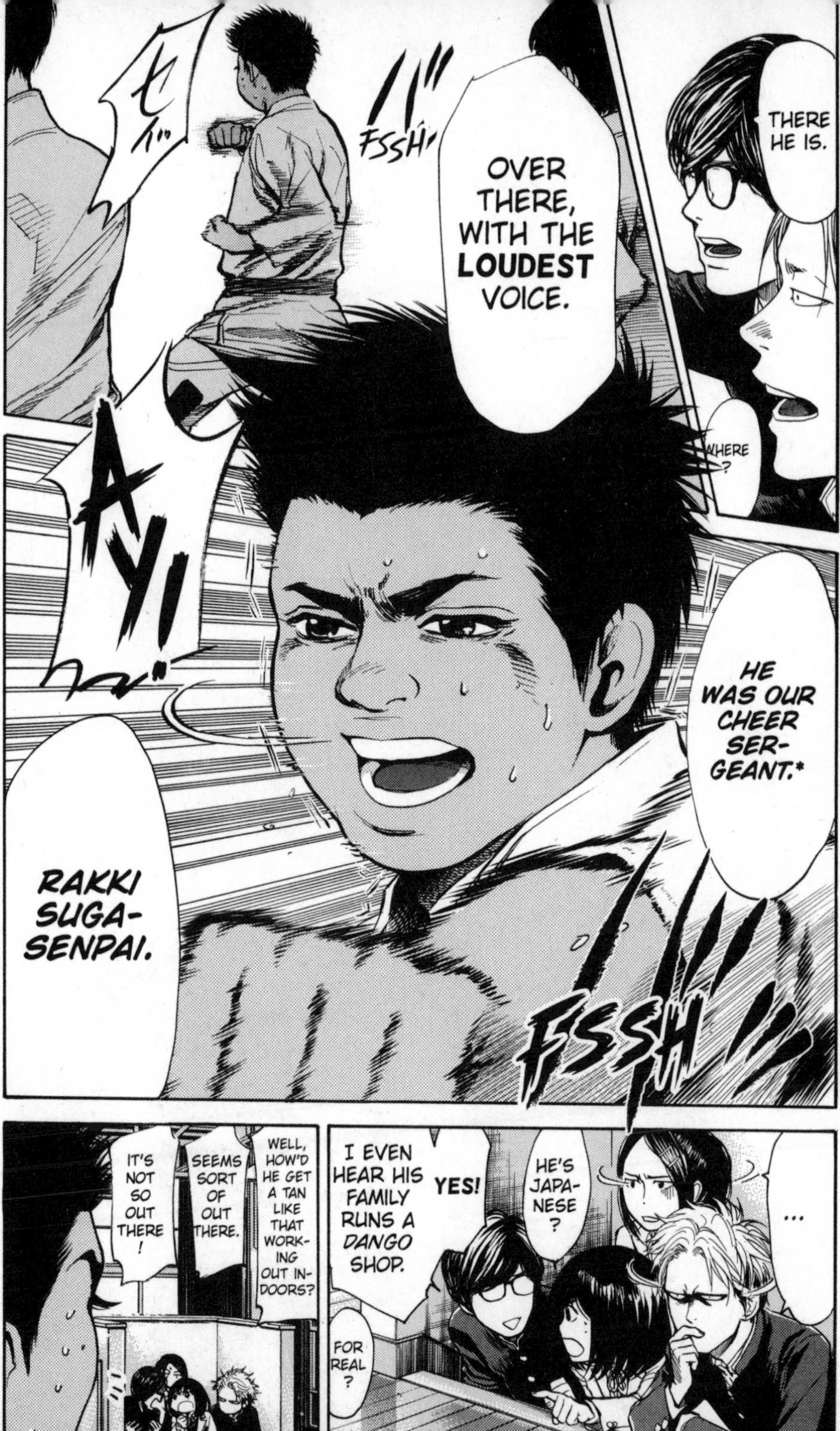
THERE HE IS.
WHERE?
OVER THERE, WITH THE LOUDEST VOICE.
FSSH
HE WAS OUR CHEER SERGEANT.*
AYI!
RAKKI SUGA-SENPAI.
FSSH
...
HE'S JAPANESE?
YES!
I EVEN HEAR HIS FAMILY RUNS A DANGO SHOP.
FOR REAL?
WELL, HOW'D HE GET A TAN LIKE THAT WORKING OUT INDOORS?
SEEMS SORT OF OUT THERE.
IT'S NOT SO OUT THERE!

*CHEER SERGEANT: AN OFFICER IN AN OUENDAN OF EQUAL RANK TO THE VICE-CAPTAIN AND SECOND IN AUTHORITY TO THE CAPTAIN.

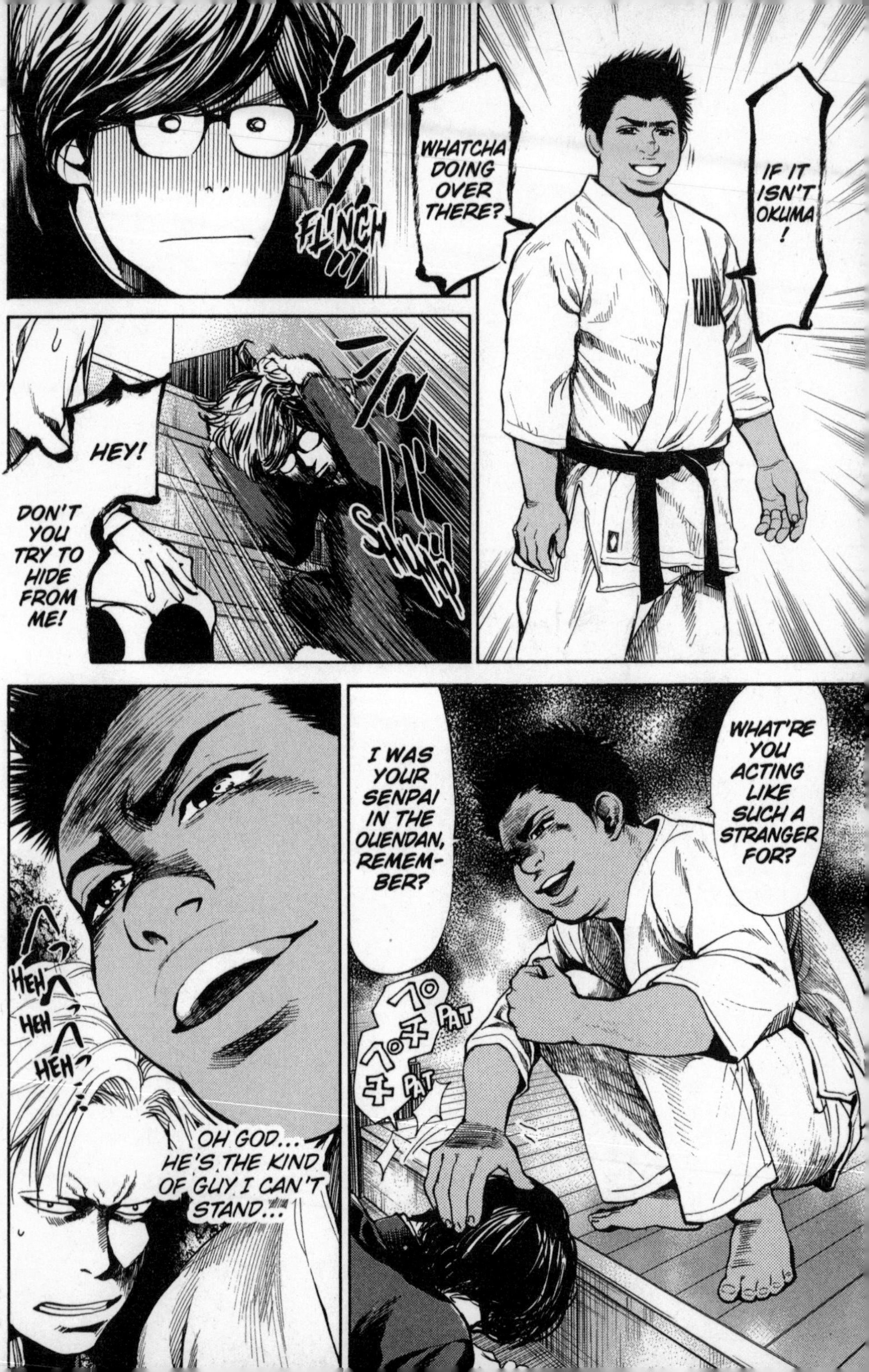
IF IT ISN'T OKUMA!
WHATCHA DOING OVER THERE?
FLINCH
HEY!
DON'T YOU TRY TO HIDE FROM ME!
WHAT'RE YOU ACTING LIKE SUCH A STRANGER FOR?
I WAS YOUR SENPAI IN THE OUENDAN, REMEMBER?
PAT
PAT
HEH
HEH
HEH
OH GOD... HE'S THE KIND OF GUY I CAN'T STAND...

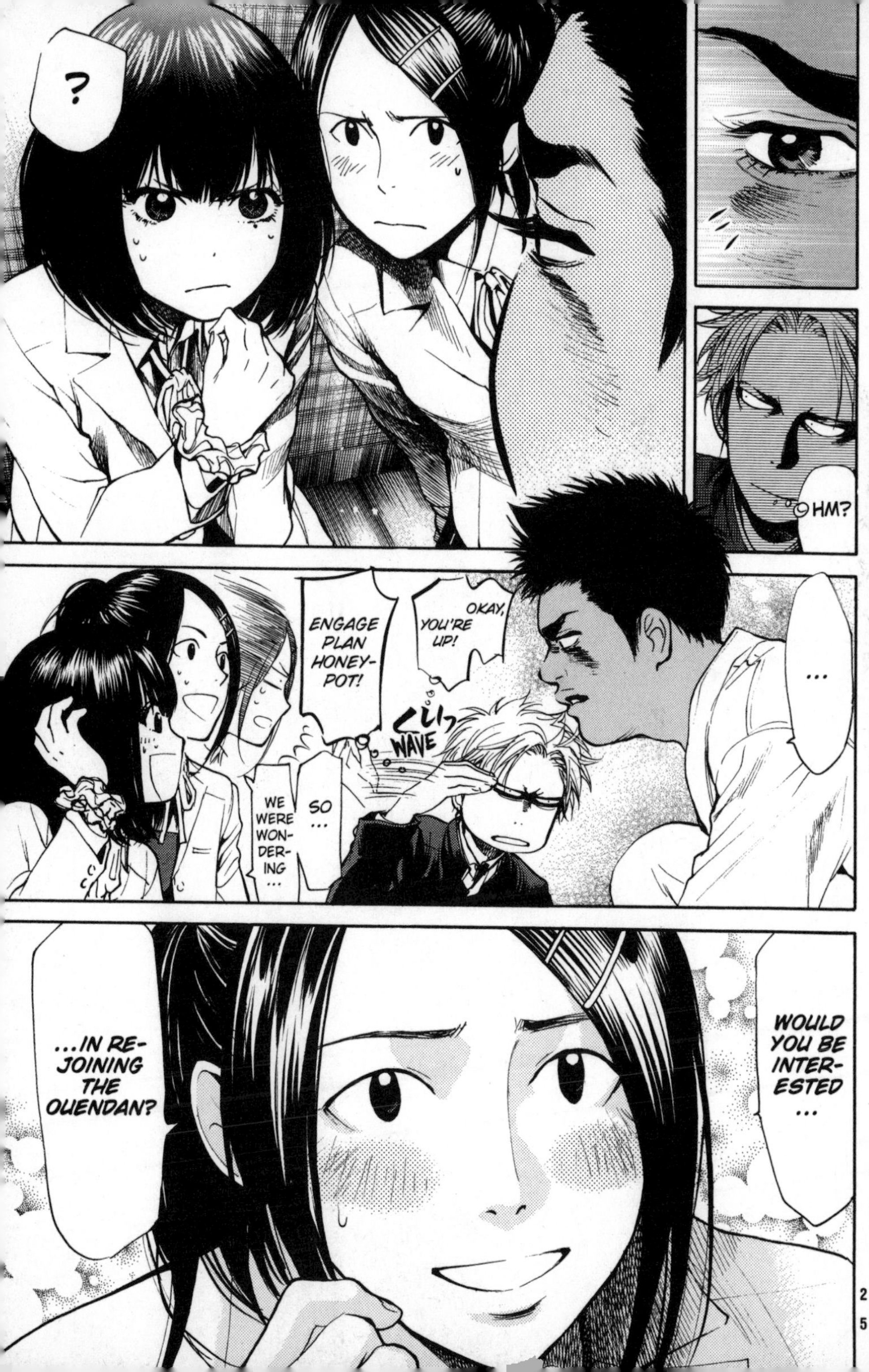
HM?
?
...
OKAY, YOU'RE UP!
ENGAGE PLAN HONEY-POT!
くいっ
WAVE
SO...
WE WERE WON-DER-ING...
WOULD YOU BE INTER-ESTED...
...IN RE-JOINING THE OUENDAN?

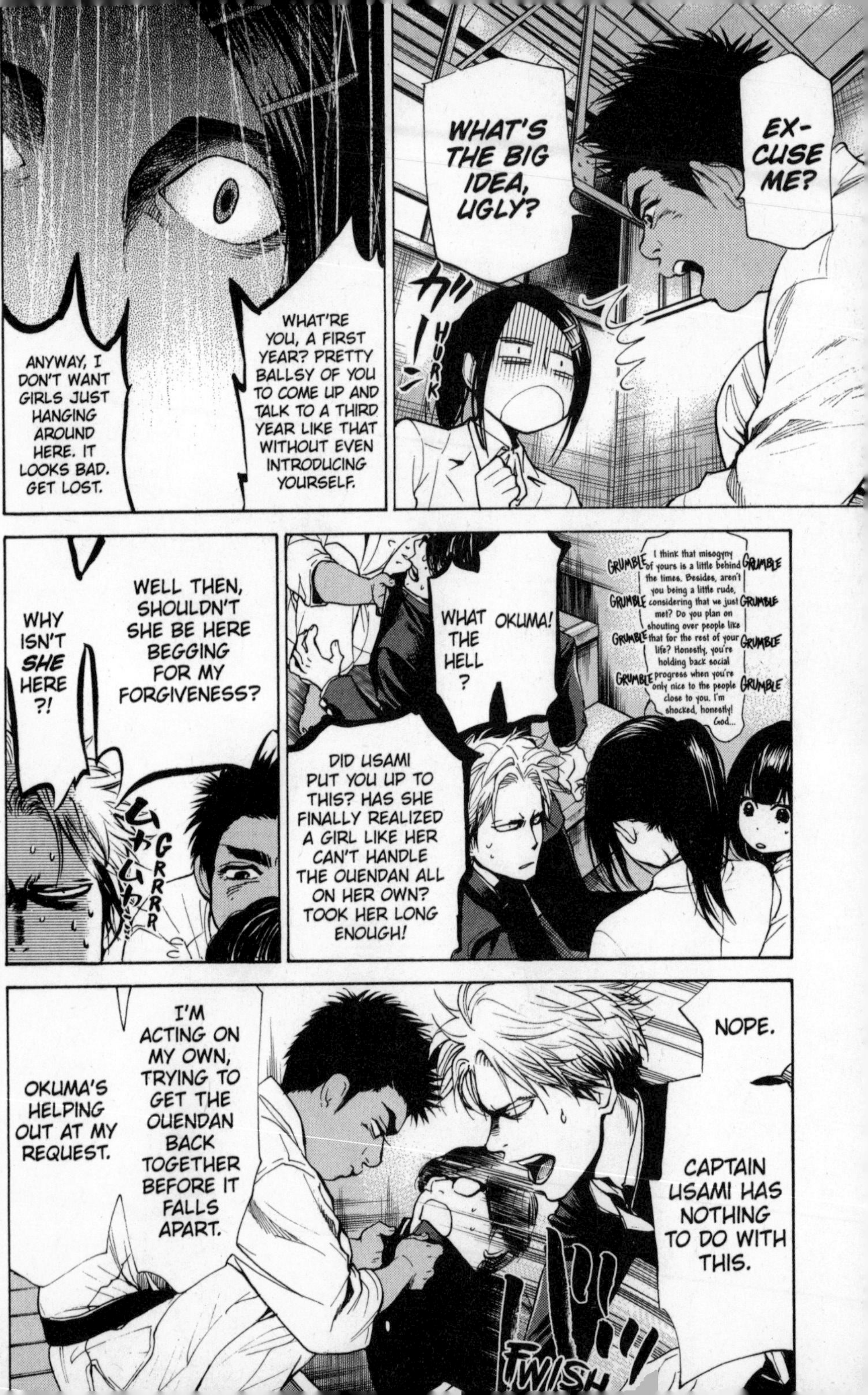
EX-CUSE ME?
WHAT'S THE BIG IDEA, UGLY?
HURK
WHAT'RE YOU, A FIRST YEAR? PRETTY BALLSY OF YOU TO COME UP AND TALK TO A THIRD YEAR LIKE THAT WITHOUT EVEN INTRODUCING YOURSELF.
ANYWAY, I DON'T WANT GIRLS JUST HANGING AROUND HERE. IT LOOKS BAD. GET LOST.
GRUMBLE GRUMBLE GRUMBLE GRUMBLE
I think that misogyny of yours is a little behind the times. Besides, aren't you being a little rude, considering that we just met? Do you plan on shouting over people like that for the rest of your life? Honestly, you're holding back social progress when you're only nice to the people close to you. I'm shocked, honestly! God...
GRUMBLE GRUMBLE GRUMBLE GRUMBLE
OKUMA!
WHAT THE HELL?
DID USAMI PUT YOU UP TO THIS? HAS SHE FINALLY REALIZED A GIRL LIKE HER CAN'T HANDLE THE OUENDAN ALL ON HER OWN? TOOK HER LONG ENOUGH!
WELL THEN, SHOULDN'T SHE BE HERE BEGGING FOR MY FORGIVENESS?
WHY ISN'T SHE HERE?!
GRRRR
NOPE.
CAPTAIN USAMI HAS NOTHING TO DO WITH THIS.
I'M ACTING ON MY OWN, TRYING TO GET THE OUENDAN BACK TOGETHER BEFORE IT FALLS APART.
OKUMA'S HELPING OUT AT MY REQUEST.
FWISH

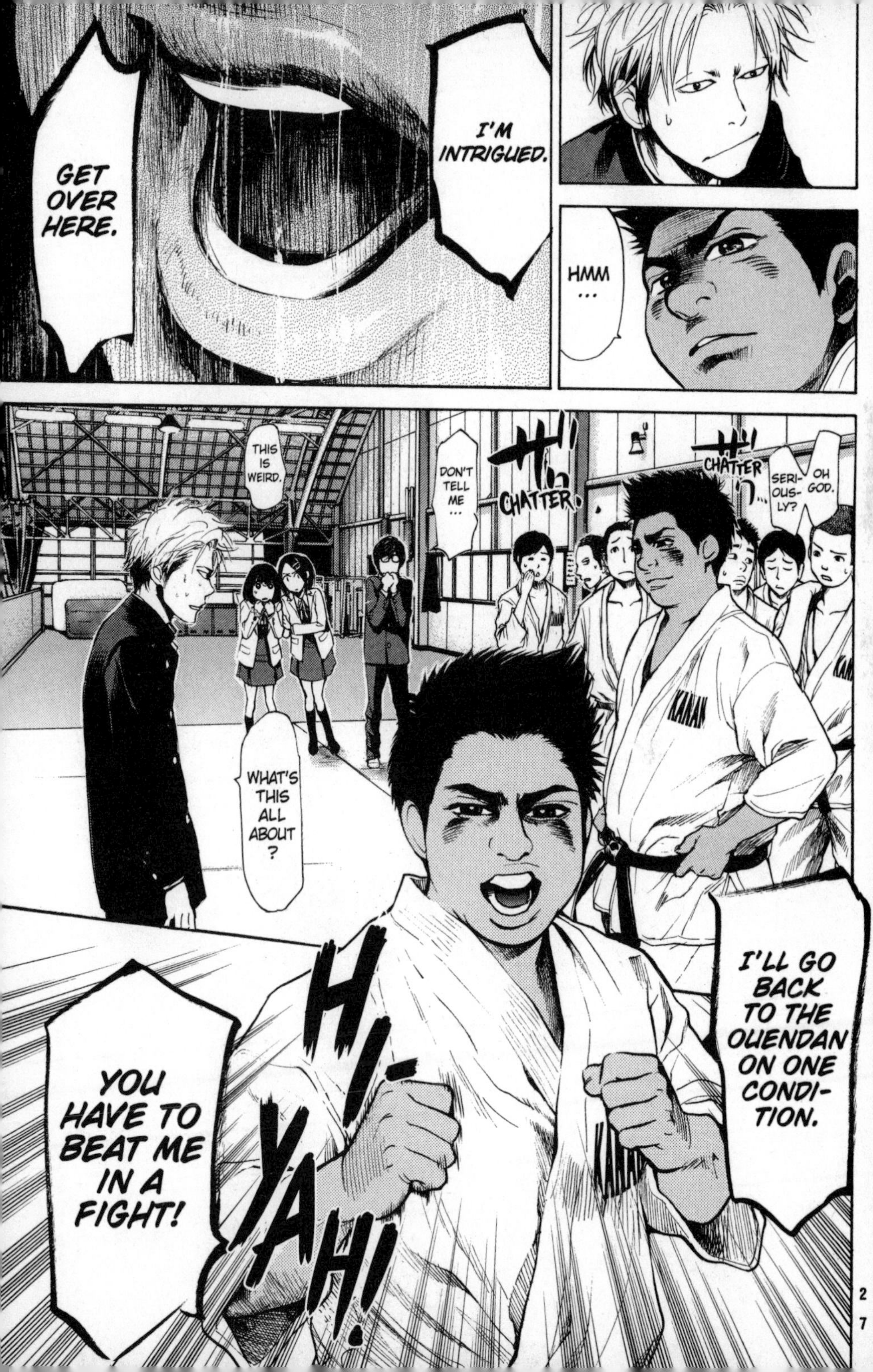
HMM ...
I'M INTRIGUED.
GET OVER HERE.
OH GOD.
SERI-OUSLY?
CHATTER
CHATTER
DON'T TELL ME ...
THIS IS WEIRD.
WHAT'S THIS ALL ABOUT ?
I'LL GO BACK TO THE OUENDAN ON ONE CONDI-TION.
HI-YAH!
YOU HAVE TO BEAT ME IN A FIGHT!

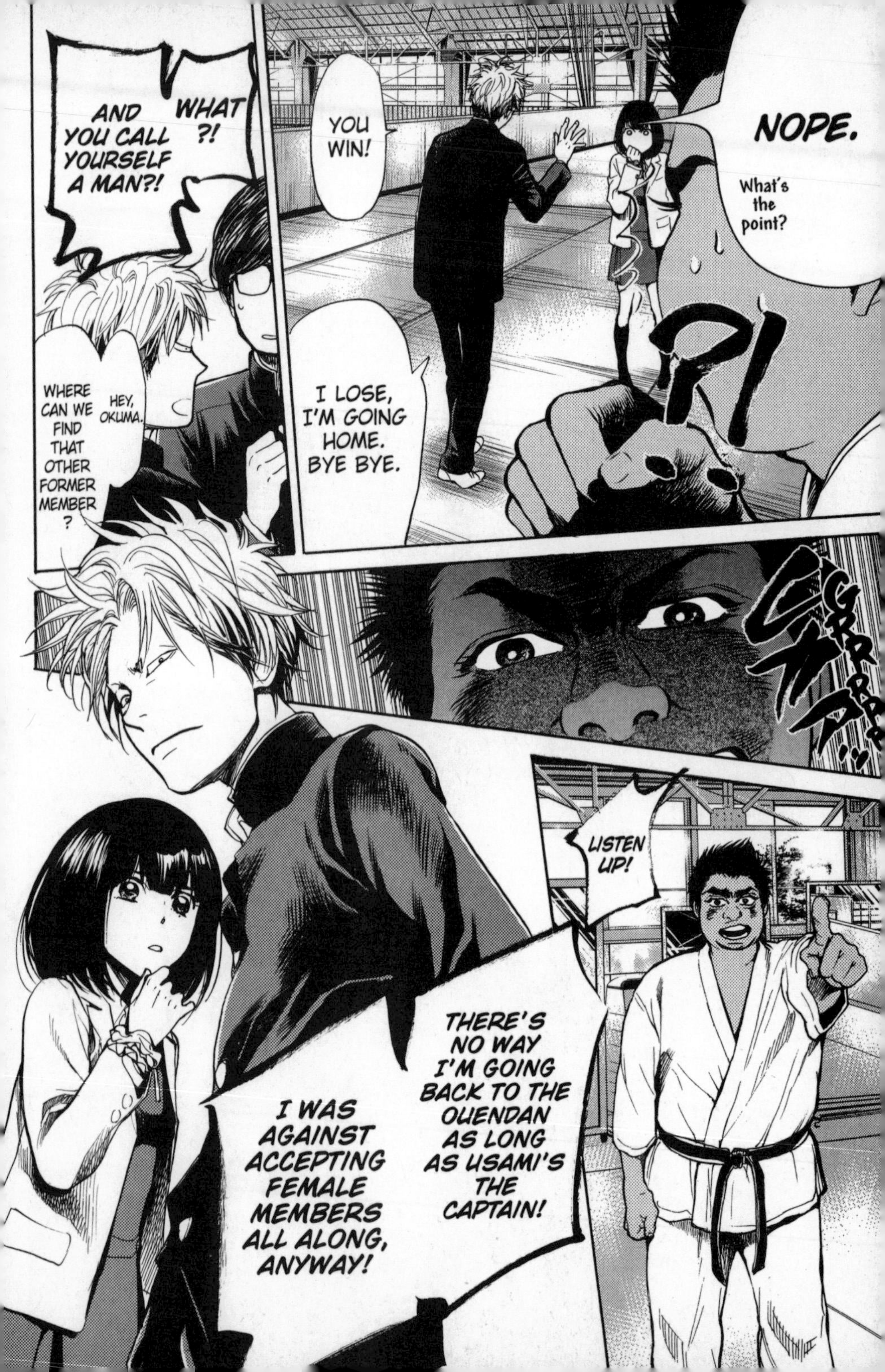
NOPE.
What's the point?
?!
YOU WIN!
I LOSE, I'M GOING HOME. BYE BYE.
WHAT?!
AND YOU CALL YOURSELF A MAN?!
HEY, OKUMA.
WHERE CAN WE FIND THAT OTHER FORMER MEMBER?
GRRRR..
LISTEN UP!
THERE'S NO WAY I'M GOING BACK TO THE OUENDAN AS LONG AS USAMI'S THE CAPTAIN!
I WAS AGAINST ACCEPTING FEMALE MEMBERS ALL ALONG, ANYWAY!

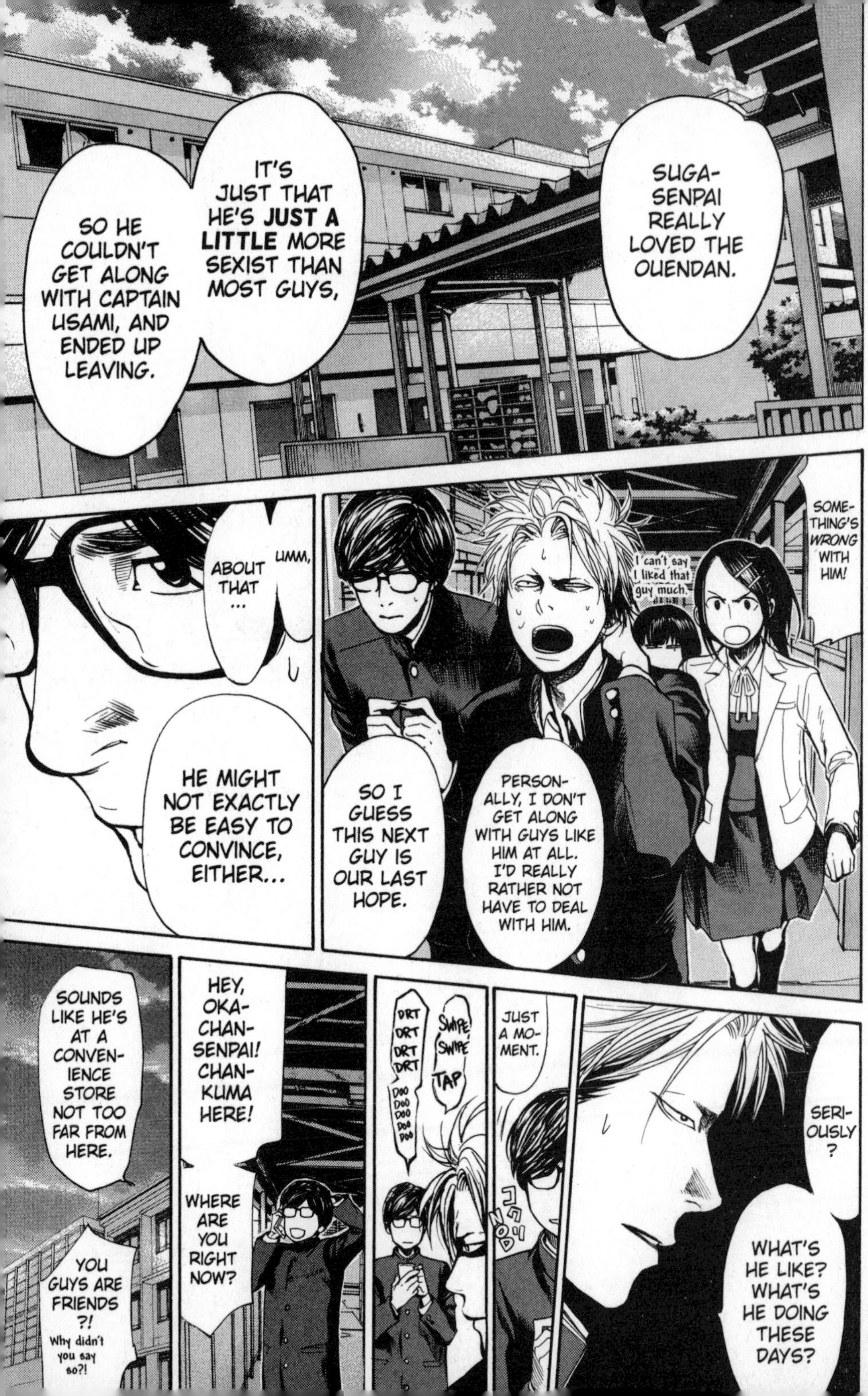
SUGA-SENPAI REALLY LOVED THE OUENDAN.
IT'S JUST THAT HE'S **JUST A LITTLE** MORE SEXIST THAN MOST GUYS,
SO HE COULDN'T GET ALONG WITH CAPTAIN USAMI, AND ENDED UP LEAVING.
SOMETHING'S *WRONG* WITH HIM!
I can't say I liked that guy much.
PERSONALLY, I DON'T GET ALONG WITH GUYS LIKE HIM AT ALL. I'D REALLY RATHER NOT HAVE TO DEAL WITH HIM.
SO I GUESS THIS NEXT GUY IS OUR LAST HOPE.
UMM,
ABOUT THAT ...
HE MIGHT NOT EXACTLY BE EASY TO CONVINCE, EITHER...
SERIOUSLY?
WHAT'S HE LIKE? WHAT'S HE DOING THESE DAYS?
JUST A MOMENT.
NOD
DRT DRT DRT DRT
SWIPE SWIPE
TAP
DOO DOO DOO DOO DOO
HEY, OKA-CHAN-SENPAI! CHANKUMA HERE!
WHERE ARE YOU RIGHT NOW?
SOUNDS LIKE HE'S AT A CONVENIENCE STORE NOT TOO FAR FROM HERE.
YOU GUYS ARE FRIENDS?!
Why didn't you say so?!

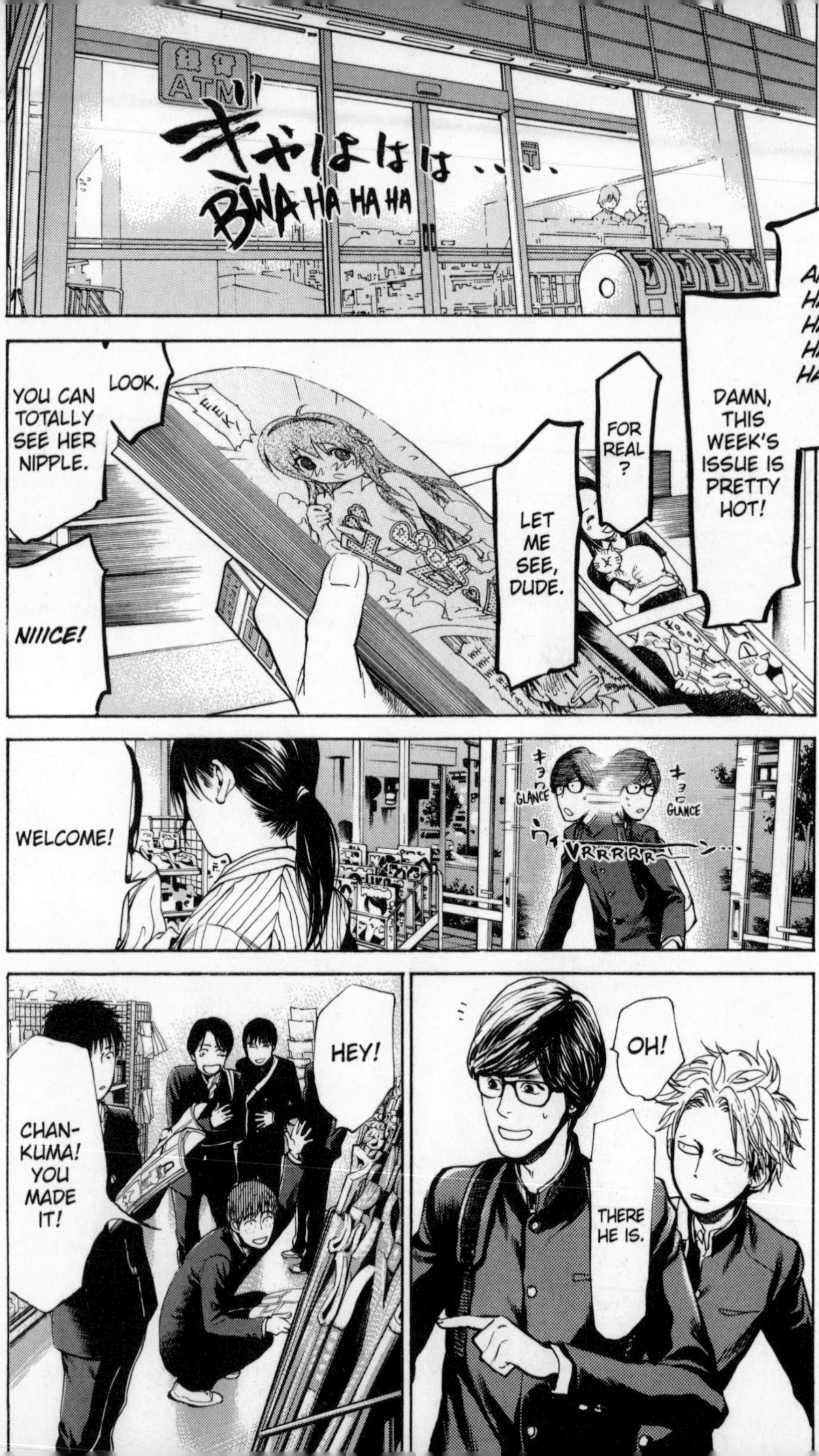
ATM
キャははは…
BWA HA HA HA
AH HA HA HA HA!
DAMN, THIS WEEK'S ISSUE IS PRETTY HOT!
FOR REAL?
LET ME SEE, DUDE.
LOOK.
YOU CAN TOTALLY SEE HER NIPPLE.
NIIICE!
GLANCE
GLANCE
VRRRRR...
WELCOME!
OH!
THERE HE IS.
HEY!
CHAN-KUMA! YOU MADE IT!

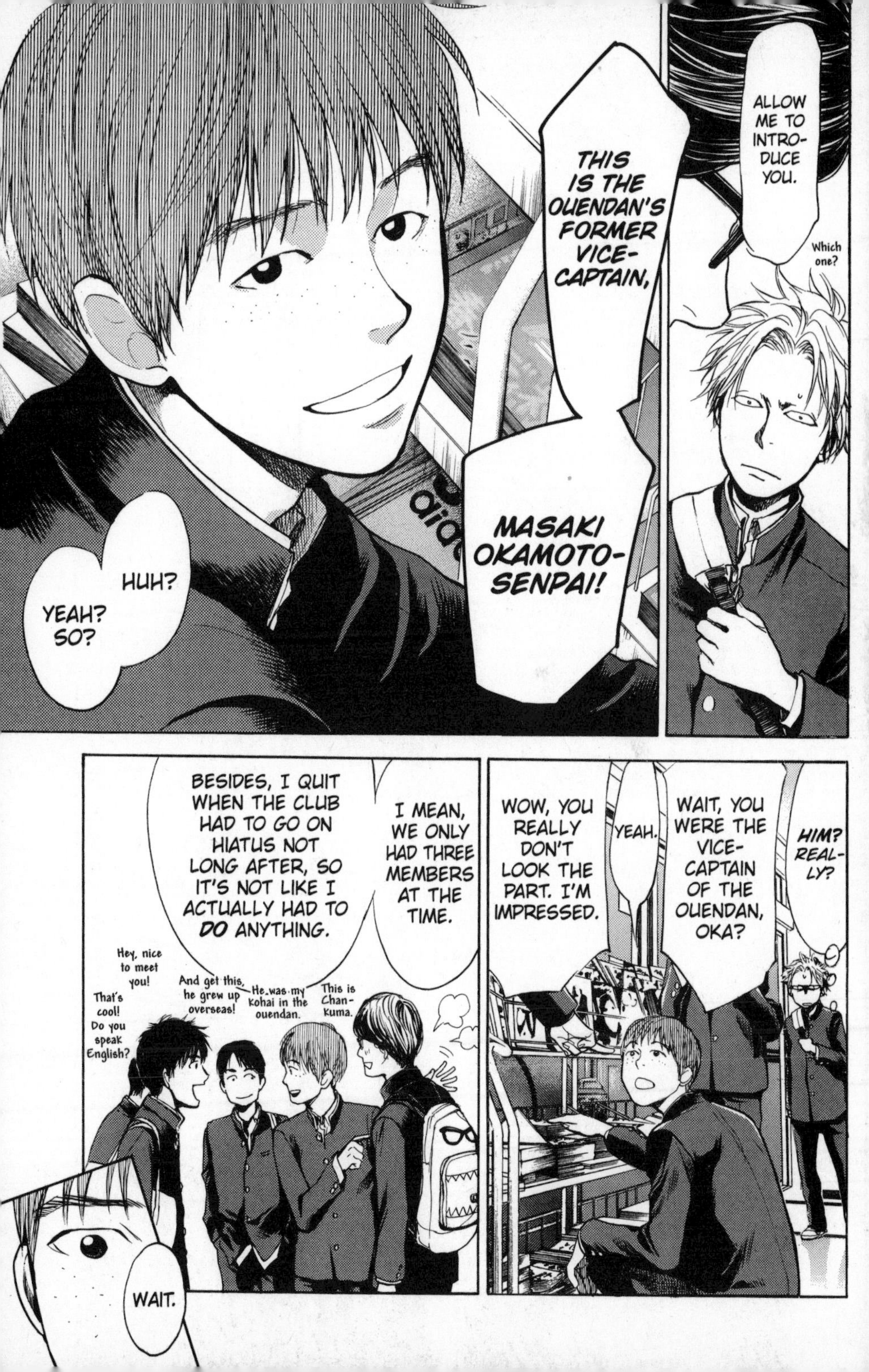
ALLOW ME TO INTRODUCE YOU.
Which one?
THIS IS THE OUENDAN'S FORMER VICE-CAPTAIN,
MASAKI OKAMOTO-SENPAI!
HUH?
YEAH? SO?
HIM? REALLY?
WAIT, YOU WERE THE VICE-CAPTAIN OF THE OUENDAN, OKA?
YEAH.
WOW, YOU REALLY DON'T LOOK THE PART. I'M IMPRESSED.
I MEAN, WE ONLY HAD THREE MEMBERS AT THE TIME.
BESIDES, I QUIT WHEN THE CLUB HAD TO GO ON HIATUS NOT LONG AFTER, SO IT'S NOT LIKE I ACTUALLY HAD TO DO ANYTHING.
This is Chan-kuma.
He was my kohai in the ouendan.
And get this, he grew up overseas!
Hey, nice to meet you!
That's cool! Do you speak English?
WAIT.

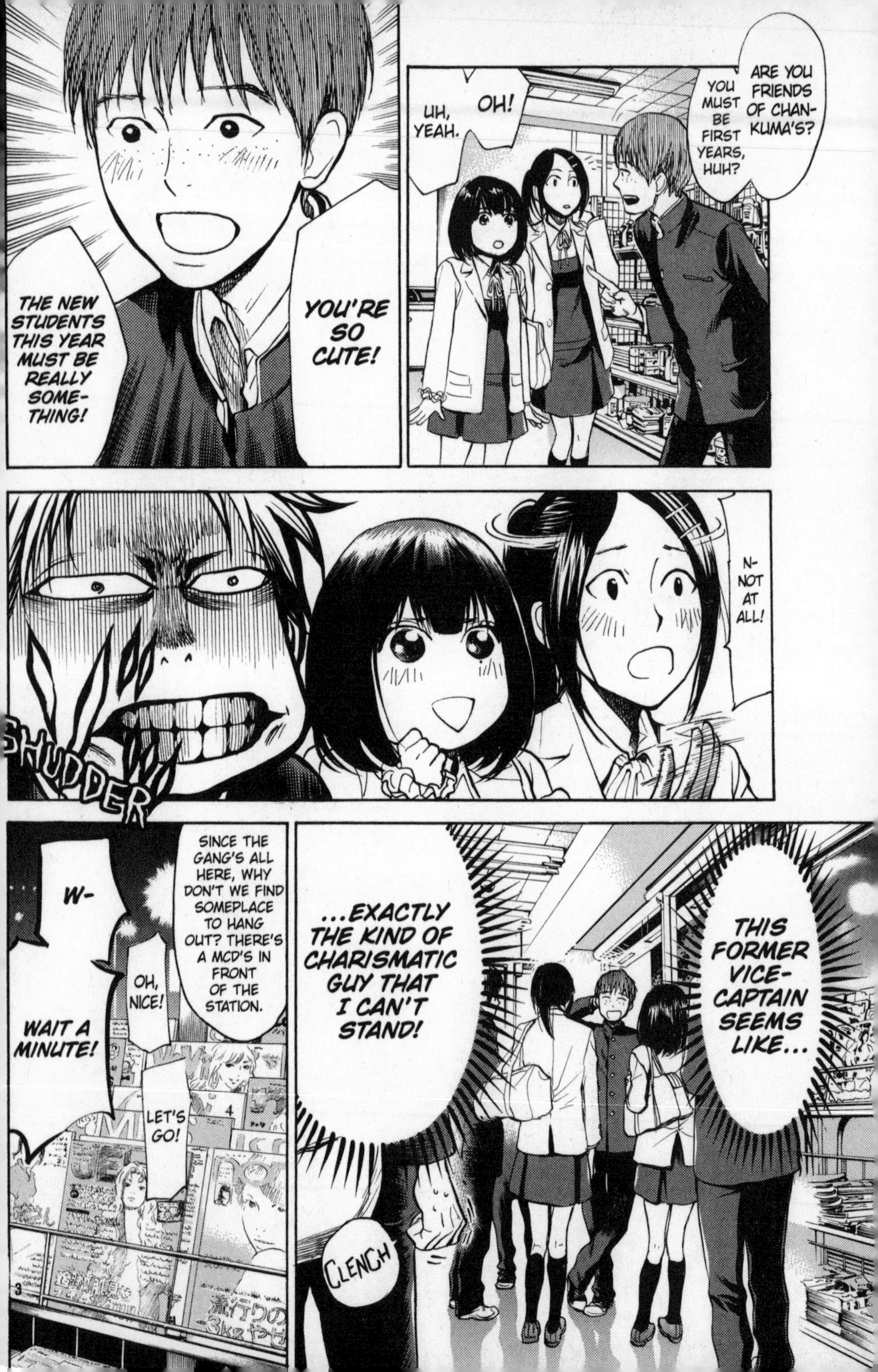
ARE YOU FRIENDS OF CHAN-KUMA'S?
YOU MUST BE FIRST YEARS, HUH?
OH!
UH, YEAH.
YOU'RE SO CUTE!
THE NEW STUDENTS THIS YEAR MUST BE REALLY SOME-THING!
N-NOT AT ALL!
SHUDDER
THIS FORMER VICE-CAPTAIN SEEMS LIKE...
...EXACTLY THE KIND OF CHARISMATIC GUY THAT I CAN'T STAND!
CLENCH
SINCE THE GANG'S ALL HERE, WHY DON'T WE FIND SOMEPLACE TO HANG OUT? THERE'S A MCD'S IN FRONT OF THE STATION.
OH, NICE!
W-
WAIT A MINUTE!
LET'S GO!

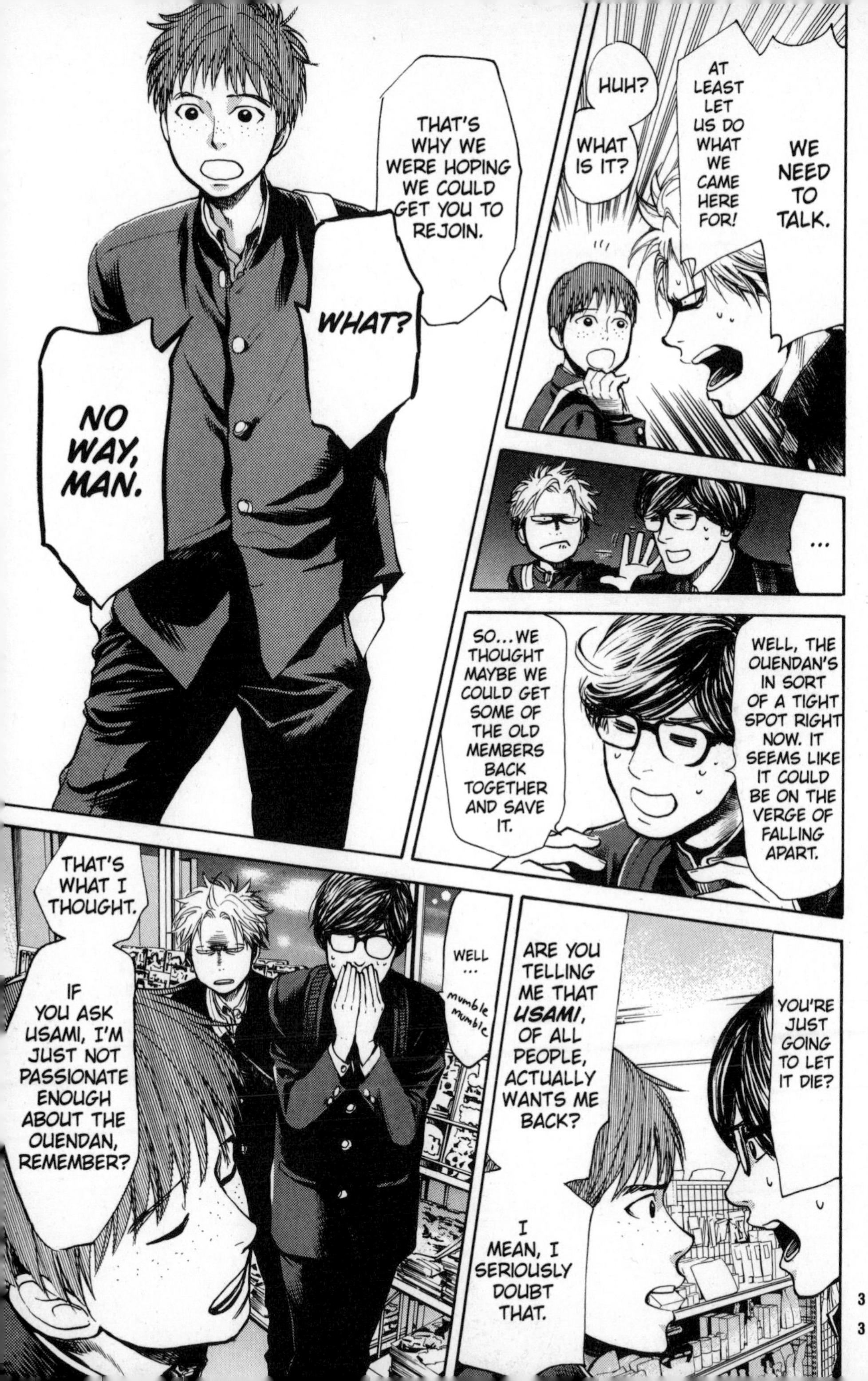
WE NEED TO TALK.
AT LEAST LET US DO WHAT WE CAME HERE FOR!
HUH?
WHAT IS IT?
...
WELL, THE OUENDAN'S IN SORT OF A TIGHT SPOT RIGHT NOW. IT SEEMS LIKE IT COULD BE ON THE VERGE OF FALLING APART.
SO...WE THOUGHT MAYBE WE COULD GET SOME OF THE OLD MEMBERS BACK TOGETHER AND SAVE IT.
THAT'S WHY WE WERE HOPING WE COULD GET YOU TO REJOIN.
WHAT?
NO WAY, MAN.
YOU'RE JUST GOING TO LET IT DIE?
ARE YOU TELLING ME THAT USAMI, OF ALL PEOPLE, ACTUALLY WANTS ME BACK?
I MEAN, I SERIOUSLY DOUBT THAT.
WELL ...
mumble mumble
THAT'S WHAT I THOUGHT.
IF YOU ASK USAMI, I'M JUST NOT PASSIONATE ENOUGH ABOUT THE OUENDAN, REMEMBER?

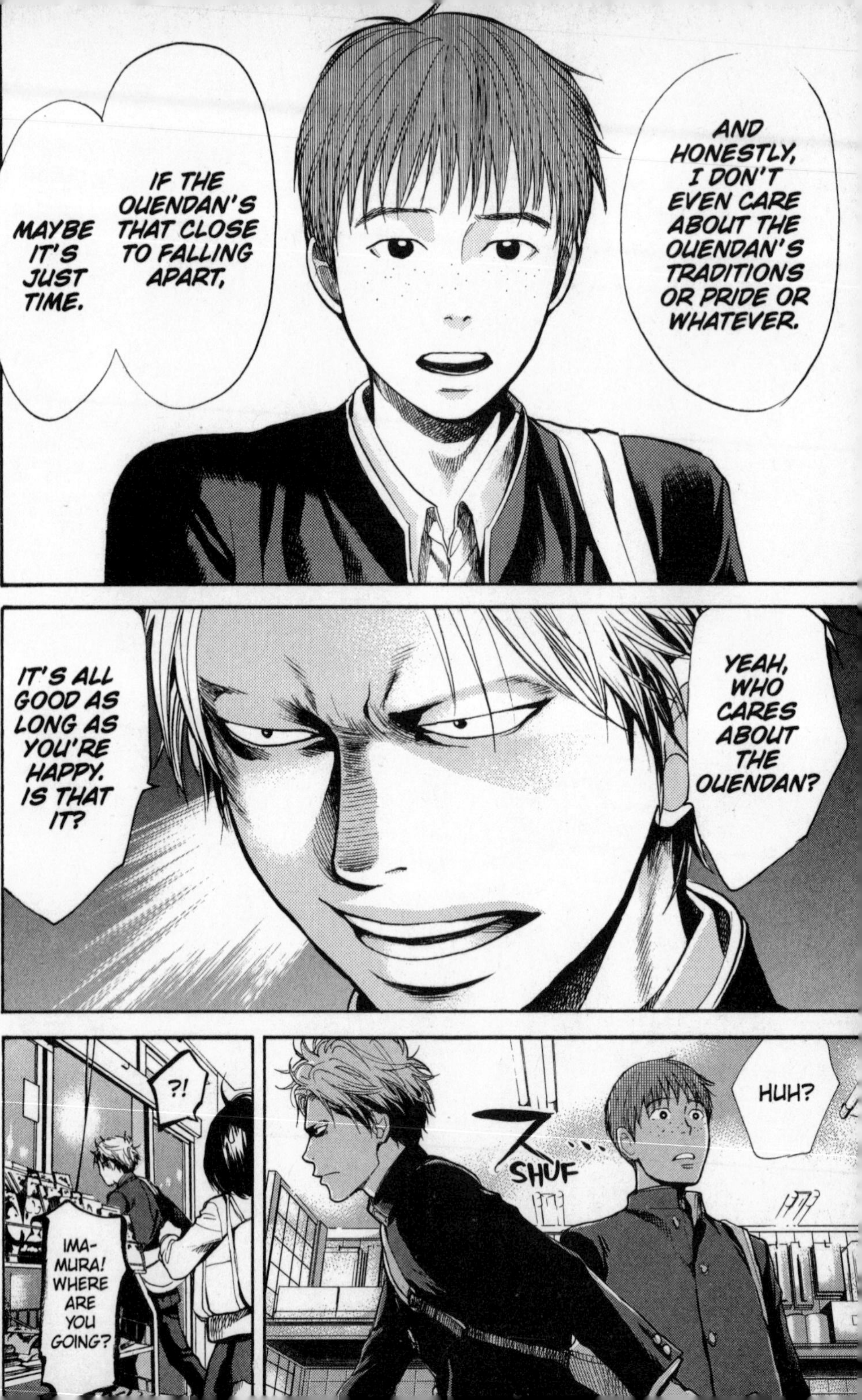
AND HONESTLY, I DON'T EVEN CARE ABOUT THE OUENDAN'S TRADITIONS OR PRIDE OR WHATEVER.
IF THE OUENDAN'S THAT CLOSE TO FALLING APART,
MAYBE IT'S JUST TIME.
YEAH, WHO CARES ABOUT THE OUENDAN?
IT'S ALL GOOD AS LONG AS YOU'RE HAPPY. IS THAT IT?
HUH?
SHUF
?!
IMA-MURA! WHERE ARE YOU GOING?

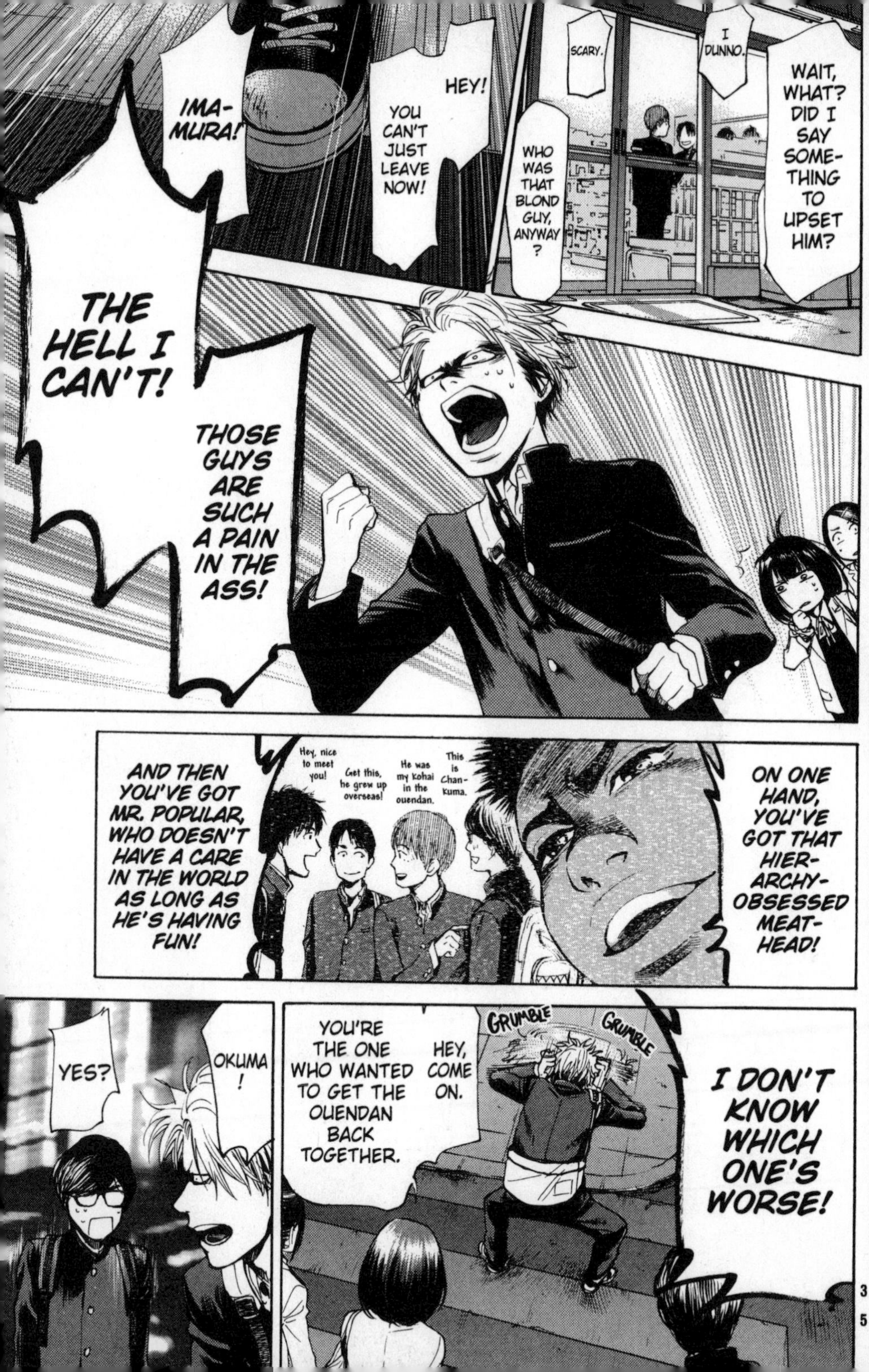
WAIT, WHAT? DID I SAY SOMETHING TO UPSET HIM?
I DUNNO.
SCARY.
WHO WAS THAT BLOND GUY, ANYWAY?
HEY!
YOU CAN'T JUST LEAVE NOW!
IMA-MURA!
THE HELL I CAN'T!
THOSE GUYS ARE SUCH A PAIN IN THE ASS!
ON ONE HAND, YOU'VE GOT THAT HIERARCHY-OBSESSED MEATHEAD!
This is Chankuma.
He was my kohai in the ouendan.
Get this, he grew up overseas!
Hey, nice to meet you!
AND THEN YOU'VE GOT MR. POPULAR, WHO DOESN'T HAVE A CARE IN THE WORLD AS LONG AS HE'S HAVING FUN!
I DON'T KNOW WHICH ONE'S WORSE!
GRUMBLE
GRUMBLE
HEY, COME ON.
YOU'RE THE ONE WHO WANTED TO GET THE OUENDAN BACK TOGETHER.
OKUMA!
YES?

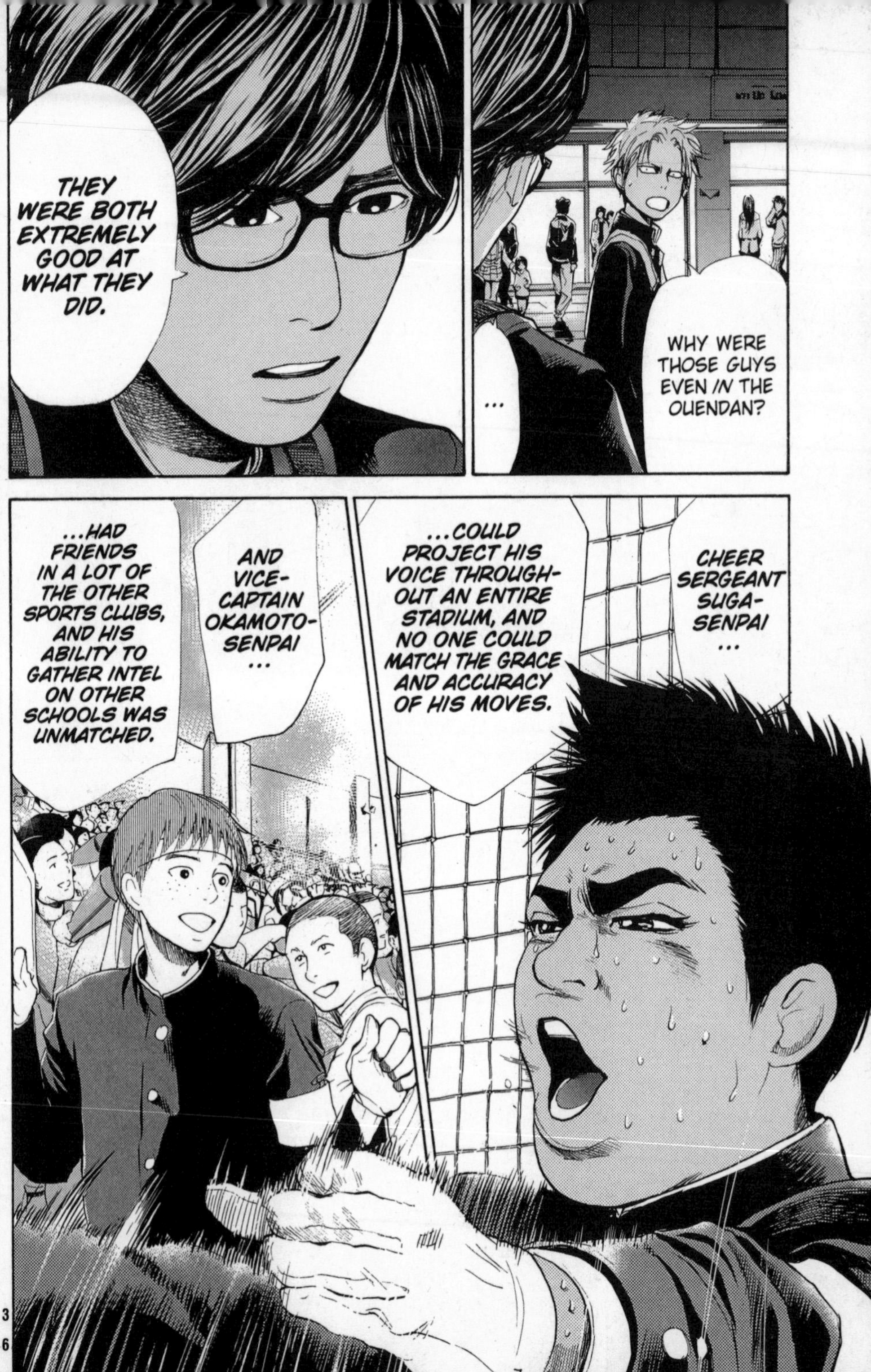
WHY WERE THOSE GUYS EVEN IN THE OUENDAN?
...
THEY WERE BOTH EXTREMELY GOOD AT WHAT THEY DID.
CHEER SERGEANT SUGA-SENPAI ...
...COULD PROJECT HIS VOICE THROUGH-OUT AN ENTIRE STADIUM, AND NO ONE COULD MATCH THE GRACE AND ACCURACY OF HIS MOVES.
AND VICE-CAPTAIN OKAMOTO-SENPAI ...
...HAD FRIENDS IN A LOT OF THE OTHER SPORTS CLUBS, AND HIS ABILITY TO GATHER INTEL ON OTHER SCHOOLS WAS UNMATCHED.

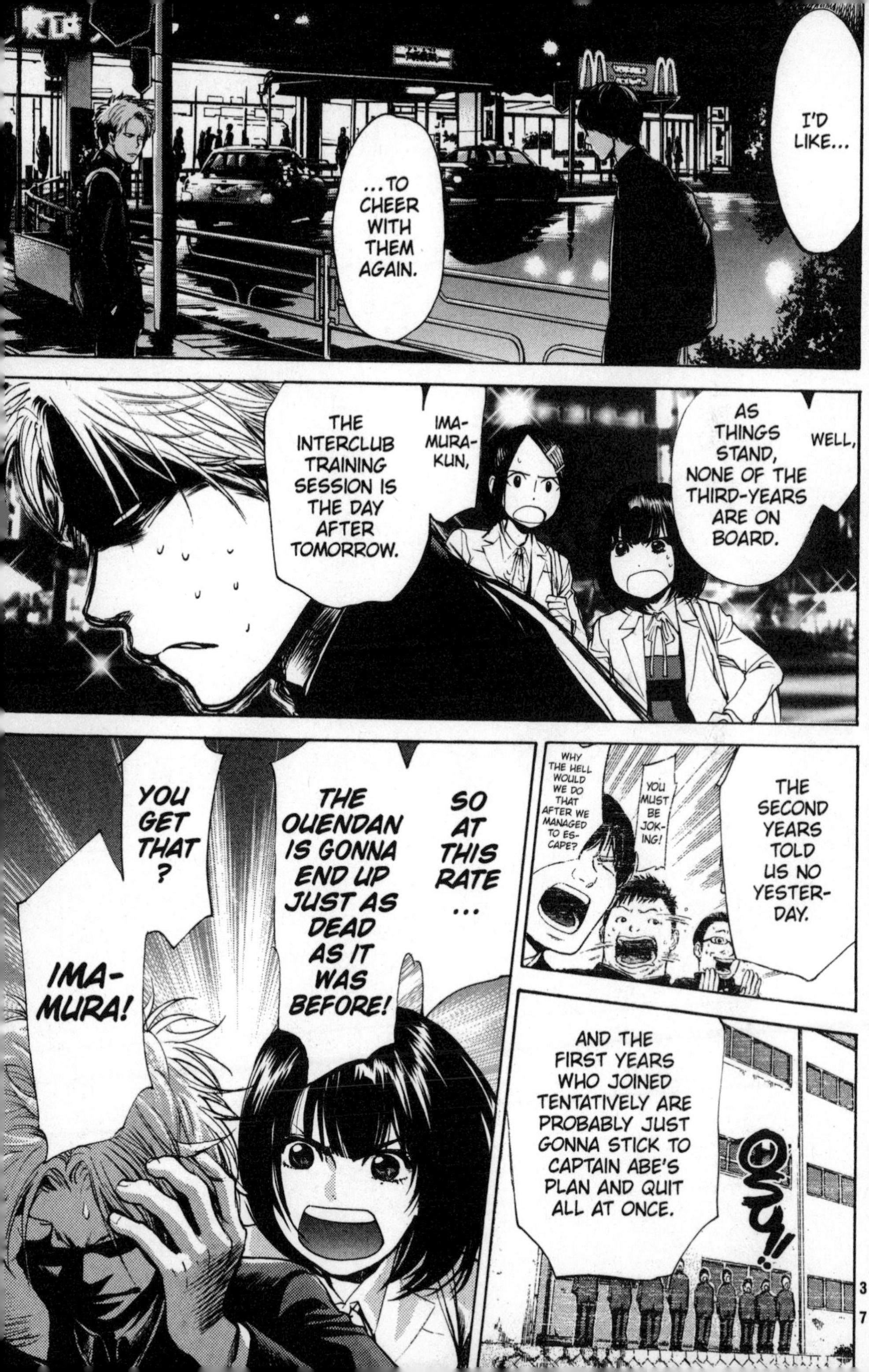
I'D LIKE...
...TO CHEER WITH THEM AGAIN.
WELL,
AS THINGS STAND, NONE OF THE THIRD-YEARS ARE ON BOARD.
IMAMURA-KUN,
THE INTERCLUB TRAINING SESSION IS THE DAY AFTER TOMORROW.
THE SECOND YEARS TOLD US NO YESTERDAY.
YOU MUST BE JOKING!
WHY THE HELL WOULD WE DO THAT AFTER WE MANAGED TO ESCAPE?
AND THE FIRST YEARS WHO JOINED TENTATIVELY ARE PROBABLY JUST GONNA STICK TO CAPTAIN ABE'S PLAN AND QUIT ALL AT ONCE.
SO AT THIS RATE...
THE OUENDAN IS GONNA END UP JUST AS DEAD AS IT WAS BEFORE!
YOU GET THAT?
IMAMURA!

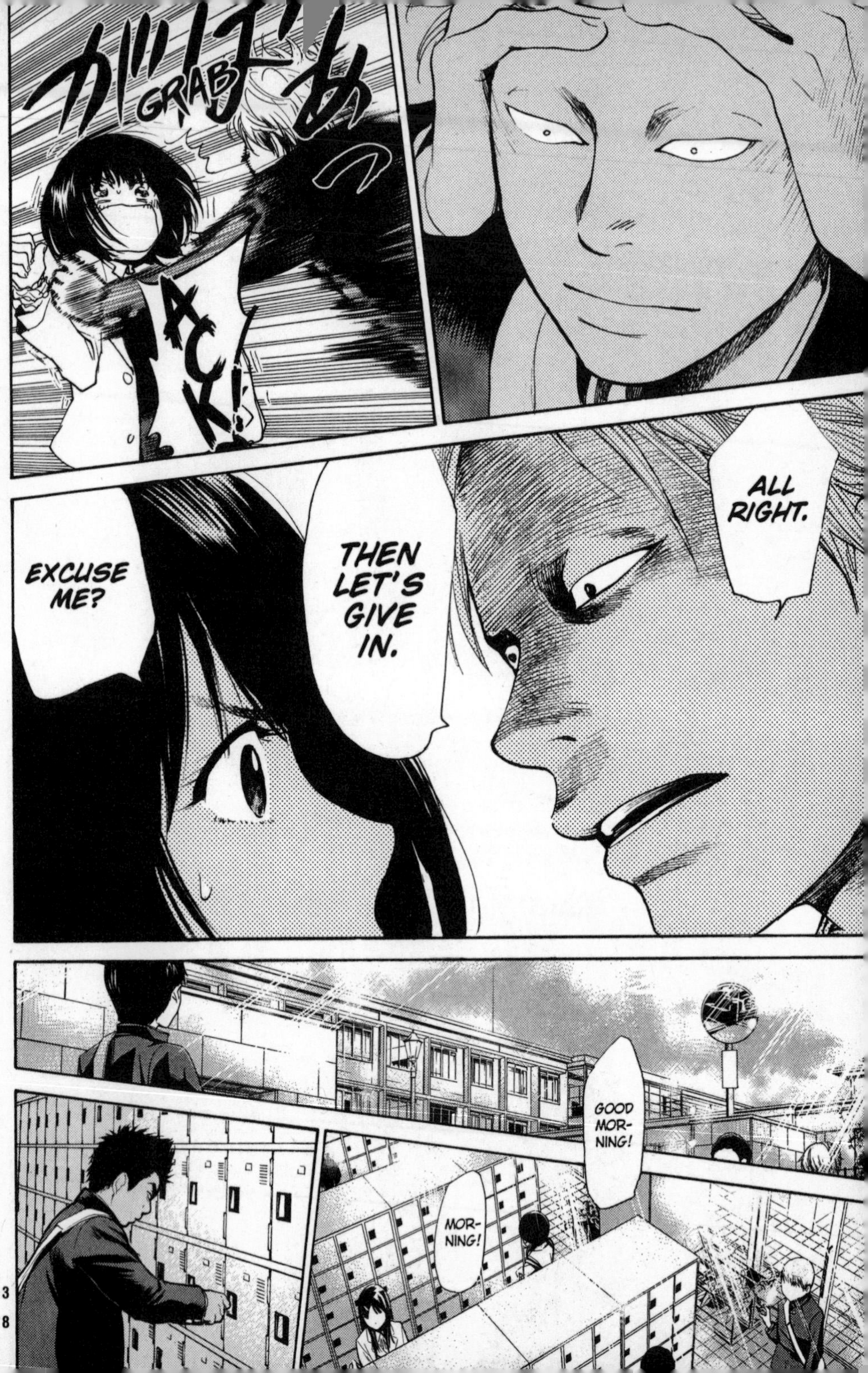
GRAB
JACK!
ALL RIGHT.
THEN LET'S GIVE IN.
EXCUSE ME?
GOOD MOR-NING!
MOR-NING!

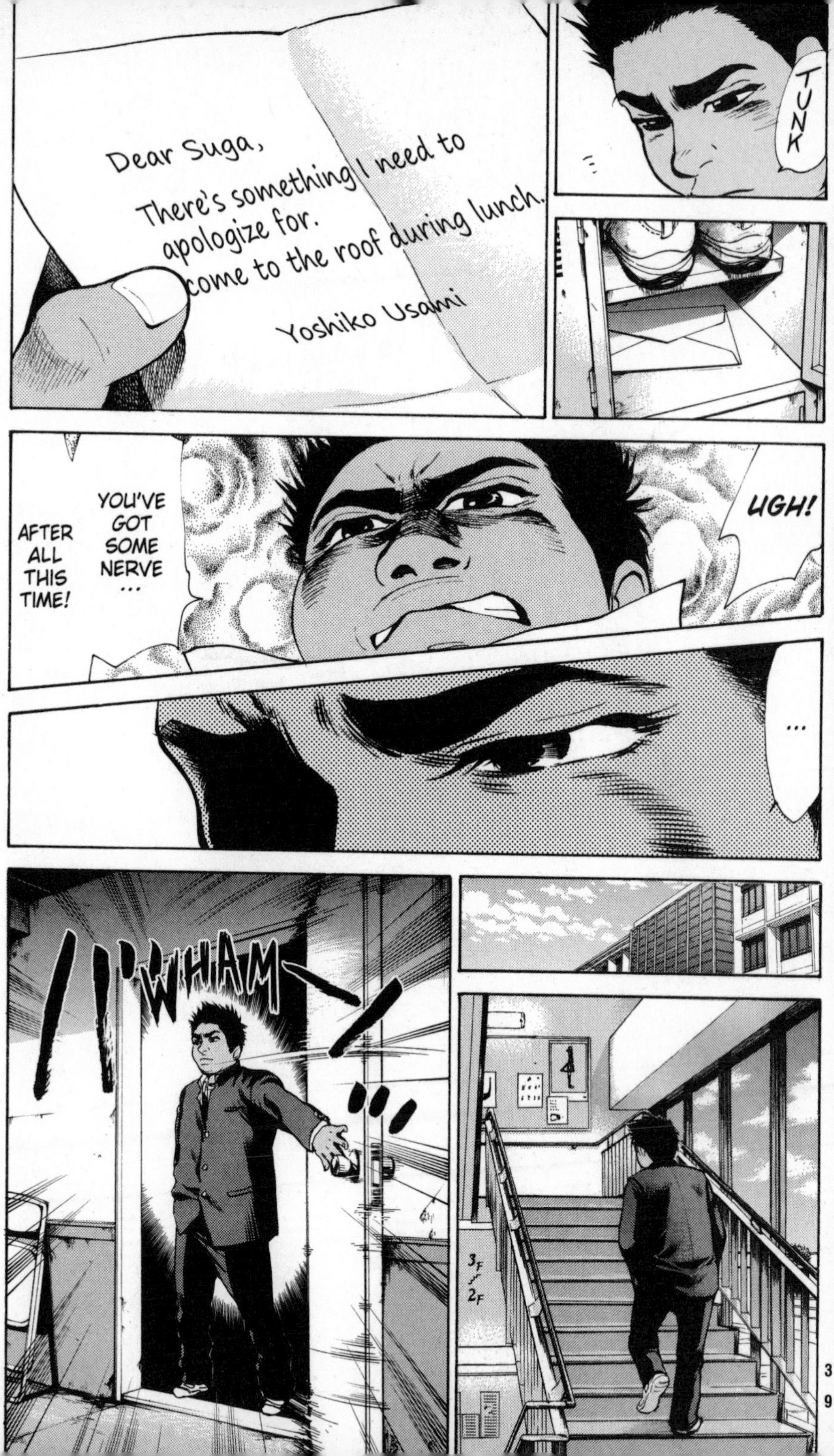
TUNK
Dear Suga,
There's something I need to apologize for.
come to the roof during lunch.
Yoshiko Usami
UGH!
YOU'VE GOT SOME NERVE...
AFTER ALL THIS TIME!
...
3F 2F
WHAM

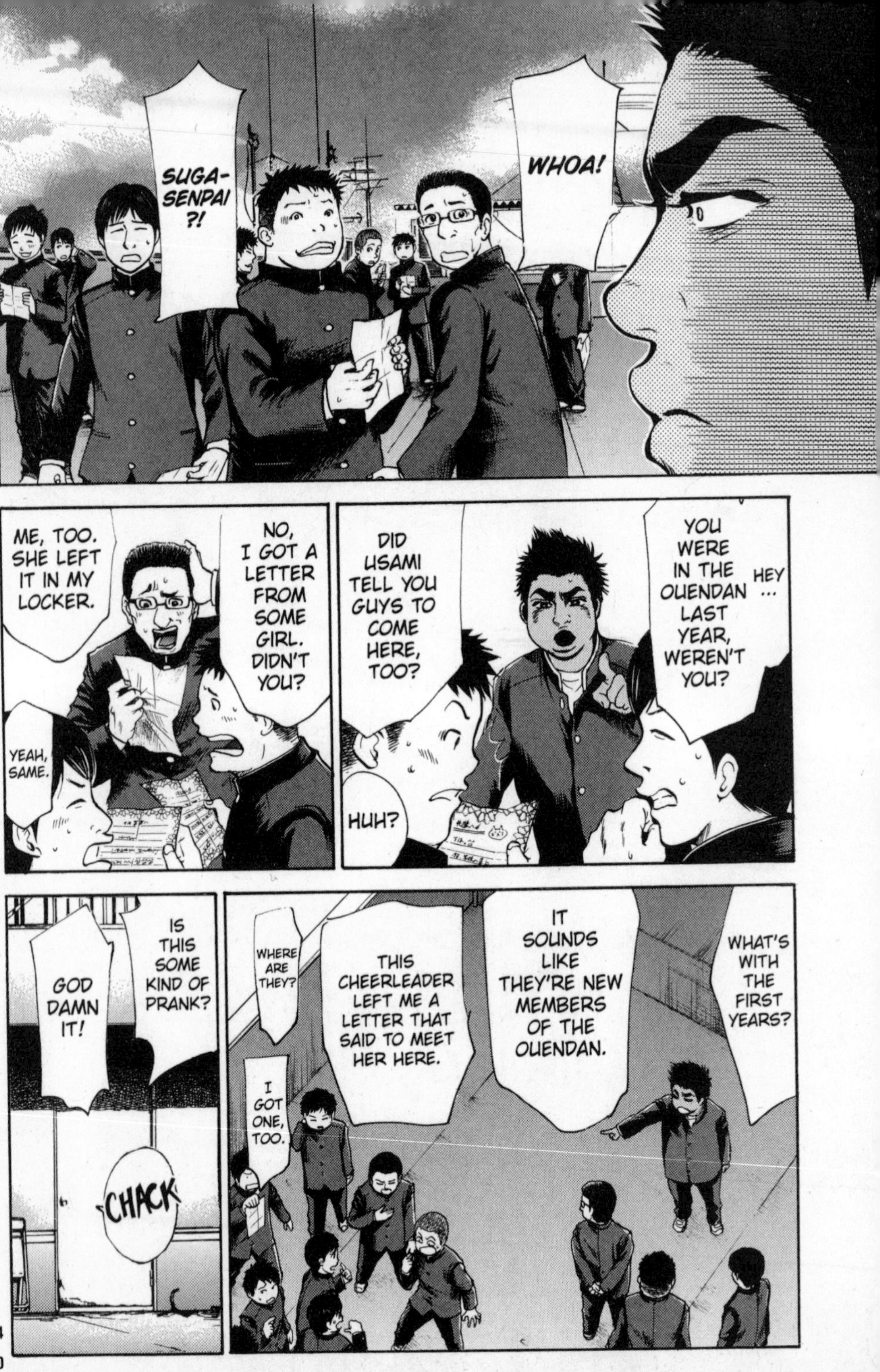
WHOA!
SUGA-SENPAI?!
HEY ...
YOU WERE IN THE OUENDAN LAST YEAR, WEREN'T YOU?
DID USAMI TELL YOU GUYS TO COME HERE, TOO?
HUH?
NO, I GOT A LETTER FROM SOME GIRL. DIDN'T YOU?
ME, TOO. SHE LEFT IT IN MY LOCKER.
YEAH, SAME.
WHAT'S WITH THE FIRST YEARS?
IT SOUNDS LIKE THEY'RE NEW MEMBERS OF THE OUENDAN.
THIS CHEERLEADER LEFT ME A LETTER THAT SAID TO MEET HER HERE.
WHERE ARE THEY?
I GOT ONE, TOO.
IS THIS SOME KIND OF PRANK?
GOD DAMN IT!
CHACK

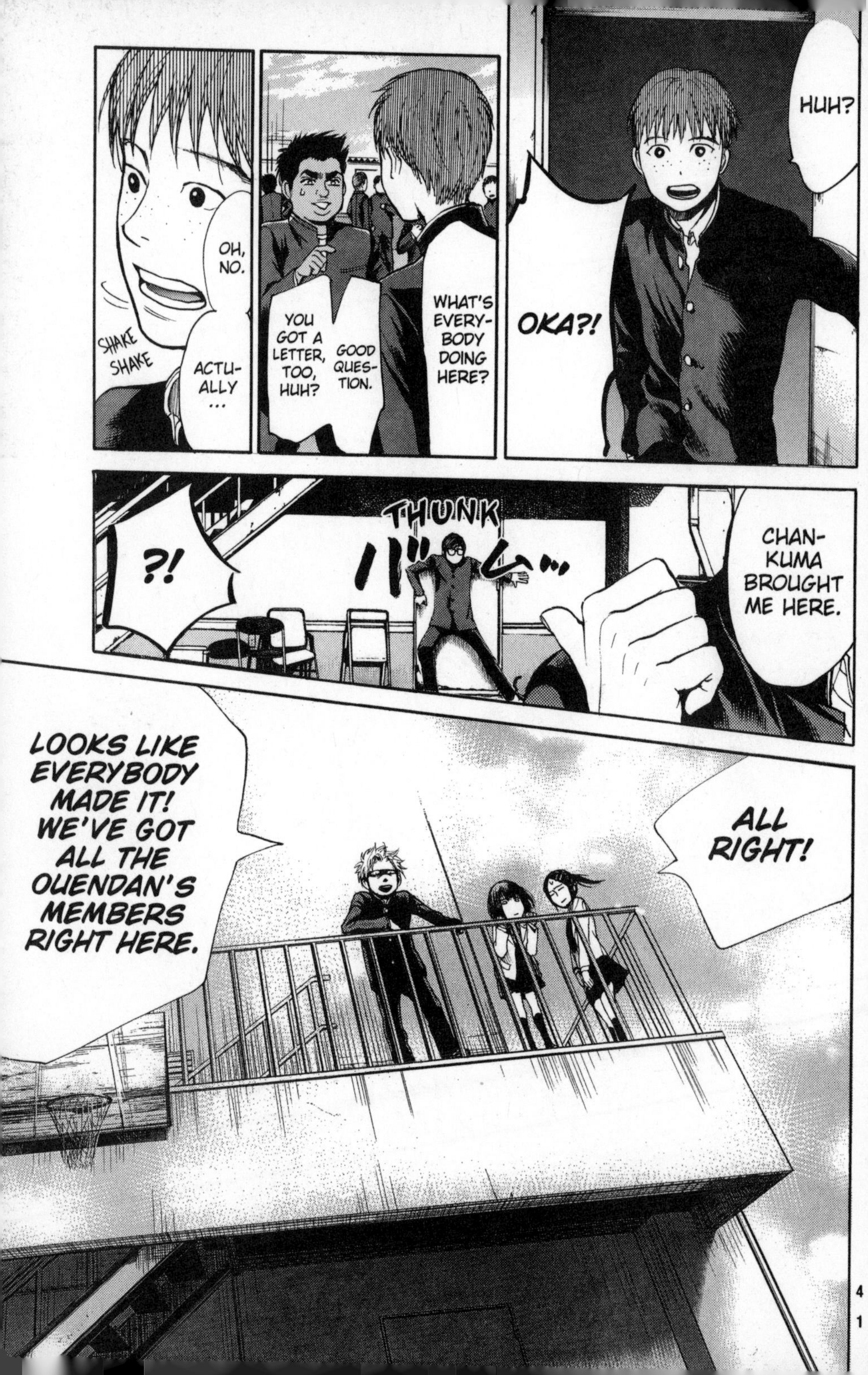
HUH?
OKA?!
WHAT'S EVERYBODY DOING HERE?
GOOD QUESTION.
YOU GOT A LETTER, TOO, HUH?
OH, NO.
ACTUALLY...
SHAKE SHAKE
CHAN-KUMA BROUGHT ME HERE.
THUNK
バム
?!
ALL RIGHT!
LOOKS LIKE EVERYBODY MADE IT! WE'VE GOT ALL THE OUENDAN'S MEMBERS RIGHT HERE.

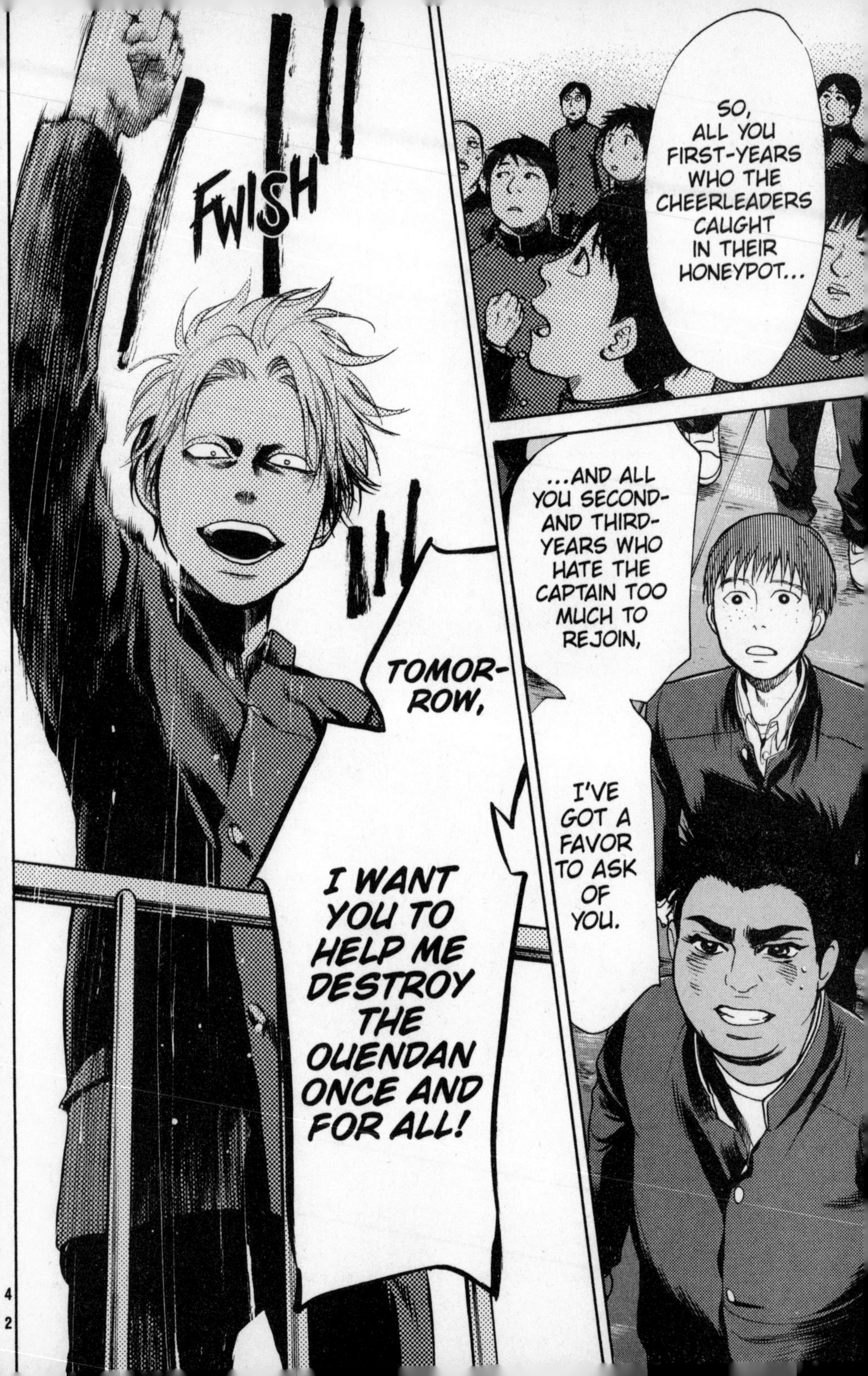
SO, ALL YOU FIRST-YEARS WHO THE CHEERLEADERS CAUGHT IN THEIR HONEYPOT...
...AND ALL YOU SECOND- AND THIRD-YEARS WHO HATE THE CAPTAIN TOO MUCH TO REJOIN,
I'VE GOT A FAVOR TO ASK OF YOU.
FWISH
TOMOR-ROW,
I WANT YOU TO HELP ME DESTROY THE OUENDAN ONCE AND FOR ALL!

12. EVERYBODY YELL NOW!

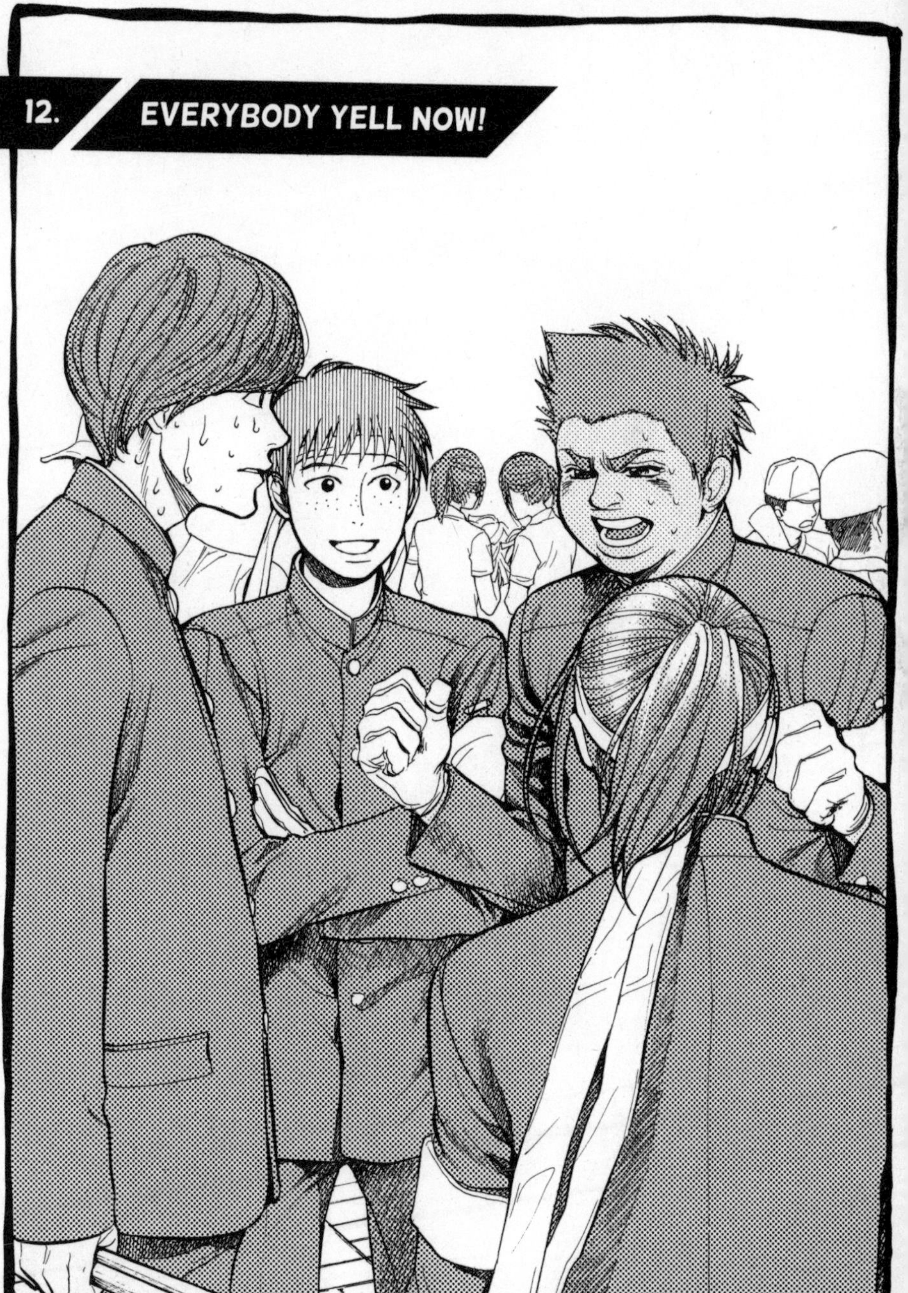

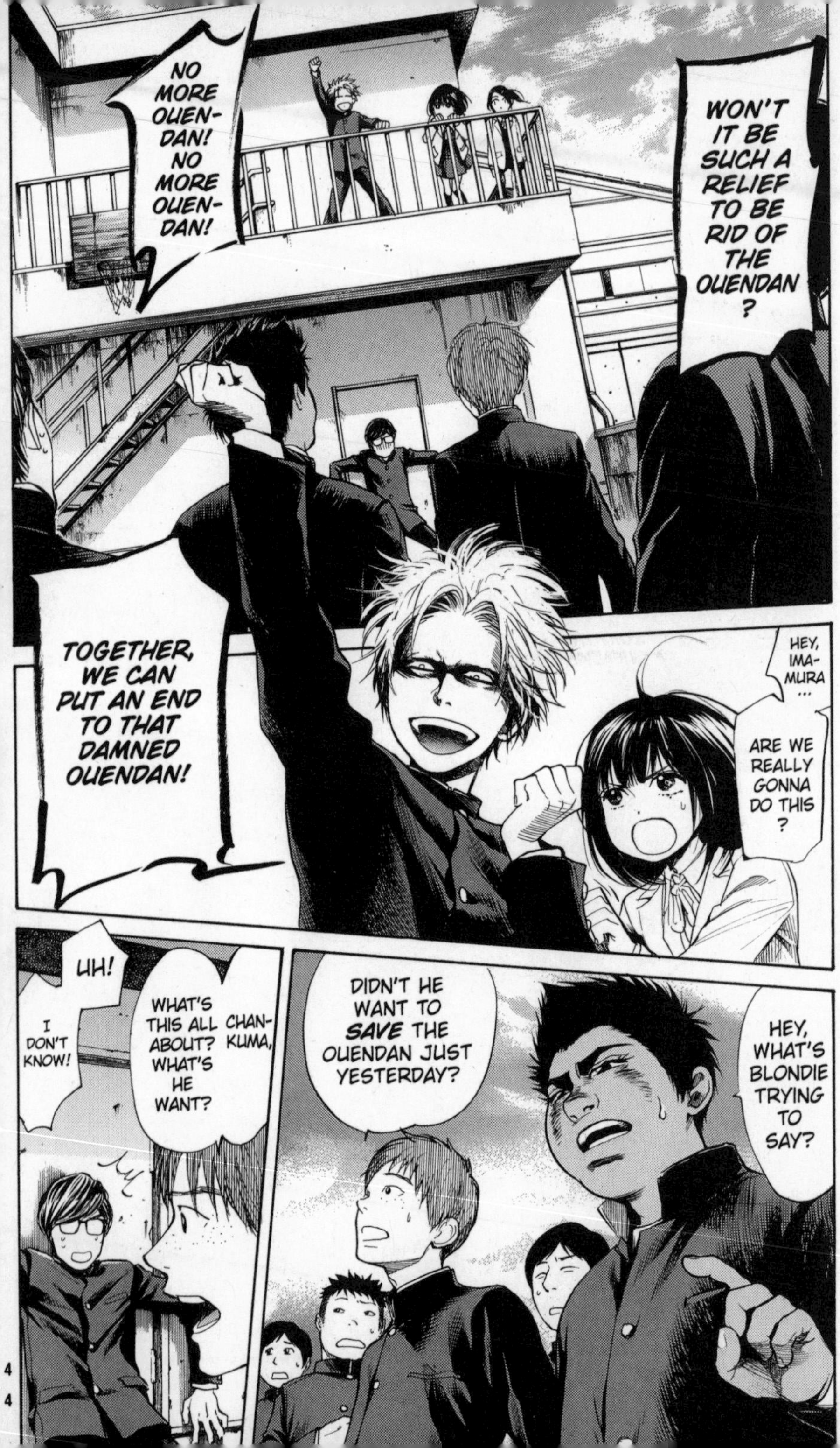
WON'T IT BE SUCH A RELIEF TO BE RID OF THE OUENDAN?
NO MORE OUENDAN! NO MORE OUENDAN!
TOGETHER, WE CAN PUT AN END TO THAT DAMNED OUENDAN!
HEY, IMAMURA...
ARE WE REALLY GONNA DO THIS?
HEY, WHAT'S BLONDIE TRYING TO SAY?
DIDN'T HE WANT TO SAVE THE OUENDAN JUST YESTERDAY?
CHANKUMA,
WHAT'S THIS ALL ABOUT? WHAT'S HE WANT?
UH!
I DON'T KNOW!

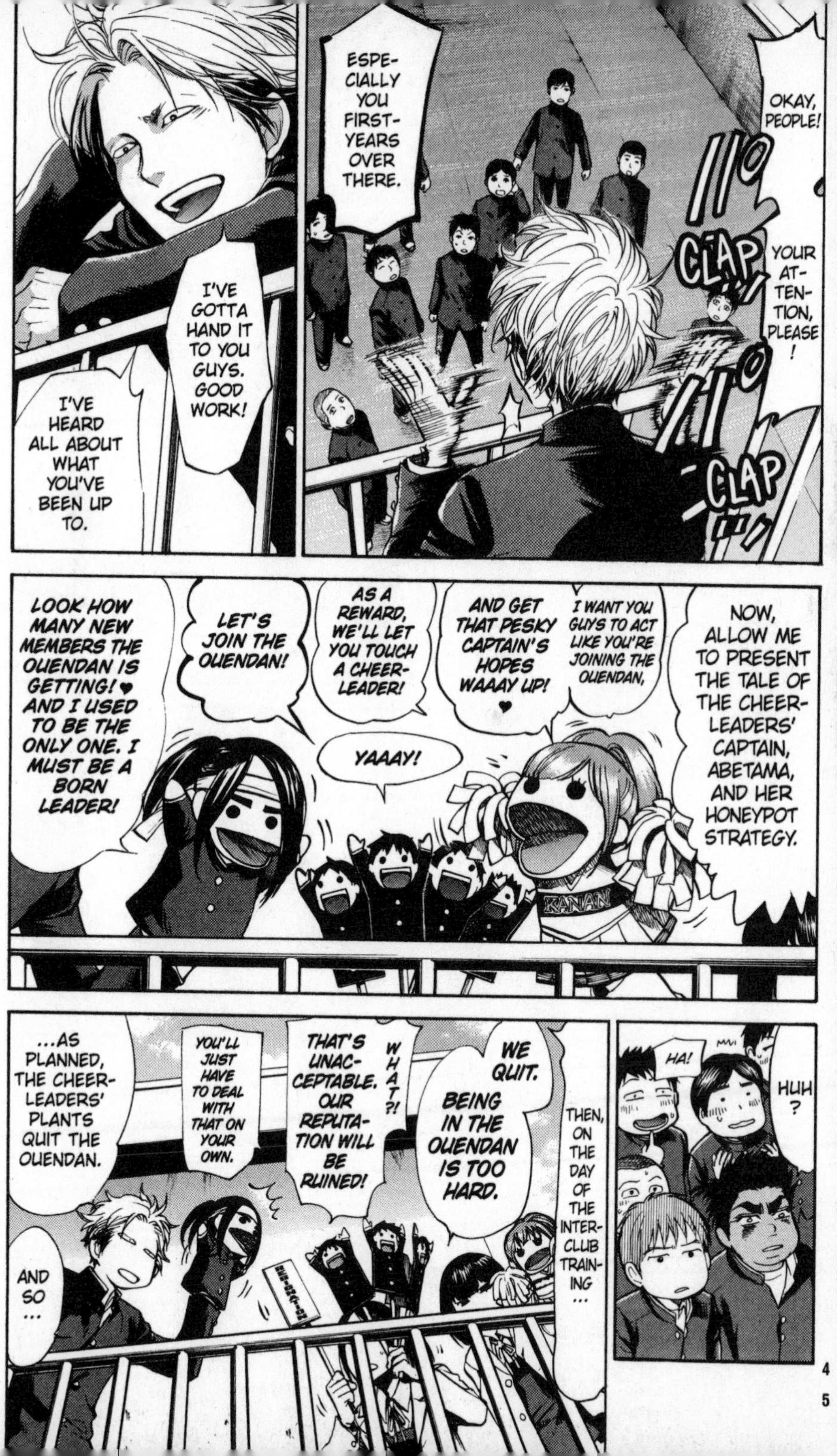
OKAY, PEOPLE!
CLAP
YOUR ATTENTION, PLEASE!
CLAP
ESPECIALLY YOU FIRST-YEARS OVER THERE.
I'VE GOTTA HAND IT TO YOU GUYS. GOOD WORK!
I'VE HEARD ALL ABOUT WHAT YOU'VE BEEN UP TO.
NOW, ALLOW ME TO PRESENT THE TALE OF THE CHEERLEADERS' CAPTAIN, ABETAMA, AND HER HONEYPOT STRATEGY.
I WANT YOU GUYS TO ACT LIKE YOU'RE JOINING THE OUENDAN,
AND GET THAT PESKY CAPTAIN'S HOPES WAAAY UP! ♥
AS A REWARD, WE'LL LET YOU TOUCH A CHEERLEADER!
LET'S JOIN THE OUENDAN!
YAAAY!
LOOK HOW MANY NEW MEMBERS THE OUENDAN IS GETTING! ♥ AND I USED TO BE THE ONLY ONE. I MUST BE A BORN LEADER!
KANAN
HUH?
HA!
THEN, ON THE DAY OF THE INTER-CLUB TRAINING...
WE QUIT.
BEING IN THE OUENDAN IS TOO HARD.
WHAT?!
THAT'S UNACCEPTABLE. OUR REPUTATION WILL BE RUINED!
YOU'LL JUST HAVE TO DEAL WITH THAT ON YOUR OWN.
...AS PLANNED, THE CHEERLEADERS' PLANTS QUIT THE OUENDAN.
AND SO...

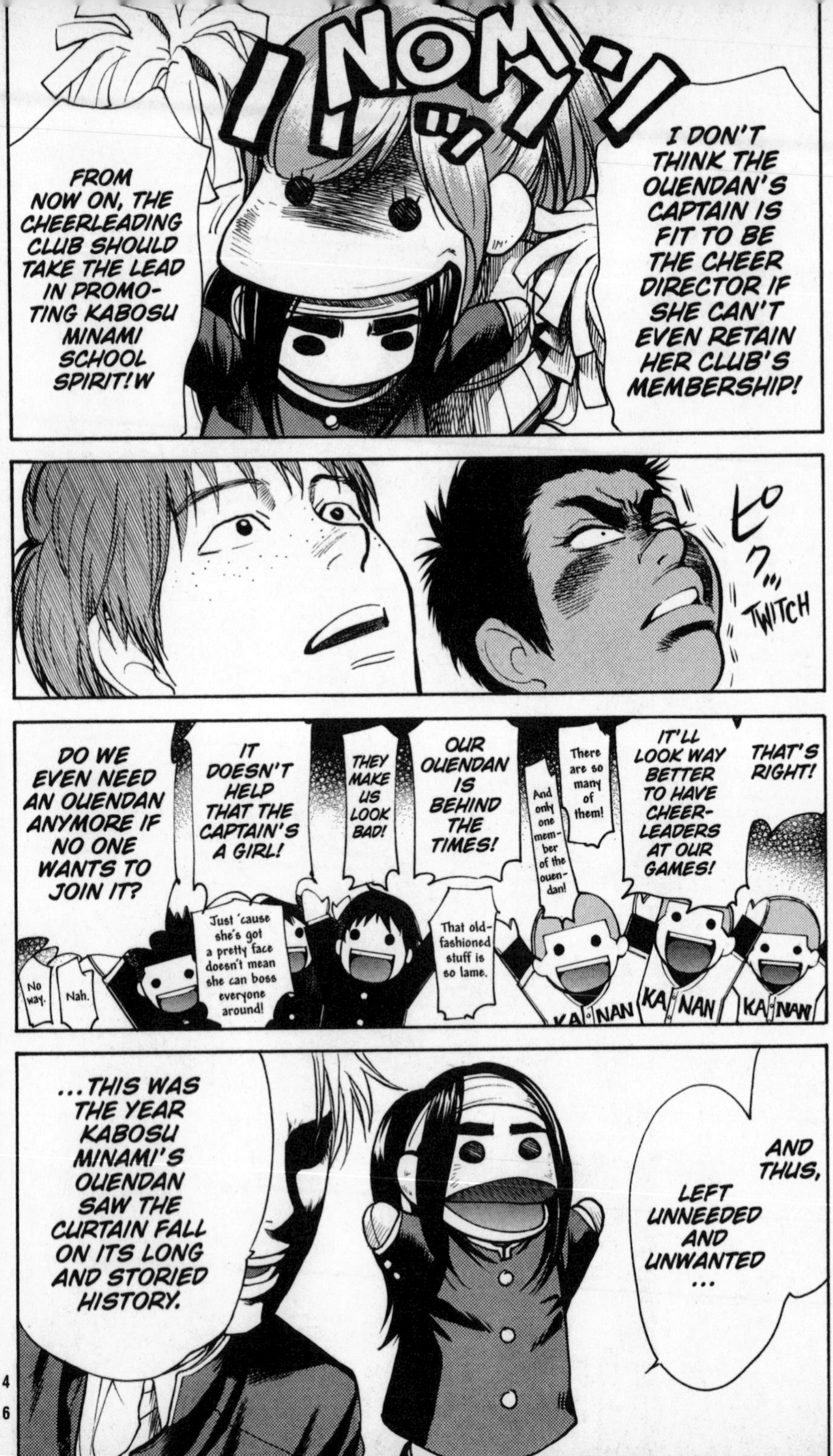
NO!!
I DON'T THINK THE OUENDAN'S CAPTAIN IS FIT TO BE THE CHEER DIRECTOR IF SHE CAN'T EVEN RETAIN HER CLUB'S MEMBERSHIP!
FROM NOW ON, THE CHEERLEADING CLUB SHOULD TAKE THE LEAD IN PROMOTING KABOSU MINAMI SCHOOL SPIRIT!W
TWITCH
THAT'S RIGHT!
IT'LL LOOK WAY BETTER TO HAVE CHEERLEADERS AT OUR GAMES!
There are so many of them!
And only one member of the ouendan!
OUR OUENDAN IS BEHIND THE TIMES!
THEY MAKE US LOOK BAD!
IT DOESN'T HELP THAT THE CAPTAIN'S A GIRL!
DO WE EVEN NEED AN OUENDAN ANYMORE IF NO ONE WANTS TO JOIN IT?
KA NAN
KA NAN
KA NAN
That old-fashioned stuff is so lame.
Just 'cause she's got a pretty face doesn't mean she can boss everyone around!
Nah.
No way.
AND THUS,
LEFT UNNEEDED AND UNWANTED...
...THIS WAS THE YEAR KABOSU MINAMI'S OUENDAN SAW THE CURTAIN FALL ON ITS LONG AND STORIED HISTORY.

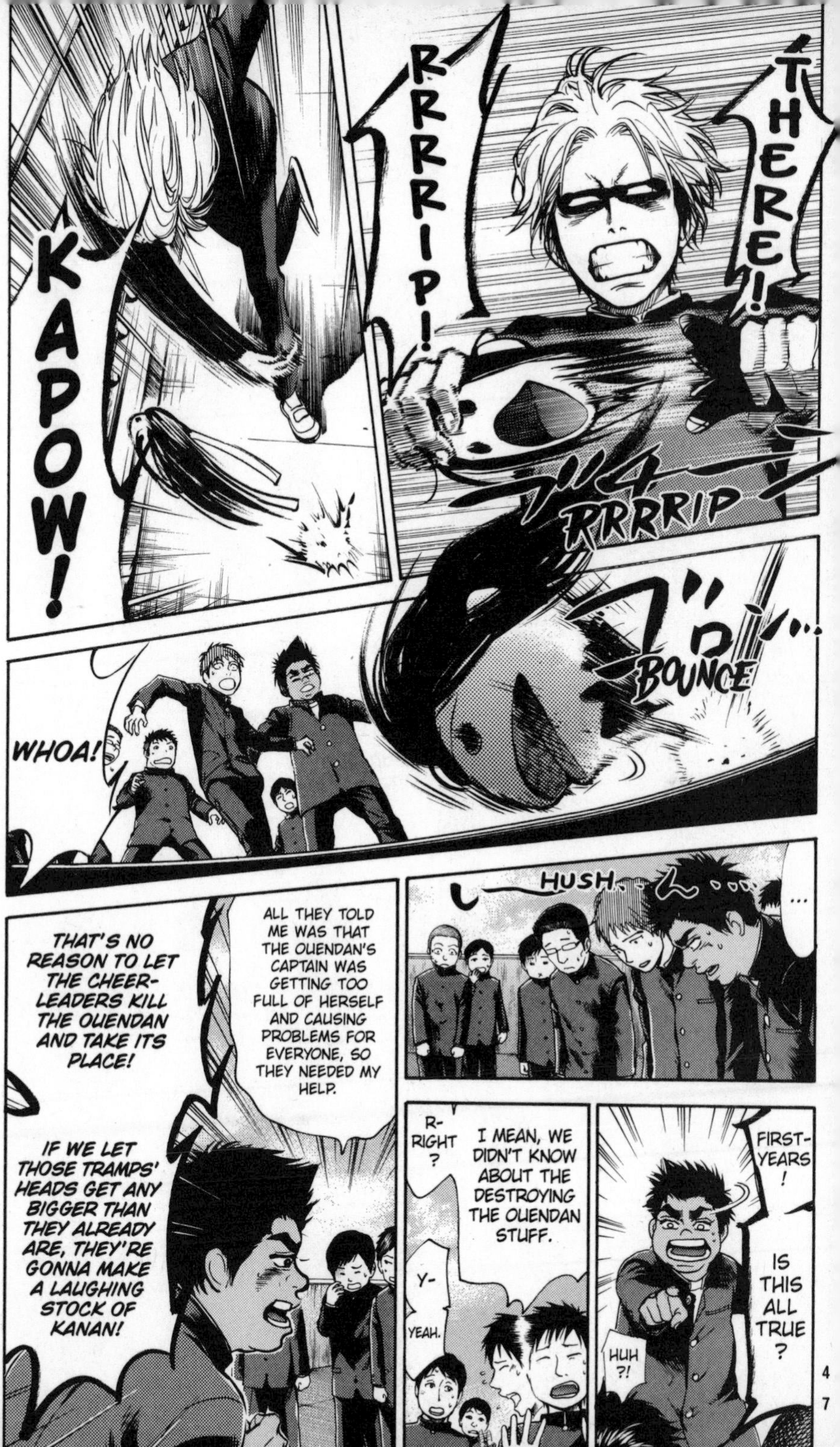
THERE!
RRRRIP!
RRRRIP
KAPOW!
BOUNCE
WHOA!
HUSH
...
FIRST-YEARS!
IS THIS ALL TRUE?
HUH?!
R-RIGHT?
I MEAN, WE DIDN'T KNOW ABOUT THE DESTROYING THE OUENDAN STUFF.
Y-YEAH.
ALL THEY TOLD ME WAS THAT THE OUENDAN'S CAPTAIN WAS GETTING TOO FULL OF HERSELF AND CAUSING PROBLEMS FOR EVERYONE, SO THEY NEEDED MY HELP.
THAT'S NO REASON TO LET THE CHEER-LEADERS KILL THE OUENDAN AND TAKE ITS PLACE!
IF WE LET THOSE TRAMPS' HEADS GET ANY BIGGER THAN THEY ALREADY ARE, THEY'RE GONNA MAKE A LAUGHING STOCK OF KANAN!

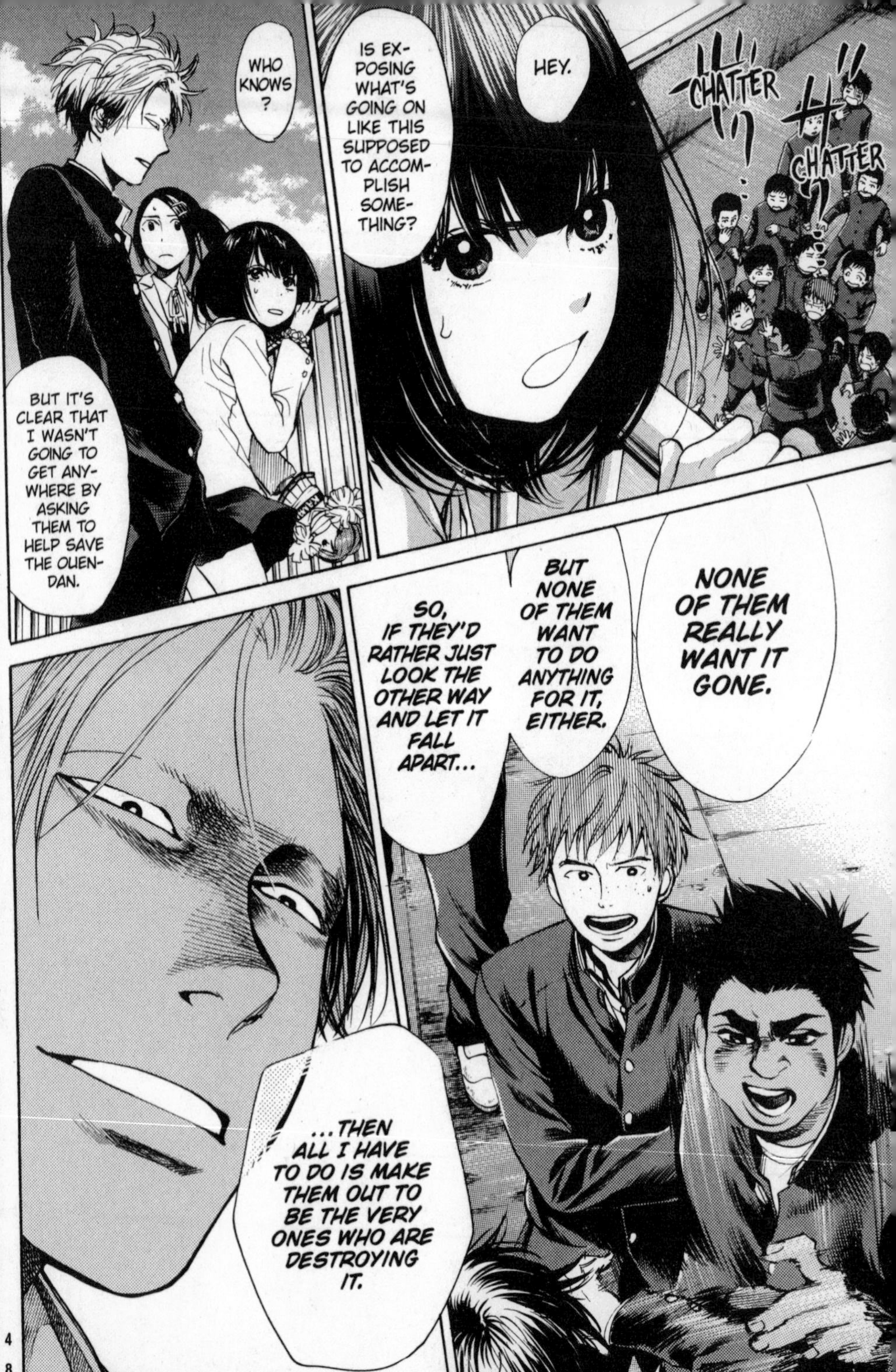
CHATTER
CHATTER
HEY.
IS EX-POSING WHAT'S GOING ON LIKE THIS SUPPOSED TO ACCOM-PLISH SOME-THING?
WHO KNOWS?
BUT IT'S CLEAR THAT I WASN'T GOING TO GET ANY-WHERE BY ASKING THEM TO HELP SAVE THE OUEN-DAN.
NONE OF THEM REALLY WANT IT GONE.
BUT NONE OF THEM WANT TO DO ANYTHING FOR IT, EITHER.
SO, IF THEY'D RATHER JUST LOOK THE OTHER WAY AND LET IT FALL APART...
...THEN ALL I HAVE TO DO IS MAKE THEM OUT TO BE THE VERY ONES WHO ARE DESTROYING IT.

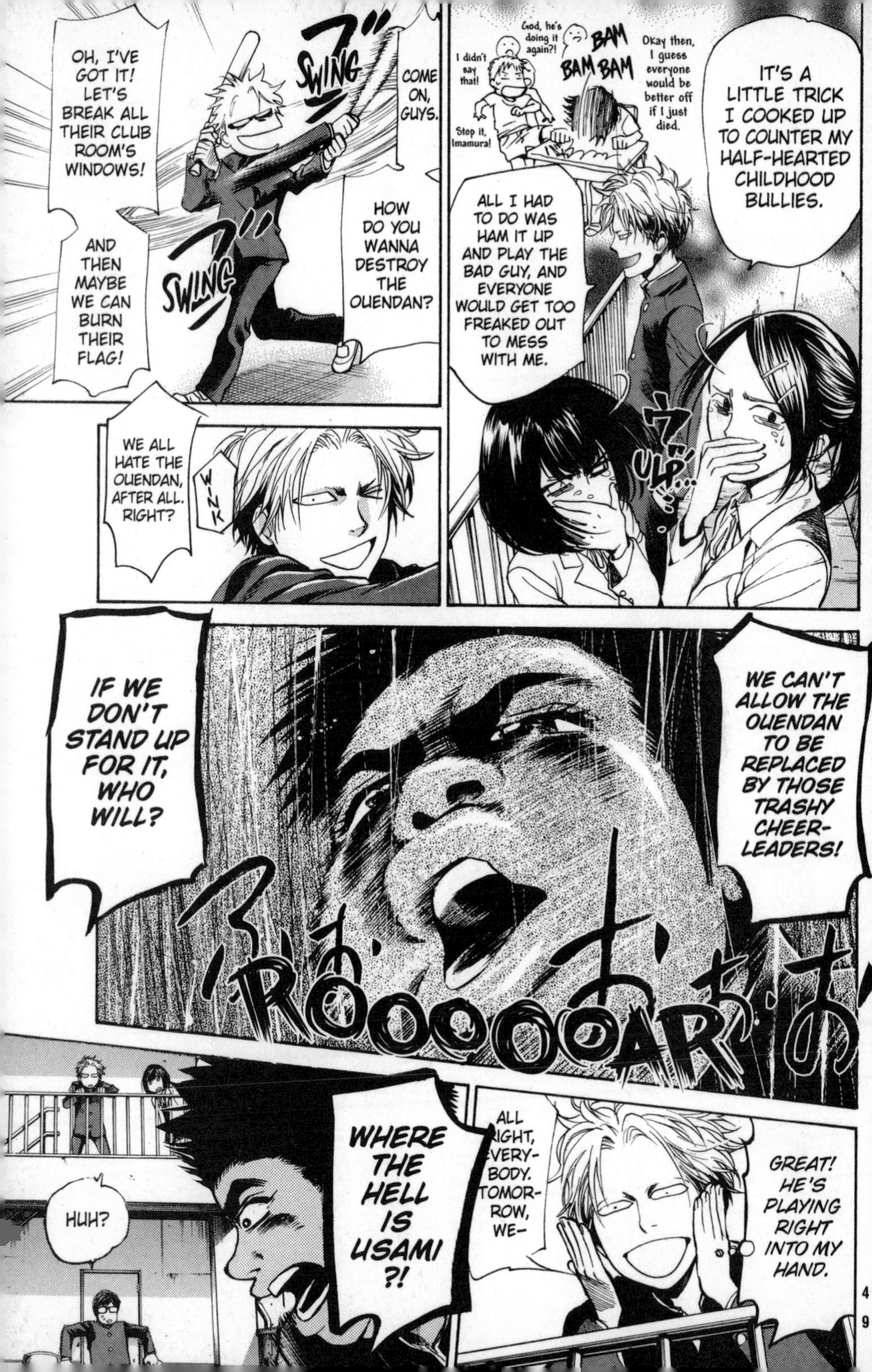
IT'S A LITTLE TRICK I COOKED UP TO COUNTER MY HALF-HEARTED CHILDHOOD BULLIES.
Okay then, I guess everyone would be better off if I just died.
BAM BAM BAM
God, he's doing it again?!
I didn't say that!
Stop it, Imamura!
ALL I HAD TO DO WAS HAM IT UP AND PLAY THE BAD GUY, AND EVERYONE WOULD GET TOO FREAKED OUT TO MESS WITH ME.
ULP...
COME ON, GUYS.
SWING
OH, I'VE GOT IT! LET'S BREAK ALL THEIR CLUB ROOM'S WINDOWS!
HOW DO YOU WANNA DESTROY THE OUENDAN?
SWING
AND THEN MAYBE WE CAN BURN THEIR FLAG!
WE ALL HATE THE OUENDAN, AFTER ALL. RIGHT?
WINK
WE CAN'T ALLOW THE OUENDAN TO BE REPLACED BY THOSE TRASHY CHEER-LEADERS!
IF WE DON'T STAND UP FOR IT, WHO WILL?
ROOOOOOAR
GREAT! HE'S PLAYING RIGHT INTO MY HAND.
ALL RIGHT, EVERY-BODY. TOMOR-ROW, WE-
WHERE THE HELL IS USAMI ?!
HUH?

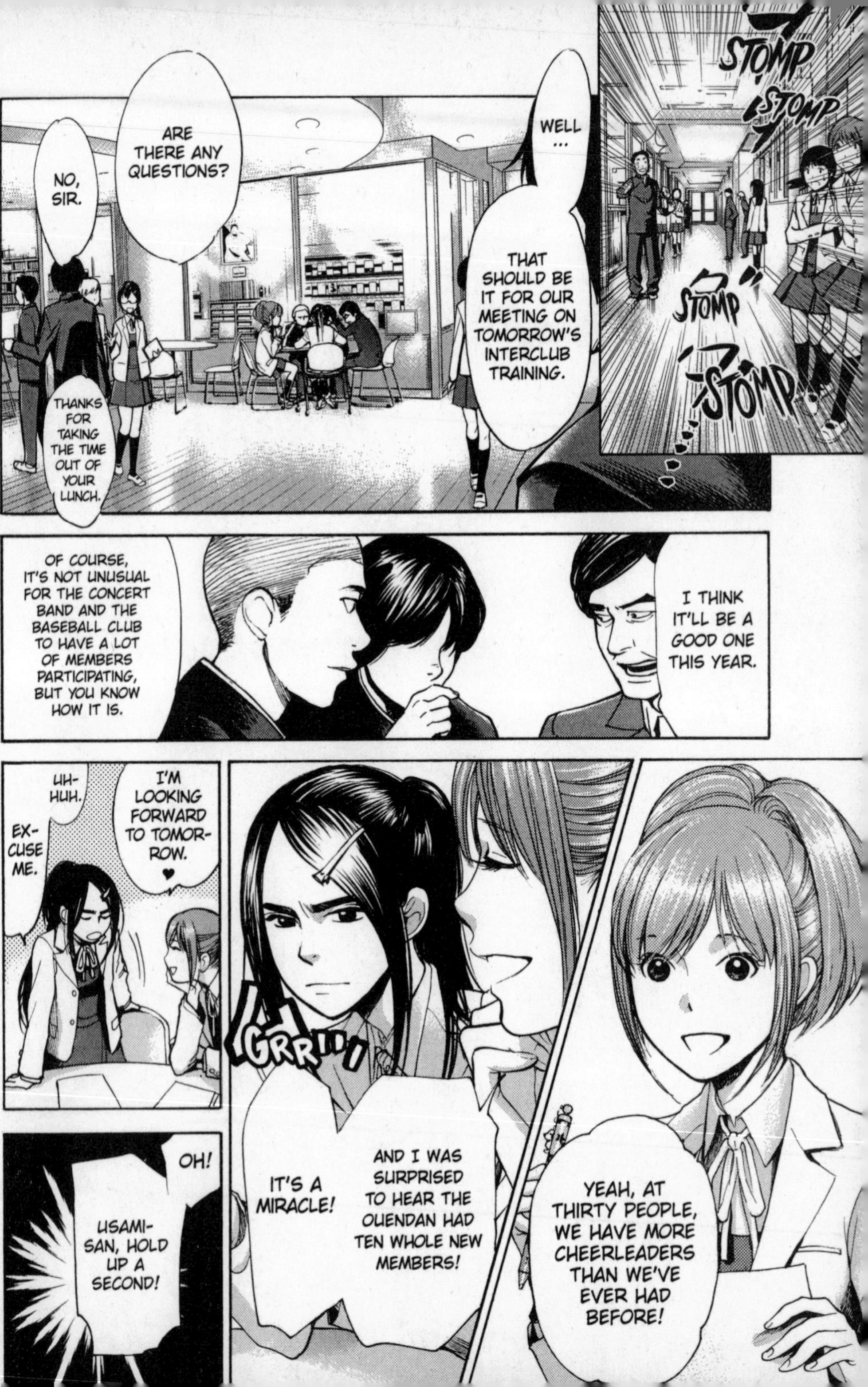
STOMP
STOMP
STOMP
STOMP
WELL ...
THAT SHOULD BE IT FOR OUR MEETING ON TOMORROW'S INTERCLUB TRAINING.
ARE THERE ANY QUESTIONS?
NO, SIR.
THANKS FOR TAKING THE TIME OUT OF YOUR LUNCH.
I THINK IT'LL BE A GOOD ONE THIS YEAR.
OF COURSE, IT'S NOT UNUSUAL FOR THE CONCERT BAND AND THE BASEBALL CLUB TO HAVE A LOT OF MEMBERS PARTICIPATING, BUT YOU KNOW HOW IT IS.
YEAH, AT THIRTY PEOPLE, WE HAVE MORE CHEERLEADERS THAN WE'VE EVER HAD BEFORE!
AND I WAS SURPRISED TO HEAR THE OUENDAN HAD TEN WHOLE NEW MEMBERS!
IT'S A MIRACLE!
GRRR
I'M LOOKING FORWARD TO TOMORROW. ♥
UH-HUH.
EXCUSE ME.
OH!
USAMI-SAN, HOLD UP A SECOND!

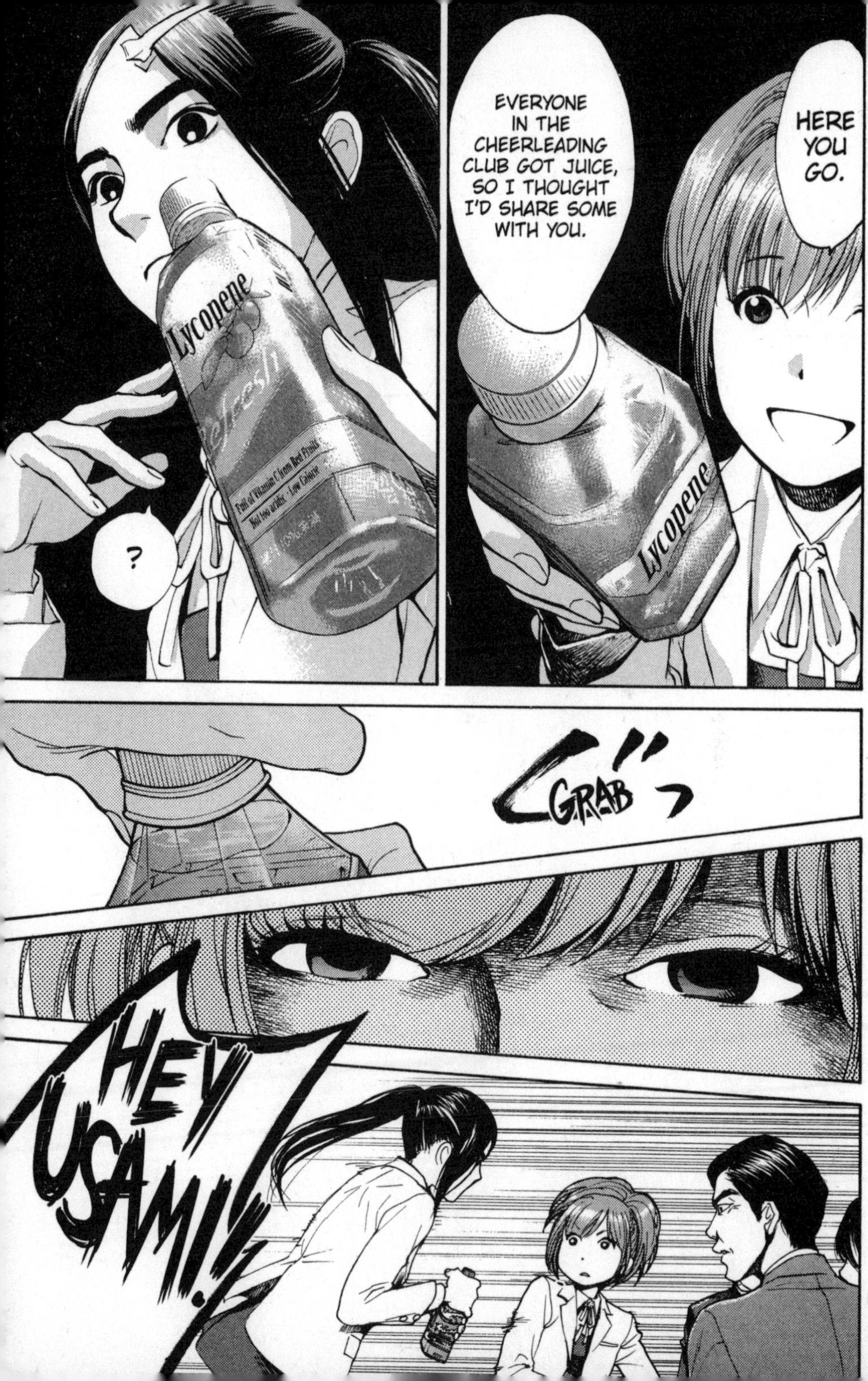
HERE YOU GO.
EVERYONE IN THE CHEERLEADING CLUB GOT JUICE, SO I THOUGHT I'D SHARE SOME WITH YOU.
Lycopene
Lycopene
?
GRAB
HEY USAMI!!

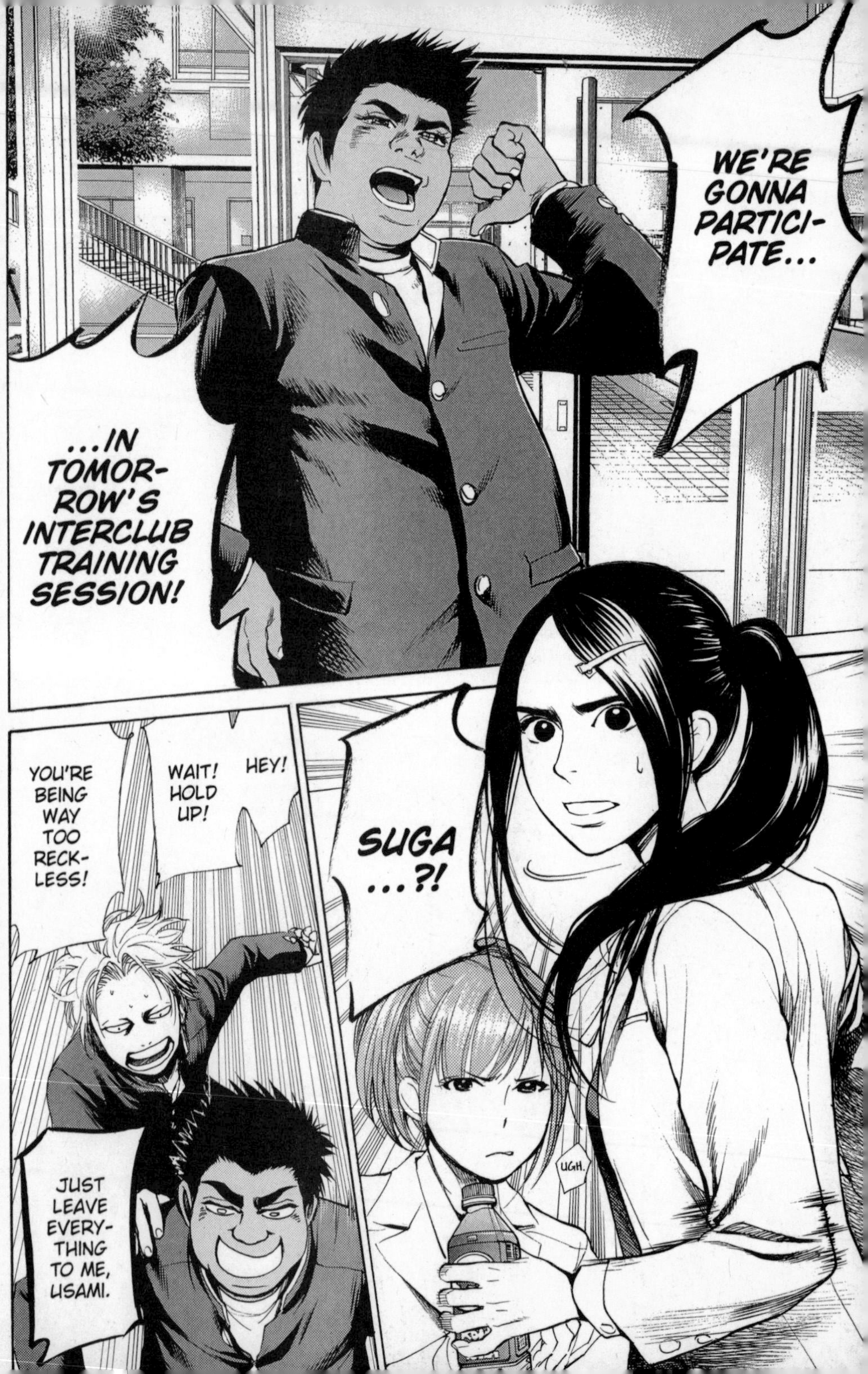
WE'RE GONNA PARTICI-PATE...
...IN TOMOR-ROW'S INTERCLUB TRAINING SESSION!
SUGA ...?!
UGH.
HEY!
WAIT! HOLD UP!
YOU'RE BEING WAY TOO RECK-LESS!
JUST LEAVE EVERY-THING TO ME, USAMI.

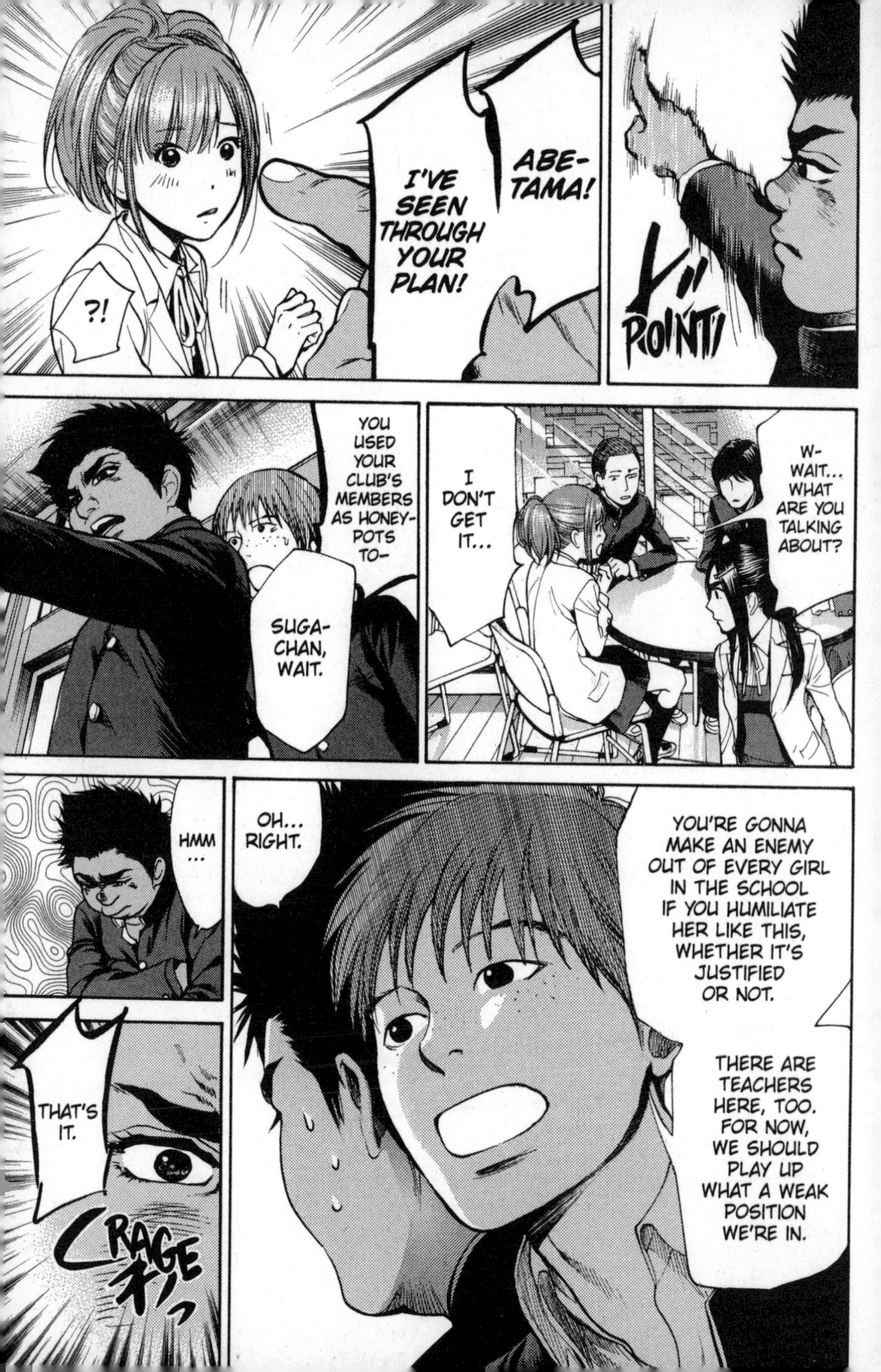
POINT!
ABE-TAMA!
I'VE SEEN THROUGH YOUR PLAN!
?!
W-WAIT... WHAT ARE YOU TALKING ABOUT?
I DON'T GET IT...
YOU USED YOUR CLUB'S MEMBERS AS HONEY-POTS TO-
SUGA-CHAN, WAIT.
YOU'RE GONNA MAKE AN ENEMY OUT OF EVERY GIRL IN THE SCHOOL IF YOU HUMILIATE HER LIKE THIS, WHETHER IT'S JUSTIFIED OR NOT.
THERE ARE TEACHERS HERE, TOO. FOR NOW, WE SHOULD PLAY UP WHAT A WEAK POSITION WE'RE IN.
OH... RIGHT.
HMM...
THAT'S IT.
RAGE

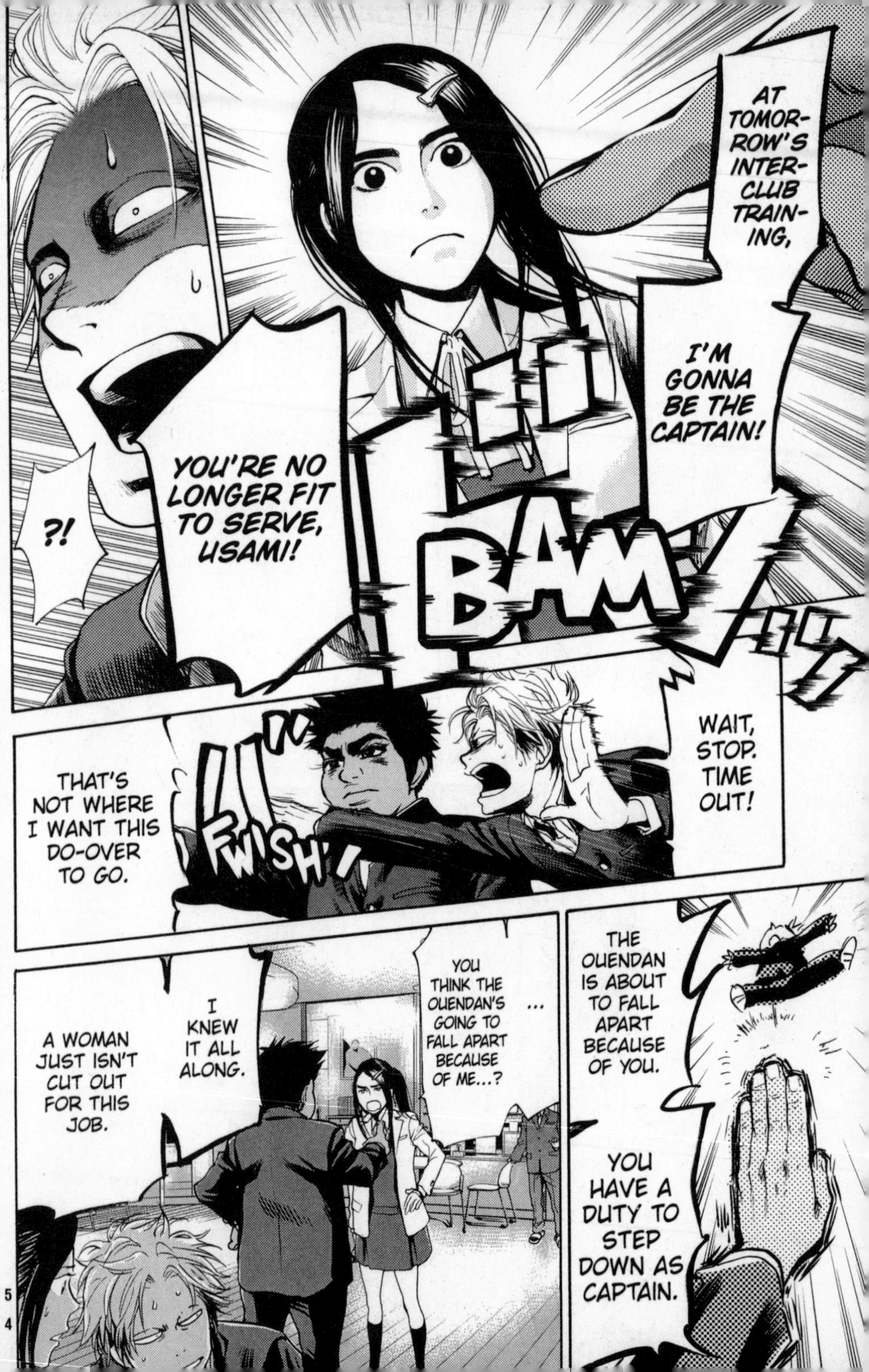
AT TOMORROW'S INTER-CLUB TRAINING,
I'M GONNA BE THE CAPTAIN!
BAM
YOU'RE NO LONGER FIT TO SERVE, USAMI!
?!
WAIT, STOP. TIME OUT!
FWISH
THAT'S NOT WHERE I WANT THIS DO-OVER TO GO.
THE OUENDAN IS ABOUT TO FALL APART BECAUSE OF YOU.
YOU HAVE A DUTY TO STEP DOWN AS CAPTAIN.
...
YOU THINK THE OUENDAN'S GOING TO FALL APART BECAUSE OF ME...?
I KNEW IT ALL ALONG.
A WOMAN JUST ISN'T CUT OUT FOR THIS JOB.

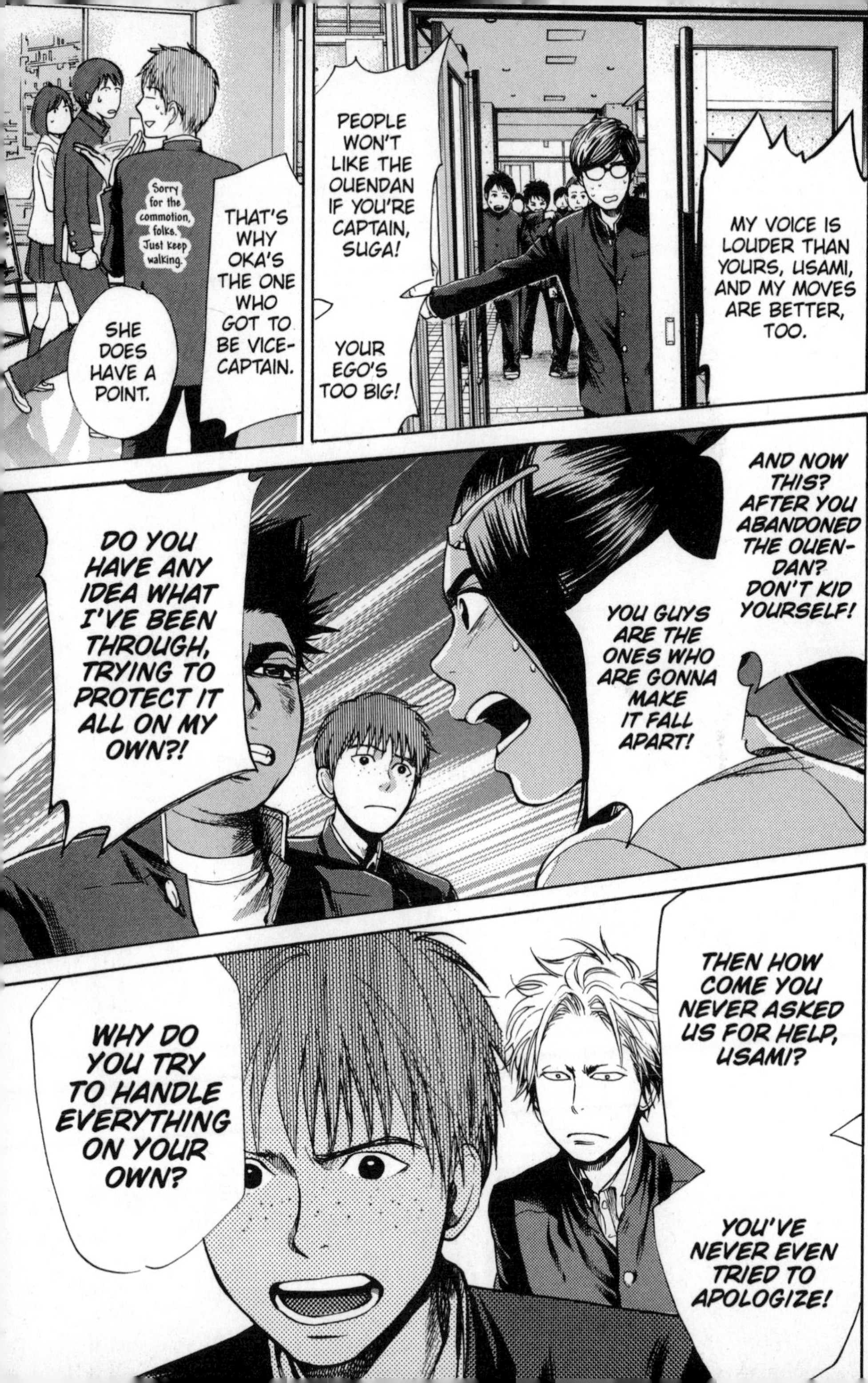
MY VOICE IS LOUDER THAN YOURS, USAMI, AND MY MOVES ARE BETTER, TOO.
PEOPLE WON'T LIKE THE OUENDAN IF YOU'RE CAPTAIN, SUGA!
YOUR EGO'S TOO BIG!
THAT'S WHY OKA'S THE ONE WHO GOT TO BE VICE-CAPTAIN.
Sorry for the commotion, folks. Just keep walking.
SHE DOES HAVE A POINT.
AND NOW THIS? AFTER YOU ABANDONED THE OUEN-DAN? DON'T KID YOURSELF!
YOU GUYS ARE THE ONES WHO ARE GONNA MAKE IT FALL APART!
DO YOU HAVE ANY IDEA WHAT I'VE BEEN THROUGH, TRYING TO PROTECT IT ALL ON MY OWN?!
THEN HOW COME YOU NEVER ASKED US FOR HELP, USAMI?
YOU'VE NEVER EVEN TRIED TO APOLOGIZE!
WHY DO YOU TRY TO HANDLE EVERYTHING ON YOUR OWN?

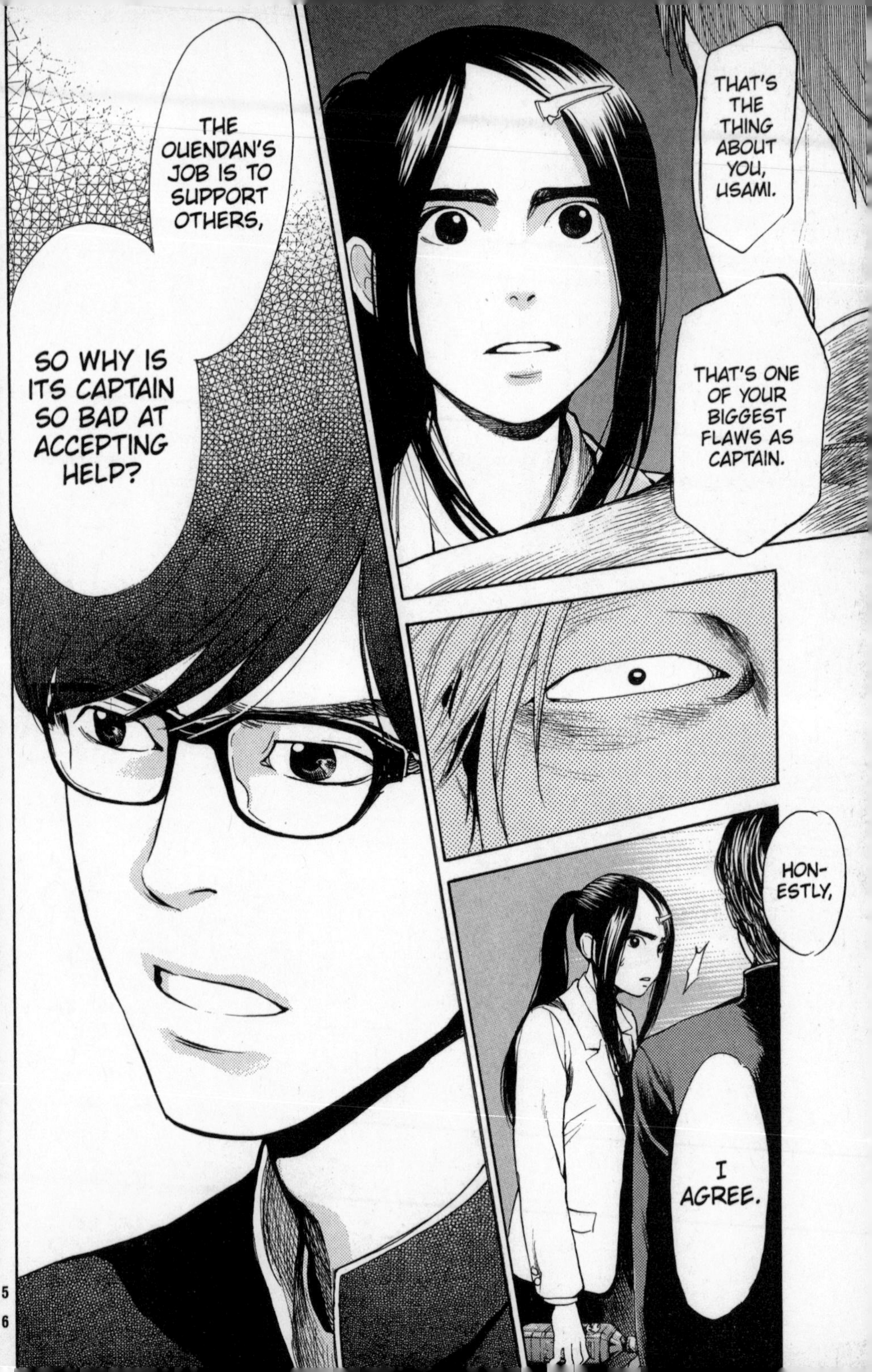
THAT'S THE THING ABOUT YOU, USAMI.
THAT'S ONE OF YOUR BIGGEST FLAWS AS CAPTAIN.
HON-ESTLY,
I AGREE.
THE OUENDAN'S JOB IS TO SUPPORT OTHERS,
SO WHY IS ITS CAPTAIN SO BAD AT ACCEPTING HELP?

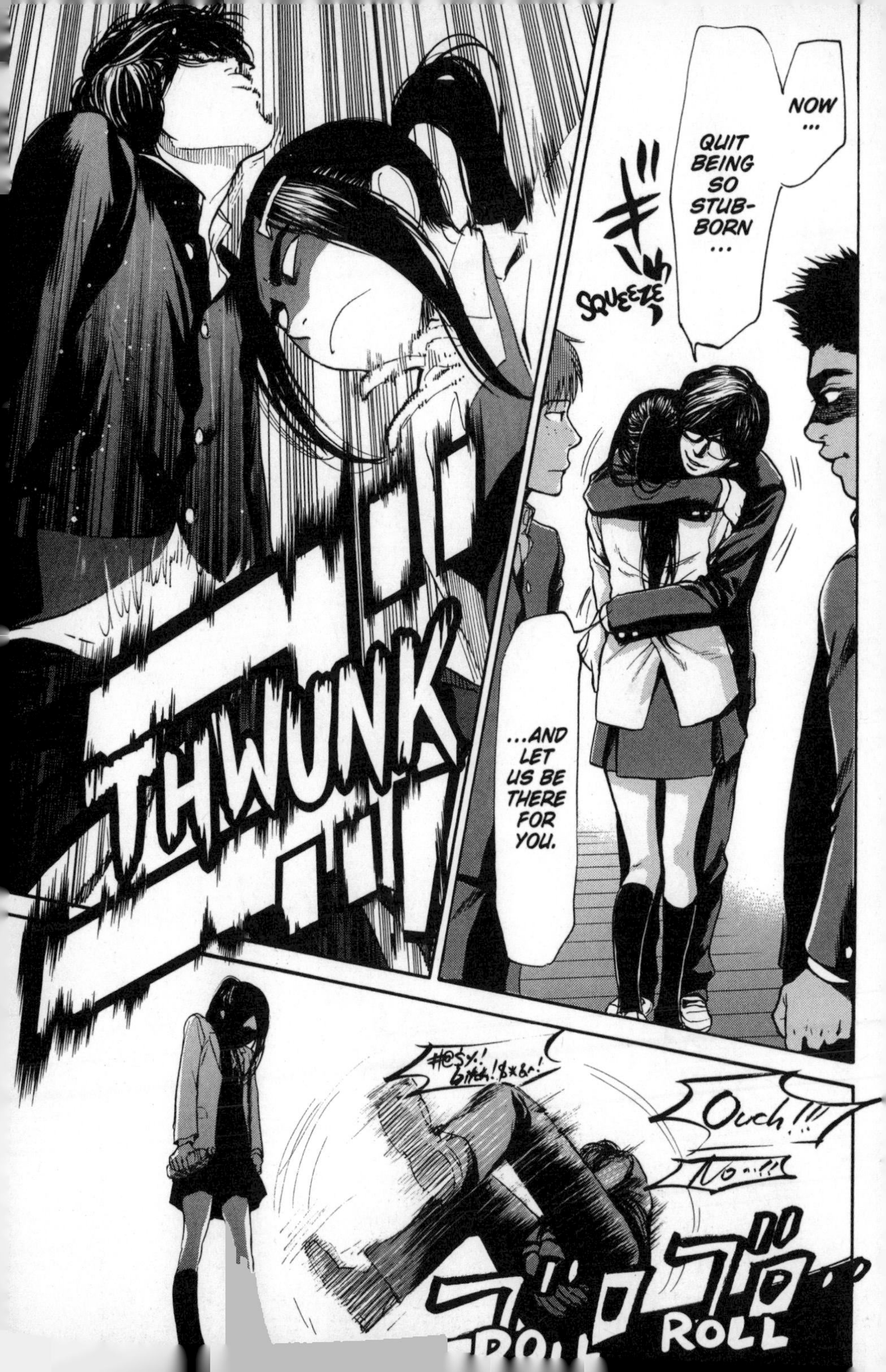
NOW...
QUIT BEING SO STUBBORN...
SQUEEZE
...AND LET US BE THERE FOR YOU.
THWUNK
Ouch!!!
No...!!
ROLL

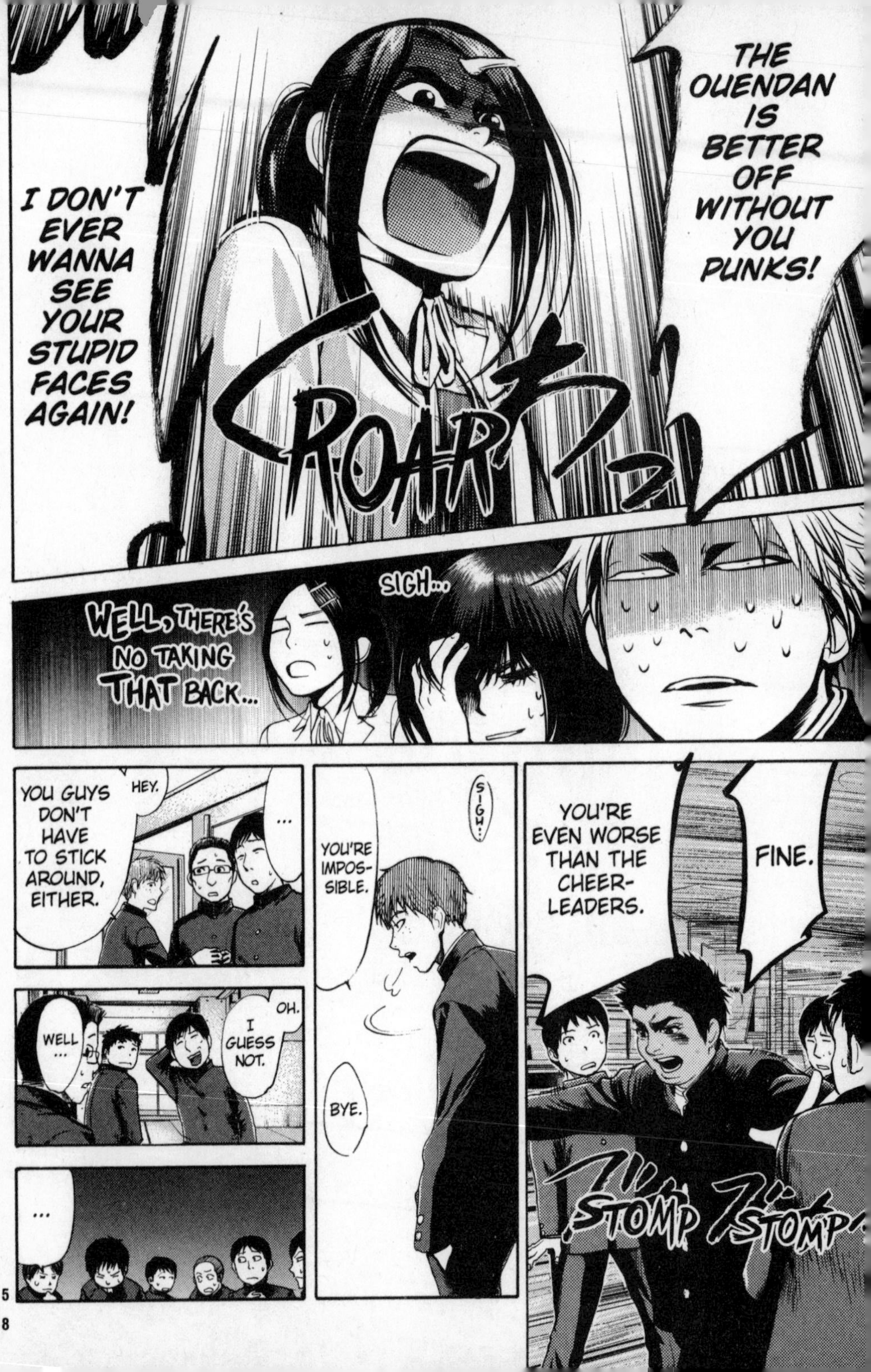
THE OUENDAN IS BETTER OFF WITHOUT YOU PUNKS!
I DON'T EVER WANNA SEE YOUR STUPID FACES AGAIN!
ROAR
SIGH...
WELL, THERE'S NO TAKING THAT BACK...
FINE.
YOU'RE EVEN WORSE THAN THE CHEER-LEADERS.
STOMP STOMP
SIGH...
YOU'RE IMPOSSIBLE.
BYE.
...
HEY.
YOU GUYS DON'T HAVE TO STICK AROUND, EITHER.
OH. I GUESS NOT.
WELL...
...

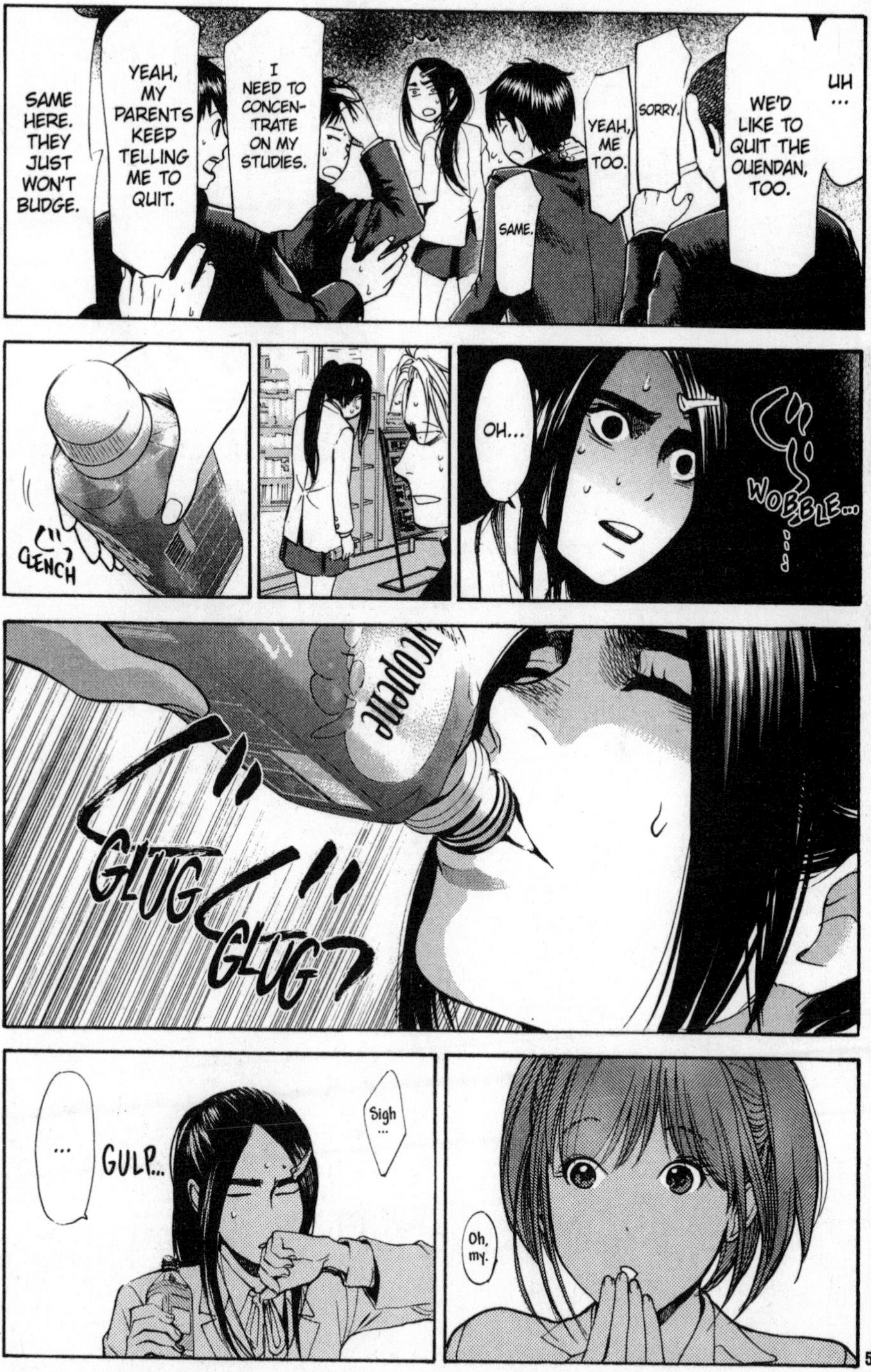
UH ...
WE'D LIKE TO QUIT THE OUENDAN, TOO.
SORRY.
YEAH, ME TOO.
SAME.
I NEED TO CONCENTRATE ON MY STUDIES.
YEAH, MY PARENTS KEEP TELLING ME TO QUIT.
SAME HERE. THEY JUST WON'T BUDGE.
WOBBLE...
OH...
CLENCH
GLUG
GLUG
Oh, my.
Sigh ...
...
GULP...

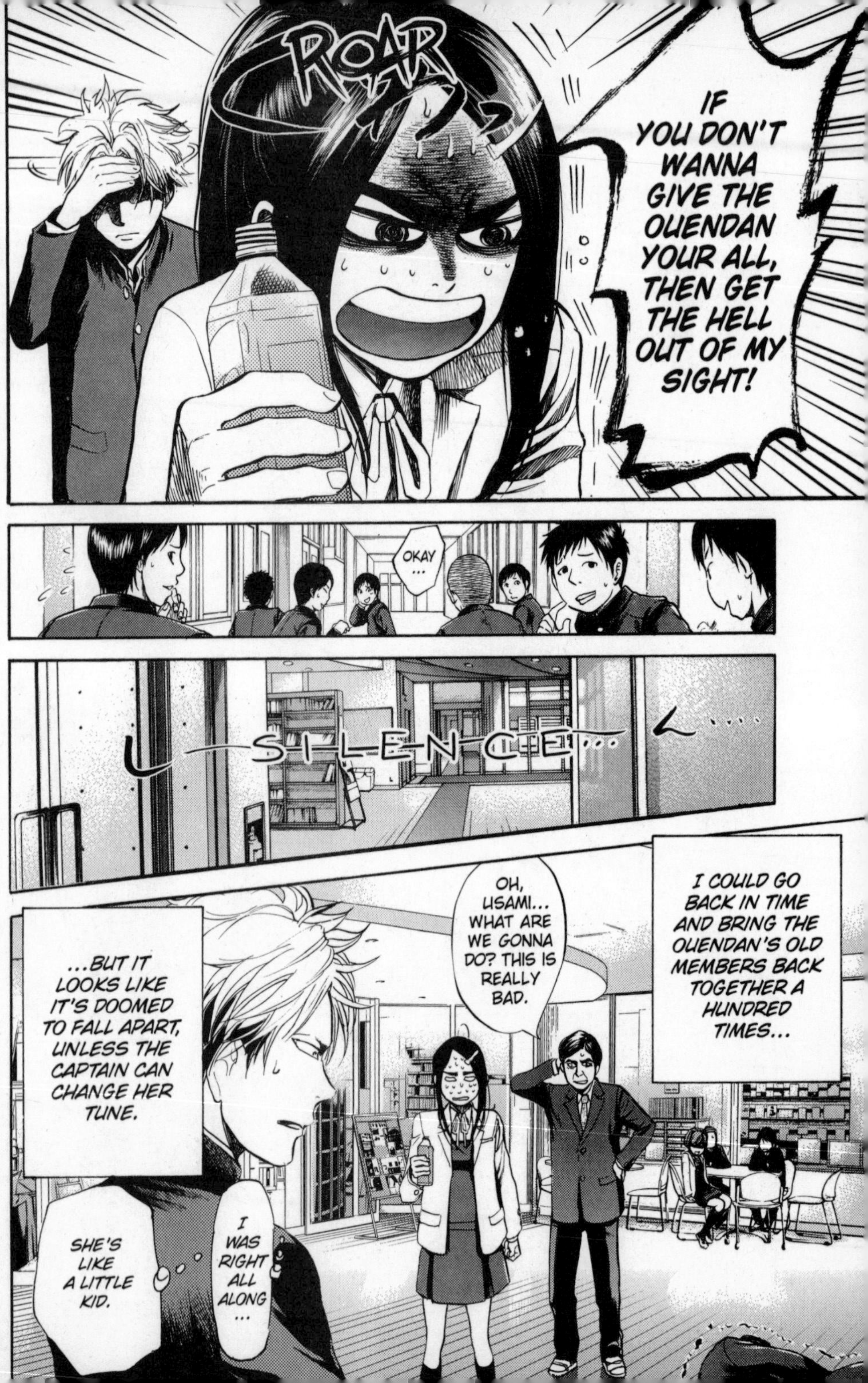
IF YOU DON'T WANNA GIVE THE OUENDAN YOUR ALL, THEN GET THE HELL OUT OF MY SIGHT!
ROAR
OKAY ...
SILENCE...
I COULD GO BACK IN TIME AND BRING THE OUENDAN'S OLD MEMBERS BACK TOGETHER A HUNDRED TIMES...
OH, USAMI... WHAT ARE WE GONNA DO? THIS IS REALLY BAD.
...BUT IT LOOKS LIKE IT'S DOOMED TO FALL APART, UNLESS THE CAPTAIN CAN CHANGE HER TUNE.
I WAS RIGHT ALL ALONG ...
SHE'S LIKE A LITTLE KID.

13. THE DAY BEFORE THE BIG DAY

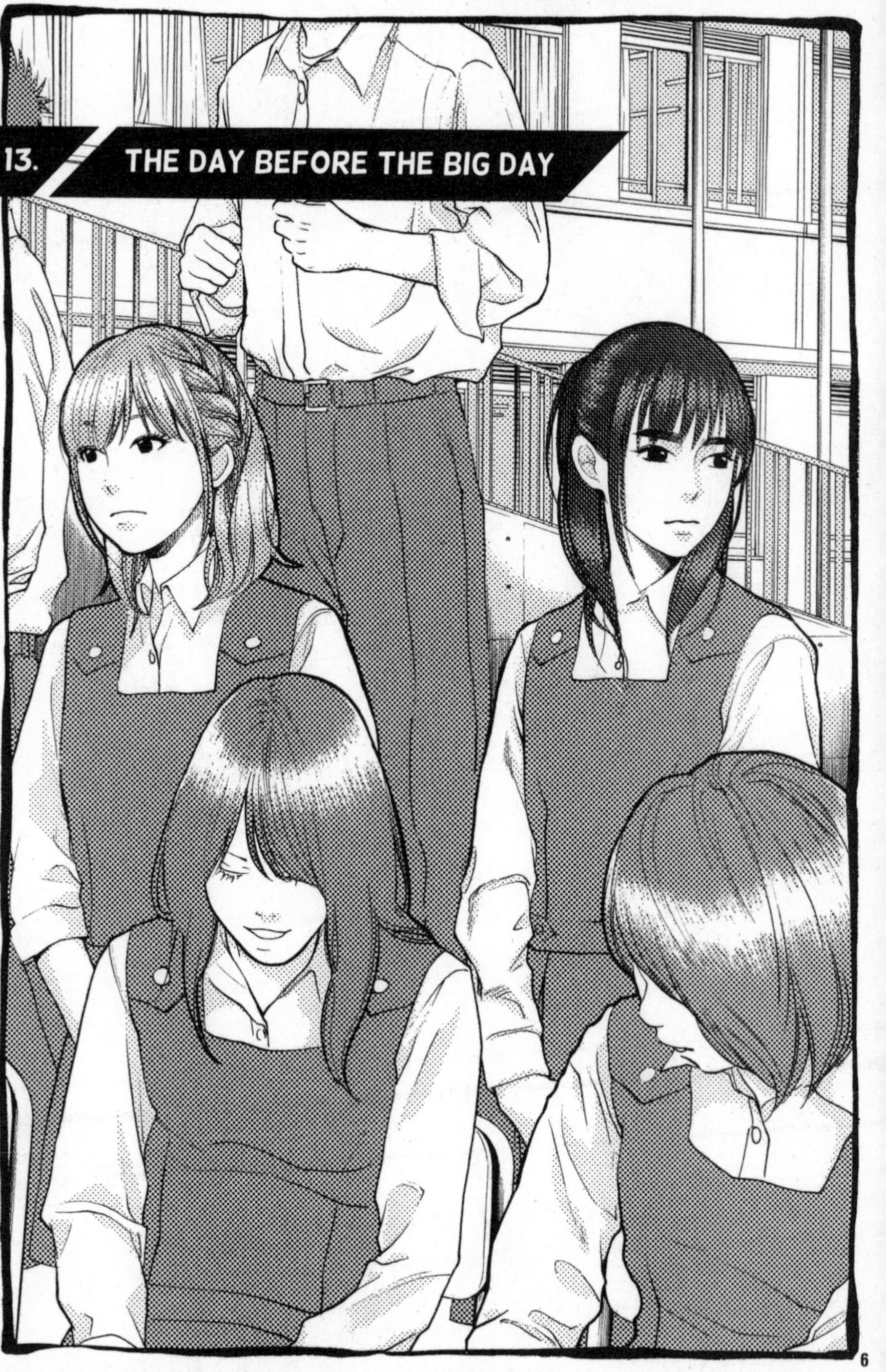

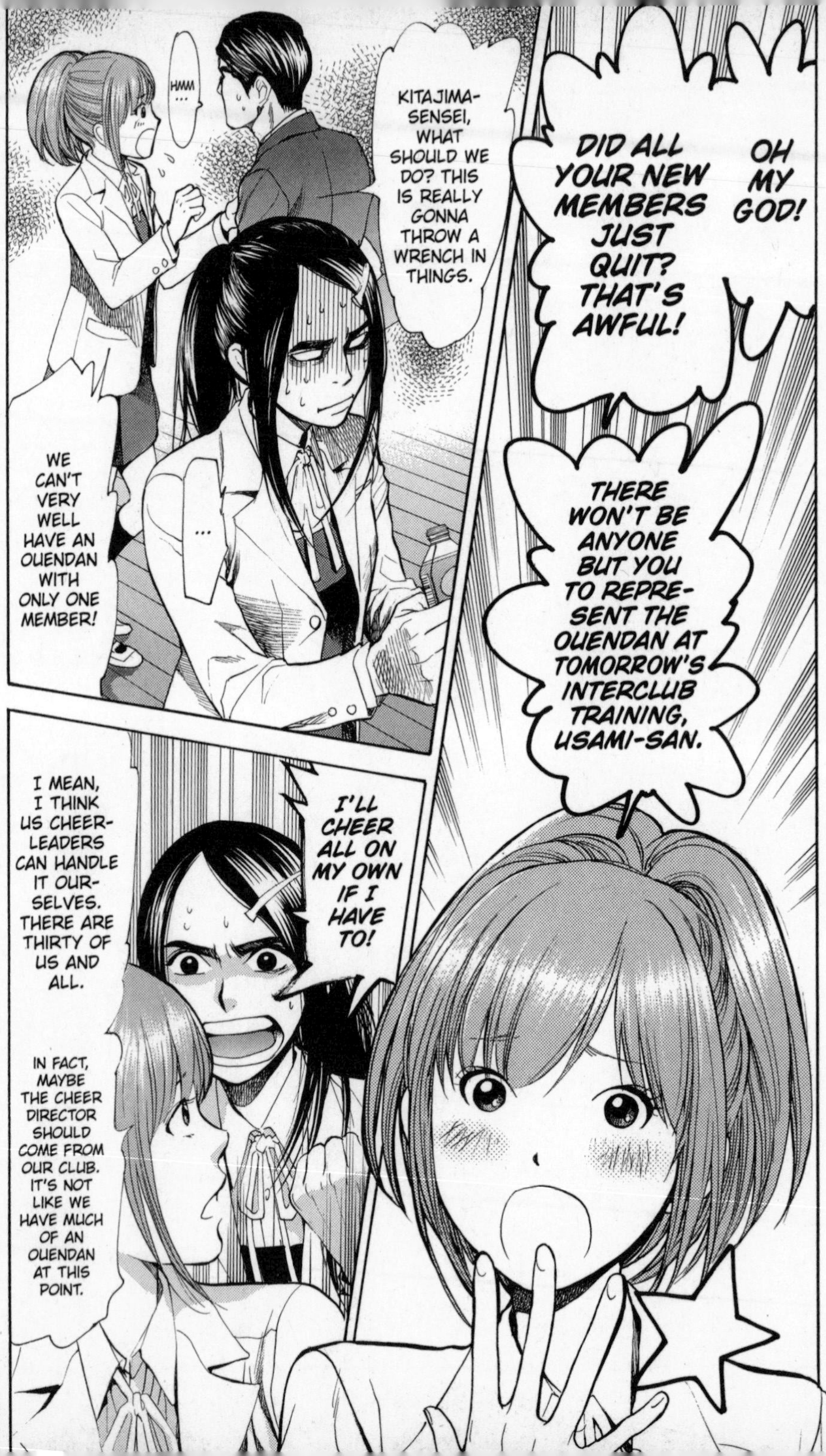
OH MY GOD!
DID ALL YOUR NEW MEMBERS JUST QUIT? THAT'S AWFUL!
THERE WON'T BE ANYONE BUT YOU TO REPRESENT THE OUENDAN AT TOMORROW'S INTERCLUB TRAINING, USAMI-SAN.
KITAJIMA-SENSEI, WHAT SHOULD WE DO? THIS IS REALLY GONNA THROW A WRENCH IN THINGS.
HMM...
WE CAN'T VERY WELL HAVE AN OUENDAN WITH ONLY ONE MEMBER!
...
I'LL CHEER ALL ON MY OWN IF I HAVE TO!
I MEAN, I THINK US CHEERLEADERS CAN HANDLE IT OURSELVES. THERE ARE THIRTY OF US AND ALL.
IN FACT, MAYBE THE CHEER DIRECTOR SHOULD COME FROM OUR CLUB. IT'S NOT LIKE WE HAVE MUCH OF AN OUENDAN AT THIS POINT.

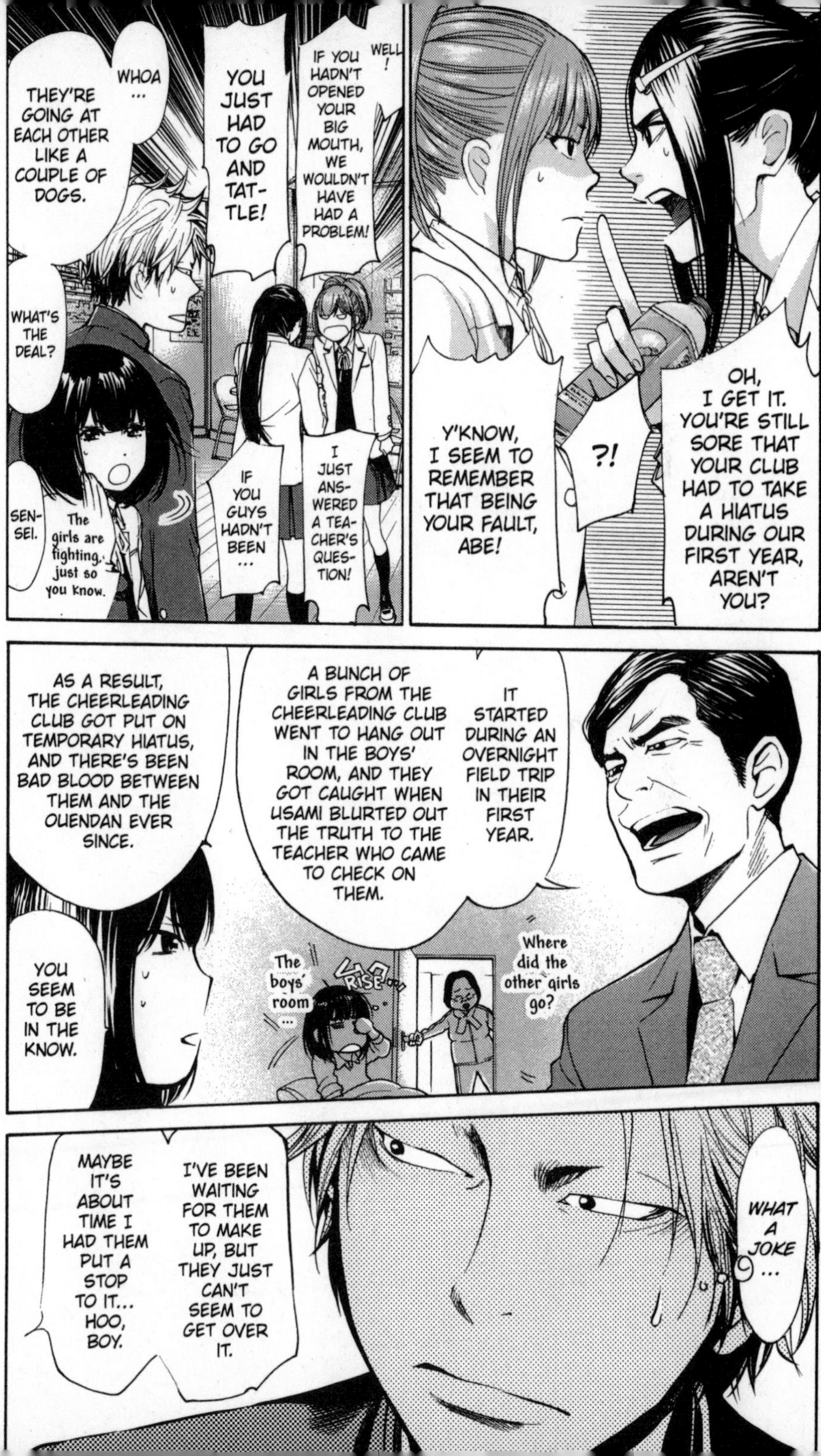
OH, I GET IT. YOU'RE STILL SORE THAT YOUR CLUB HAD TO TAKE A HIATUS DURING OUR FIRST YEAR, AREN'T YOU?
?!
Y'KNOW, I SEEM TO REMEMBER THAT BEING YOUR FAULT, ABE!
WELL!
IF YOU HADN'T OPENED YOUR BIG MOUTH, WE WOULDN'T HAVE HAD A PROBLEM!
YOU JUST HAD TO GO AND TAT-TLE!
WHOA...
THEY'RE GOING AT EACH OTHER LIKE A COUPLE OF DOGS.
WHAT'S THE DEAL?
I JUST ANS-WERED A TEA-CHER'S QUES-TION!
IF YOU GUYS HADN'T BEEN...
SEN-SEI.
The girls are fighting, just so you know.
IT STARTED DURING AN OVERNIGHT FIELD TRIP IN THEIR FIRST YEAR.
A BUNCH OF GIRLS FROM THE CHEERLEADING CLUB WENT TO HANG OUT IN THE BOYS' ROOM, AND THEY GOT CAUGHT WHEN USAMI BLURTED OUT THE TRUTH TO THE TEACHER WHO CAME TO CHECK ON THEM.
AS A RESULT, THE CHEERLEADING CLUB GOT PUT ON TEMPORARY HIATUS, AND THERE'S BEEN BAD BLOOD BETWEEN THEM AND THE OUENDAN EVER SINCE.
Where did the other girls go?
RISE
The boys' room...
YOU SEEM TO BE IN THE KNOW.
WHAT A JOKE...
I'VE BEEN WAITING FOR THEM TO MAKE UP, BUT THEY JUST CAN'T SEEM TO GET OVER IT.
MAYBE IT'S ABOUT TIME I HAD THEM PUT A STOP TO IT... HOO, BOY.

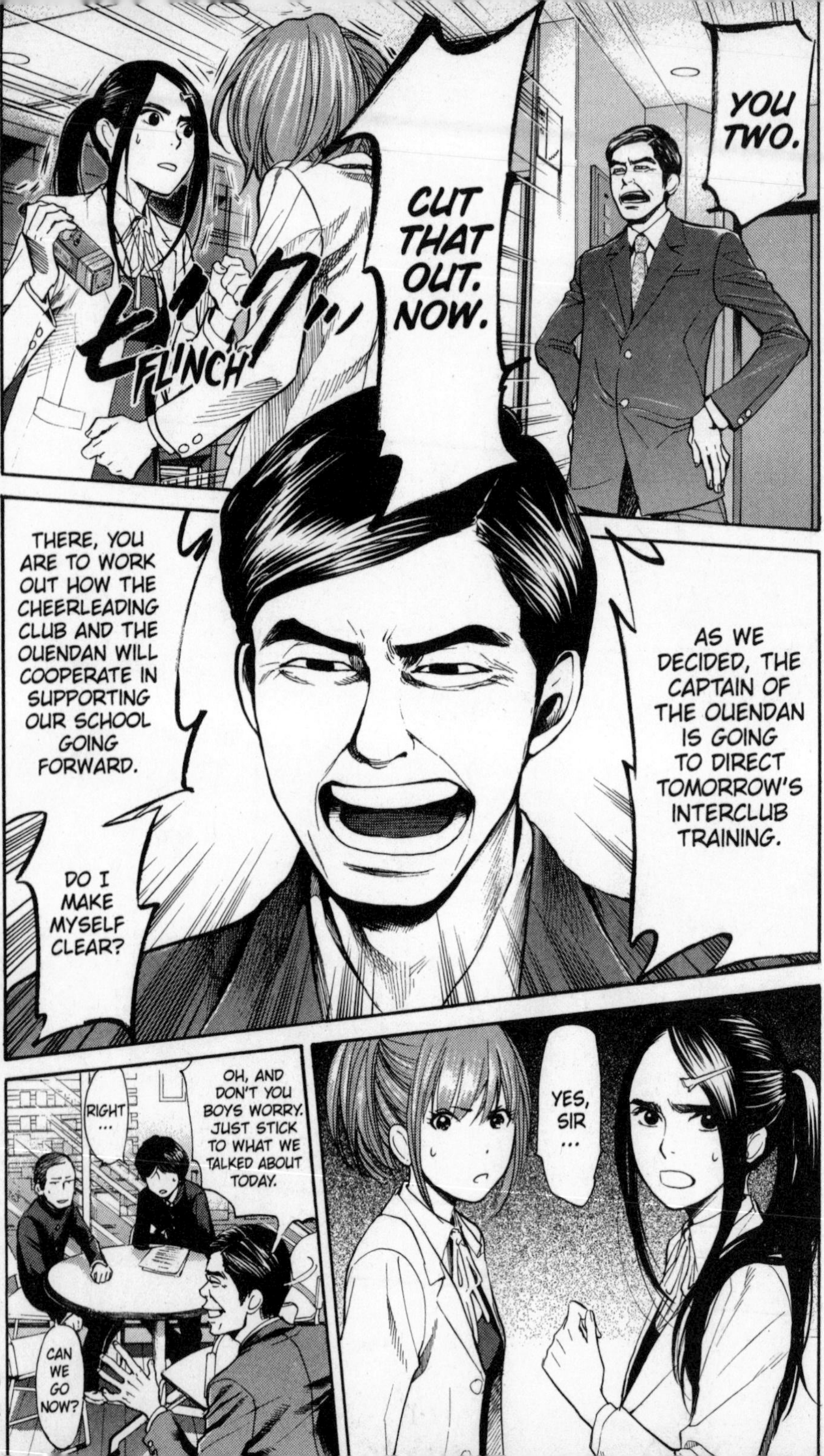
YOU TWO.
CUT THAT OUT. NOW.
FLINCH
AS WE DECIDED, THE CAPTAIN OF THE OUENDAN IS GOING TO DIRECT TOMORROW'S INTERCLUB TRAINING.
THERE, YOU ARE TO WORK OUT HOW THE CHEERLEADING CLUB AND THE OUENDAN WILL COOPERATE IN SUPPORTING OUR SCHOOL GOING FORWARD.
DO I MAKE MYSELF CLEAR?
YES, SIR ...
OH, AND DON'T YOU BOYS WORRY. JUST STICK TO WHAT WE TALKED ABOUT TODAY.
RIGHT ...
CAN WE GO NOW?

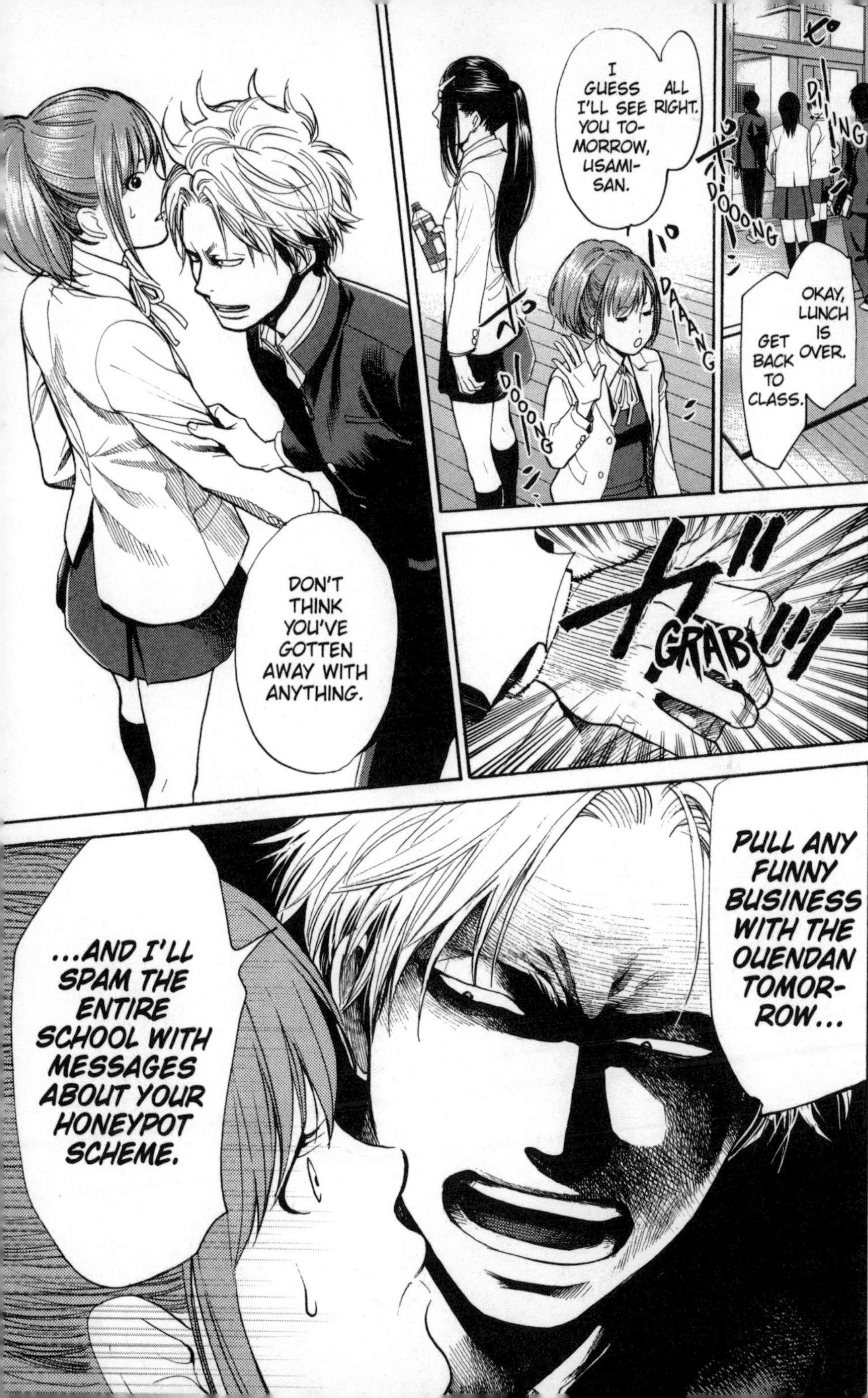

DIIING
DOOONG
OKAY, LUNCH IS OVER. GET BACK TO CLASS.
ALL RIGHT.
I GUESS I'LL SEE YOU TO-MORROW, USAMI-SAN.
DAAANG
DOOONG
GRAB
DON'T THINK YOU'VE GOTTEN AWAY WITH ANYTHING.
PULL ANY FUNNY BUSINESS WITH THE OUENDAN TOMOR-ROW...
...AND I'LL SPAM THE ENTIRE SCHOOL WITH MESSAGES ABOUT YOUR HONEYPOT SCHEME.

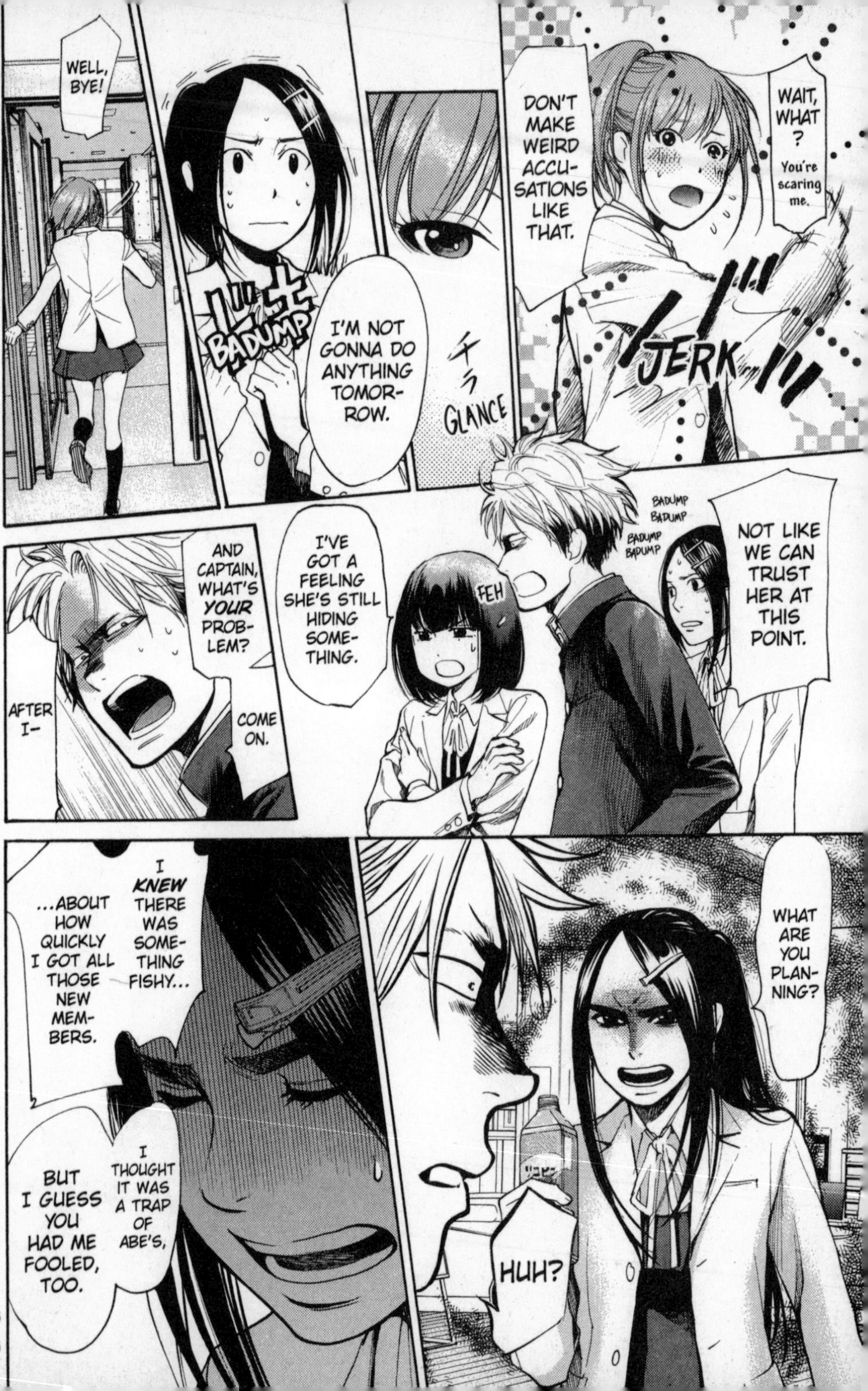
WAIT, WHAT?
You're scaring me.
JERK
DON'T MAKE WEIRD ACCUSATIONS LIKE THAT.
チラ
GLANCE
I'M NOT GONNA DO ANYTHING TOMORROW.
BADUMP
WELL, BYE!
BADUMP BADUMP BADUMP BADUMP
NOT LIKE WE CAN TRUST HER AT THIS POINT.
FEH
I'VE GOT A FEELING SHE'S STILL HIDING SOMETHING.
AND CAPTAIN, WHAT'S *YOUR* PROBLEM?
COME ON.
AFTER I-
WHAT ARE YOU PLANNING?
HUH?
I *KNEW* THERE WAS SOMETHING FISHY...
...ABOUT HOW QUICKLY I GOT ALL THOSE NEW MEMBERS.
I THOUGHT IT WAS A TRAP OF ABE'S,
BUT I GUESS YOU HAD ME FOOLED, TOO.

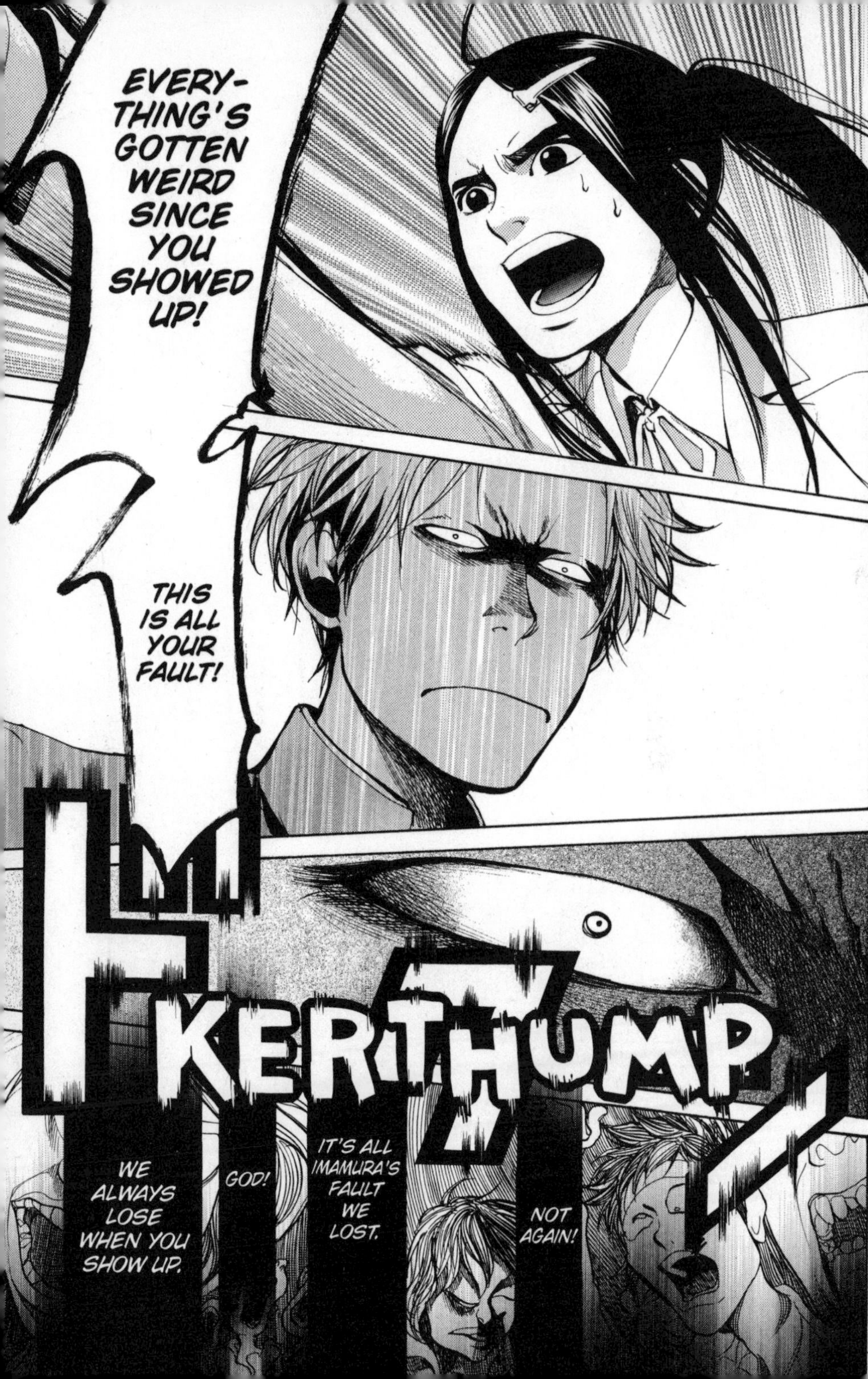
EVERY-THING'S GOTTEN WEIRD SINCE YOU SHOWED UP!
THIS IS ALL YOUR FAULT!
KERTHUMP
NOT AGAIN!
IT'S ALL IMAMURA'S FAULT WE LOST.
GOD!
WE ALWAYS LOSE WHEN YOU SHOW UP.

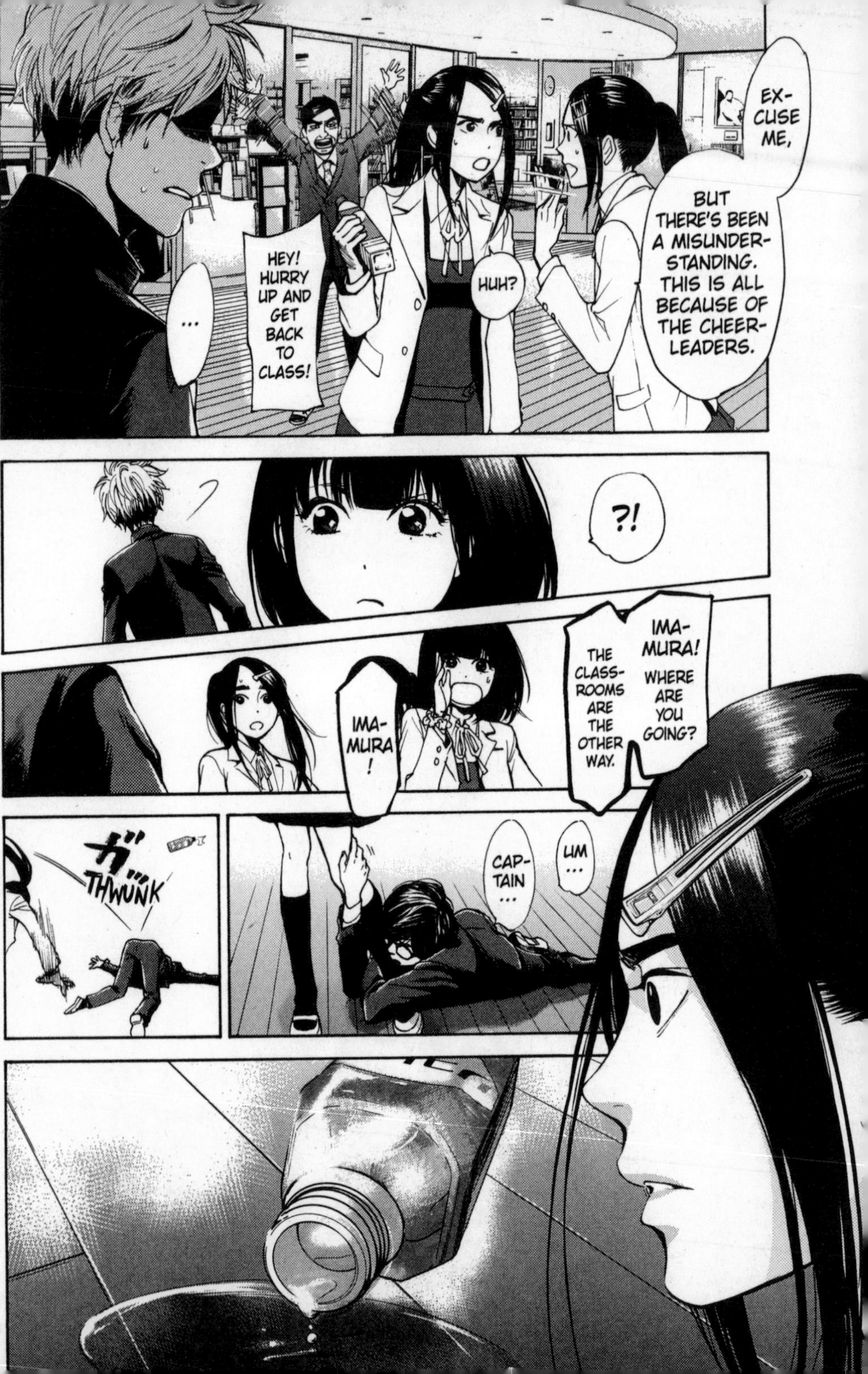
EX-CUSE ME,
BUT THERE'S BEEN A MISUNDER-STANDING. THIS IS ALL BECAUSE OF THE CHEER-LEADERS.
HUH?
HEY! HURRY UP AND GET BACK TO CLASS!
...
?!
IMA-MURA! WHERE ARE YOU GOING?
THE CLASS-ROOMS ARE THE OTHER WAY.
IMA-MURA!
UM...
CAP-TAIN...
ガ
THWUNK

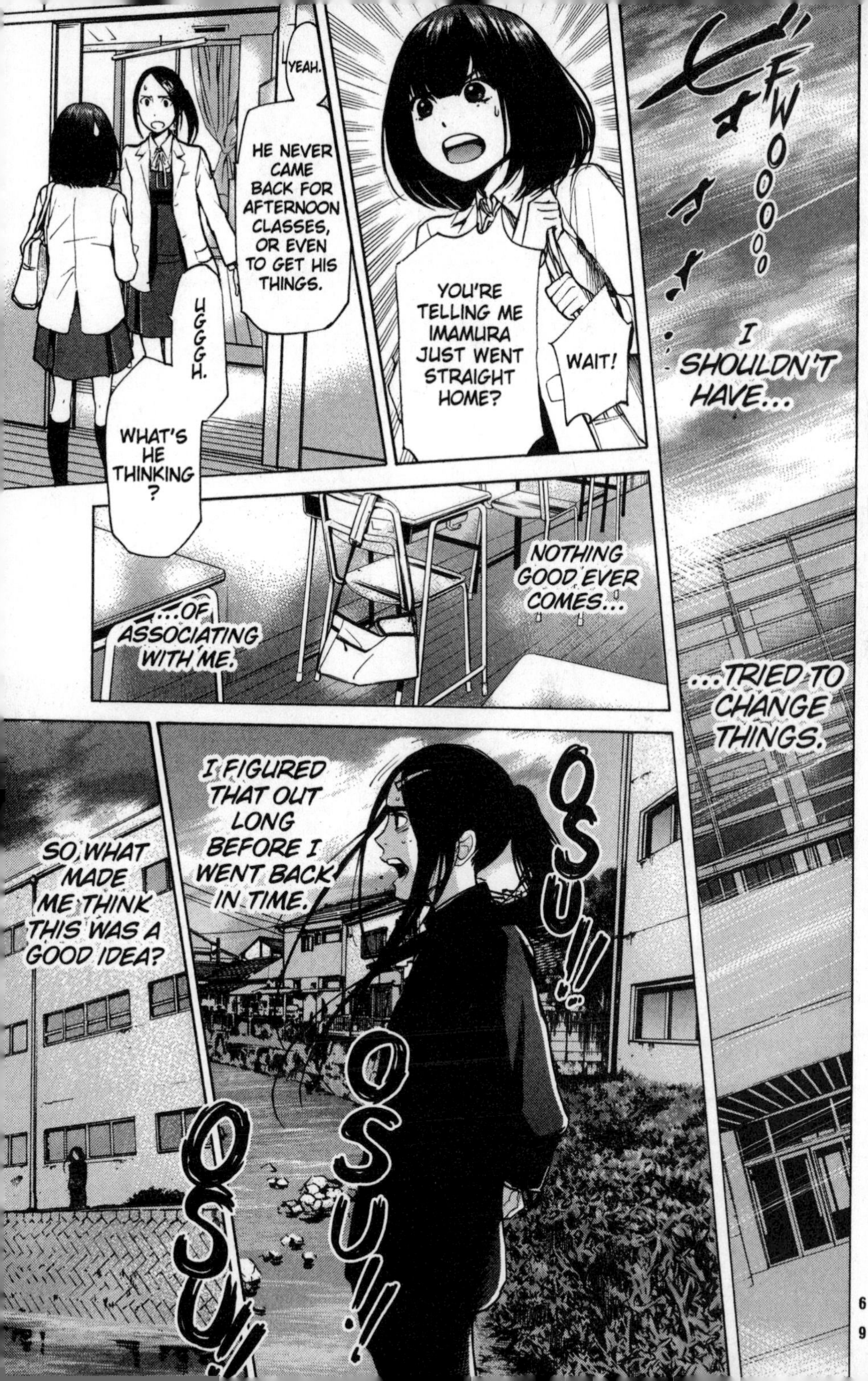
FWOOOOO
I SHOULDN'T HAVE...
...TRIED TO CHANGE THINGS.
WAIT!
YOU'RE TELLING ME IMAMURA JUST WENT STRAIGHT HOME?
YEAH.
HE NEVER CAME BACK FOR AFTERNOON CLASSES, OR EVEN TO GET HIS THINGS.
UGGGH.
WHAT'S HE THINKING?
NOTHING GOOD EVER COMES...
...OF ASSOCIATING WITH ME.
OSU!!
I FIGURED THAT OUT LONG BEFORE I WENT BACK IN TIME.
SO WHAT MADE ME THINK THIS WAS A GOOD IDEA?
OSU!!
OSU!!

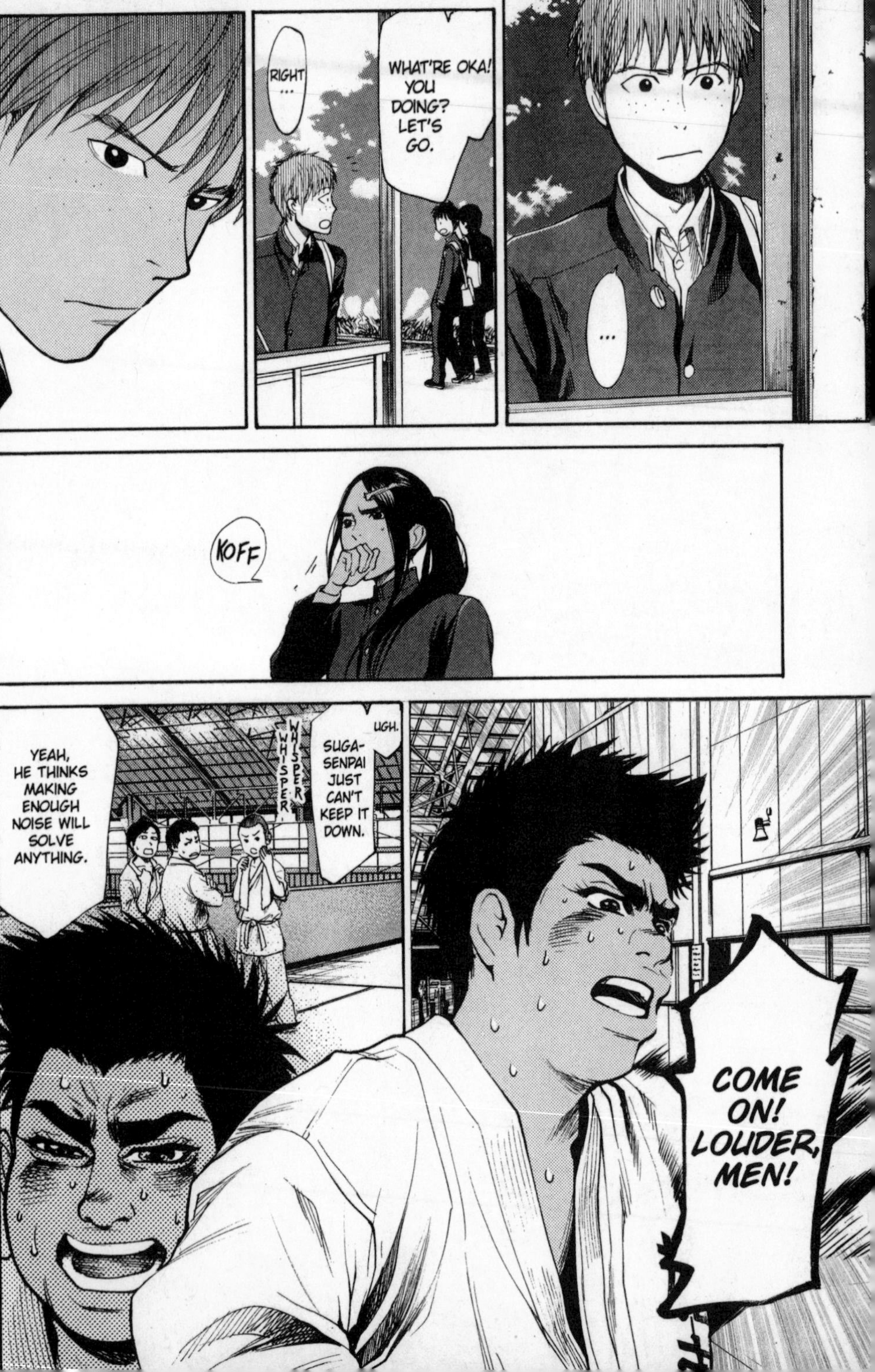
...
OKA! WHAT'RE YOU DOING? LET'S GO.
RIGHT ...
KOFF
COME ON! LOUDER, MEN!
UGH.
SUGA-SENPAI JUST CAN'T KEEP IT DOWN.
WHISPER WHISPER
YEAH, HE THINKS MAKING ENOUGH NOISE WILL SOLVE ANYTHING.

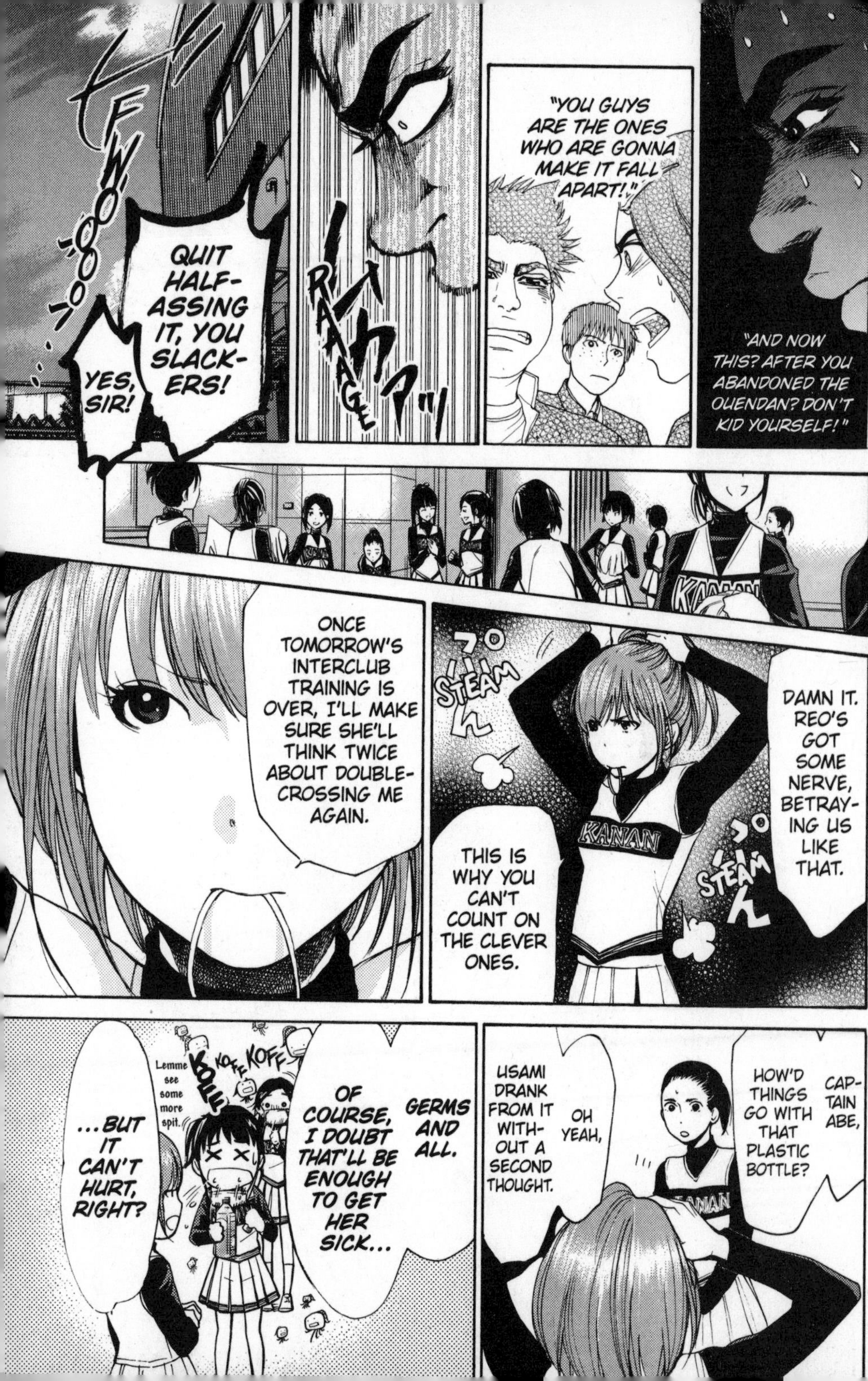
"AND NOW THIS? AFTER YOU ABANDONED THE OUENDAN? DON'T KID YOURSELF!"
"YOU GUYS ARE THE ONES WHO ARE GONNA MAKE IT FALL APART!"
RAAAGE
FWOOOO...
QUIT HALF-ASSING IT, YOU SLACKERS!
YES, SIR!
DAMN IT. REO'S GOT SOME NERVE, BETRAYING US LIKE THAT.
STEAM
STEAM
THIS IS WHY YOU CAN'T COUNT ON THE CLEVER ONES.
KANAN
ONCE TOMORROW'S INTERCLUB TRAINING IS OVER, I'LL MAKE SURE SHE'LL THINK TWICE ABOUT DOUBLE-CROSSING ME AGAIN.
CAPTAIN ABE,
HOW'D THINGS GO WITH THAT PLASTIC BOTTLE?
OH YEAH,
USAMI DRANK FROM IT WITHOUT A SECOND THOUGHT.
GERMS AND ALL.
OF COURSE, I DOUBT THAT'LL BE ENOUGH TO GET HER SICK...
KOFF KOFF KOFF
Lemme see some more spit.
...BUT IT CAN'T HURT, RIGHT?

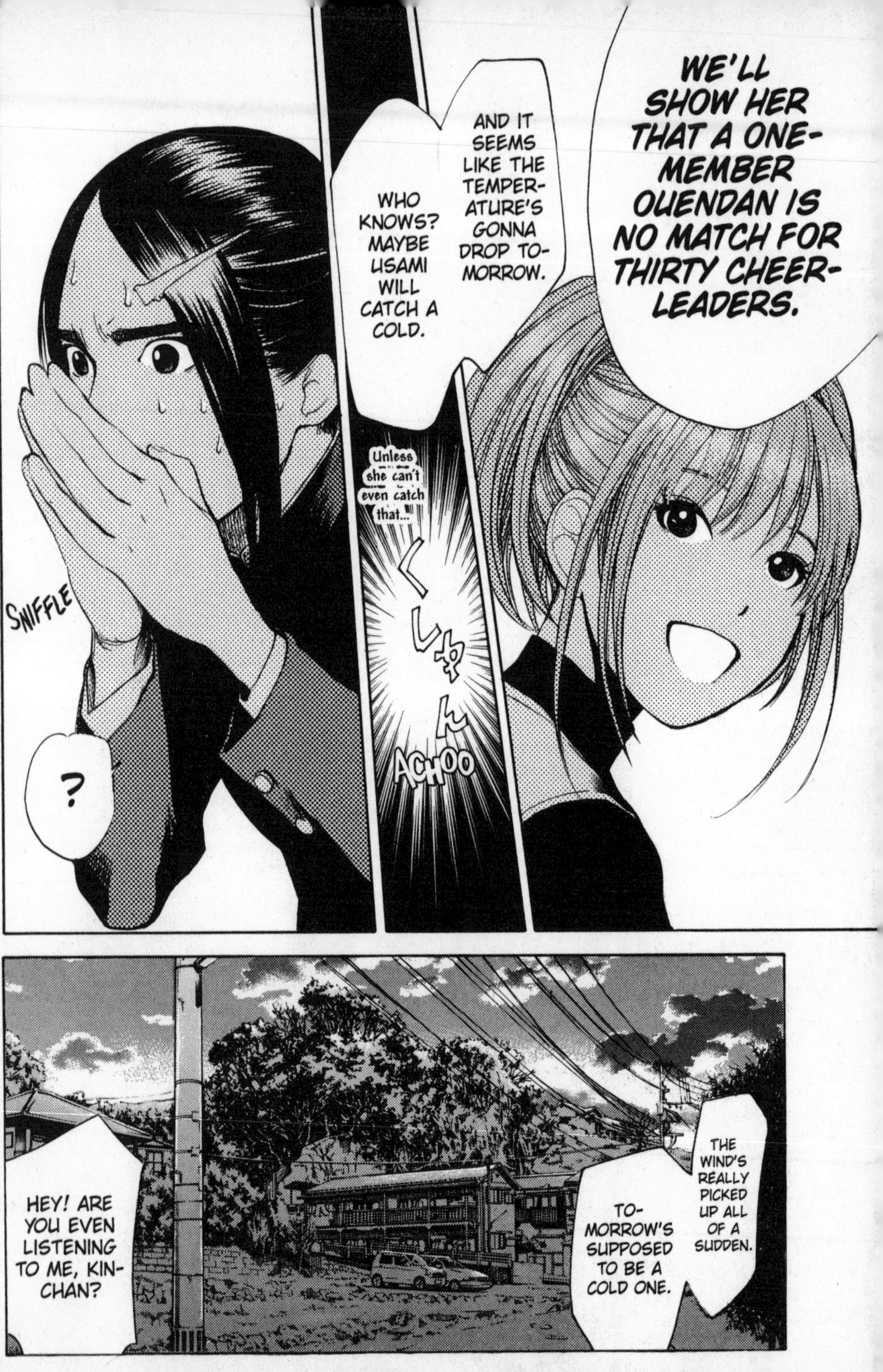
WE'LL SHOW HER THAT A ONE-MEMBER OUENDAN IS NO MATCH FOR THIRTY CHEER-LEADERS.
AND IT SEEMS LIKE THE TEMPER-ATURE'S GONNA DROP TO-MORROW.
WHO KNOWS? MAYBE USAMI WILL CATCH A COLD.
Unless she can't even catch that...
くしゅん
ACHOO
SNIFFLE
?
THE WIND'S REALLY PICKED UP ALL OF A SUDDEN.
TO-MORROW'S SUPPOSED TO BE A COLD ONE.
HEY! ARE YOU EVEN LISTENING TO ME, KIN-CHAN?

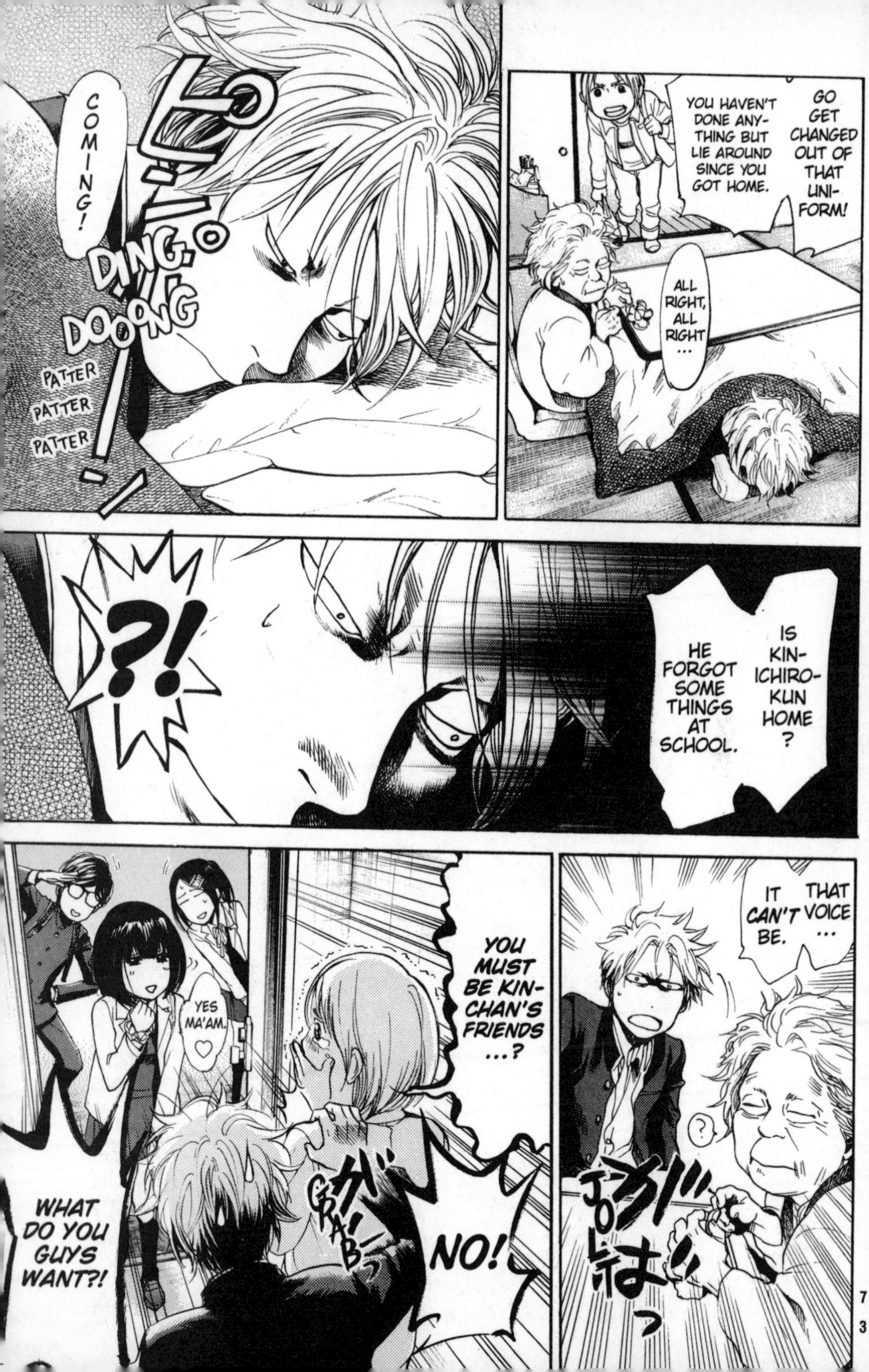
GO GET CHANGED OUT OF THAT UNIFORM!
YOU HAVEN'T DONE ANYTHING BUT LIE AROUND SINCE YOU GOT HOME.
ALL RIGHT, ALL RIGHT...
DING DOOONG
COMING!
PATTER PATTER PATTER
IS KIN-ICHIRO-KUN HOME?
HE FORGOT SOME THINGS AT SCHOOL.
?!
THAT VOICE...
IT CAN'T BE.
?
JOLT
YOU MUST BE KIN-CHAN'S FRIENDS...?
YES MA'AM. ♡
NO!
GRAB
WHAT DO YOU GUYS WANT?!

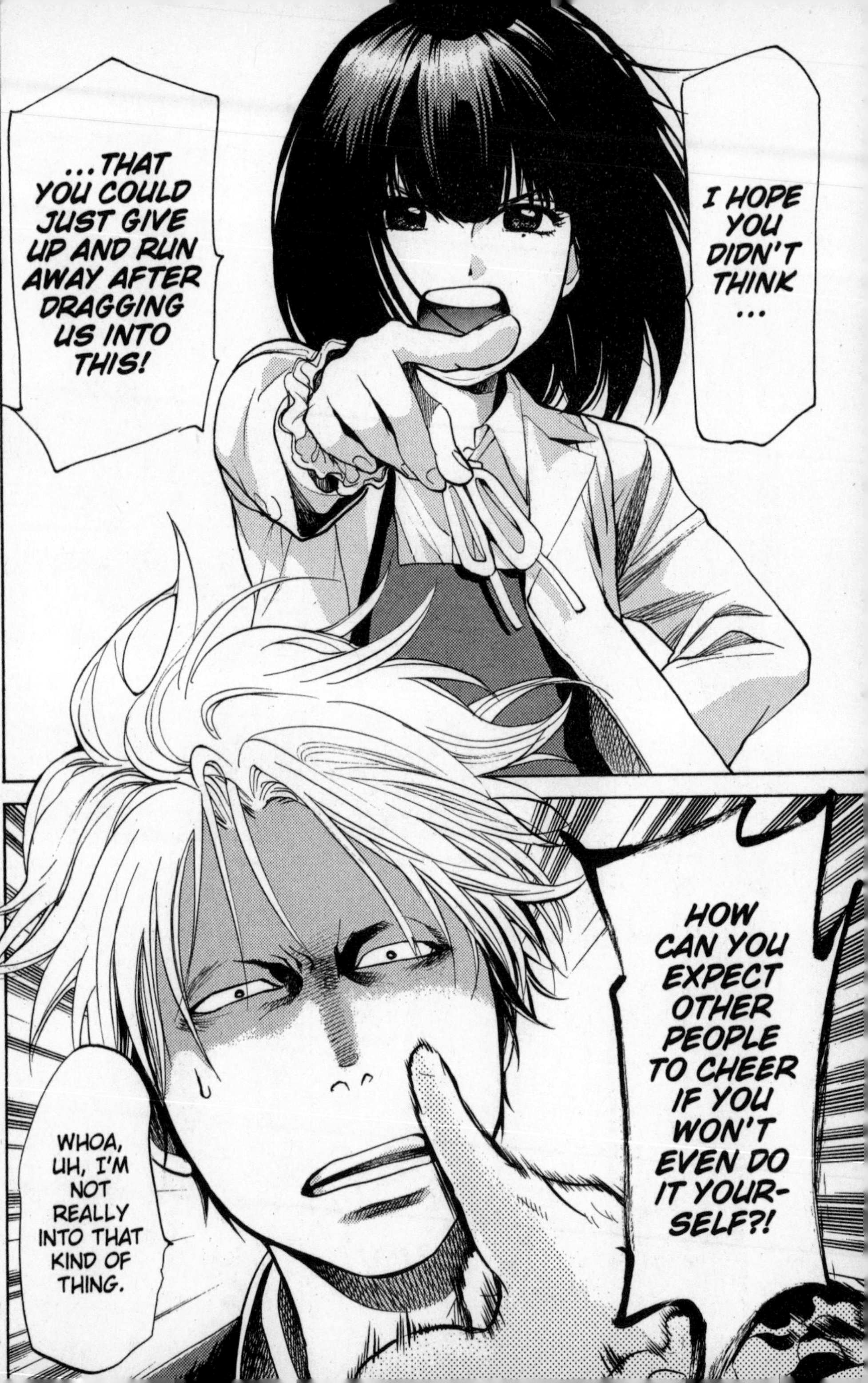
I HOPE YOU DIDN'T THINK...
...THAT YOU COULD JUST GIVE UP AND RUN AWAY AFTER DRAGGING US INTO THIS!
HOW CAN YOU EXPECT OTHER PEOPLE TO CHEER IF YOU WON'T EVEN DO IT YOUR-SELF?!
WHOA, UH, I'M NOT REALLY INTO THAT KIND OF THING.

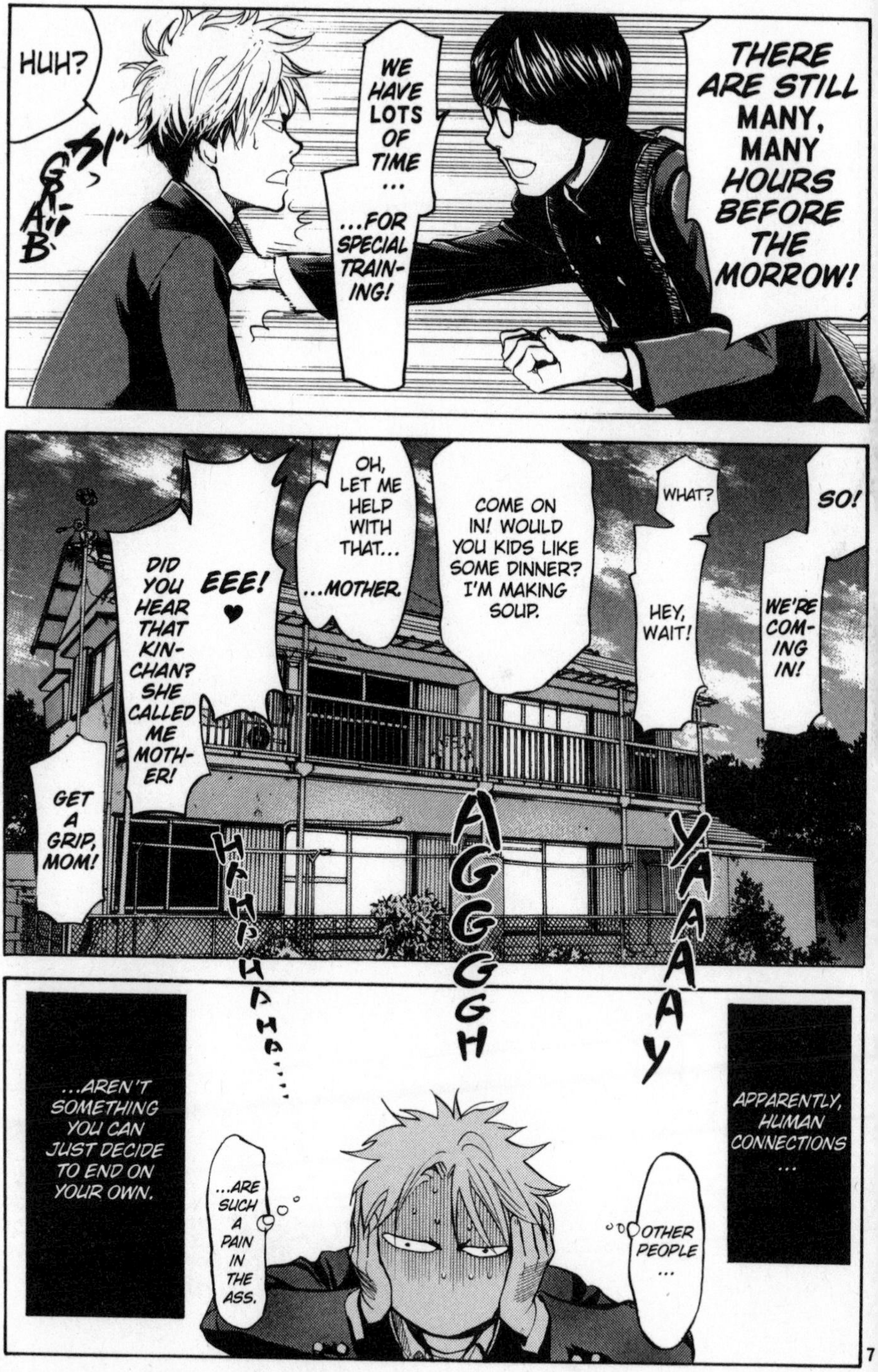
THERE ARE STILL MANY, MANY HOURS BEFORE THE MORROW!
WE HAVE LOTS OF TIME...
...FOR SPECIAL TRAINING!
GRAB
HUH?
SO!
WE'RE COMING IN!
WHAT?
HEY, WAIT!
COME ON IN! WOULD YOU KIDS LIKE SOME DINNER? I'M MAKING SOUP.
OH, LET ME HELP WITH THAT...
...MOTHER.
EEE! ♥
DID YOU HEAR THAT KIN-CHAN? SHE CALLED ME MOTHER!
GET A GRIP, MOM!
YAAAAAY
AGGGGH
HAHAHAHA....
APPARENTLY, HUMAN CONNECTIONS...
OTHER PEOPLE...
...ARE SUCH A PAIN IN THE ASS.
...AREN'T SOMETHING YOU CAN JUST DECIDE TO END ON YOUR OWN.

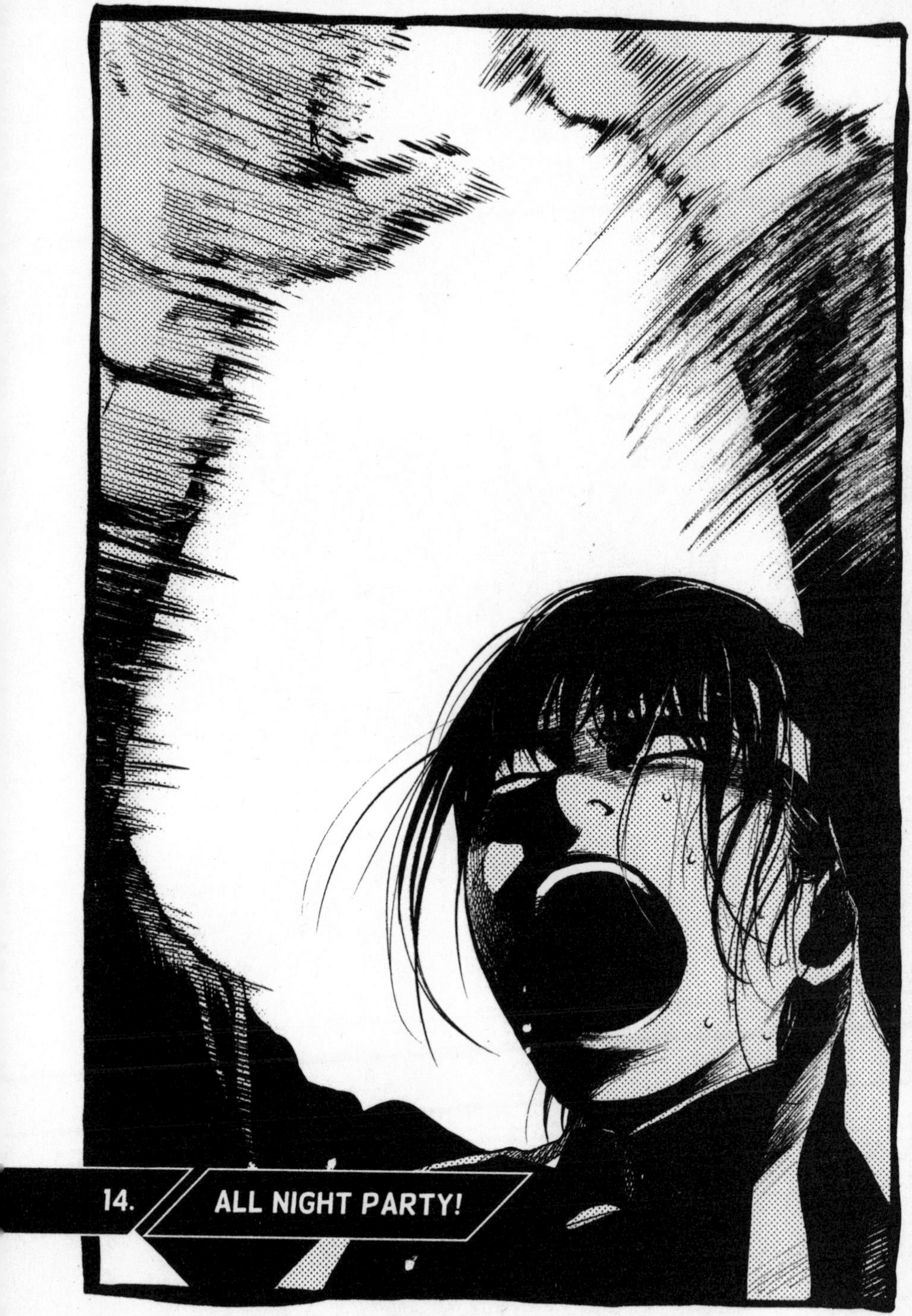
14.
ALL NIGHT PARTY!

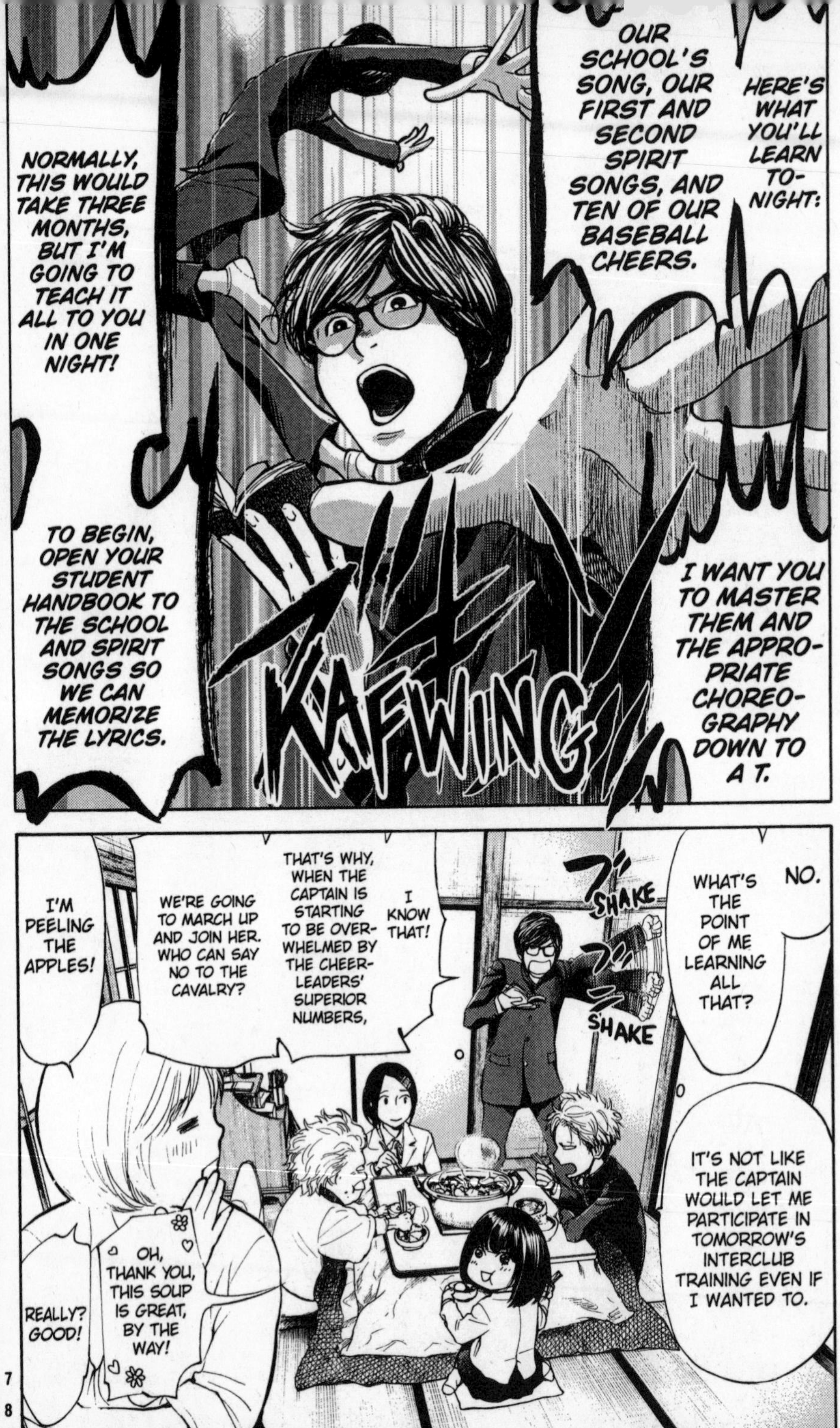
HERE'S WHAT YOU'LL LEARN TO-NIGHT:
OUR SCHOOL'S SONG, OUR FIRST AND SECOND SPIRIT SONGS, AND TEN OF OUR BASEBALL CHEERS.
NORMALLY, THIS WOULD TAKE THREE MONTHS, BUT I'M GOING TO TEACH IT ALL TO YOU IN ONE NIGHT!
I WANT YOU TO MASTER THEM AND THE APPRO-PRIATE CHOREO-GRAPHY DOWN TO A T.
KAFWING
TO BEGIN, OPEN YOUR STUDENT HANDBOOK TO THE SCHOOL AND SPIRIT SONGS SO WE CAN MEMORIZE THE LYRICS.
NO.
WHAT'S THE POINT OF ME LEARNING ALL THAT?
SHAKE
SHAKE
IT'S NOT LIKE THE CAPTAIN WOULD LET ME PARTICIPATE IN TOMORROW'S INTERCLUB TRAINING EVEN IF I WANTED TO.
I KNOW THAT!
THAT'S WHY, WHEN THE CAPTAIN IS STARTING TO BE OVER-WHELMED BY THE CHEER-LEADERS' SUPERIOR NUMBERS,
WE'RE GOING TO MARCH UP AND JOIN HER. WHO CAN SAY NO TO THE CAVALRY?
I'M PEELING THE APPLES!
OH, THANK YOU, THIS SOUP IS GREAT, BY THE WAY!
REALLY? GOOD!

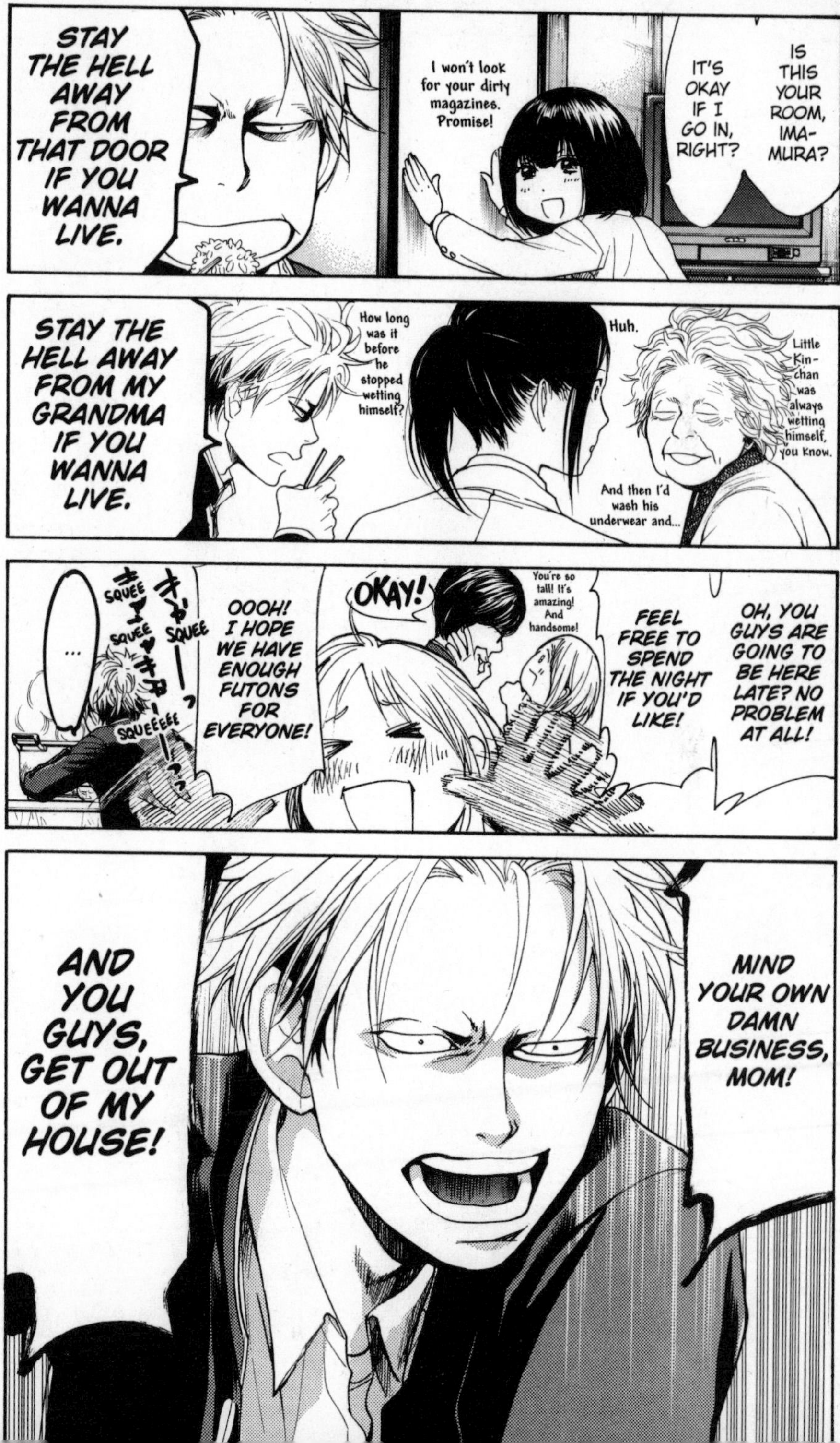
IS THIS YOUR ROOM, IMAMURA?
IT'S OKAY IF I GO IN, RIGHT?
I won't look for your dirty magazines. Promise!
STAY THE HELL AWAY FROM THAT DOOR IF YOU WANNA LIVE.
Little Kin-chan was always wetting himself, you know.
And then I'd wash his underwear and...
Huh.
How long was it before he stopped wetting himself?
STAY THE HELL AWAY FROM MY GRANDMA IF YOU WANNA LIVE.
OH, YOU GUYS ARE GOING TO BE HERE LATE? NO PROBLEM AT ALL!
FEEL FREE TO SPEND THE NIGHT IF YOU'D LIKE!
You're so tall! It's amazing! And handsome!
OKAY!
OOOH! I HOPE WE HAVE ENOUGH FUTONS FOR EVERYONE!
SQUEE
SQUEE
SQUEE
SQUEEEEE
...
MIND YOUR OWN DAMN BUSINESS, MOM!
AND YOU GUYS, GET OUT OF MY HOUSE!

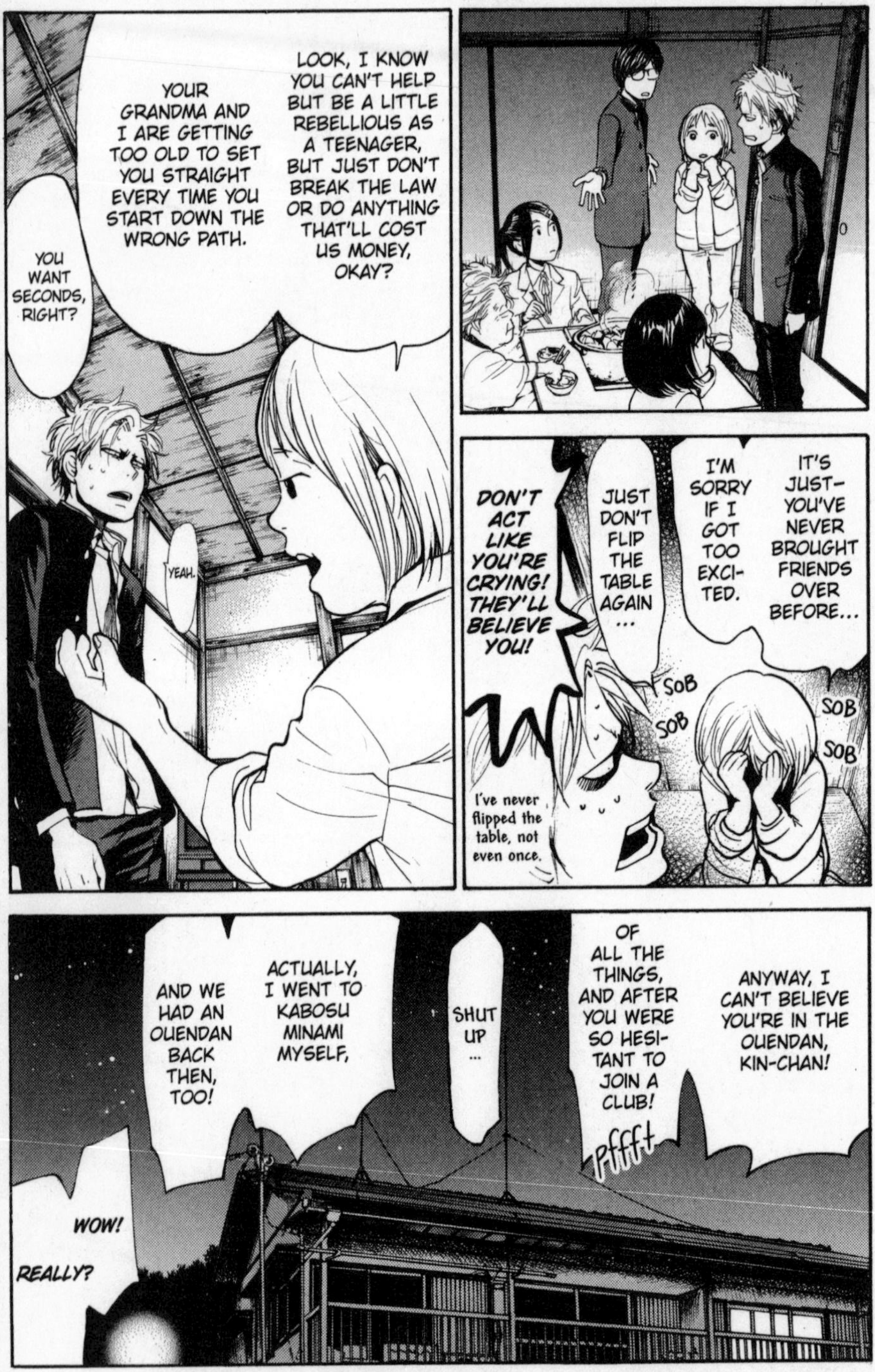
IT'S JUST— YOU'VE NEVER BROUGHT FRIENDS OVER BEFORE...
I'M SORRY IF I GOT TOO EXCITED.
JUST DON'T FLIP THE TABLE AGAIN...
DON'T ACT LIKE YOU'RE CRYING! THEY'LL BELIEVE YOU!
SOB SOB
SOB SOB
I've never flipped the table, not even once.
LOOK, I KNOW YOU CAN'T HELP BUT BE A LITTLE REBELLIOUS AS A TEENAGER, BUT JUST DON'T BREAK THE LAW OR DO ANYTHING THAT'LL COST US MONEY, OKAY?
YOUR GRANDMA AND I ARE GETTING TOO OLD TO SET YOU STRAIGHT EVERY TIME YOU START DOWN THE WRONG PATH.
YOU WANT SECONDS, RIGHT?
YEAH.
ANYWAY, I CAN'T BELIEVE YOU'RE IN THE OUENDAN, KIN-CHAN!
OF ALL THE THINGS, AND AFTER YOU WERE SO HESI-TANT TO JOIN A CLUB!
pffft
SHUT UP...
ACTUALLY, I WENT TO KABOSU MINAMI MYSELF,
AND WE HAD AN OUENDAN BACK THEN, TOO!
WOW!
REALLY?

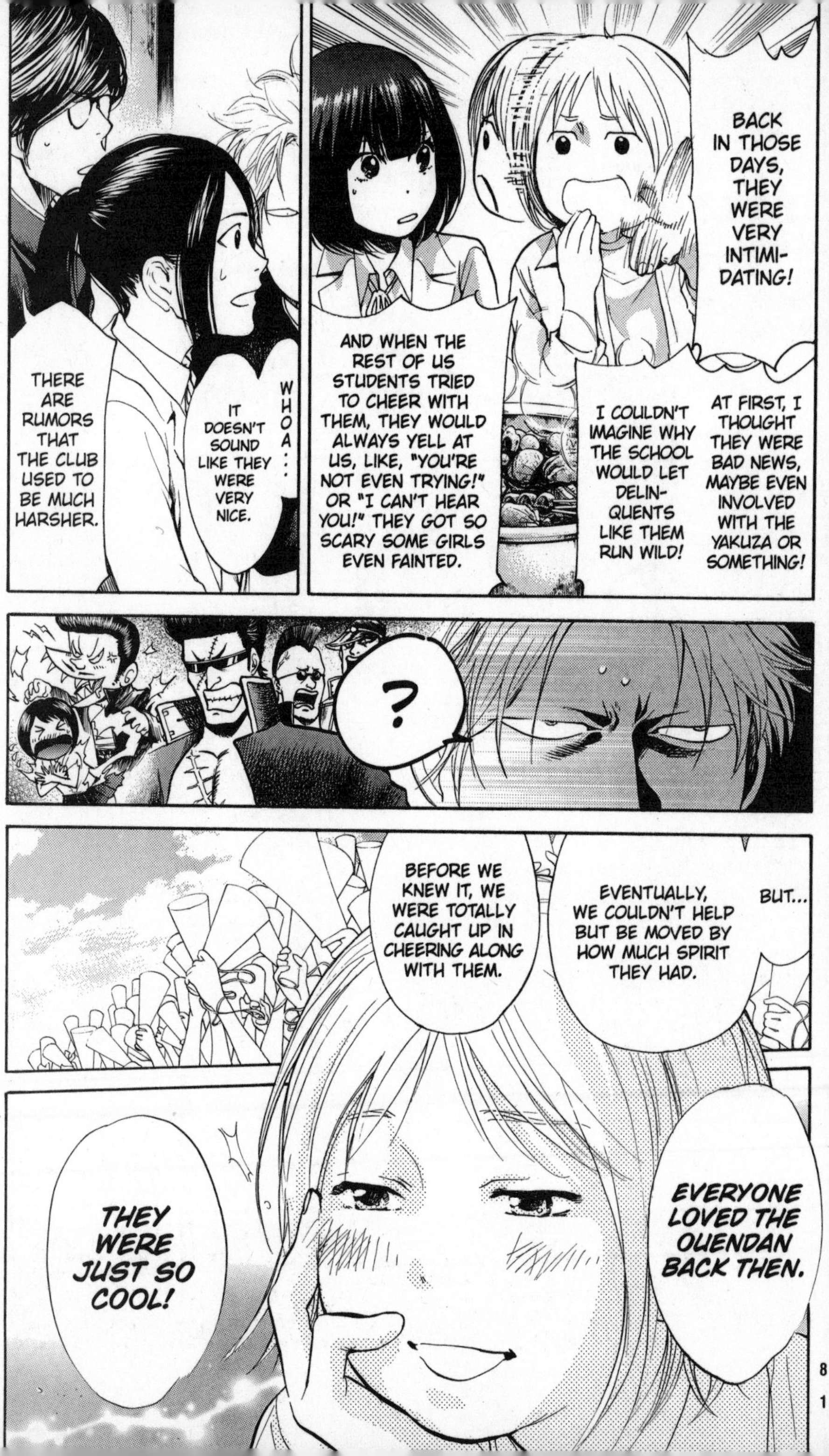
BACK IN THOSE DAYS, THEY WERE VERY INTIMIDATING!
AT FIRST, I THOUGHT THEY WERE BAD NEWS, MAYBE EVEN INVOLVED WITH THE YAKUZA OR SOMETHING!
I COULDN'T IMAGINE WHY THE SCHOOL WOULD LET DELINQUENTS LIKE THEM RUN WILD!
AND WHEN THE REST OF US STUDENTS TRIED TO CHEER WITH THEM, THEY WOULD ALWAYS YELL AT US, LIKE, "YOU'RE NOT EVEN TRYING!" OR "I CAN'T HEAR YOU!" THEY GOT SO SCARY SOME GIRLS EVEN FAINTED.
WHOA...
IT DOESN'T SOUND LIKE THEY WERE VERY NICE.
THERE ARE RUMORS THAT THE CLUB USED TO BE MUCH HARSHER.
?
BUT...
EVENTUALLY, WE COULDN'T HELP BUT BE MOVED BY HOW MUCH SPIRIT THEY HAD.
BEFORE WE KNEW IT, WE WERE TOTALLY CAUGHT UP IN CHEERING ALONG WITH THEM.
EVERYONE LOVED THE OUENDAN BACK THEN.
THEY WERE JUST SO COOL!

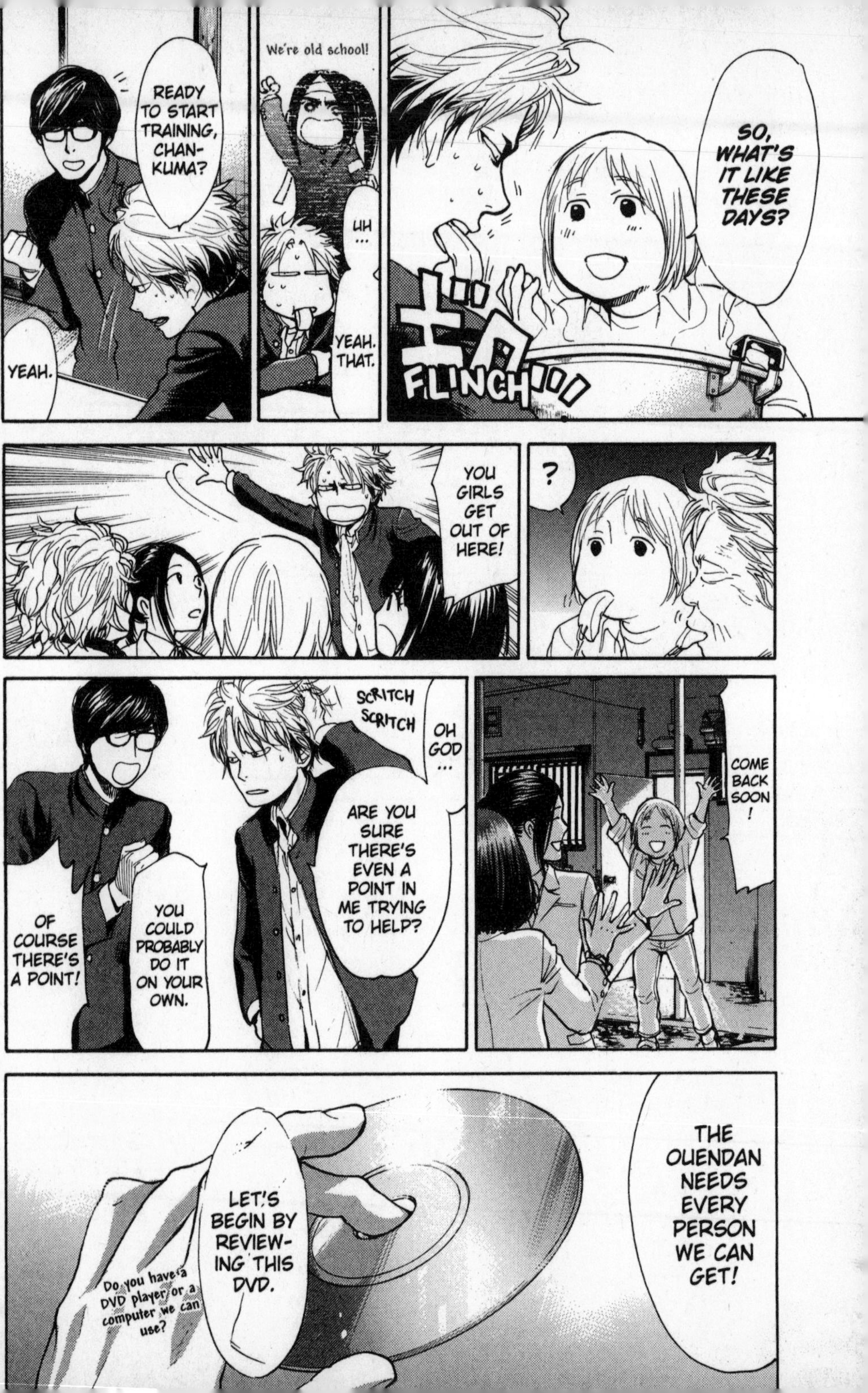
SO, WHAT'S IT LIKE THESE DAYS?
FLINCH
We're old school!
UH ...
YEAH. THAT.
READY TO START TRAINING, CHAN-KUMA?
YEAH.
?
YOU GIRLS GET OUT OF HERE!
COME BACK SOON!
SCRITCH SCRITCH
OH GOD ...
ARE YOU SURE THERE'S EVEN A POINT IN ME TRYING TO HELP?
YOU COULD PROBABLY DO IT ON YOUR OWN.
OF COURSE THERE'S A POINT!
THE OUENDAN NEEDS EVERY PERSON WE CAN GET!
LET'S BEGIN BY REVIEWING THIS DVD.
Do you have a DVD player or a computer we can use?

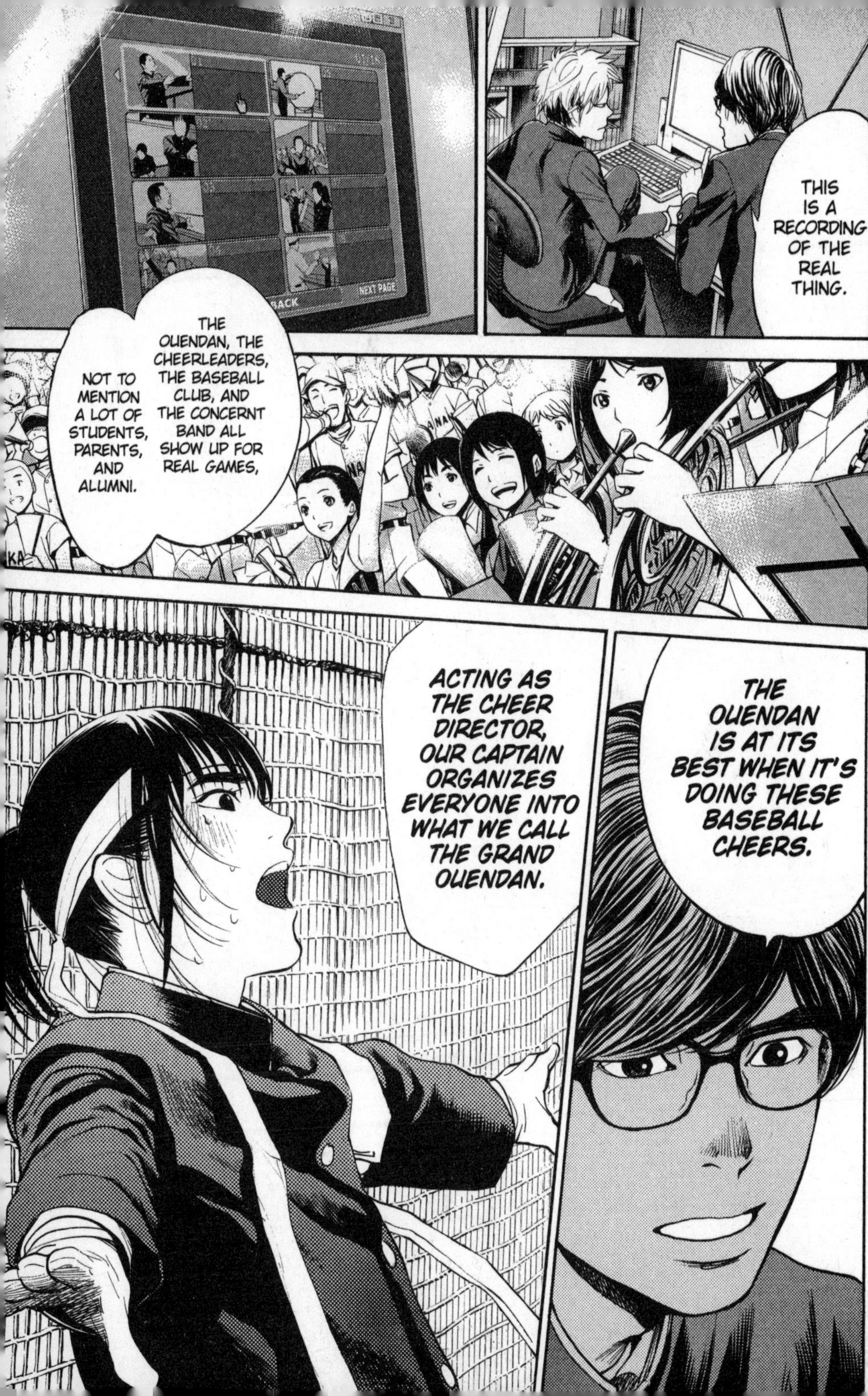
THIS IS A RECORDING OF THE REAL THING.
BACK
NEXT PAGE
THE OUENDAN, THE CHEERLEADERS, THE BASEBALL CLUB, AND THE CONCERNT BAND ALL SHOW UP FOR REAL GAMES,
NOT TO MENTION A LOT OF STUDENTS, PARENTS, AND ALUMNI.
THE OUENDAN IS AT ITS BEST WHEN IT'S DOING THESE BASEBALL CHEERS.
ACTING AS THE CHEER DIRECTOR, OUR CAPTAIN ORGANIZES EVERYONE INTO WHAT WE CALL THE GRAND OUENDAN.

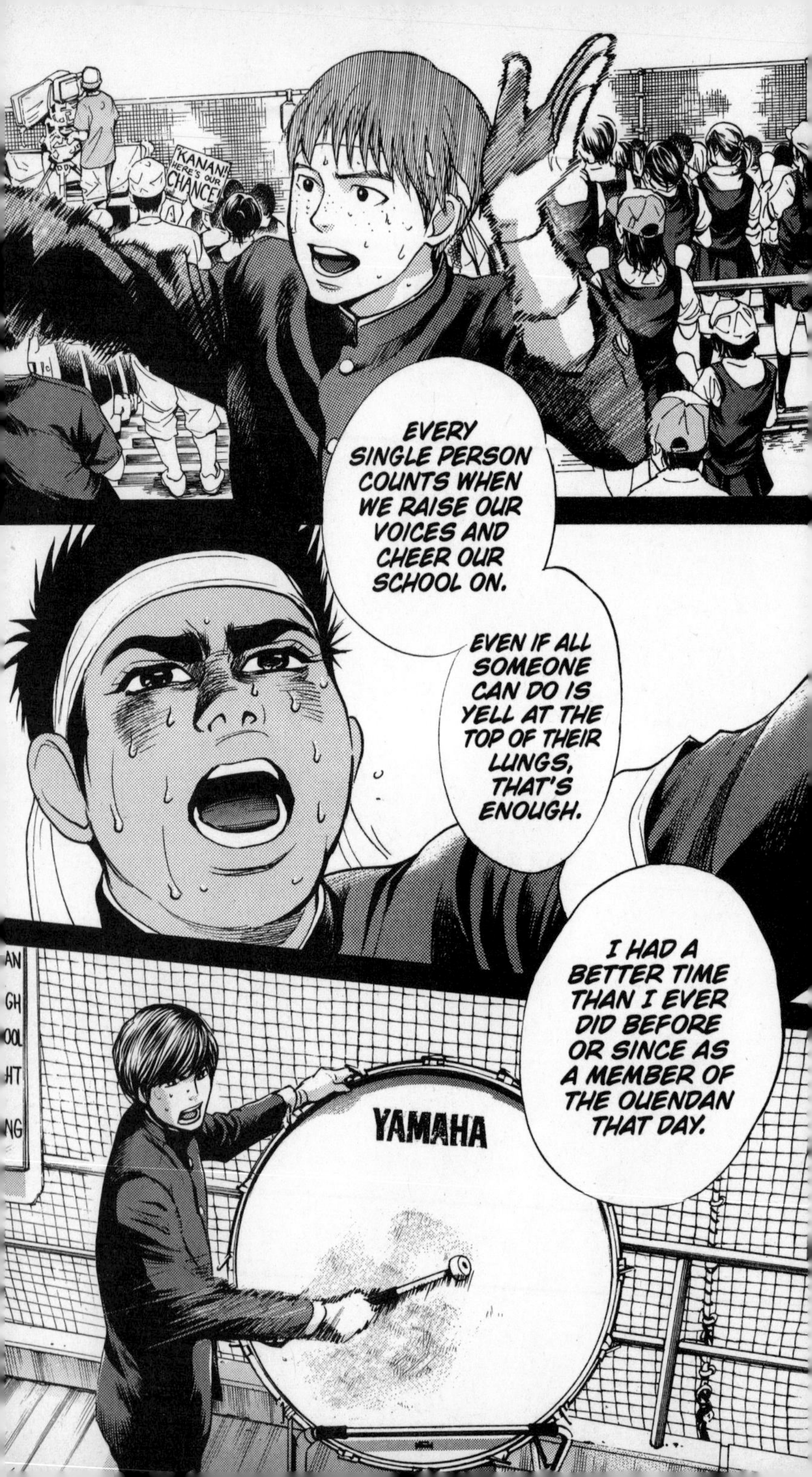
"KANAN! HERE'S OUR CHANCE!"
EVERY SINGLE PERSON COUNTS WHEN WE RAISE OUR VOICES AND CHEER OUR SCHOOL ON.
EVEN IF ALL SOMEONE CAN DO IS YELL AT THE TOP OF THEIR LUNGS, THAT'S ENOUGH.
I HAD A BETTER TIME THAN I EVER DID BEFORE OR SINCE AS A MEMBER OF THE OUENDAN THAT DAY.
YAMAHA

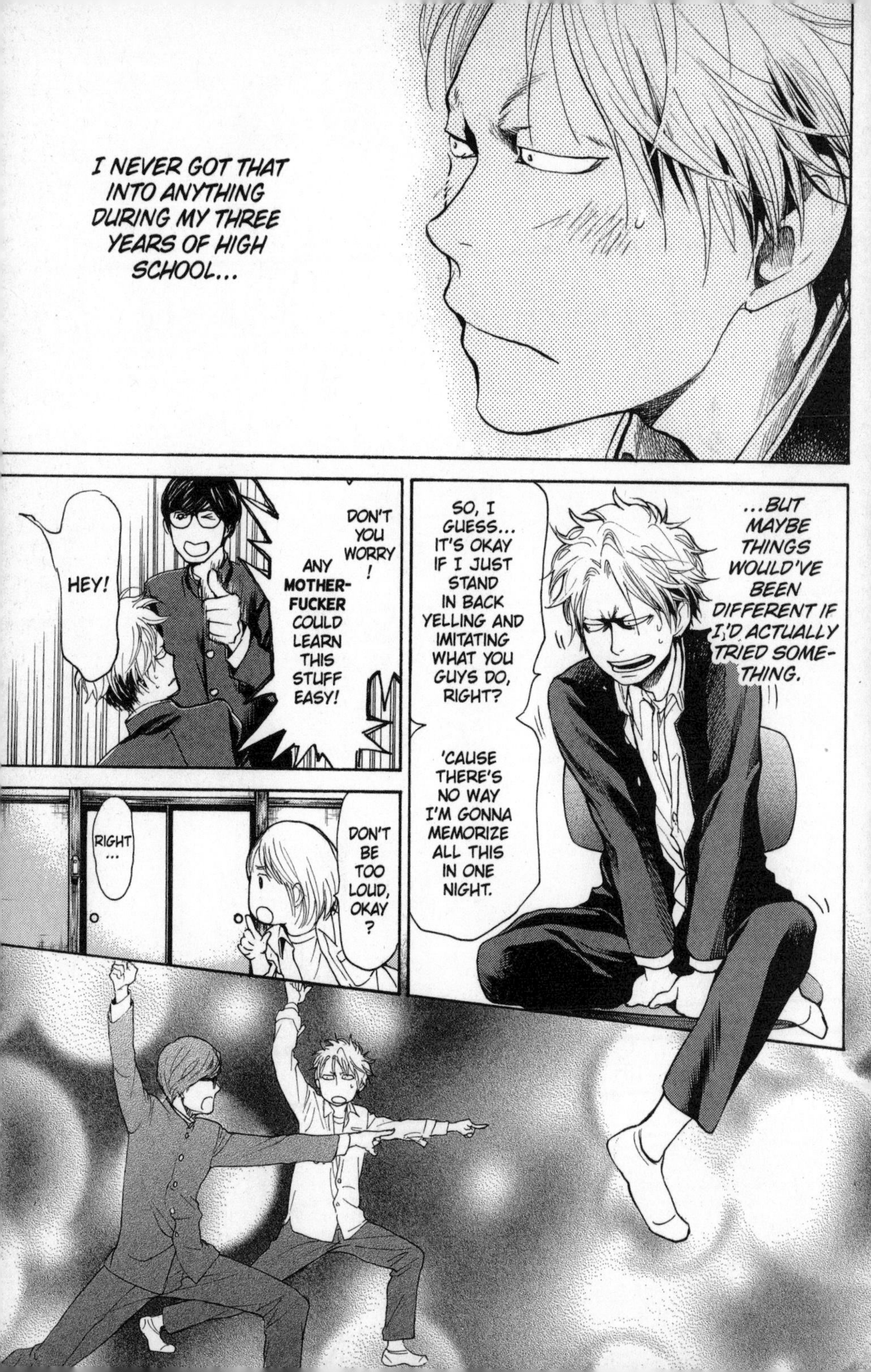
I NEVER GOT THAT INTO ANYTHING DURING MY THREE YEARS OF HIGH SCHOOL...
...BUT MAYBE THINGS WOULD'VE BEEN DIFFERENT IF I'D ACTUALLY TRIED SOMETHING.
SO, I GUESS... IT'S OKAY IF I JUST STAND IN BACK YELLING AND IMITATING WHAT YOU GUYS DO, RIGHT?
'CAUSE THERE'S NO WAY I'M GONNA MEMORIZE ALL THIS IN ONE NIGHT.
DON'T YOU WORRY!
ANY **MOTHER-FUCKER** COULD LEARN THIS STUFF EASY!
HEY!
DON'T BE TOO LOUD, OKAY?
RIGHT...

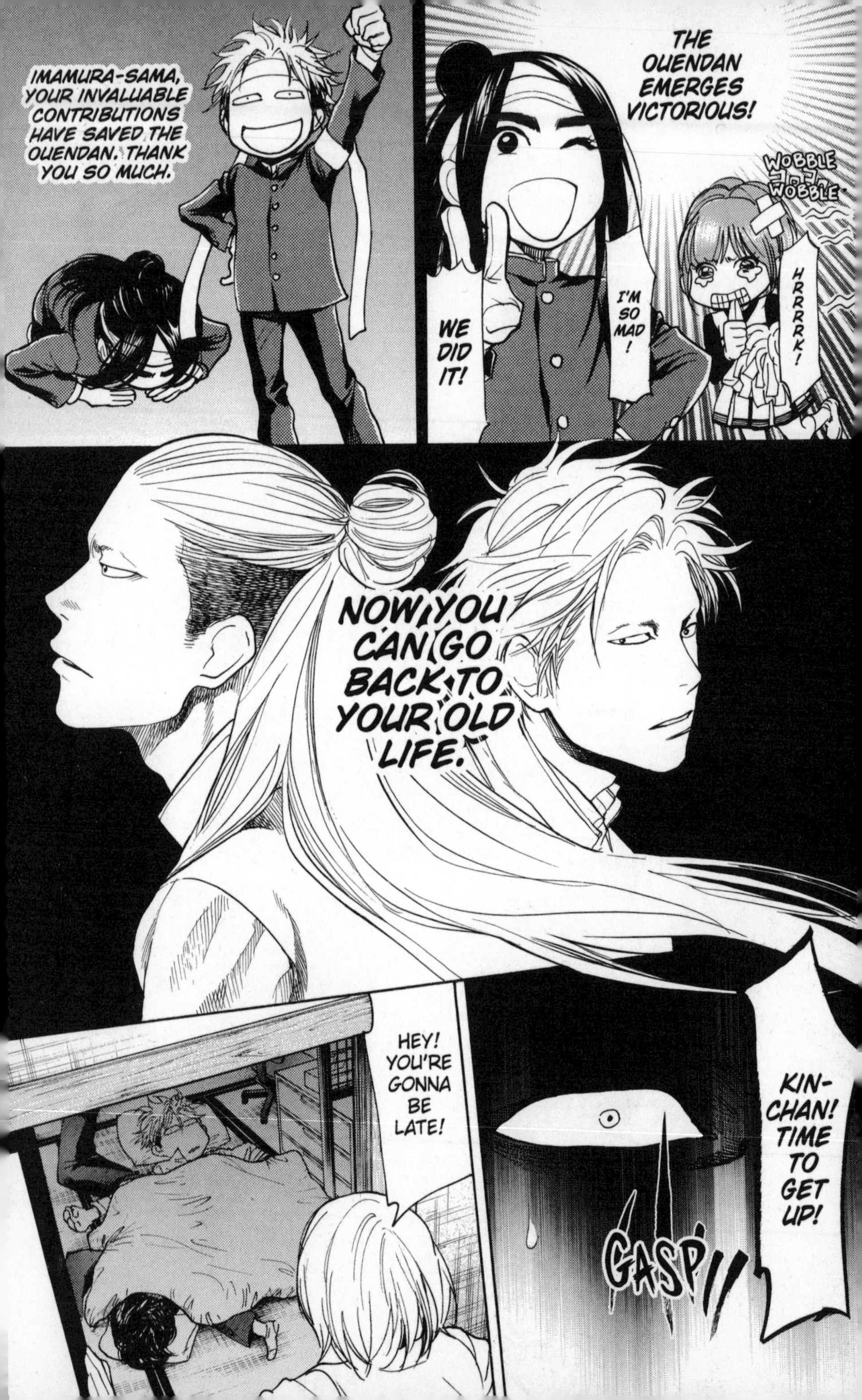
THE OUENDAN EMERGES VICTORIOUS!
WOBBLE WOBBLE
HRRRRK!
I'M SO MAD!
WE DID IT!
IMAMURA-SAMA, YOUR INVALUABLE CONTRIBUTIONS HAVE SAVED THE OUENDAN. THANK YOU SO MUCH.
NOW YOU CAN GO BACK TO YOUR OLD LIFE.
KIN-CHAN! TIME TO GET UP!
GASP
HEY! YOU'RE GONNA BE LATE!

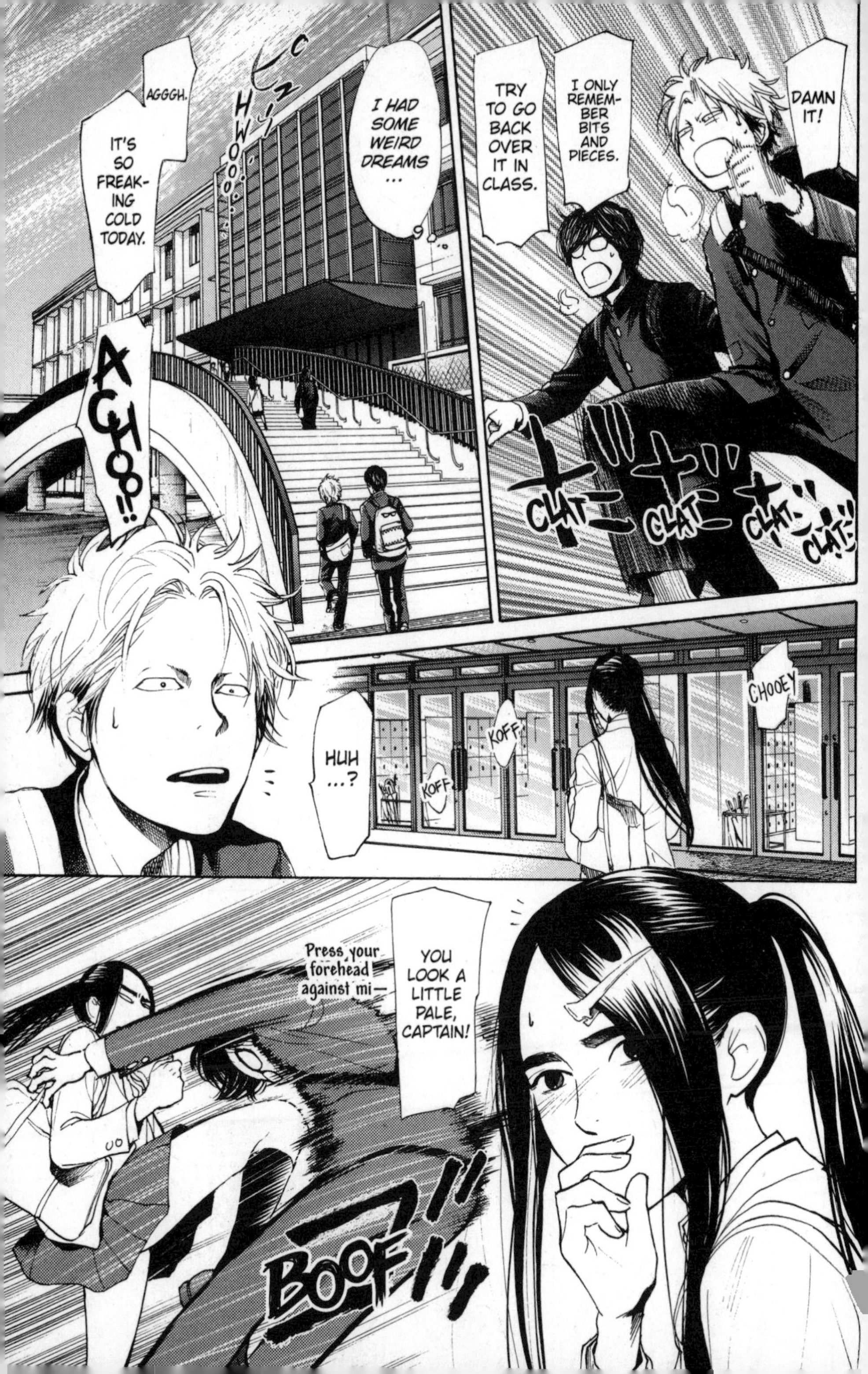

DAMN IT!
I ONLY REMEMBER BITS AND PIECES.
TRY TO GO BACK OVER IT IN CLASS.
CLAT CLAT CLAT CLAT
CHOOEY
KOFF
KOFF
I HAD SOME WEIRD DREAMS...
HWOOO...
AGGGH.
IT'S SO FREAKING COLD TODAY.
ACHOO!!
HUH...?
YOU LOOK A LITTLE PALE, CAPTAIN!
Press your forehead against mi—
BOOF!!

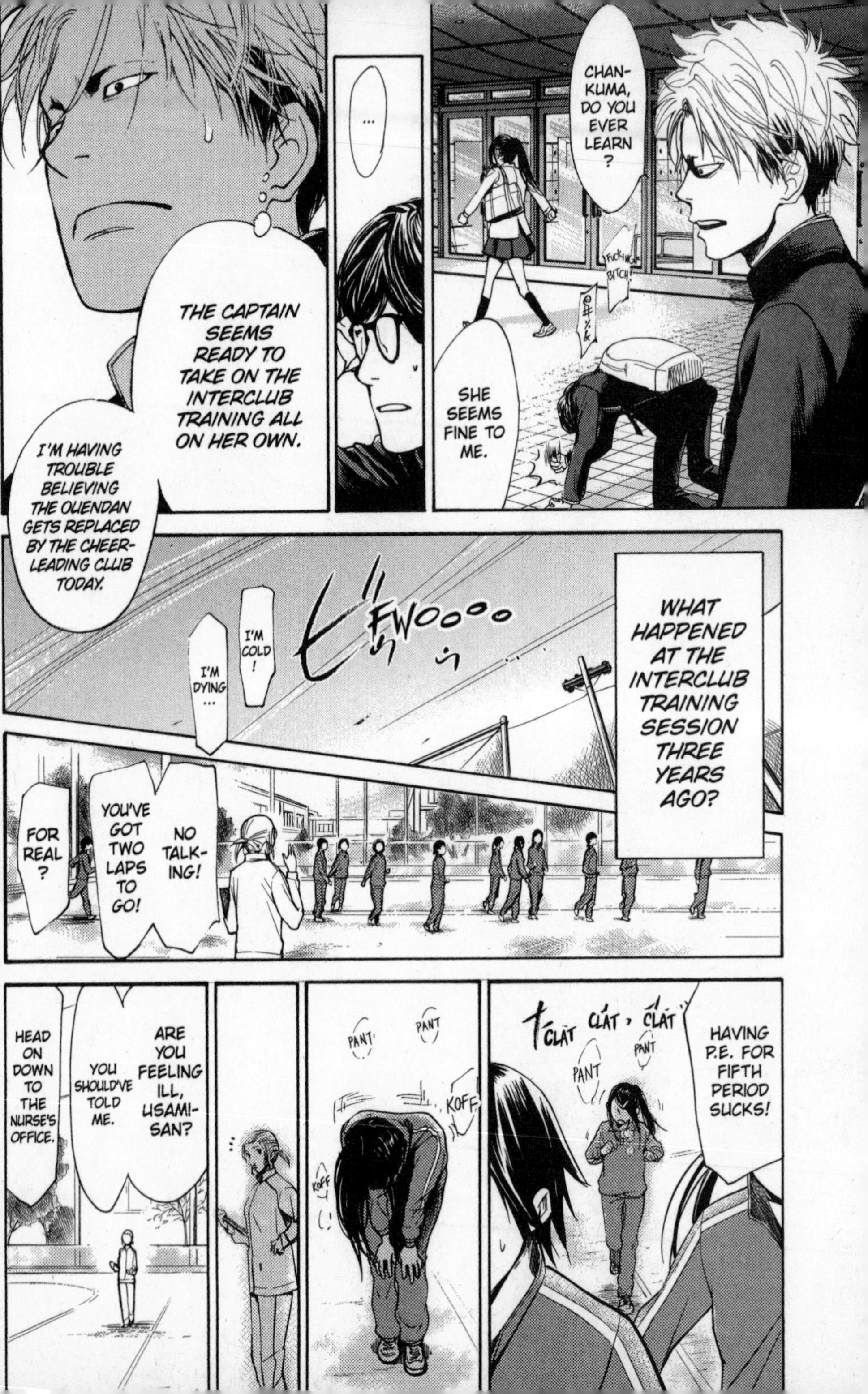
CHAN-KUMA, DO YOU EVER LEARN?
FUCKING BITCH!
SHE SEEMS FINE TO ME.
...
THE CAPTAIN SEEMS READY TO TAKE ON THE INTERCLUB TRAINING ALL ON HER OWN.
I'M HAVING TROUBLE BELIEVING THE OUENDAN GETS REPLACED BY THE CHEER-LEADING CLUB TODAY.
WHAT HAPPENED AT THE INTERCLUB TRAINING SESSION THREE YEARS AGO?
FWOOOOO
I'M COLD!
I'M DYING...
NO TALKING!
YOU'VE GOT TWO LAPS TO GO!
FOR REAL?
CLAT CLAT, CLAT
HAVING P.E. FOR FIFTH PERIOD SUCKS!
PANT
PANT
PANT
PANT
KOFF
KOFF
ARE YOU FEELING ILL, USAMI-SAN?
YOU SHOULD'VE TOLD ME.
HEAD ON DOWN TO THE NURSE'S OFFICE.

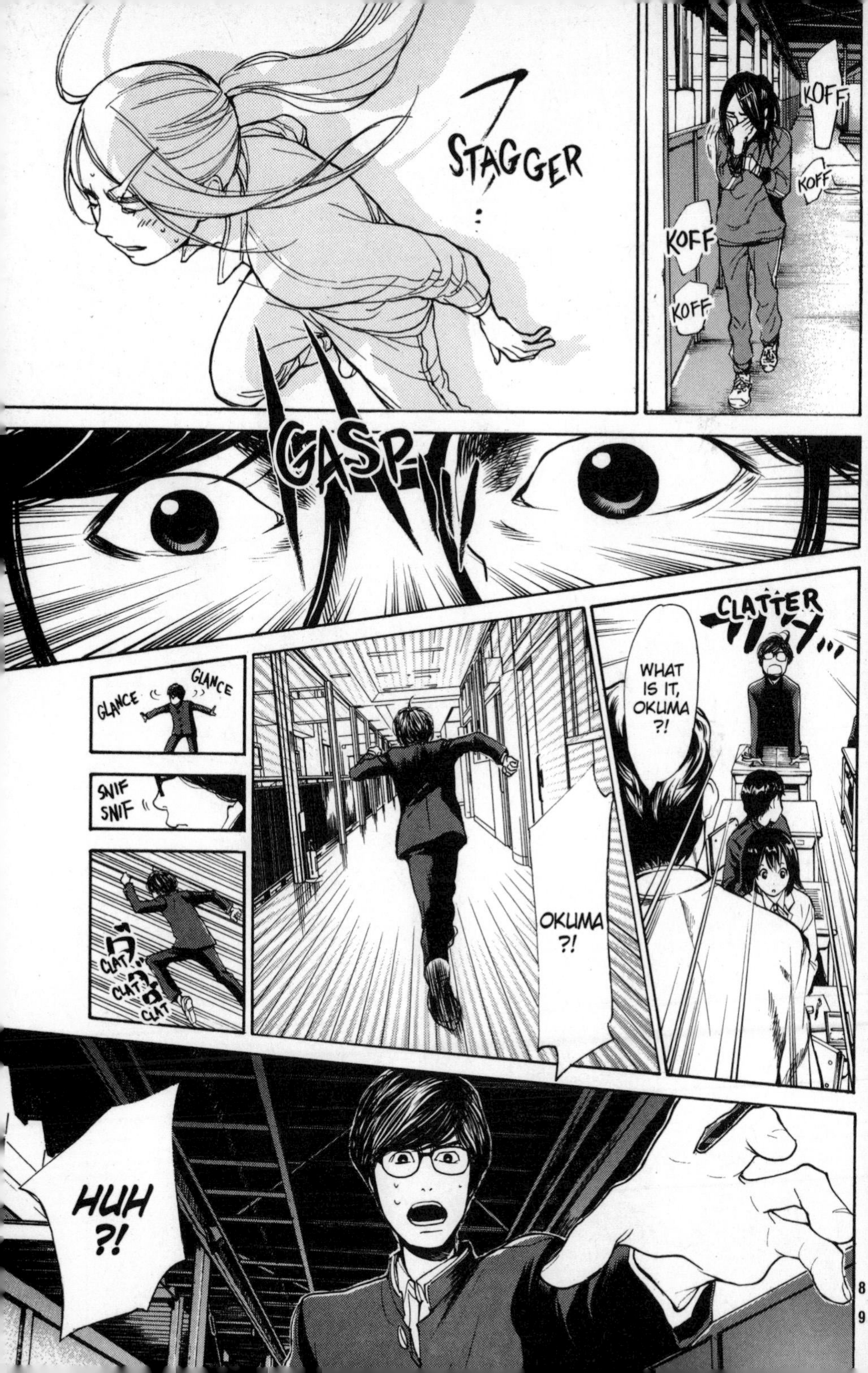
KOFF
KOFF
KOFF
KOFF
STAGGER
GASP
CLATTER
WHAT IS IT, OKUMA?!
OKUMA?!
GLANCE
GLANCE
SNIF SNIF
CLAT
CLAT
CLAT
HUH?!

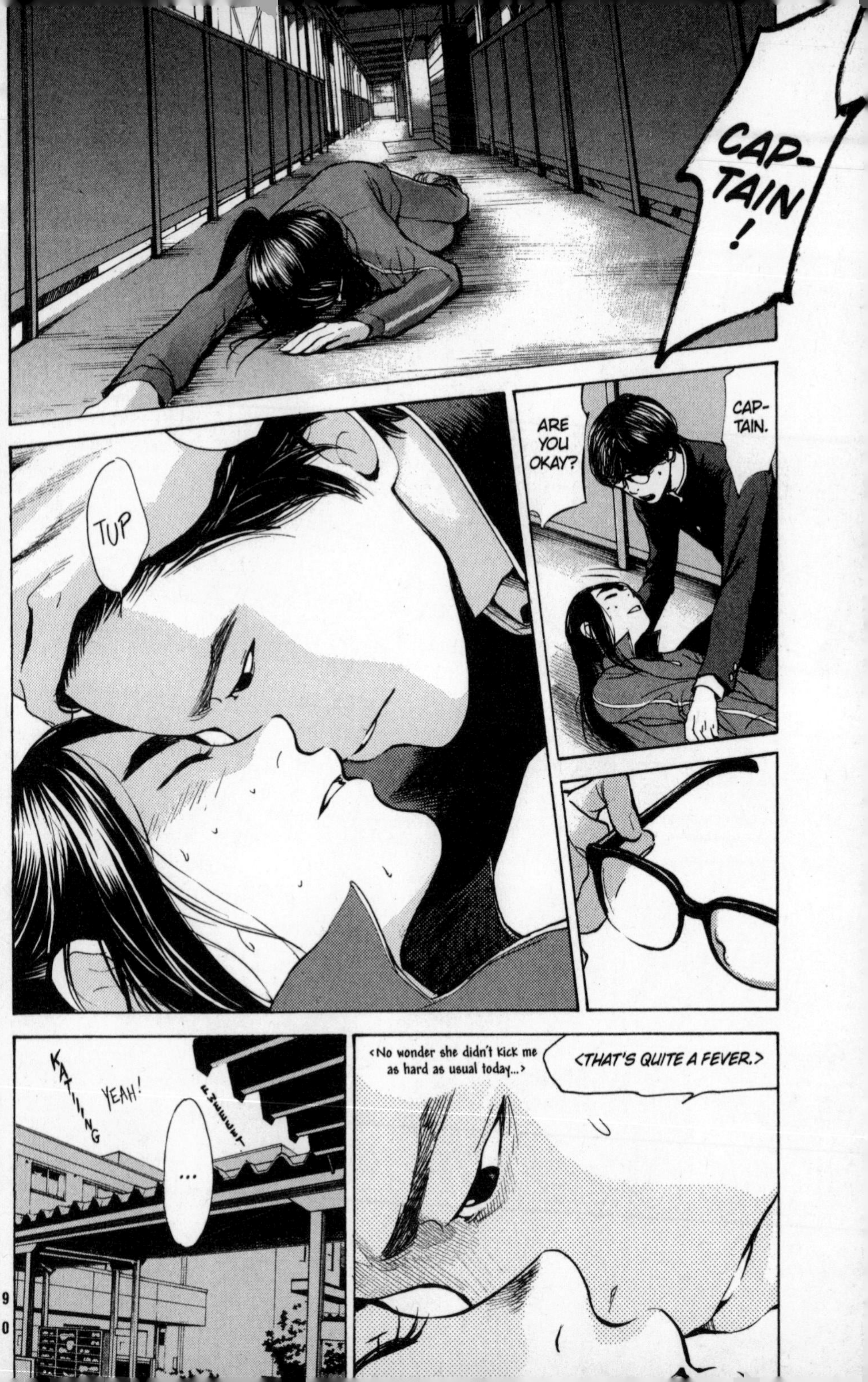
CAP-TAIN!
CAP-TAIN.
ARE YOU OKAY?
TUP
<THAT'S QUITE A FEVER.>
<No wonder she didn't kick me as hard as usual today...>
YEAH!
KATIIIING
...

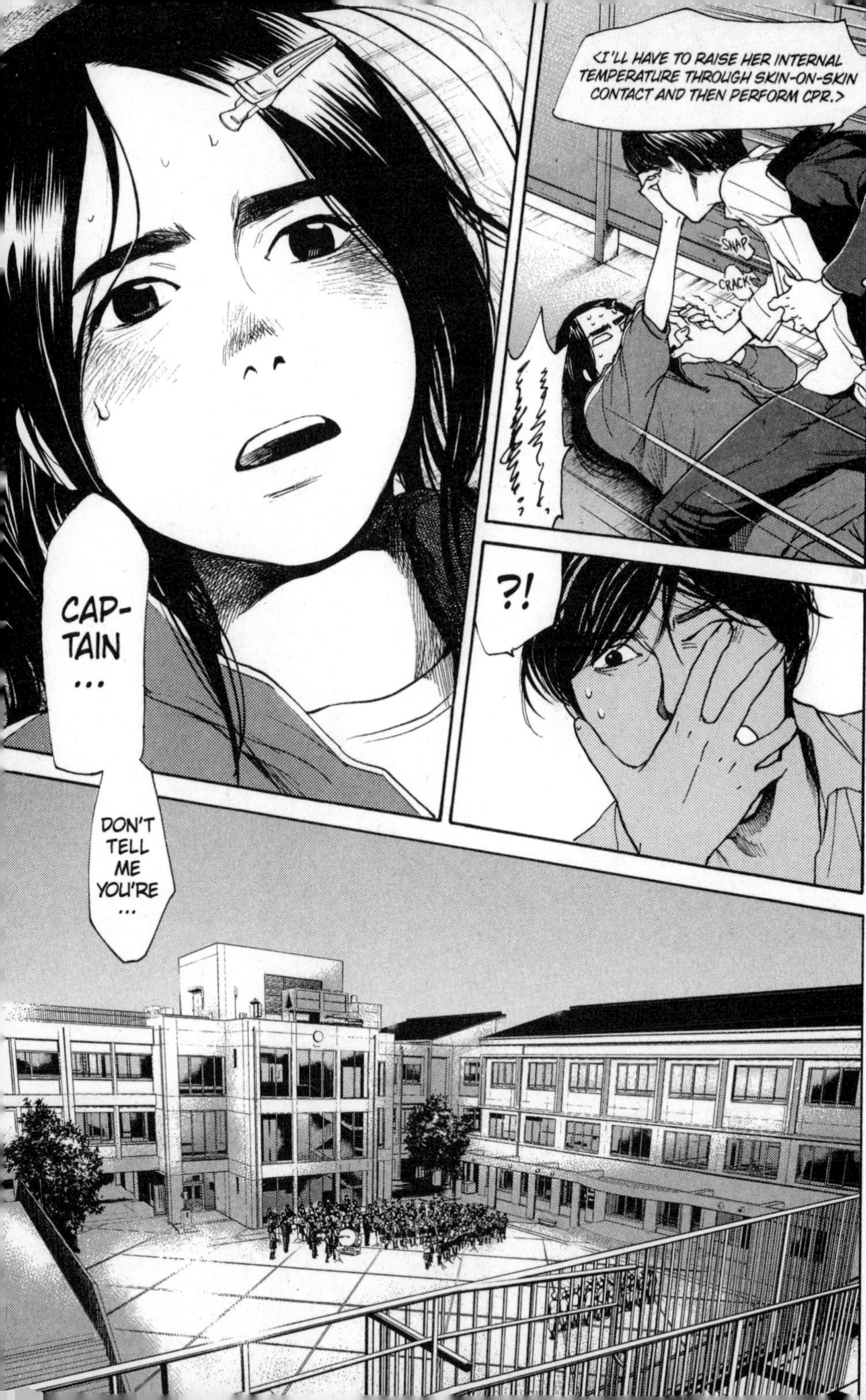
<I'LL HAVE TO RAISE HER INTERNAL TEMPERATURE THROUGH SKIN-ON-SKIN CONTACT AND THEN PERFORM CPR.>
SNAP
CRACK
?!
CAP-TAIN ...
DON'T TELL ME YOU'RE ...

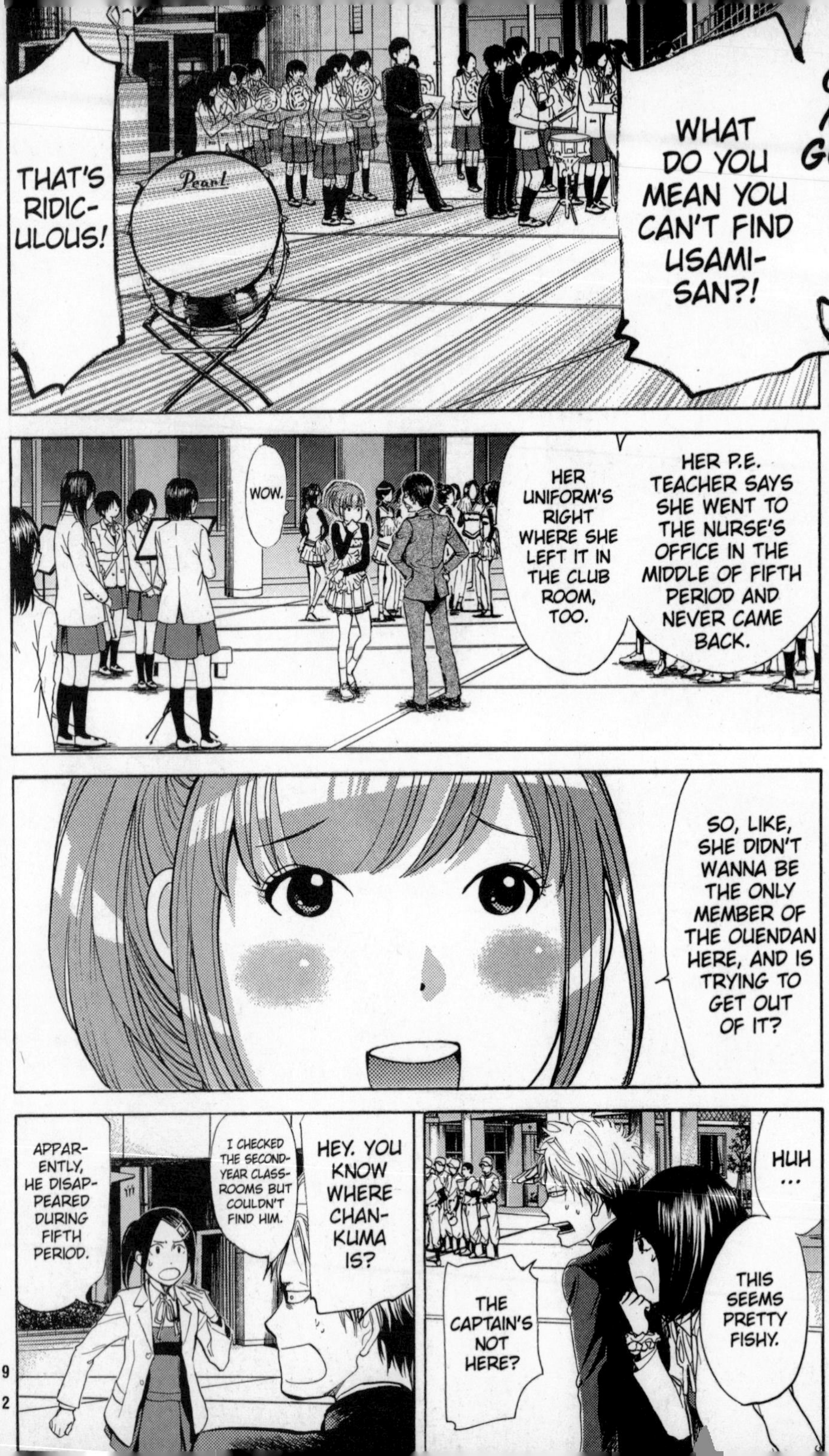
OH MY GOD!
WHAT DO YOU MEAN YOU CAN'T FIND USAMI-SAN?!
THAT'S RIDIC-ULOUS!
HER P.E. TEACHER SAYS SHE WENT TO THE NURSE'S OFFICE IN THE MIDDLE OF FIFTH PERIOD AND NEVER CAME BACK.
HER UNIFORM'S RIGHT WHERE SHE LEFT IT IN THE CLUB ROOM, TOO.
WOW.
SO, LIKE, SHE DIDN'T WANNA BE THE ONLY MEMBER OF THE OUENDAN HERE, AND IS TRYING TO GET OUT OF IT?
HUH ...
THIS SEEMS PRETTY FISHY.
THE CAPTAIN'S NOT HERE?
HEY. YOU KNOW WHERE CHAN-KUMA IS?
I CHECKED THE SECOND-YEAR CLASS-ROOMS BUT COULDN'T FIND HIM.
APPAR-ENTLY, HE DISAP-PEARED DURING FIFTH PERIOD.

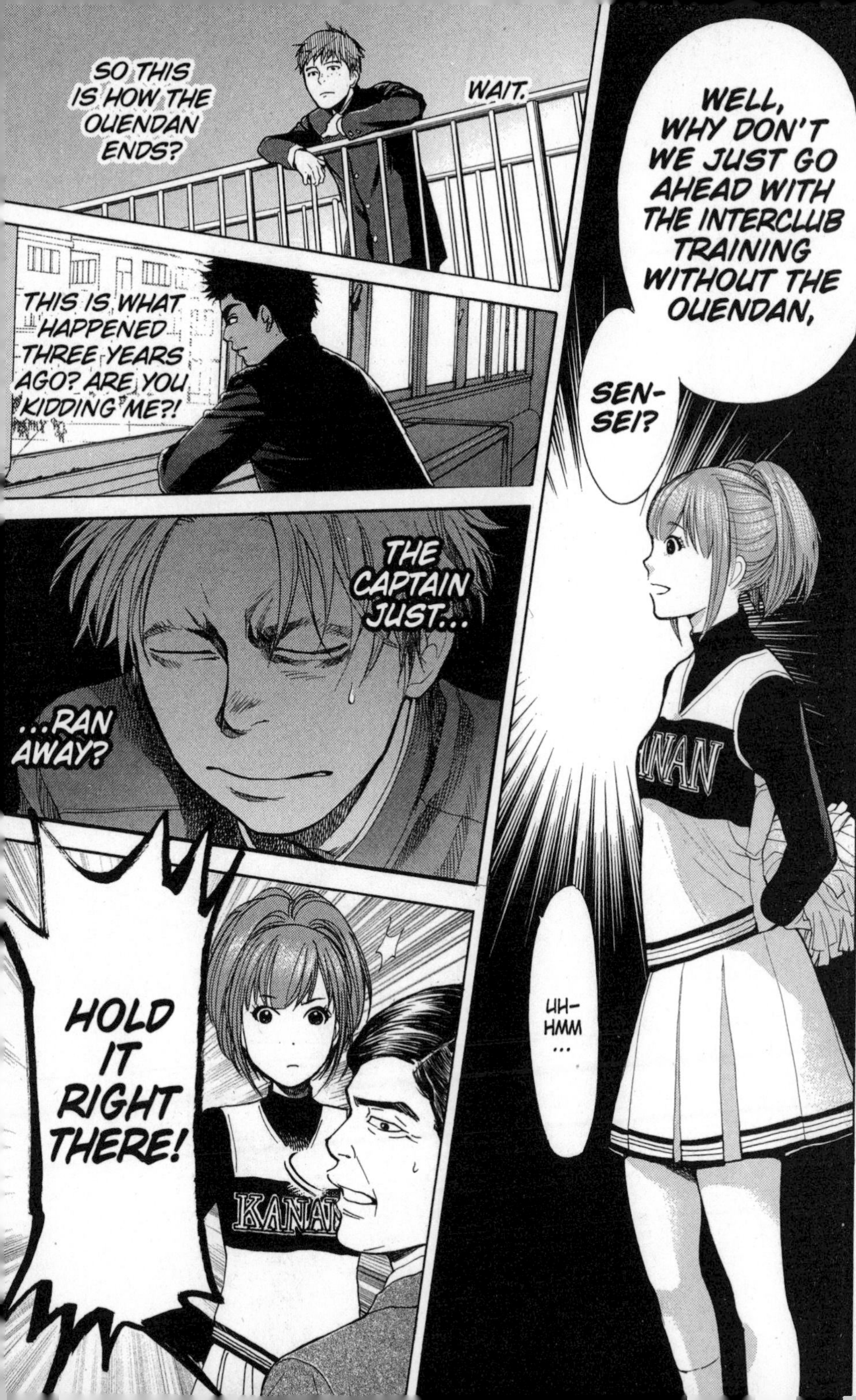
WELL, WHY DON'T WE JUST GO AHEAD WITH THE INTERCLUB TRAINING WITHOUT THE OUENDAN,
SEN-SEI?
UH-HMM...
WAIT.
SO THIS IS HOW THE OUENDAN ENDS?
THIS IS WHAT HAPPENED THREE YEARS AGO? ARE YOU KIDDING ME?!
THE CAPTAIN JUST...
...RAN AWAY?
HOLD IT RIGHT THERE!

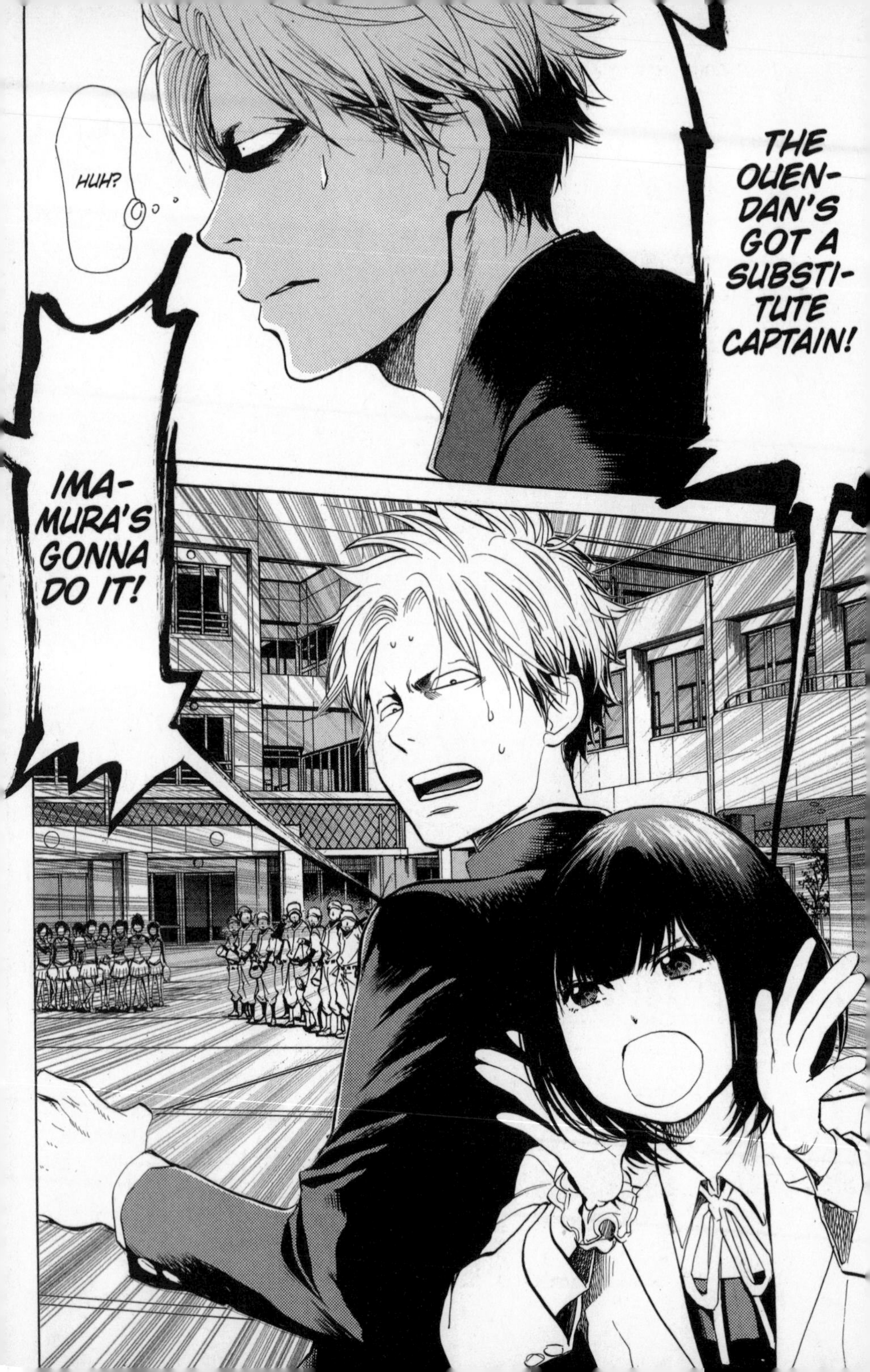
THE OUEN-DAN'S GOT A SUBSTITUTE CAPTAIN!
HUH?
IMAMURA'S GONNA DO IT!

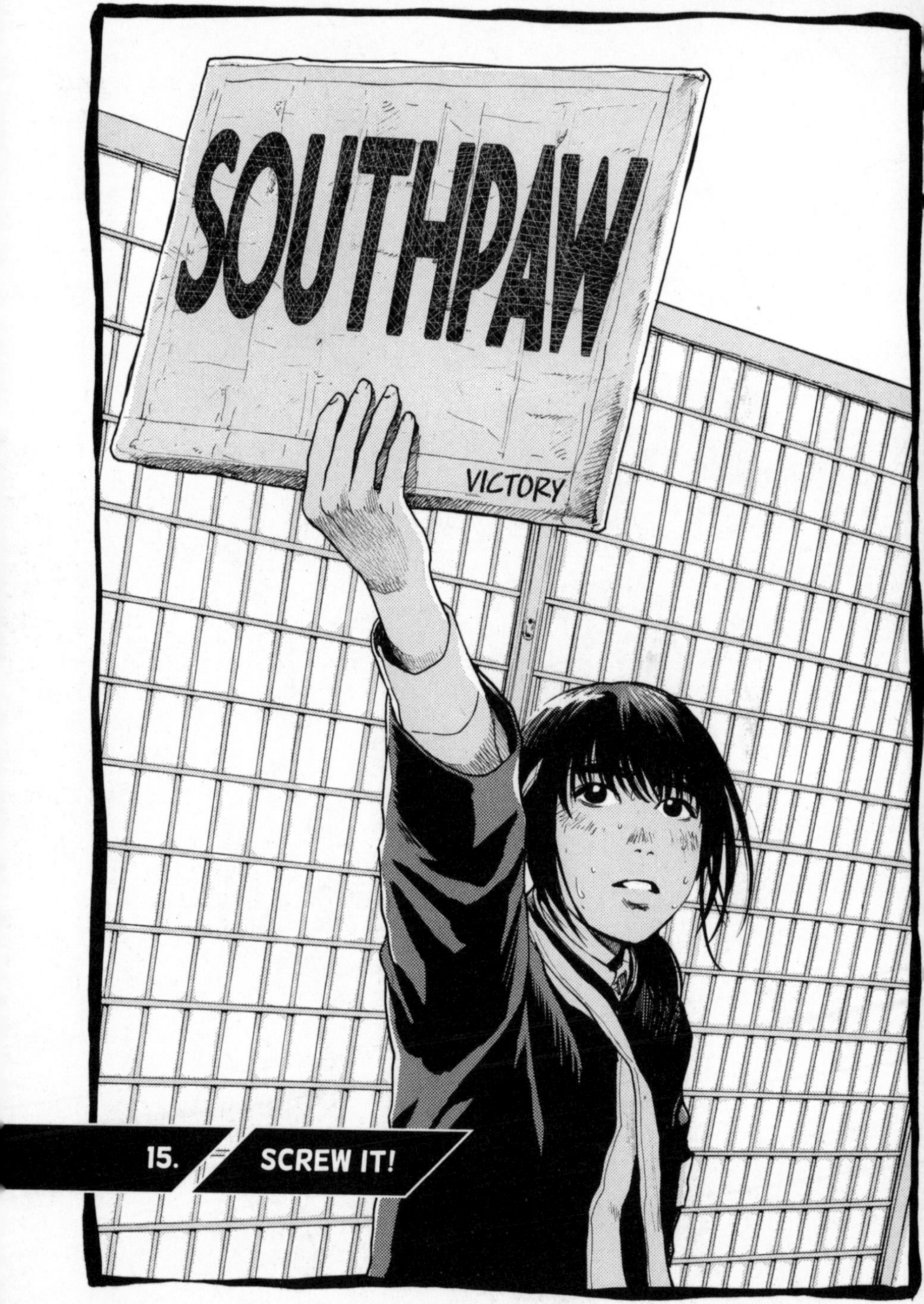
SOUTHPAW
VICTORY
15.
SCREW IT!

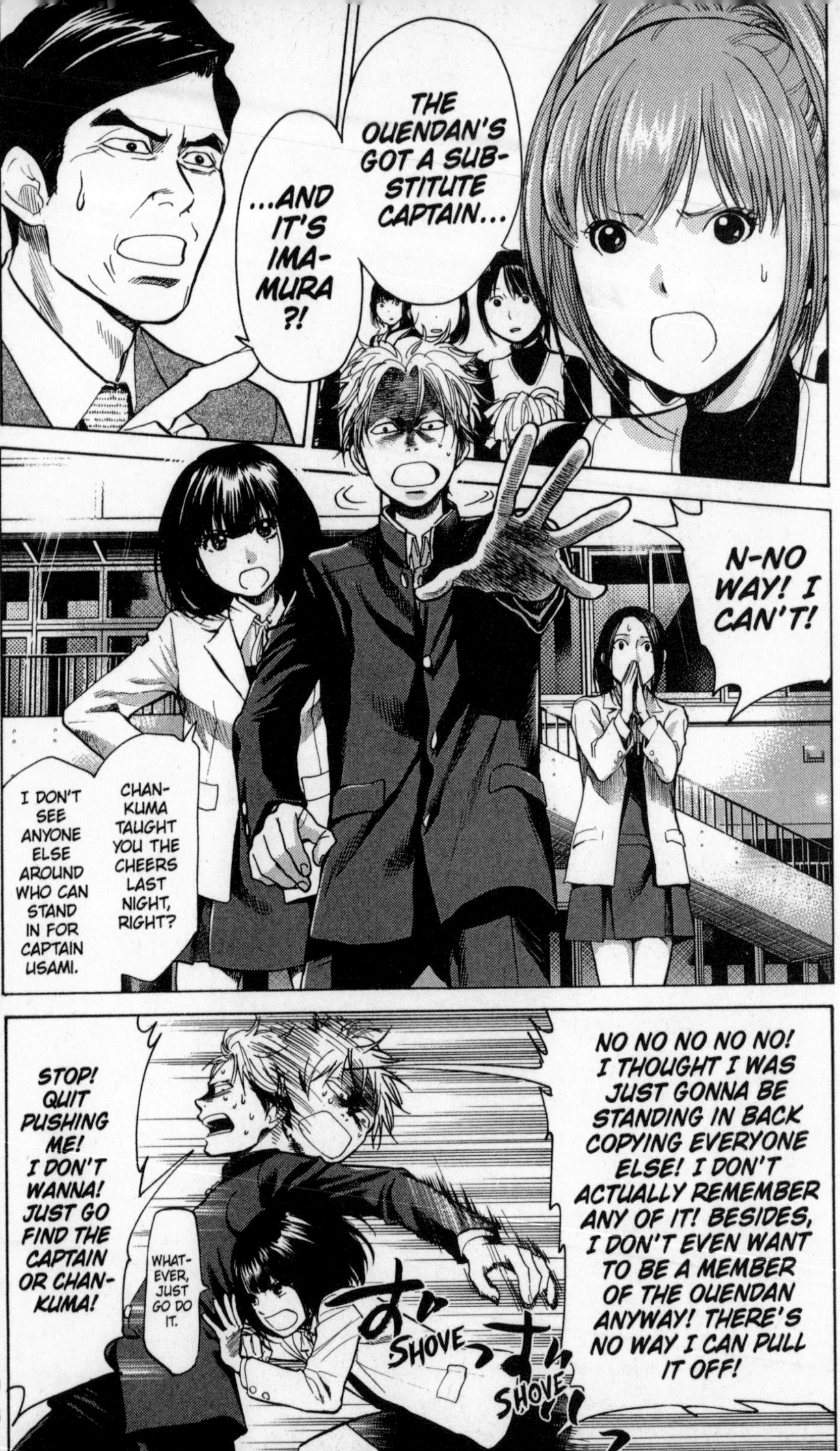
THE OUENDAN'S GOT A SUB-STITUTE CAPTAIN...
...AND IT'S IMAMURA?!
N-NO WAY! I CAN'T!
CHAN-KUMA TAUGHT YOU THE CHEERS LAST NIGHT, RIGHT?
I DON'T SEE ANYONE ELSE AROUND WHO CAN STAND IN FOR CAPTAIN USAMI.
NO NO NO NO NO! I THOUGHT I WAS JUST GONNA BE STANDING IN BACK COPYING EVERYONE ELSE! I DON'T ACTUALLY REMEMBER ANY OF IT! BESIDES, I DON'T EVEN WANT TO BE A MEMBER OF THE OUENDAN ANYWAY! THERE'S NO WAY I CAN PULL IT OFF!
STOP! QUIT PUSHING ME! I DON'T WANNA! JUST GO FIND THE CAPTAIN OR CHAN-KUMA!
WHAT-EVER, JUST GO DO IT.
SHOVE
SHOVE

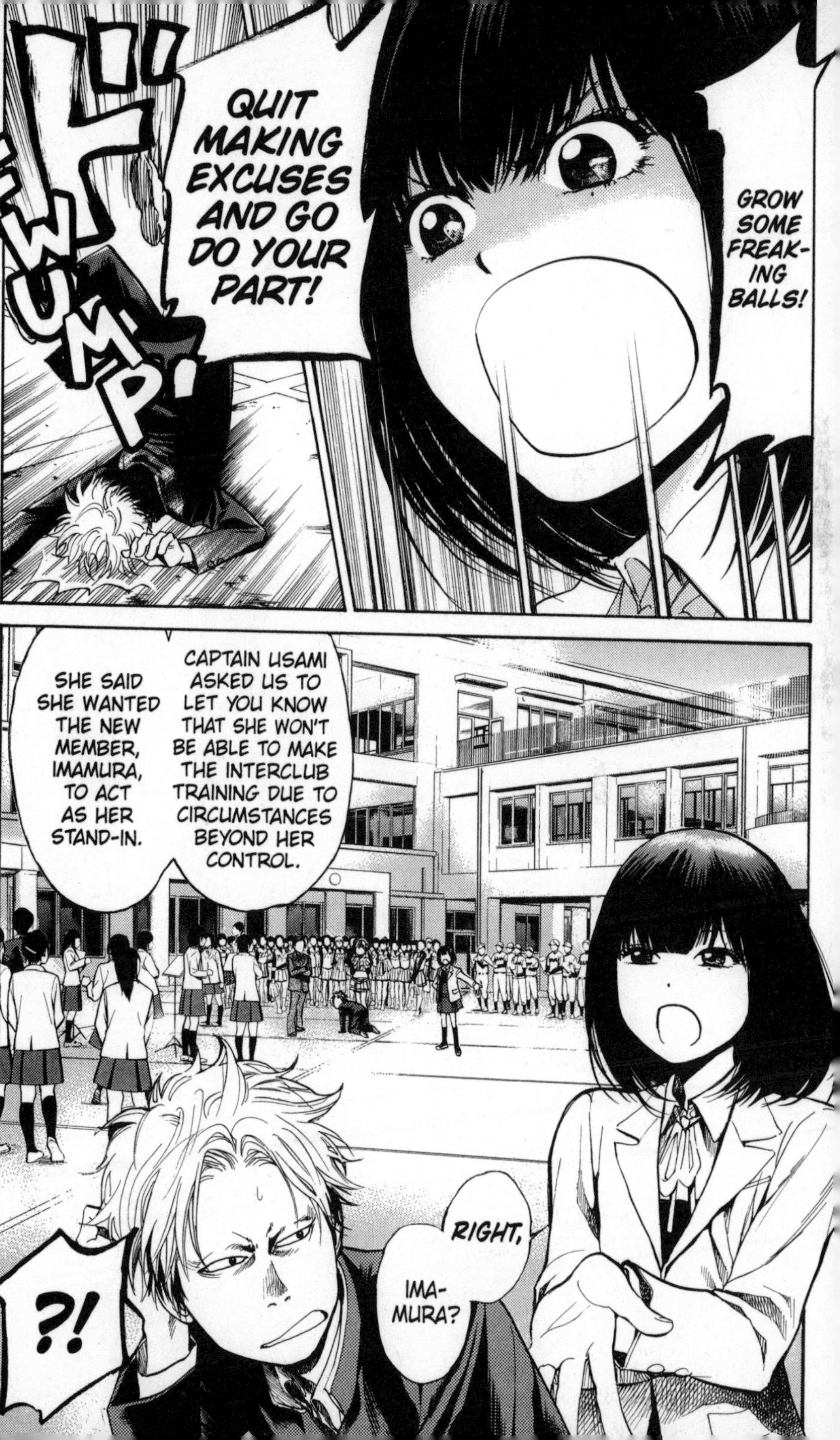
GROW SOME FREAKING BALLS!
QUIT MAKING EXCUSES AND GO DO YOUR PART!
FWUMP
CAPTAIN USAMI ASKED US TO LET YOU KNOW THAT SHE WON'T BE ABLE TO MAKE THE INTERCLUB TRAINING DUE TO CIRCUMSTANCES BEYOND HER CONTROL.
SHE SAID SHE WANTED THE NEW MEMBER, IMAMURA, TO ACT AS HER STAND-IN.
RIGHT,
IMAMURA?
?!

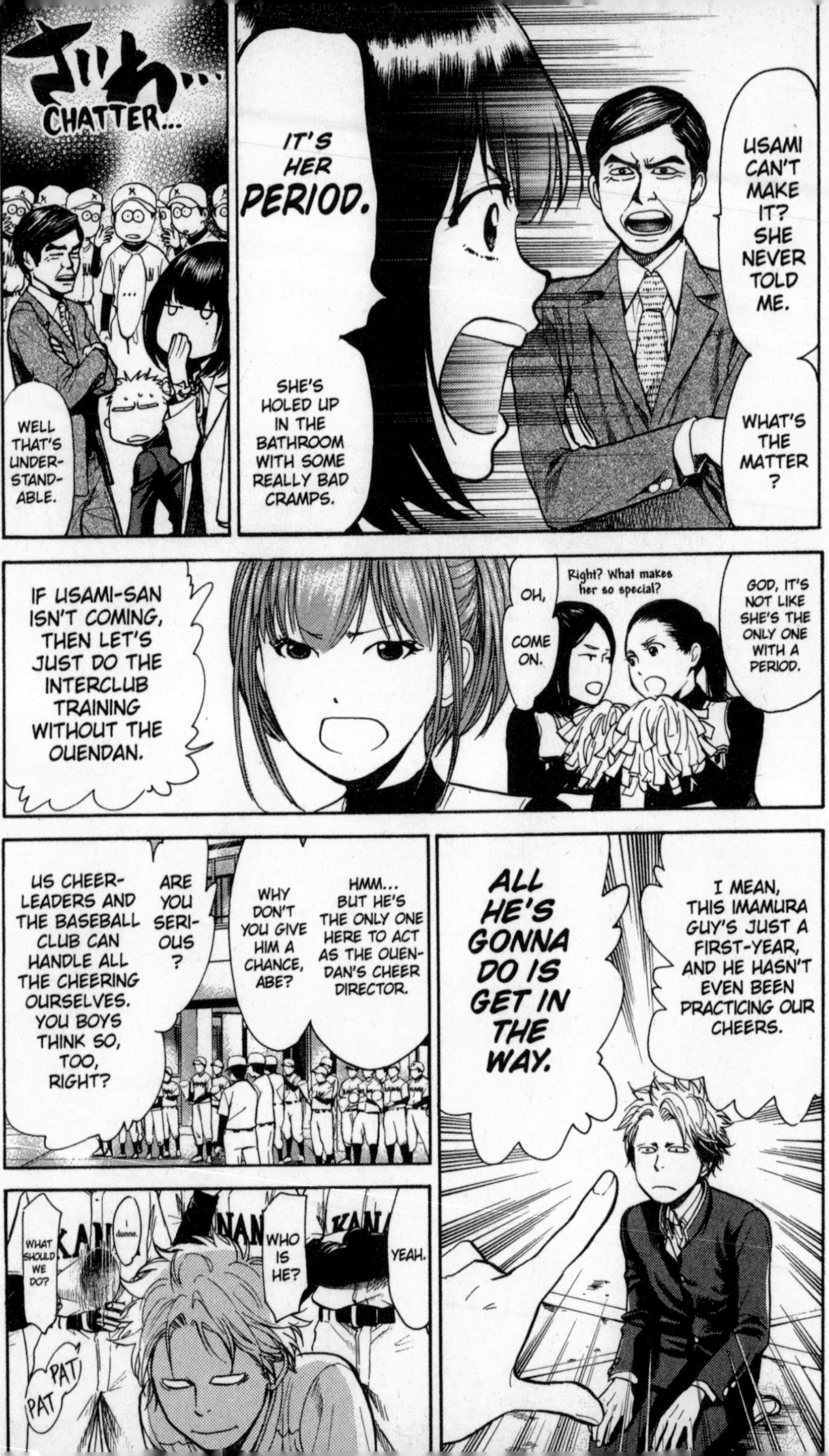
USAMI CAN'T MAKE IT? SHE NEVER TOLD ME.
WHAT'S THE MATTER?
IT'S HER PERIOD.
SHE'S HOLED UP IN THE BATHROOM WITH SOME REALLY BAD CRAMPS.
CHATTER...
...
WELL THAT'S UNDERSTANDABLE.
GOD, IT'S NOT LIKE SHE'S THE ONLY ONE WITH A PERIOD.
Right? What makes her so special?
OH, COME ON.
IF USAMI-SAN ISN'T COMING, THEN LET'S JUST DO THE INTERCLUB TRAINING WITHOUT THE OUENDAN.
I MEAN, THIS IMAMURA GUY'S JUST A FIRST-YEAR, AND HE HASN'T EVEN BEEN PRACTICING OUR CHEERS.
ALL HE'S GONNA DO IS GET IN THE WAY.
HMM... BUT HE'S THE ONLY ONE HERE TO ACT AS THE OUENDAN'S CHEER DIRECTOR.
WHY DON'T YOU GIVE HIM A CHANCE, ABE?
ARE YOU SERIOUS?
US CHEERLEADERS AND THE BASEBALL CLUB CAN HANDLE ALL THE CHEERING OURSELVES. YOU BOYS THINK SO, TOO, RIGHT?
YEAH.
WHO IS HE?
I dunno.
WHAT SHOULD WE DO?
PAT
PAT

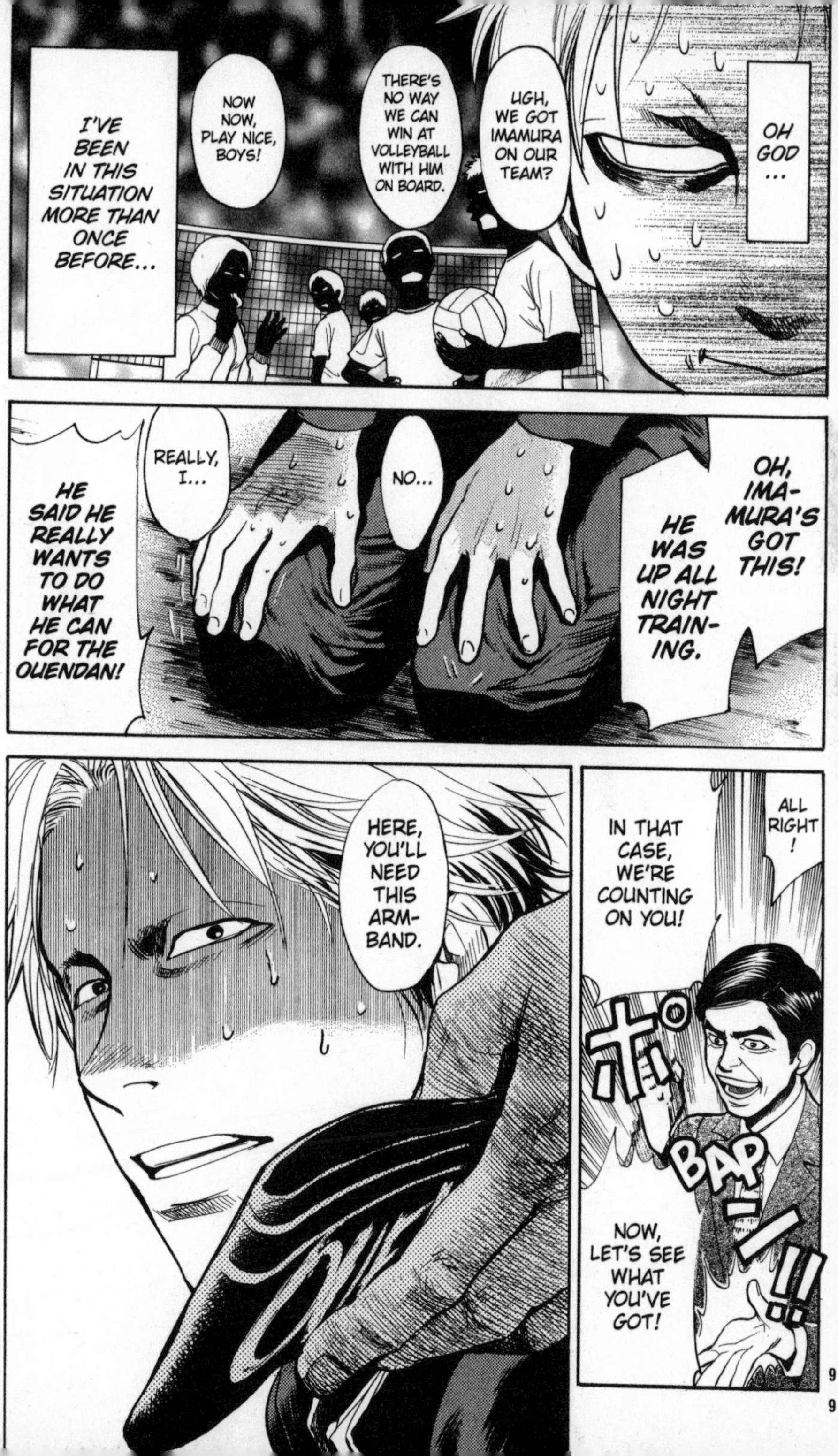
OH GOD ...
UGH, WE GOT IMAMURA ON OUR TEAM?
THERE'S NO WAY WE CAN WIN AT VOLLEYBALL WITH HIM ON BOARD.
NOW NOW, PLAY NICE, BOYS!
I'VE BEEN IN THIS SITUATION MORE THAN ONCE BEFORE...
OH, IMAMURA'S GOT THIS!
HE WAS UP ALL NIGHT TRAINING.
NO...
REALLY, I...
HE SAID HE REALLY WANTS TO DO WHAT HE CAN FOR THE OUENDAN!
ALL RIGHT!
IN THAT CASE, WE'RE COUNTING ON YOU!
ポ
BAP—!!
NOW, LET'S SEE WHAT YOU'VE GOT!
HERE, YOU'LL NEED THIS ARMBAND.

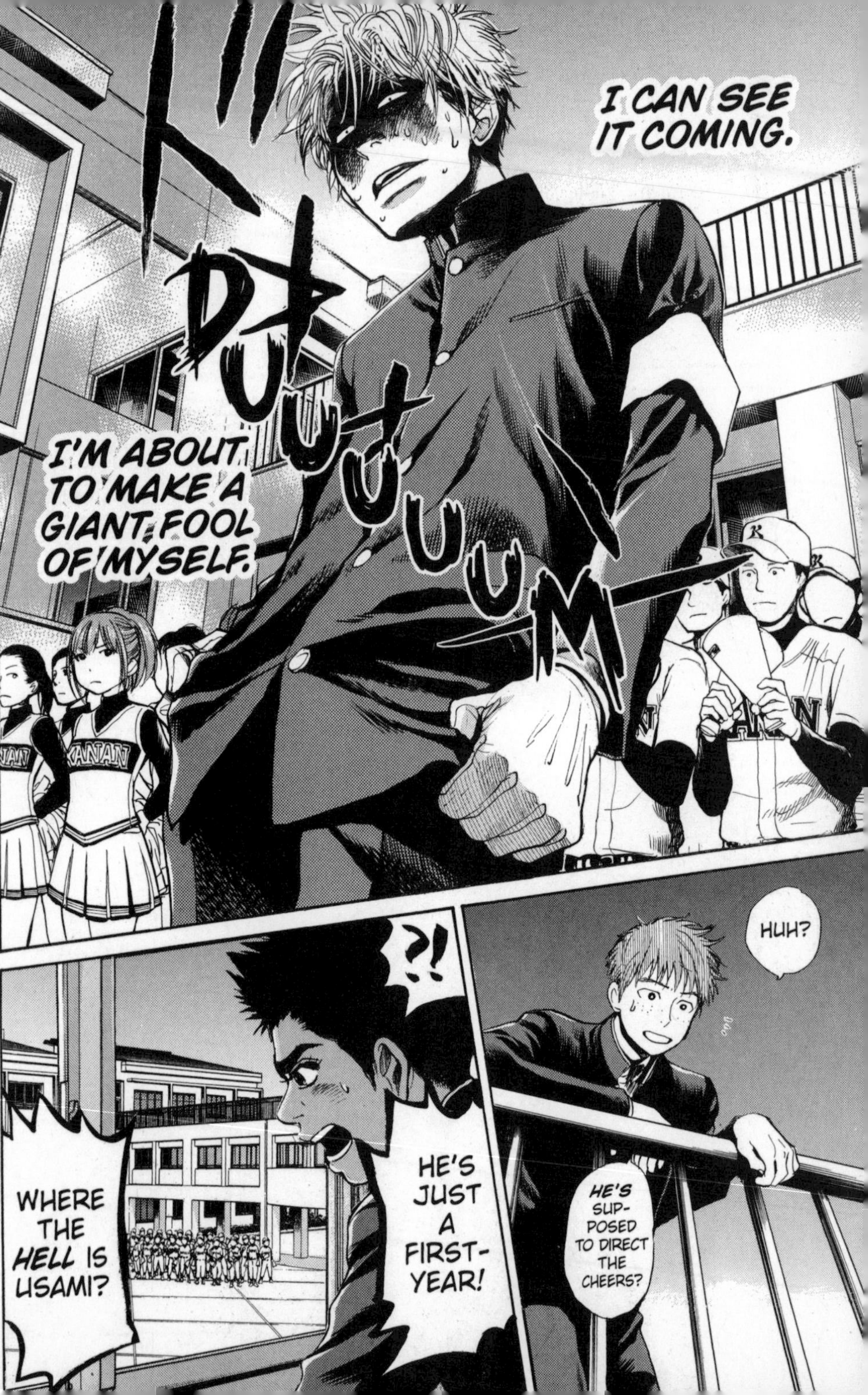
I CAN SEE IT COMING.
DUUUUUM
I'M ABOUT TO MAKE A GIANT FOOL OF MYSELF.
HUH?
HE'S SUP-POSED TO DIRECT THE CHEERS?
?!
HE'S JUST A FIRST-YEAR!
WHERE THE *HELL* IS USAMI?

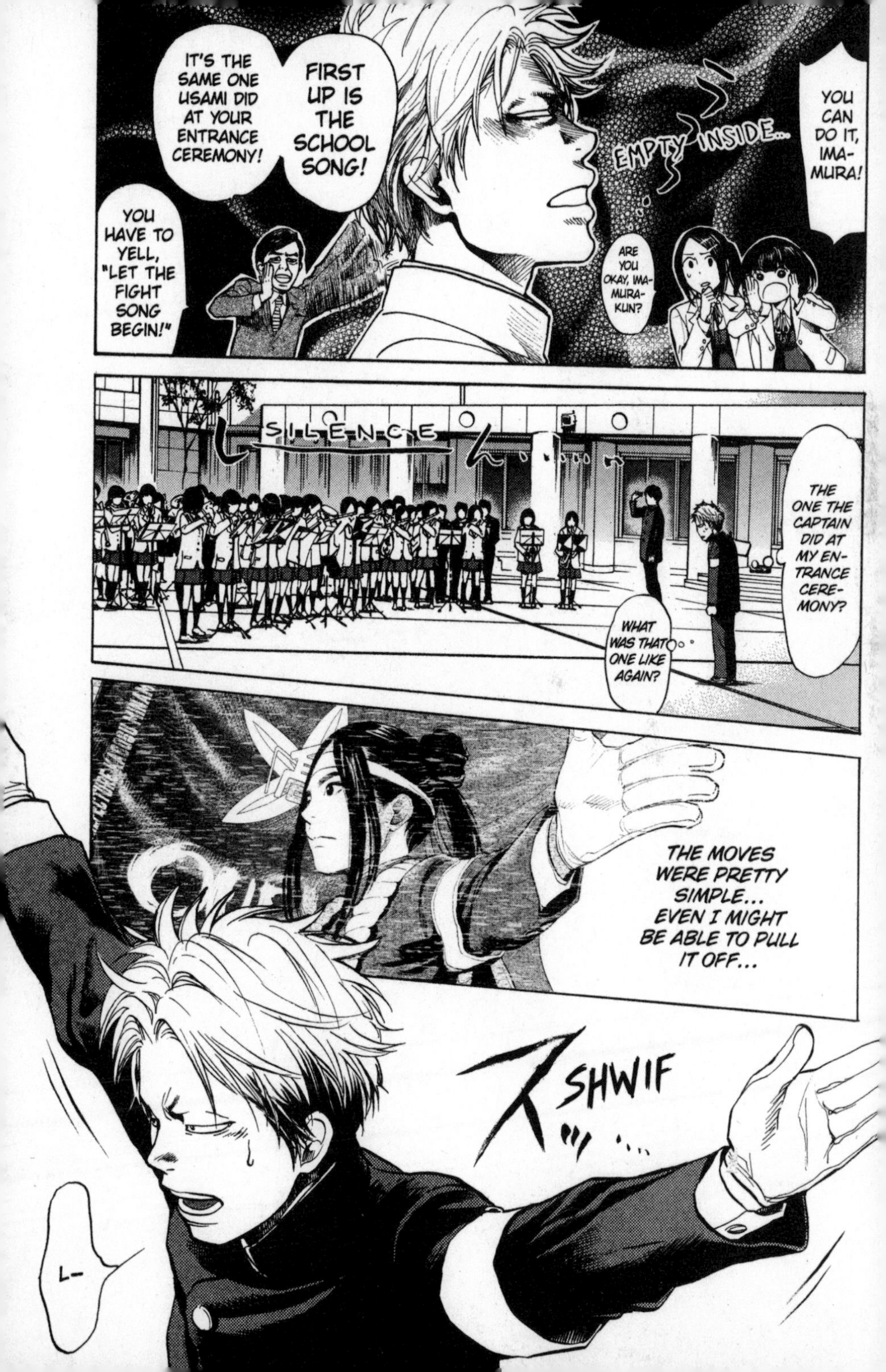
YOU CAN DO IT, IMA-MURA!
EMPTY INSIDE...
ARE YOU OKAY, IMA-MURA-KUN?
FIRST UP IS THE SCHOOL SONG!
IT'S THE SAME ONE USAMI DID AT YOUR ENTRANCE CEREMONY!
YOU HAVE TO YELL, "LET THE FIGHT SONG BEGIN!"
SILENCE
THE ONE THE CAPTAIN DID AT MY EN-TRANCE CERE-MONY?
WHAT WAS THAT ONE LIKE AGAIN?
THE MOVES WERE PRETTY SIMPLE... EVEN I MIGHT BE ABLE TO PULL IT OFF...
SHWIF
L-

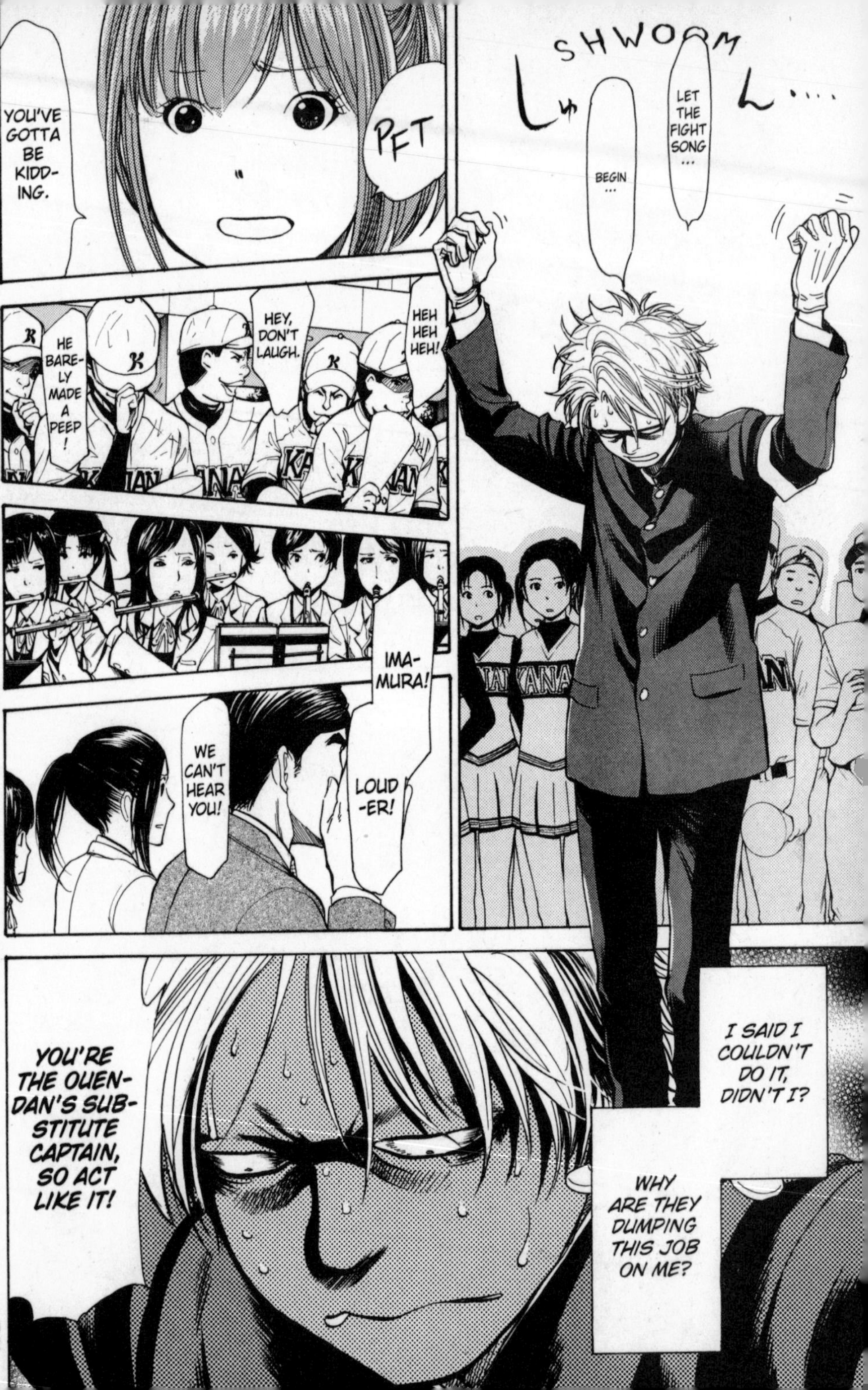
SHWOOM
しゅん....
LET THE FIGHT SONG ...
BEGIN ...
PFT
YOU'VE GOTTA BE KIDDING.
HEH HEH HEH!
HEY, DON'T LAUGH.
HE BARELY MADE A PEEP!
IMAMURA!
LOUDER!
WE CAN'T HEAR YOU!
I SAID I COULDN'T DO IT, DIDN'T I?
WHY ARE THEY DUMPING THIS JOB ON ME?
YOU'RE THE OUENDAN'S SUBSTITUTE CAPTAIN, SO ACT LIKE IT!

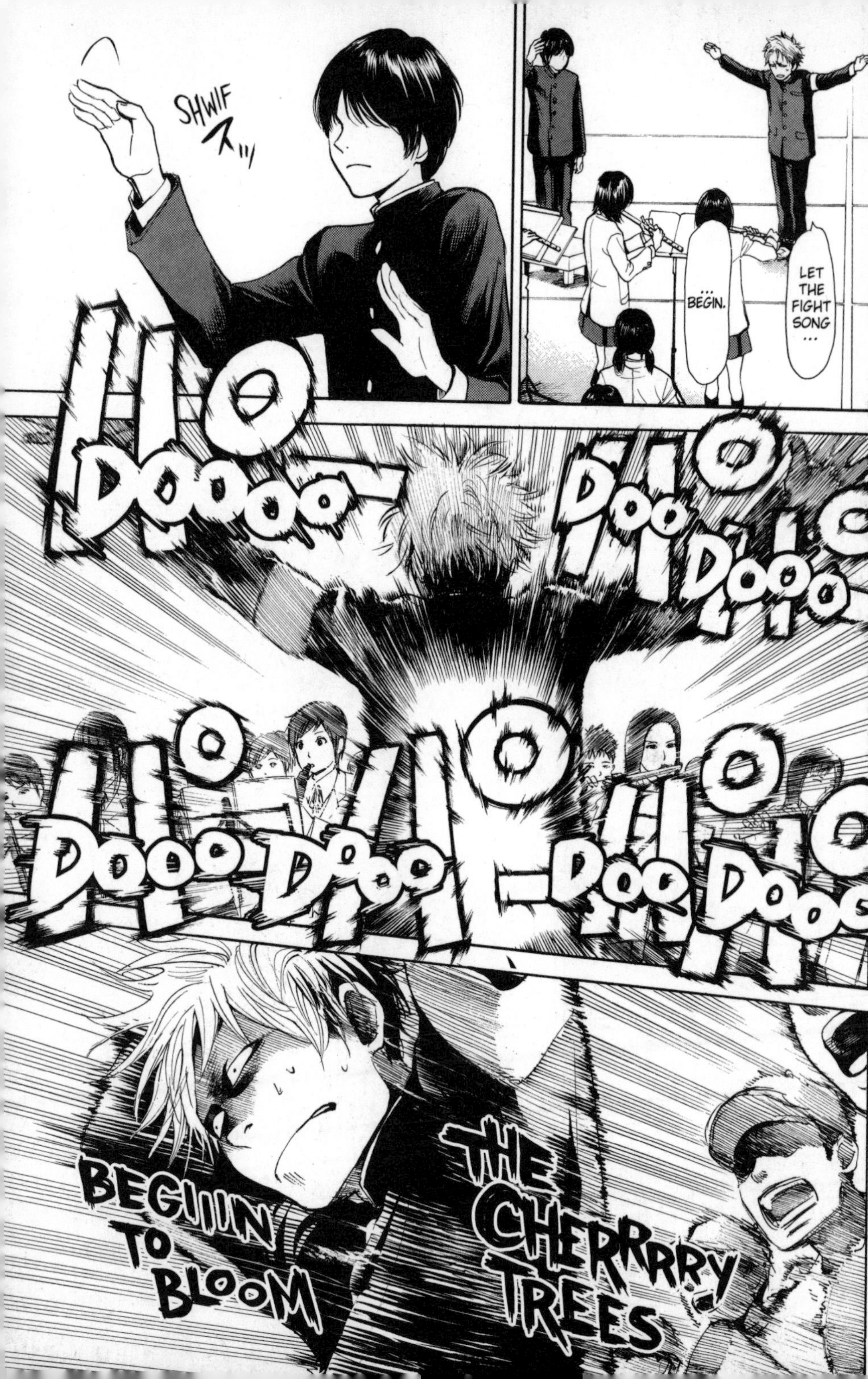
LET THE FIGHT SONG...
...BEGIN.
SHWIF
スッ
DOOOO
DOOO DOOO
DOOO DOOO-DOOO DOOOO
THE CHERRRRY TREES
BEGIIIN TO BLOOM

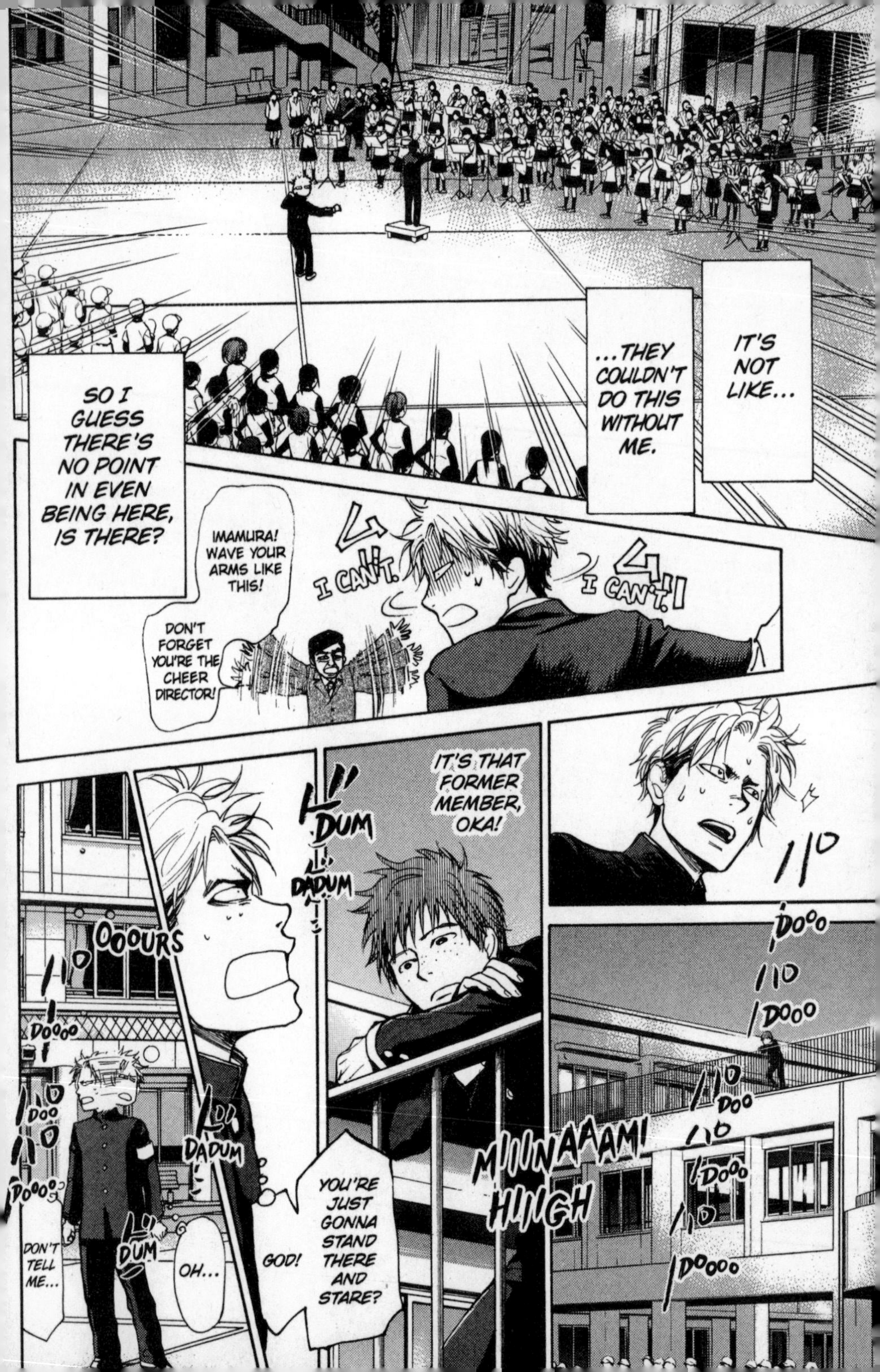
IT'S NOT LIKE...
...THEY COULDN'T DO THIS WITHOUT ME.
SO I GUESS THERE'S NO POINT IN EVEN BEING HERE, IS THERE?
I CAN'T.
I CAN'T.
IMAMURA! WAVE YOUR ARMS LIKE THIS!
DON'T FORGET YOU'RE THE CHEER DIRECTOR!
DOOO
DOOO
MIIINAAAMI HIIIGH
DOO
DOOO
DOOOO
IT'S THAT FORMER MEMBER, OKA!
DUM
DADUM
YOU'RE JUST GONNA STAND THERE AND STARE?
GOD!
OOOURS
DOOOO
DOO
DOOOO
DADUM
DUM
OH...
DON'T TELL ME...

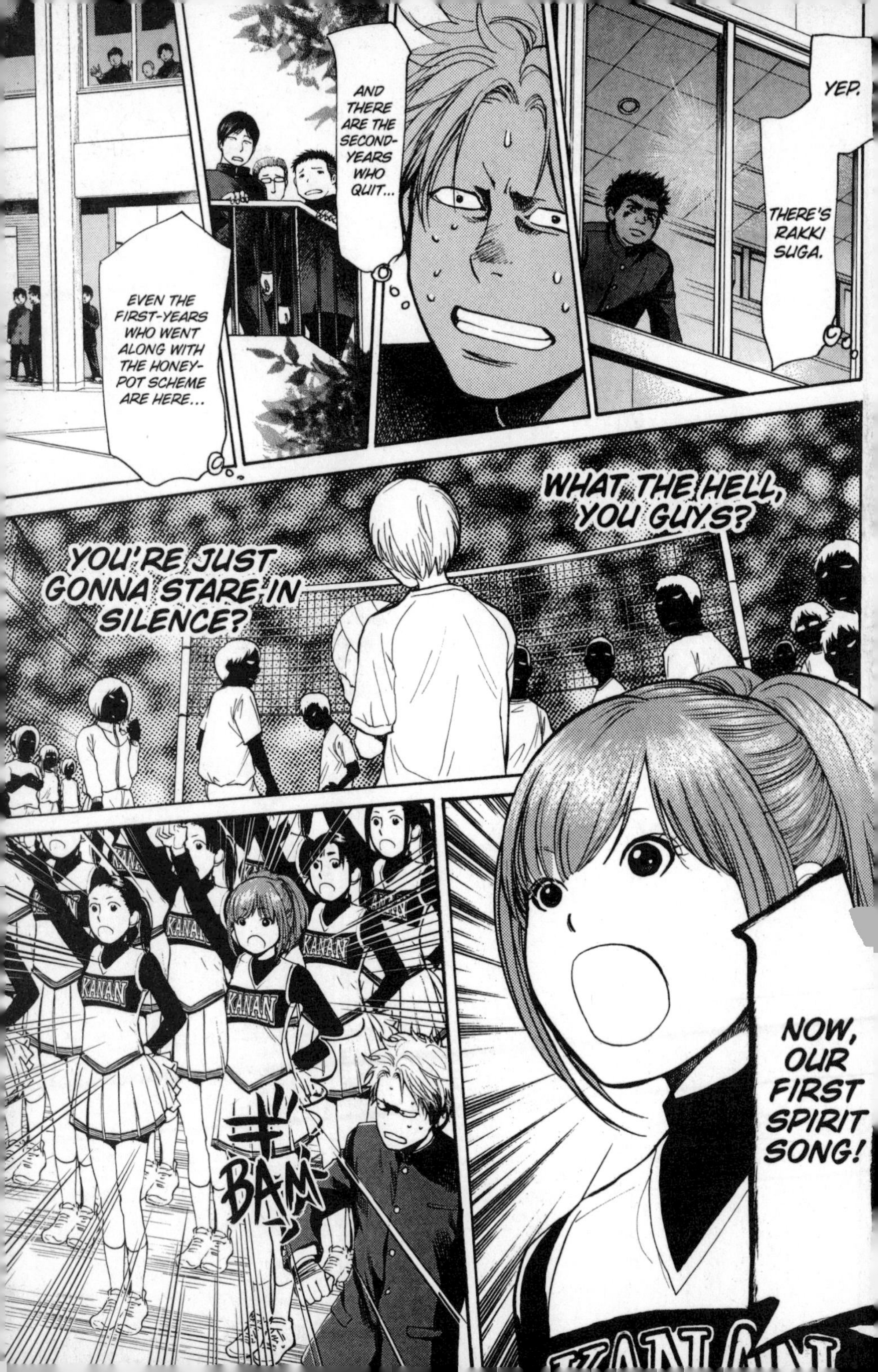
YEP.
THERE'S RAKKI SUGA.
AND THERE ARE THE SECOND-YEARS WHO QUIT...
EVEN THE FIRST-YEARS WHO WENT ALONG WITH THE HONEY-POT SCHEME ARE HERE...
WHAT THE HELL, YOU GUYS?
YOU'RE JUST GONNA STARE IN SILENCE?
NOW, OUR FIRST SPIRIT SONG!
KANAN
KANAN
KANAN
KANAN
BAM

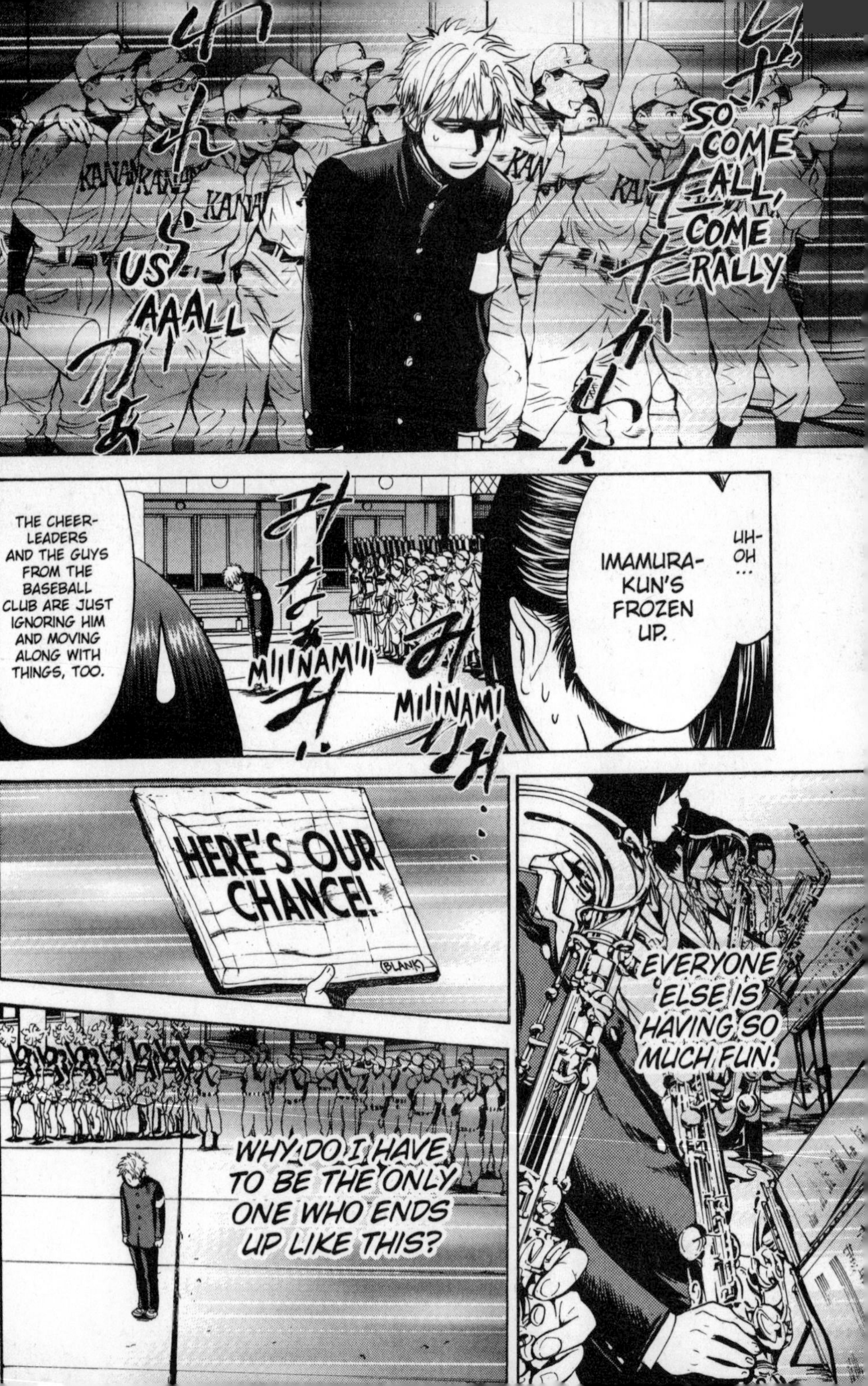
SO COME ALL, COME RALLY
US AAALL
UH-OH...
IMAMURA-KUN'S FROZEN UP.
MIIINAMI
MIIINAMI
THE CHEER-LEADERS AND THE GUYS FROM THE BASEBALL CLUB ARE JUST IGNORING HIM AND MOVING ALONG WITH THINGS, TOO.
EVERYONE ELSE IS HAVING SO MUCH FUN.
HERE'S OUR CHANCE!
(BLANK)
WHY DO I HAVE TO BE THE ONLY ONE WHO ENDS UP LIKE THIS?

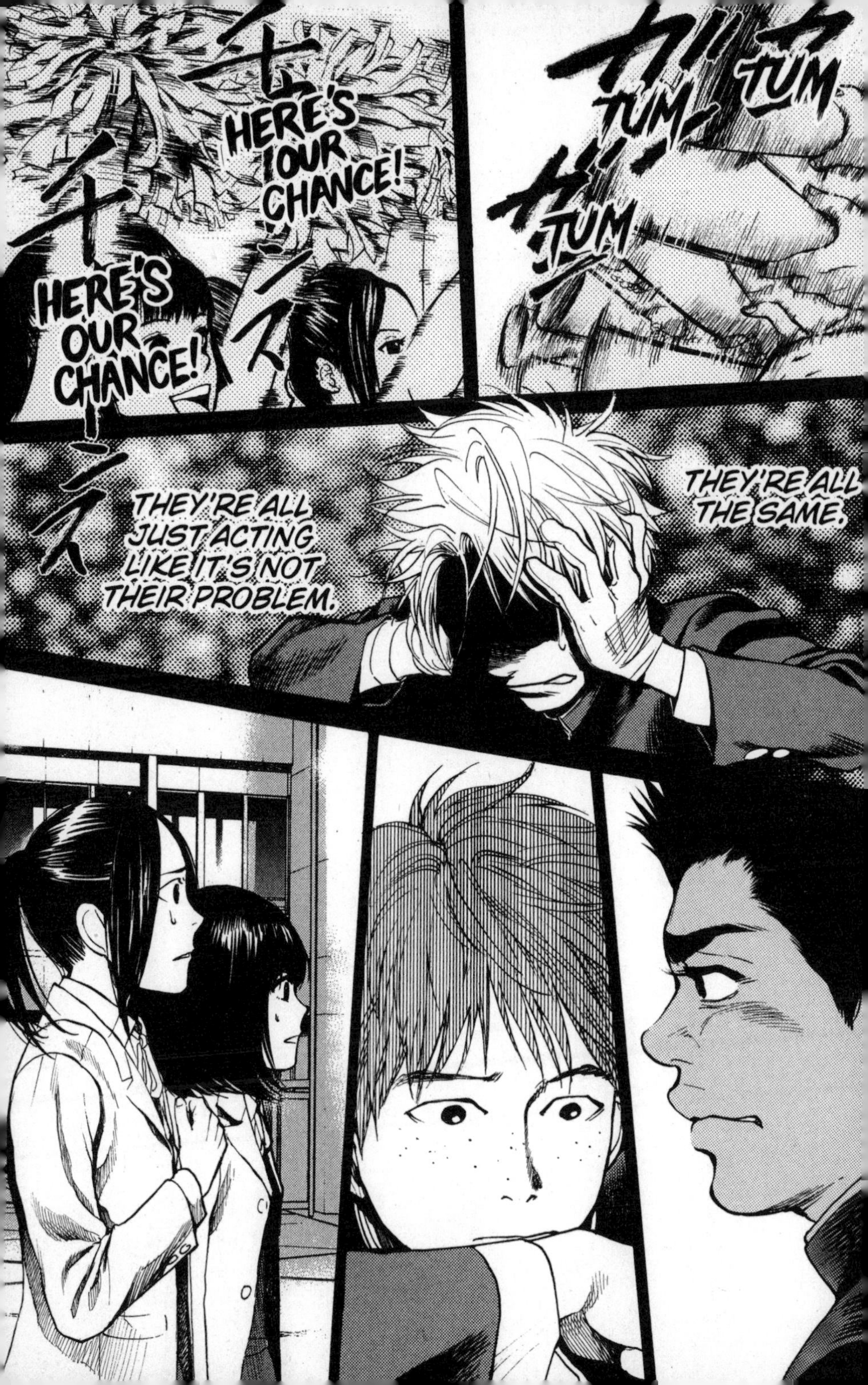
TUM
TUM
TUM
TUM
HERE'S OUR CHANCE!
HERE'S OUR CHANCE!
THEY'RE ALL THE SAME.
THEY'RE ALL JUST ACTING LIKE IT'S NOT THEIR PROBLEM.

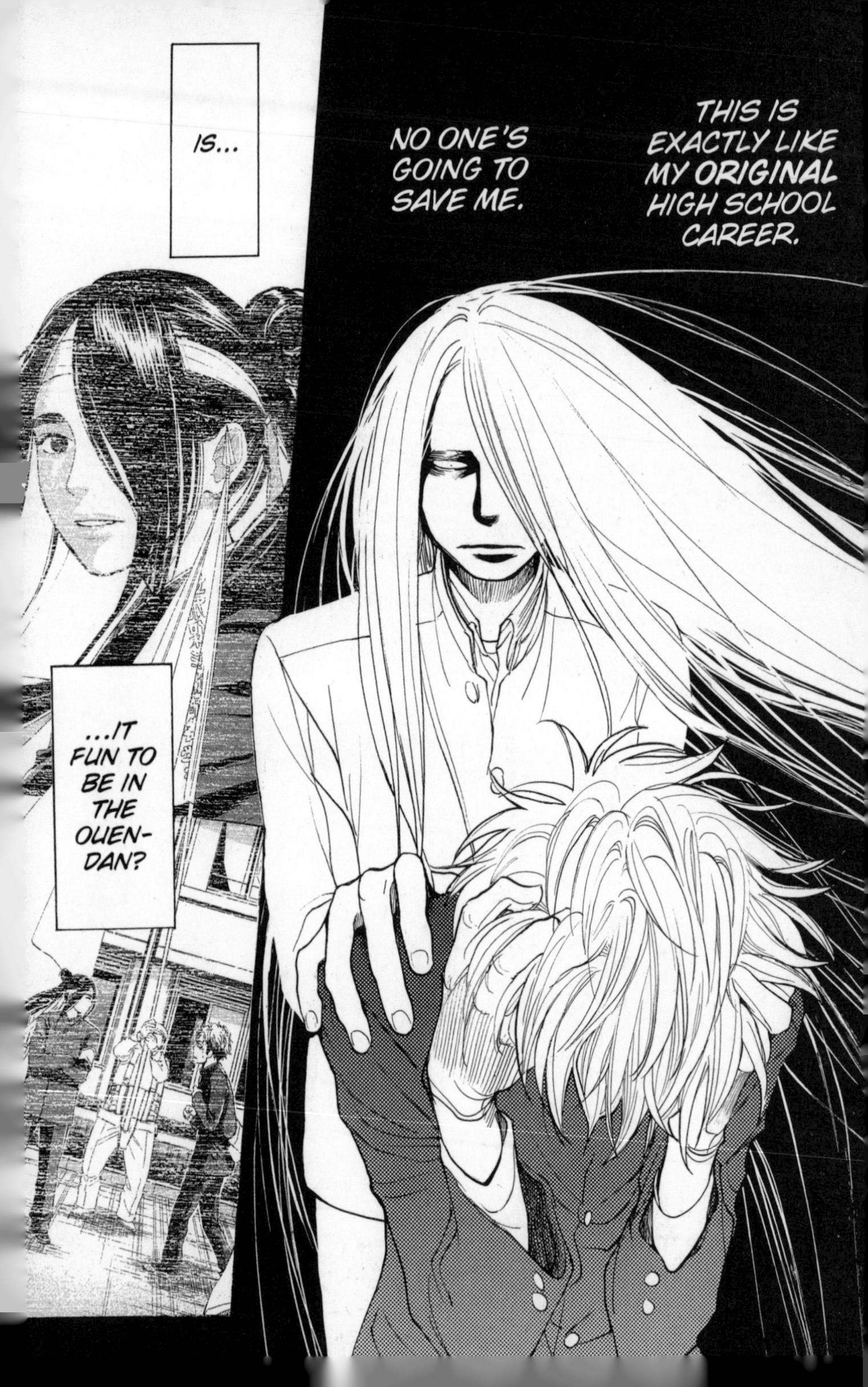
THIS IS EXACTLY LIKE MY **ORIGINAL** HIGH SCHOOL CAREER.
NO ONE'S GOING TO SAVE ME.
IS...
...IT FUN TO BE IN THE OUEN-DAN?

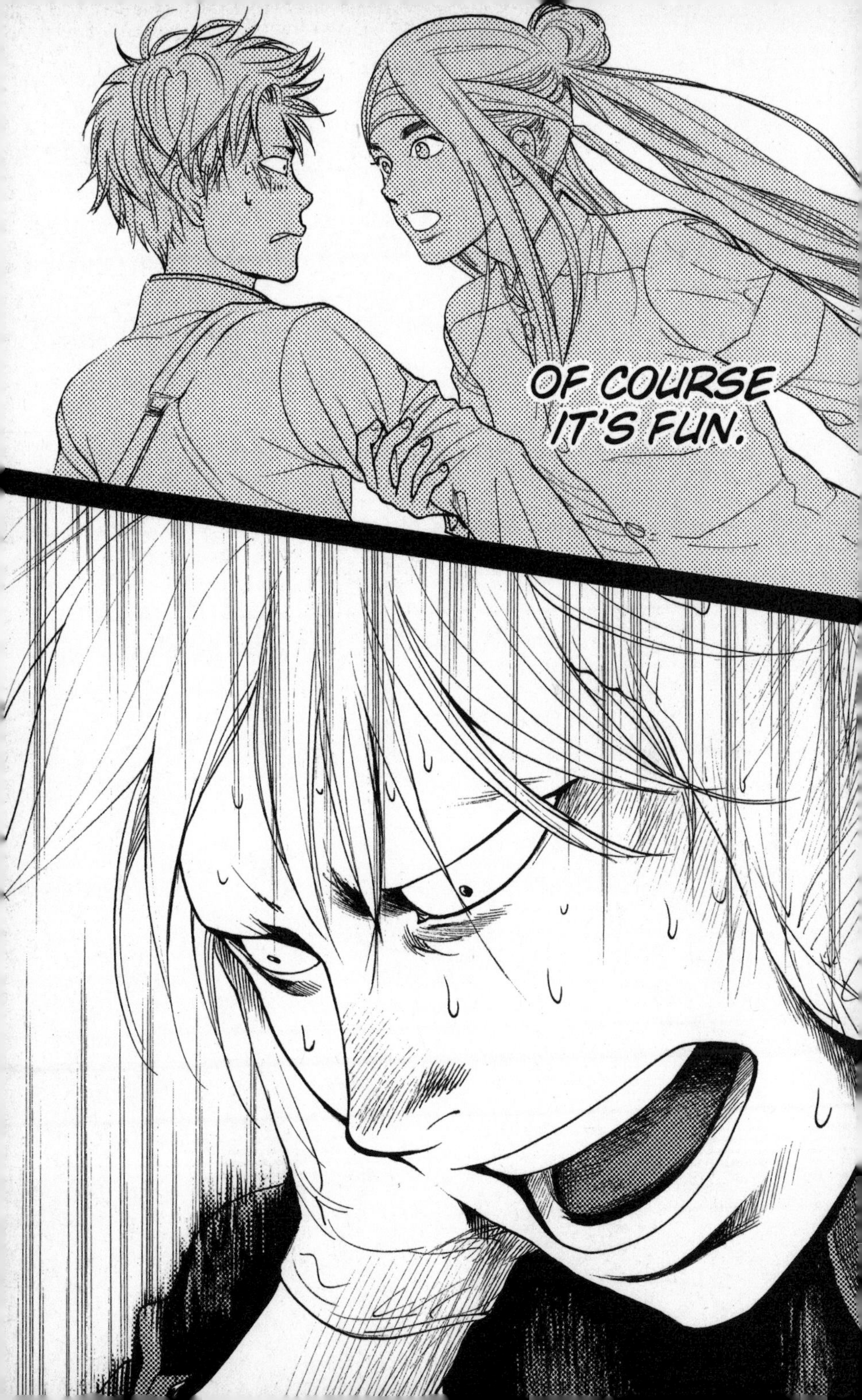
OF COURSE IT'S FUN.

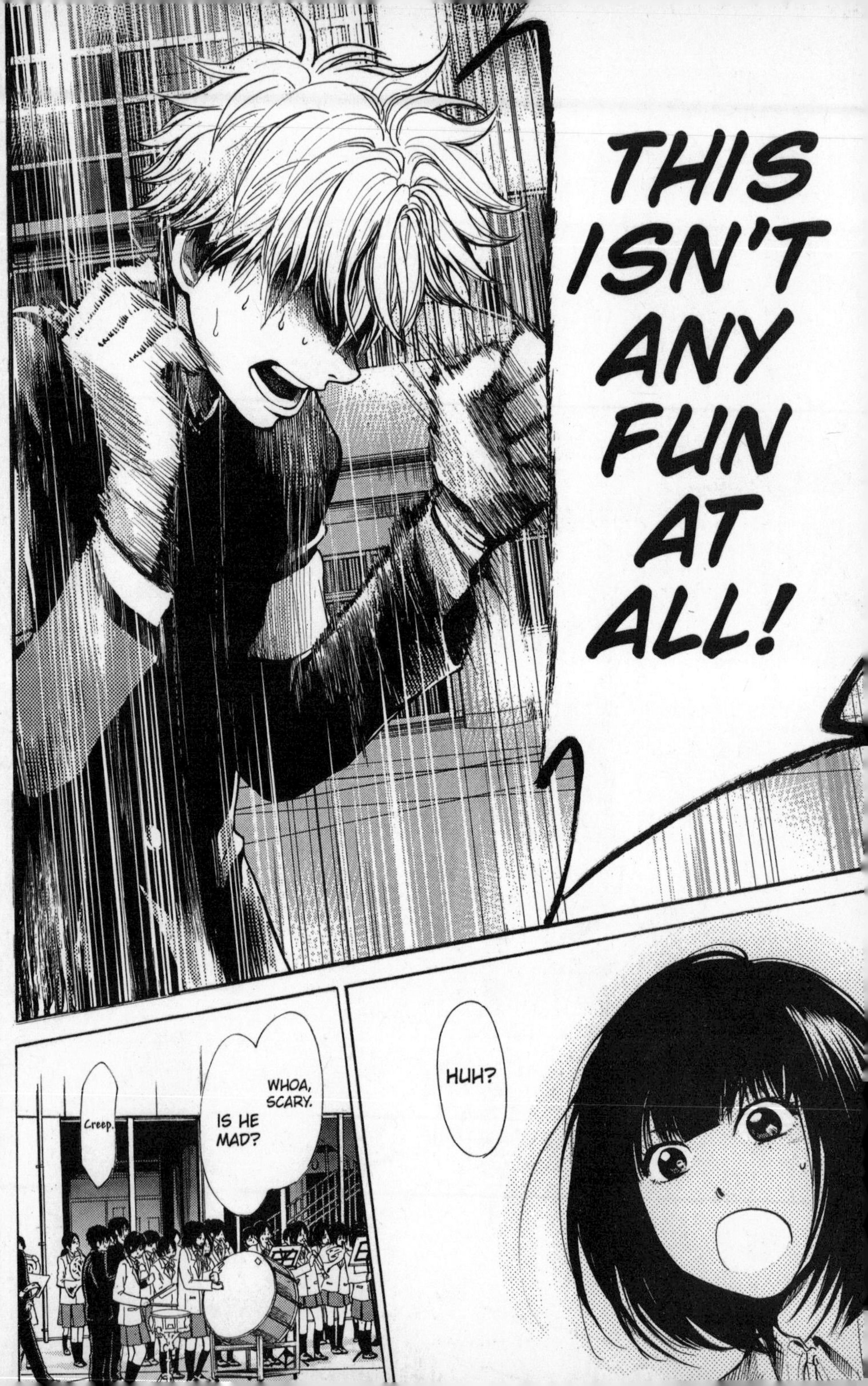
THIS ISN'T ANY FUN AT ALL!
HUH?
WHOA, SCARY.
IS HE MAD?
Creep.

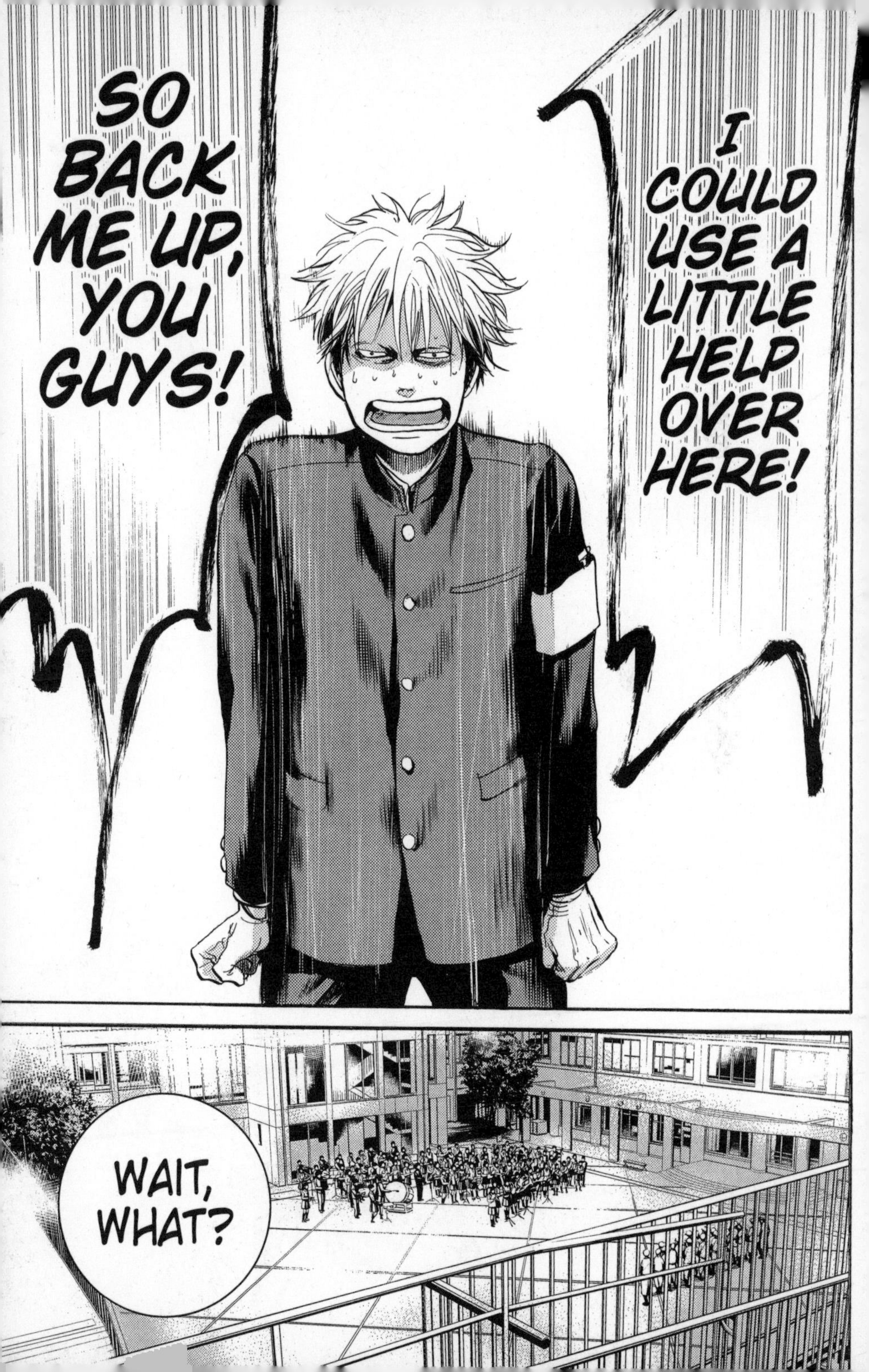
I COULD USE A LITTLE HELP OVER HERE!
SO BACK ME UP, YOU GUYS!
WAIT, WHAT?

Again!!

アゲイン!!

16. RAW FEELINGS

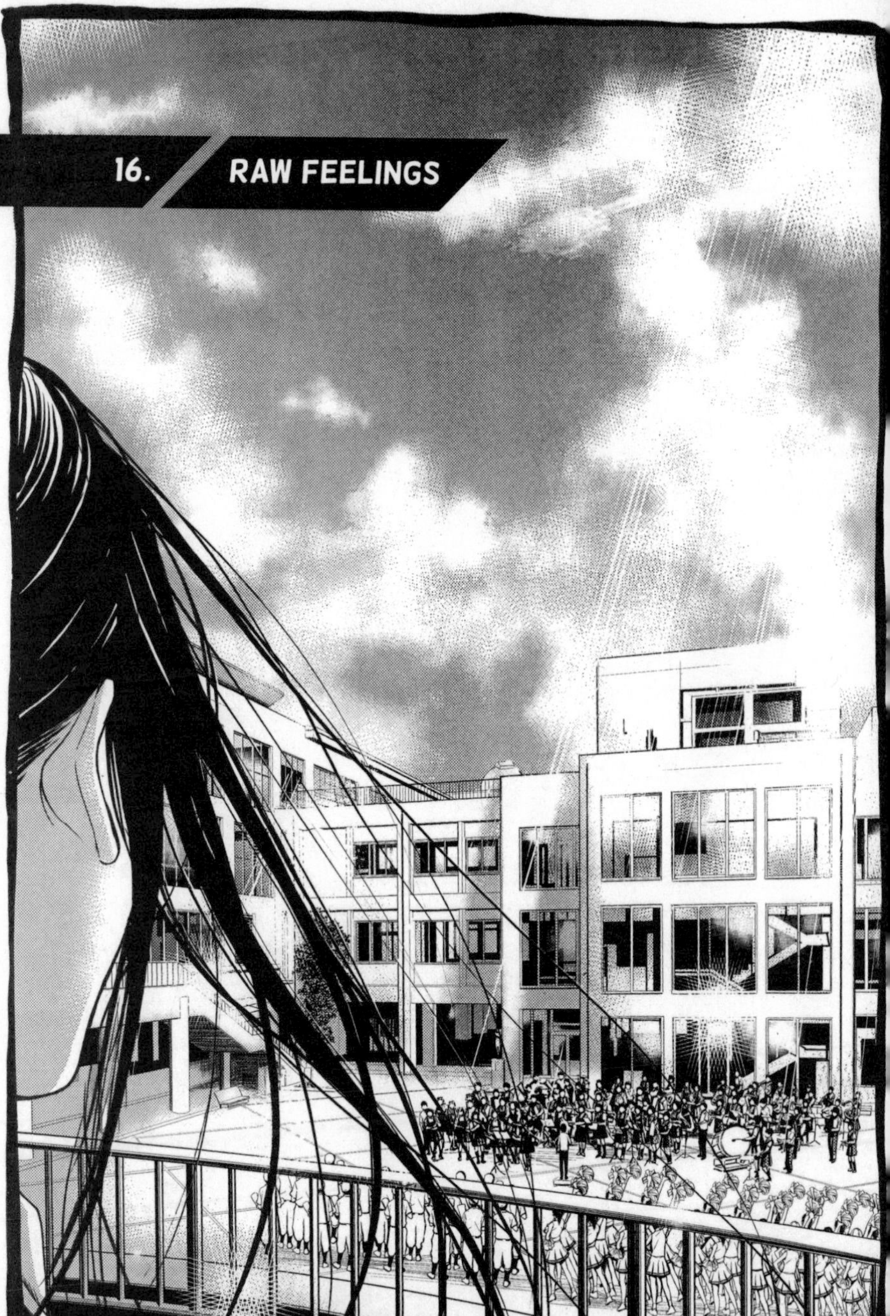

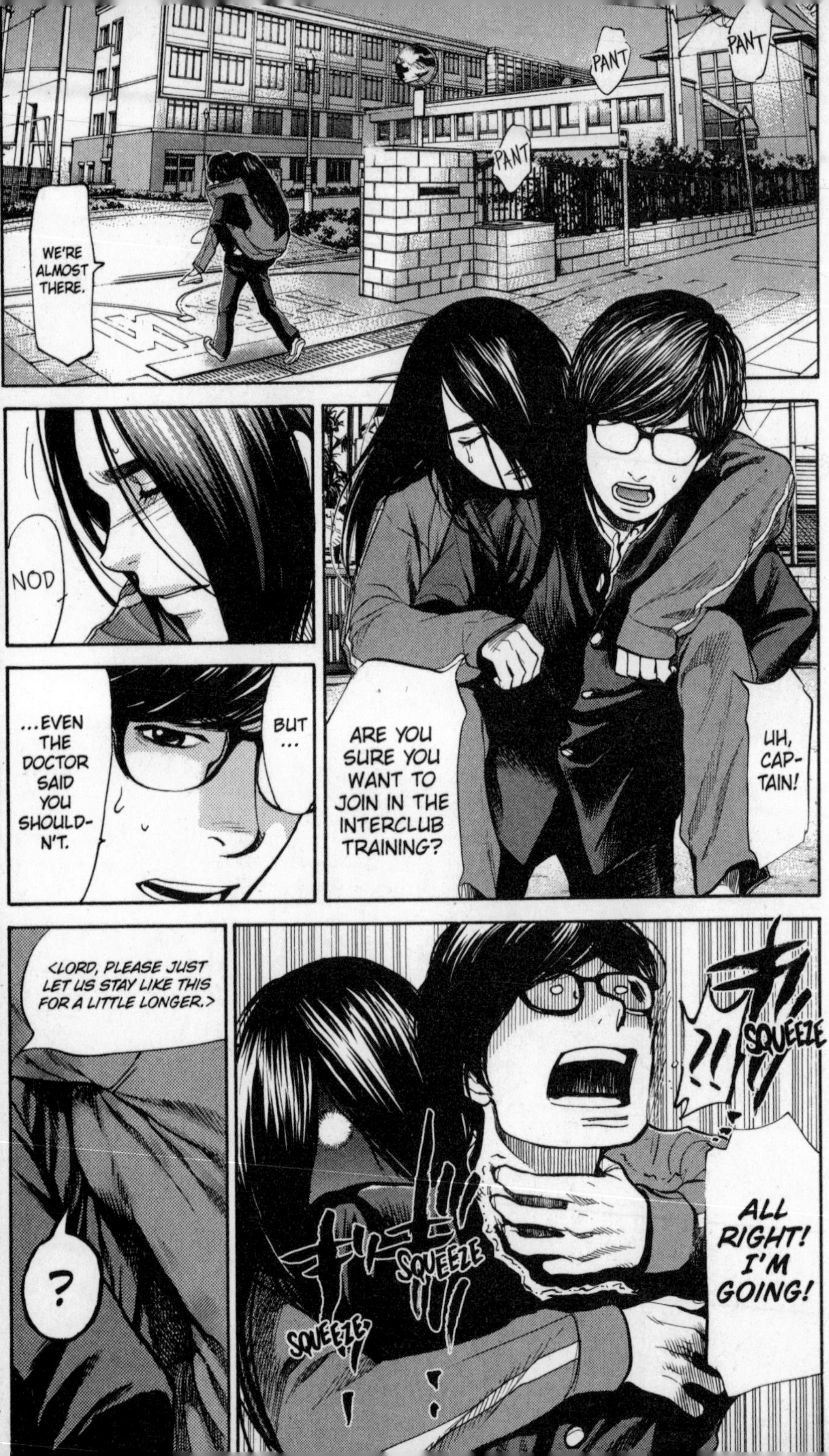
PANT
PANT
PANT
WE'RE ALMOST THERE.
UH, CAPTAIN!
ARE YOU SURE YOU WANT TO JOIN IN THE INTERCLUB TRAINING?
NOD
BUT...
...EVEN THE DOCTOR SAID YOU SHOULDN'T.
!!
SQUEEZE
ALL RIGHT! I'M GOING!
SQUEEZE
SQUEEZE
<LORD, PLEASE JUST LET US STAY LIKE THIS FOR A LITTLE LONGER.>
?

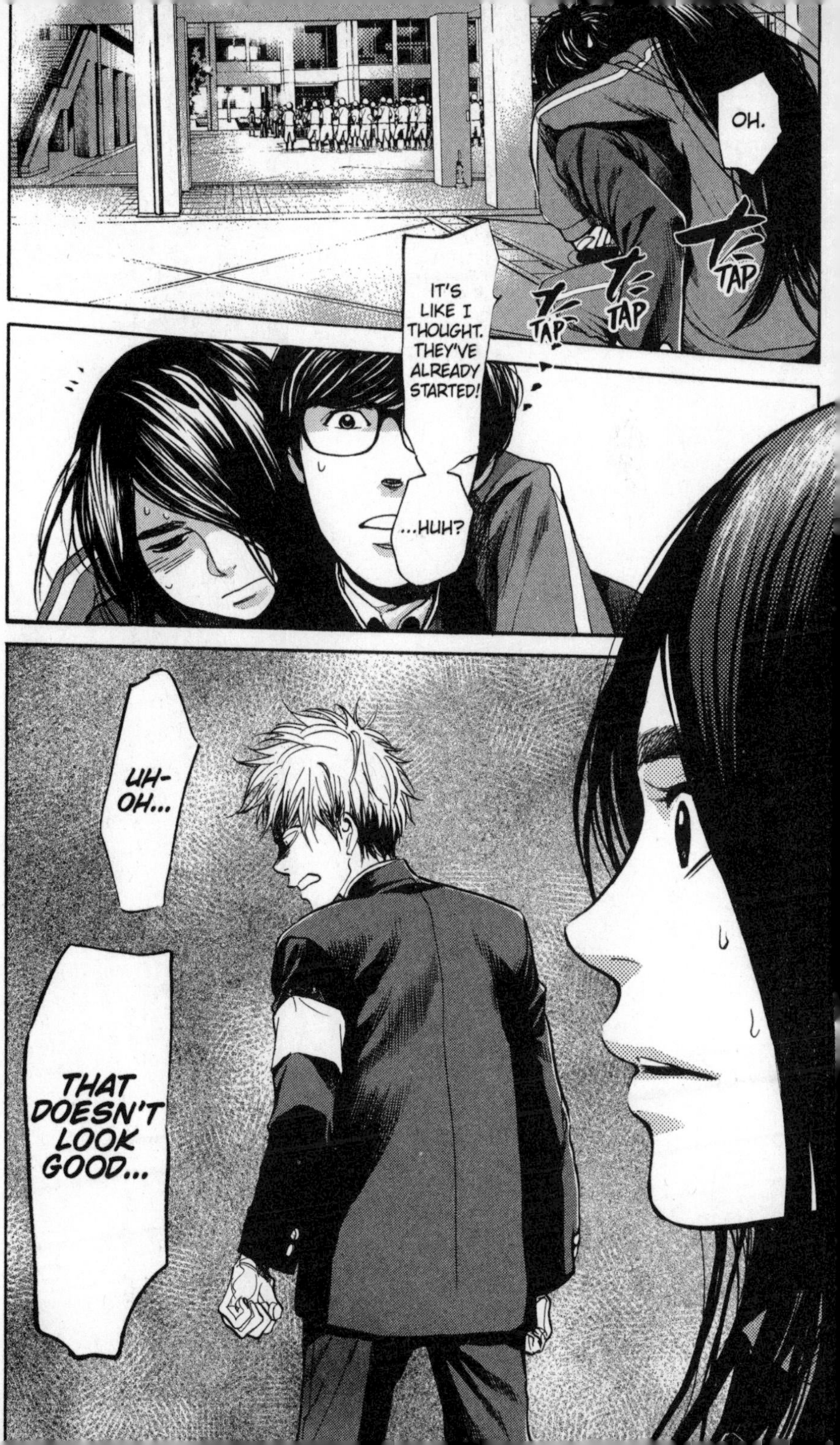
OH.
TAP
TAP
TAP
IT'S LIKE I THOUGHT. THEY'VE ALREADY STARTED!
...HUH?
UH-OH...
THAT DOESN'T LOOK GOOD...

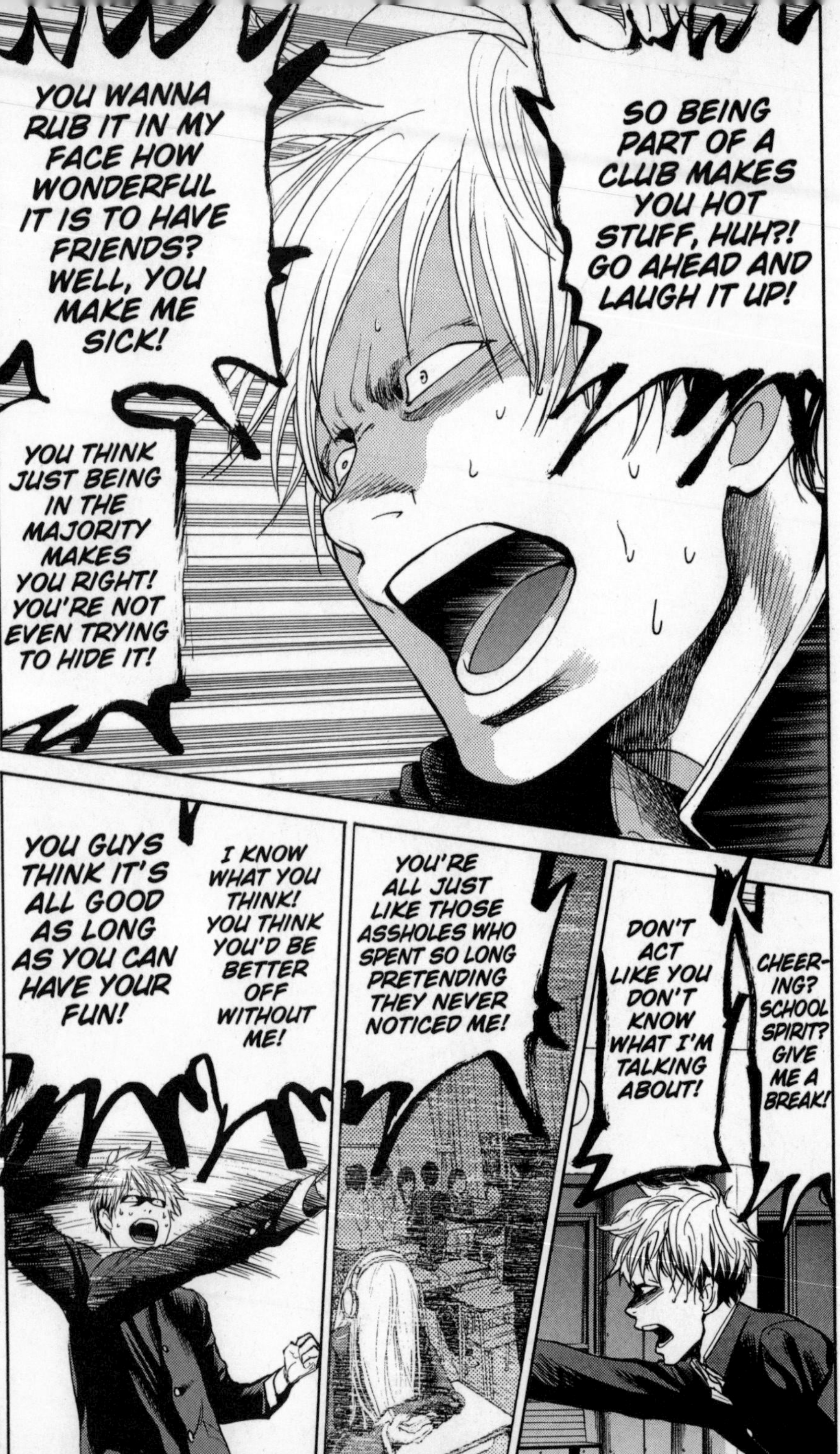
SO BEING PART OF A CLUB MAKES YOU HOT STUFF, HUH?! GO AHEAD AND LAUGH IT UP!
YOU WANNA RUB IT IN MY FACE HOW WONDERFUL IT IS TO HAVE FRIENDS? WELL, YOU MAKE ME SICK!
YOU THINK JUST BEING IN THE MAJORITY MAKES YOU RIGHT! YOU'RE NOT EVEN TRYING TO HIDE IT!
CHEER-ING? SCHOOL SPIRIT? GIVE ME A BREAK!
DON'T ACT LIKE YOU DON'T KNOW WHAT I'M TALKING ABOUT!
YOU'RE ALL JUST LIKE THOSE ASSHOLES WHO SPENT SO LONG PRETENDING THEY NEVER NOTICED ME!
I KNOW WHAT YOU THINK! YOU THINK YOU'D BE BETTER OFF WITHOUT ME!
YOU GUYS THINK IT'S ALL GOOD AS LONG AS YOU CAN HAVE YOUR FUN!

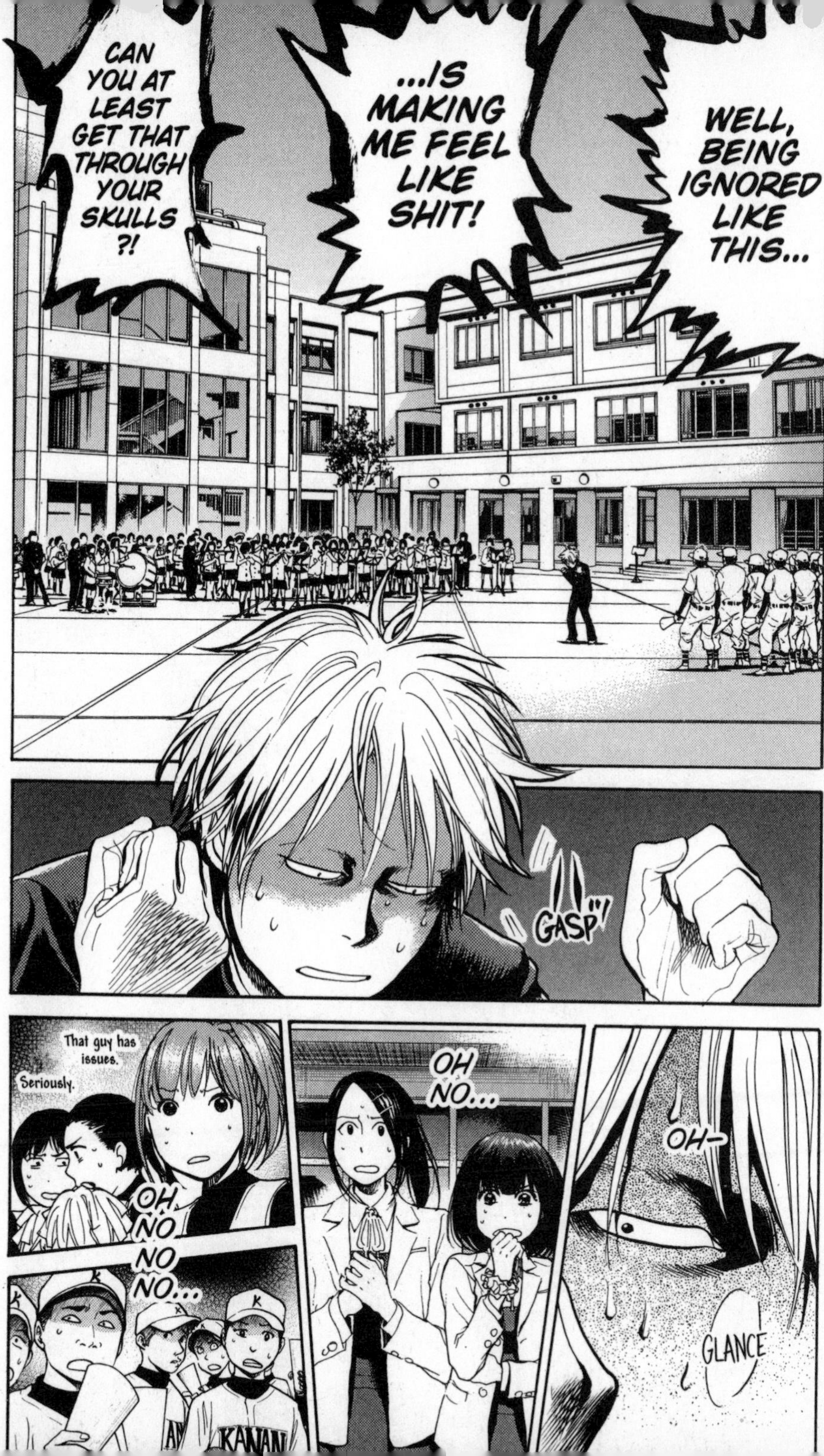
WELL, BEING IGNORED LIKE THIS...
...IS MAKING ME FEEL LIKE SHIT!
CAN YOU AT LEAST GET THAT THROUGH YOUR SKULLS ?!
GASP
OH-
GLANCE
OH NO...
That guy has issues.
Seriously.
OH NO NO NO...
KANAN

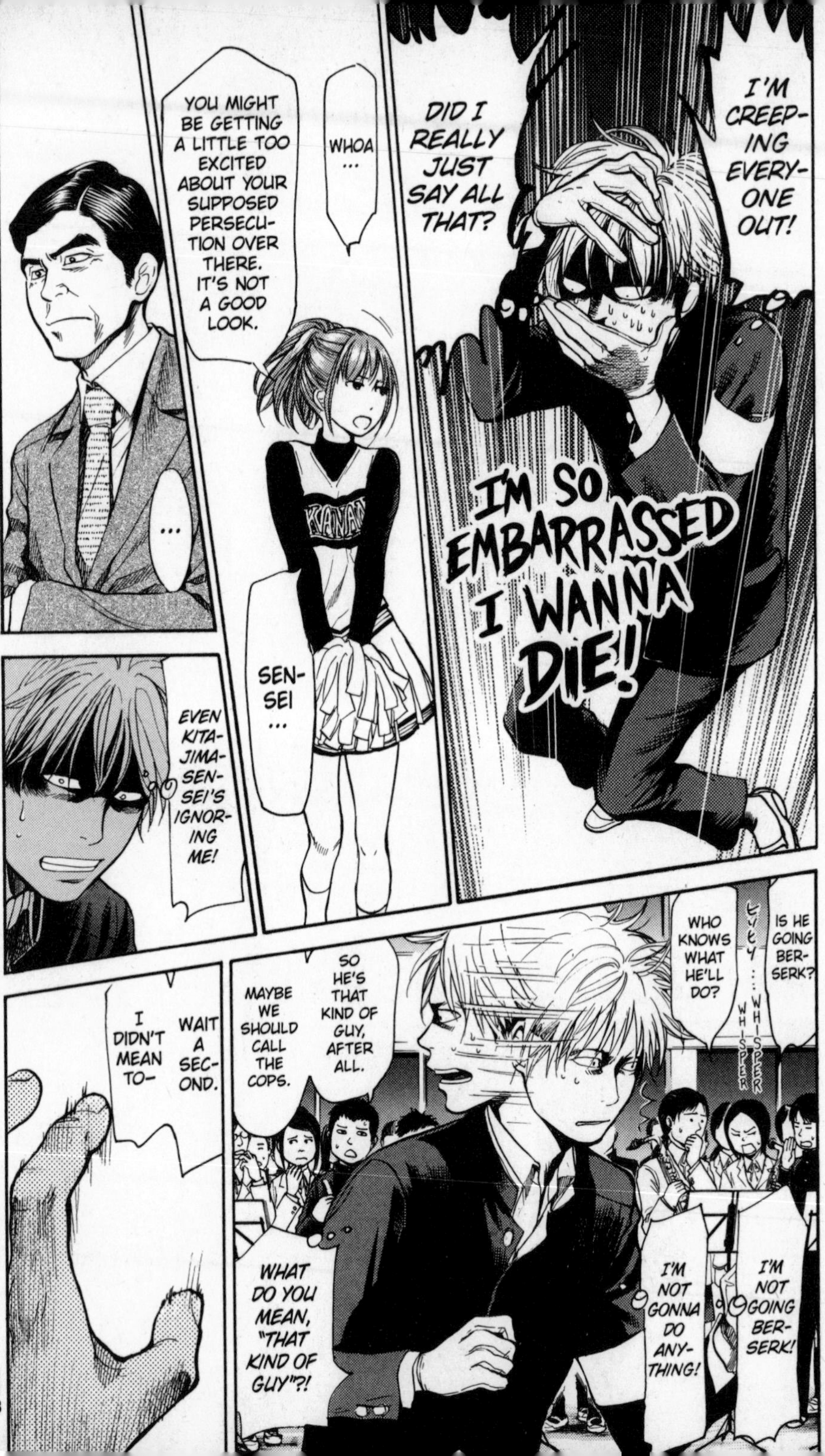

I'M CREEPING EVERYONE OUT!
DID I REALLY JUST SAY ALL THAT?
I'M SO EMBARRASSED I WANNA DIE!
WHOA ...
SEN-SEI ...
YOU MIGHT BE GETTING A LITTLE TOO EXCITED ABOUT YOUR SUPPOSED PERSECUTION OVER THERE. IT'S NOT A GOOD LOOK.
...
EVEN KITAJIMA-SENSEI'S IGNORING ME!
IS HE GOING BERSERK?
ヒソヒソ ... WHISPER WHISPER
WHO KNOWS WHAT HE'LL DO?
SO HE'S THAT KIND OF GUY, AFTER ALL.
MAYBE WE SHOULD CALL THE COPS.
I'M NOT GOING BERSERK!
I'M NOT GONNA DO ANYTHING!
WHAT DO YOU MEAN, "THAT KIND OF GUY"?!
WAIT A SECOND.
I DIDN'T MEAN TO-

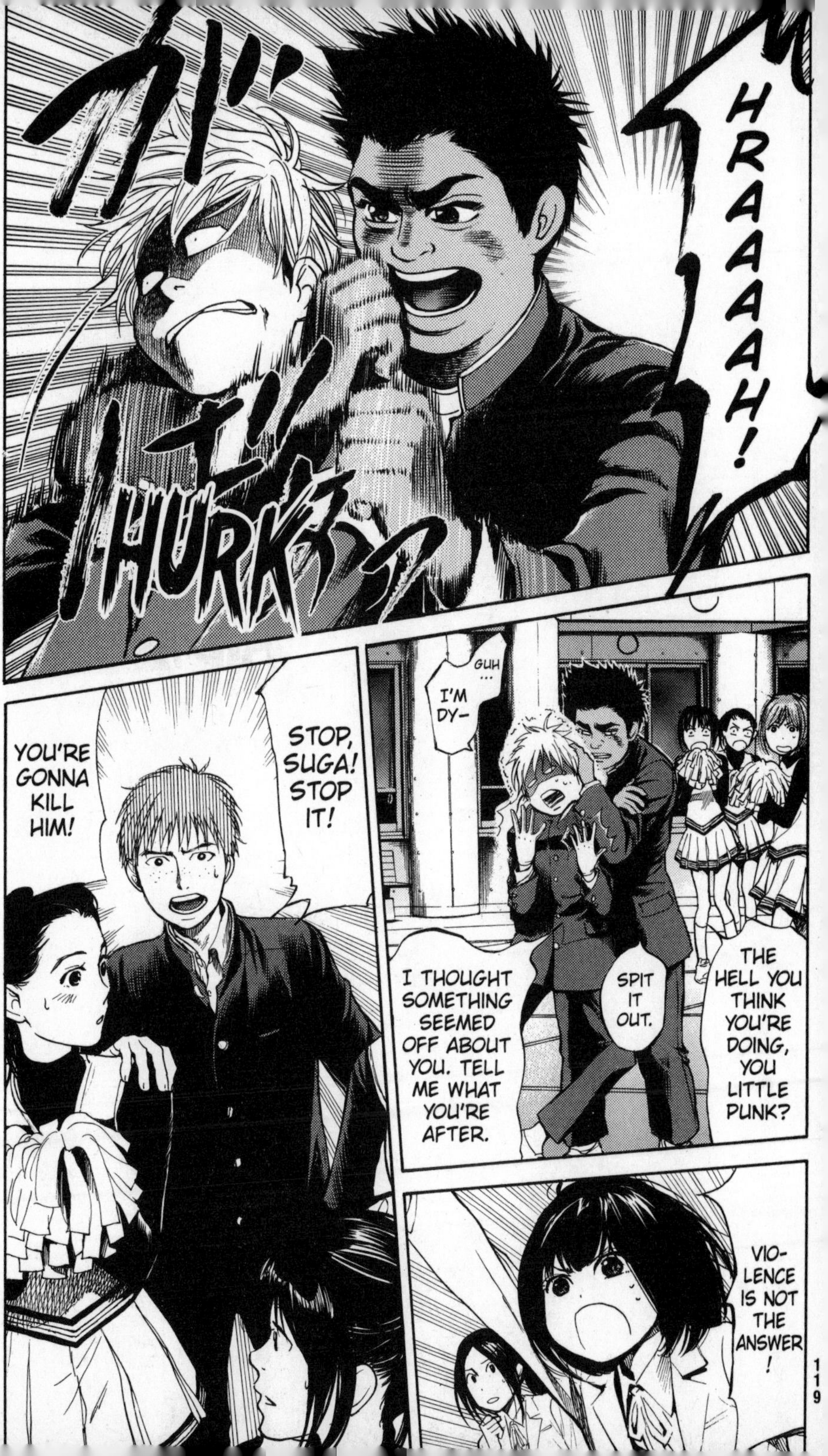
HRAAAAH!
HURK
GUH... I'M DY–
THE HELL YOU THINK YOU'RE DOING, YOU LITTLE PUNK?
SPIT IT OUT.
I THOUGHT SOMETHING SEEMED OFF ABOUT YOU. TELL ME WHAT YOU'RE AFTER.
VIO-LENCE IS NOT THE ANSWER!
STOP, SUGA! STOP IT!
YOU'RE GONNA KILL HIM!

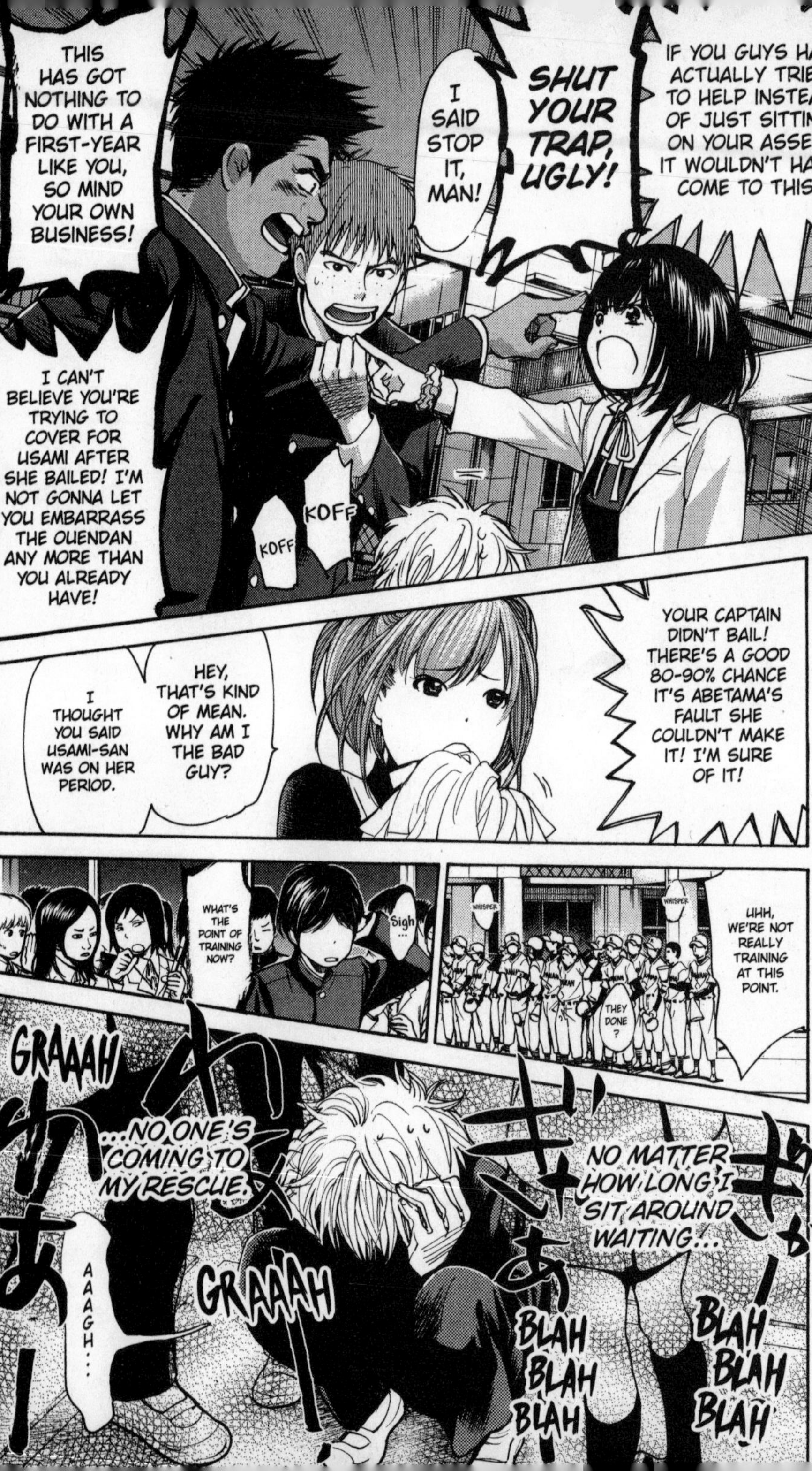
IF YOU GUYS HAD ACTUALLY TRIED TO HELP INSTEAD OF JUST SITTING ON YOUR ASSES, IT WOULDN'T HAVE COME TO THIS!
SHUT YOUR TRAP, UGLY!
I SAID STOP IT, MAN!
THIS HAS GOT NOTHING TO DO WITH A FIRST-YEAR LIKE YOU, SO MIND YOUR OWN BUSINESS!
I CAN'T BELIEVE YOU'RE TRYING TO COVER FOR USAMI AFTER SHE BAILED! I'M NOT GONNA LET YOU EMBARRASS THE OUENDAN ANY MORE THAN YOU ALREADY HAVE!
KOFF
KOFF
YOUR CAPTAIN DIDN'T BAIL! THERE'S A GOOD 80-90% CHANCE IT'S ABETAMA'S FAULT SHE COULDN'T MAKE IT! I'M SURE OF IT!
HEY, THAT'S KIND OF MEAN. WHY AM I THE BAD GUY?
I THOUGHT YOU SAID USAMI-SAN WAS ON HER PERIOD.
UHH, WE'RE NOT REALLY TRAINING AT THIS POINT.
WHISPER
THEY DONE?
WHISPER
Sigh...
WHAT'S THE POINT OF TRAINING NOW?
NO MATTER HOW LONG I SIT AROUND WAITING...
...NO ONE'S COMING TO MY RESCUE.
BLAH BLAH BLAH
BLAH BLAH BLAH
GRAAAH
AAAGH...
GRAAAH

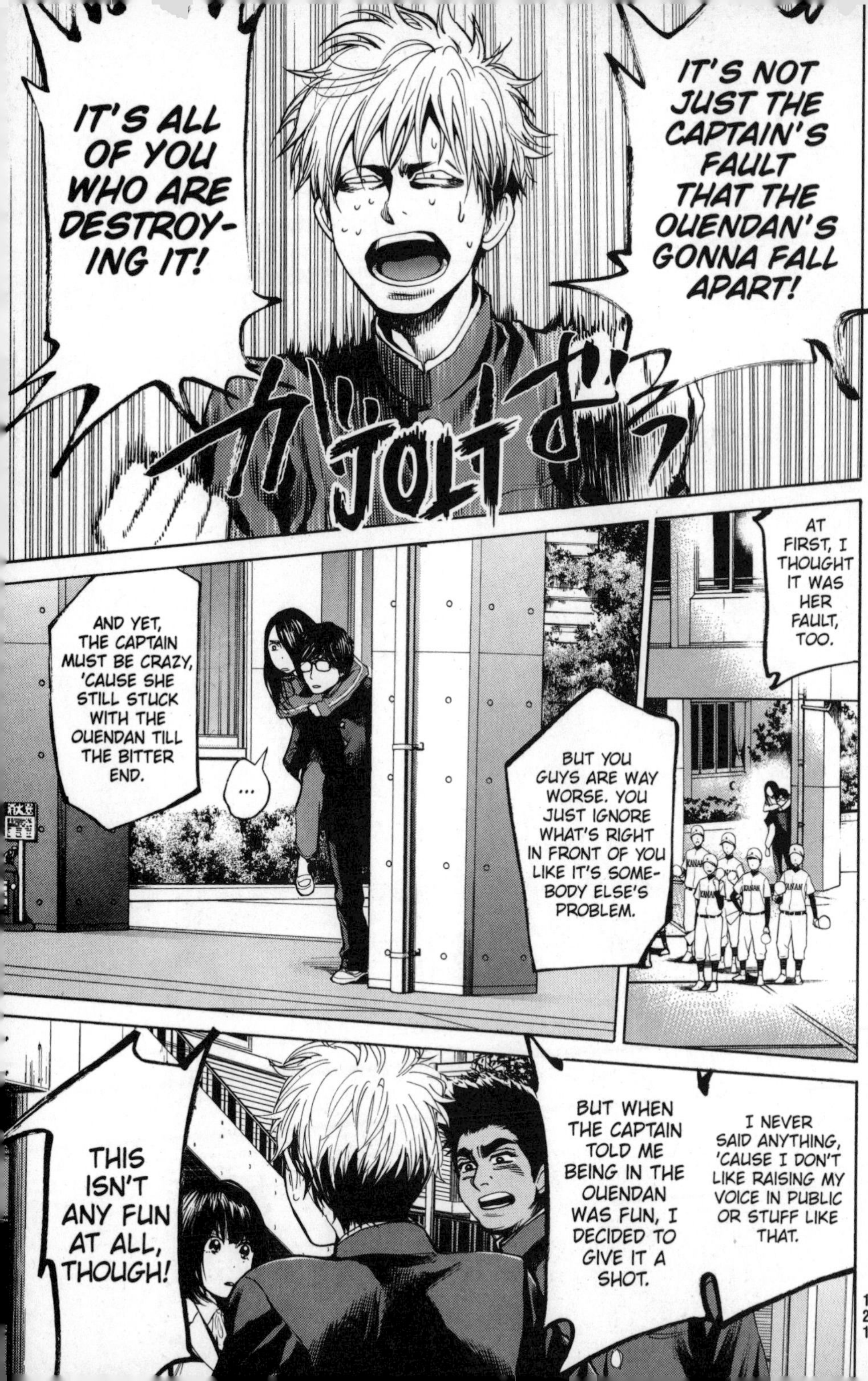
IT'S NOT JUST THE CAPTAIN'S FAULT THAT THE OUENDAN'S GONNA FALL APART!
IT'S ALL OF YOU WHO ARE DESTROY-ING IT!
JOLT
AT FIRST, I THOUGHT IT WAS HER FAULT, TOO.
BUT YOU GUYS ARE WAY WORSE. YOU JUST IGNORE WHAT'S RIGHT IN FRONT OF YOU LIKE IT'S SOME-BODY ELSE'S PROBLEM.
AND YET, THE CAPTAIN MUST BE CRAZY, 'CAUSE SHE STILL STUCK WITH THE OUENDAN TILL THE BITTER END.
...
I NEVER SAID ANYTHING, 'CAUSE I DON'T LIKE RAISING MY VOICE IN PUBLIC OR STUFF LIKE THAT.
BUT WHEN THE CAPTAIN TOLD ME BEING IN THE OUENDAN WAS FUN, I DECIDED TO GIVE IT A SHOT.
THIS ISN'T ANY FUN AT ALL, THOUGH!

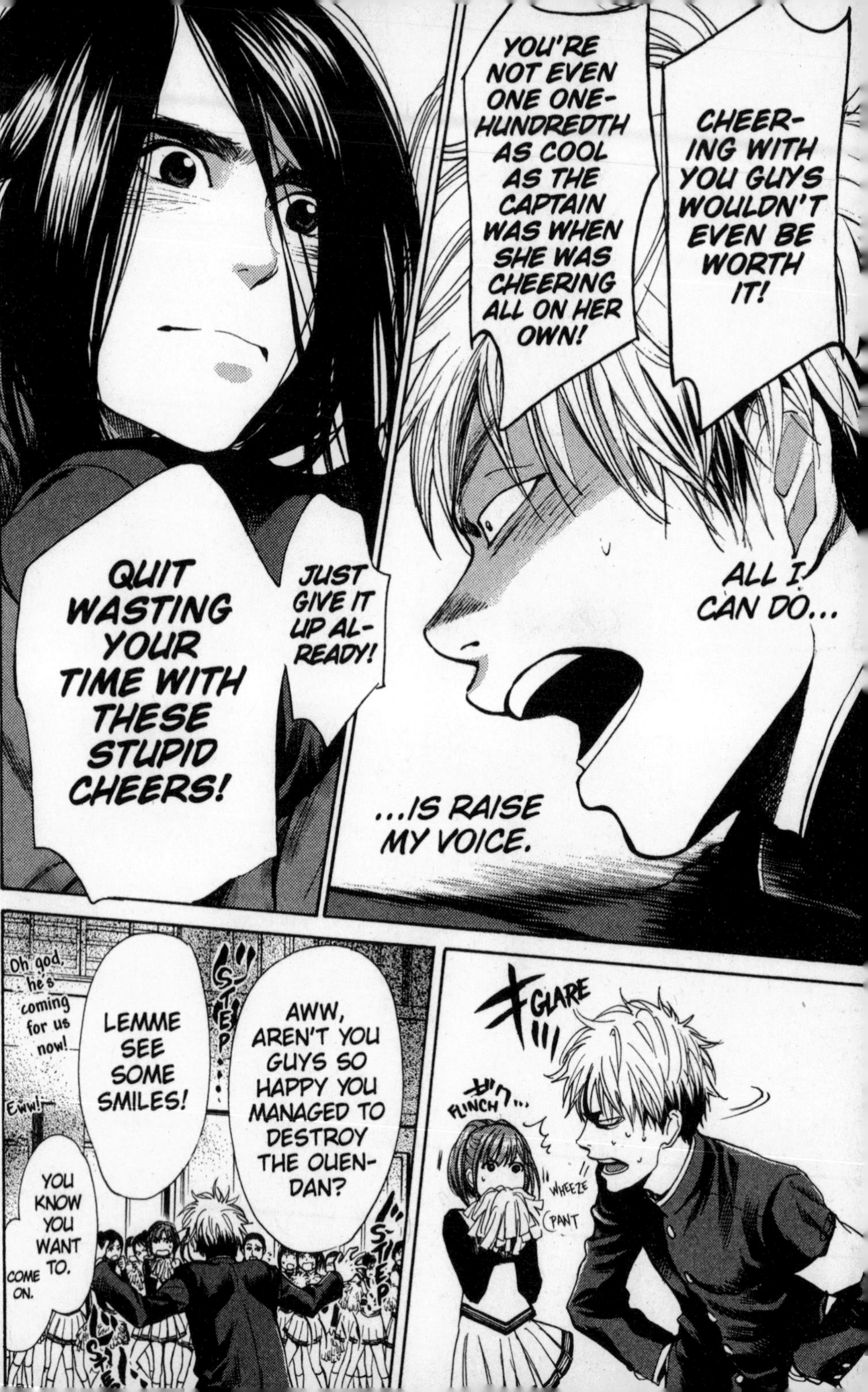
CHEER-ING WITH YOU GUYS WOULDN'T EVEN BE WORTH IT!
YOU'RE NOT EVEN ONE ONE-HUNDREDTH AS COOL AS THE CAPTAIN WAS WHEN SHE WAS CHEERING ALL ON HER OWN!
ALL I CAN DO...
...IS RAISE MY VOICE.
JUST GIVE IT UP AL-READY!
QUIT WASTING YOUR TIME WITH THESE STUPID CHEERS!
GLARE
FLINCH...
WHEEZE
PANT
AWW, AREN'T YOU GUYS SO HAPPY YOU MANAGED TO DESTROY THE OUEN-DAN?
STEP...
STEP
LEMME SEE SOME SMILES!
Oh god, he's coming for us now!
Eww!
YOU KNOW YOU WANT TO.
COME ON.

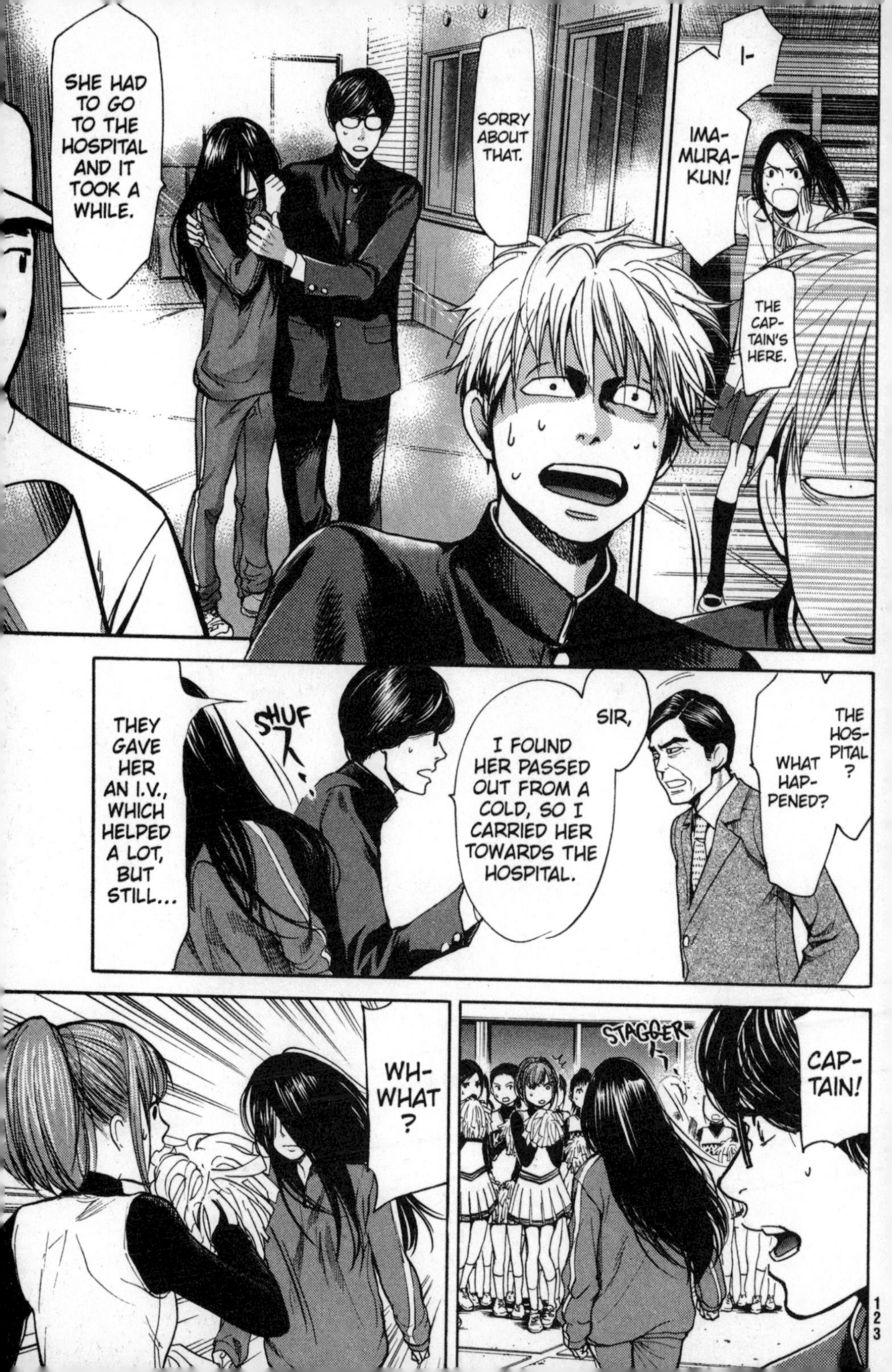
I-
IMA-MURA-KUN!
THE CAP-TAIN'S HERE.
SORRY ABOUT THAT.
SHE HAD TO GO TO THE HOSPITAL AND IT TOOK A WHILE.
THE HOS-PITAL?
WHAT HAP-PENED?
SIR,
I FOUND HER PASSED OUT FROM A COLD, SO I CARRIED HER TOWARDS THE HOSPITAL.
SHUF
THEY GAVE HER AN I.V., WHICH HELPED A LOT, BUT STILL...
CAP-TAIN!
STAGGER
WH-WHAT?

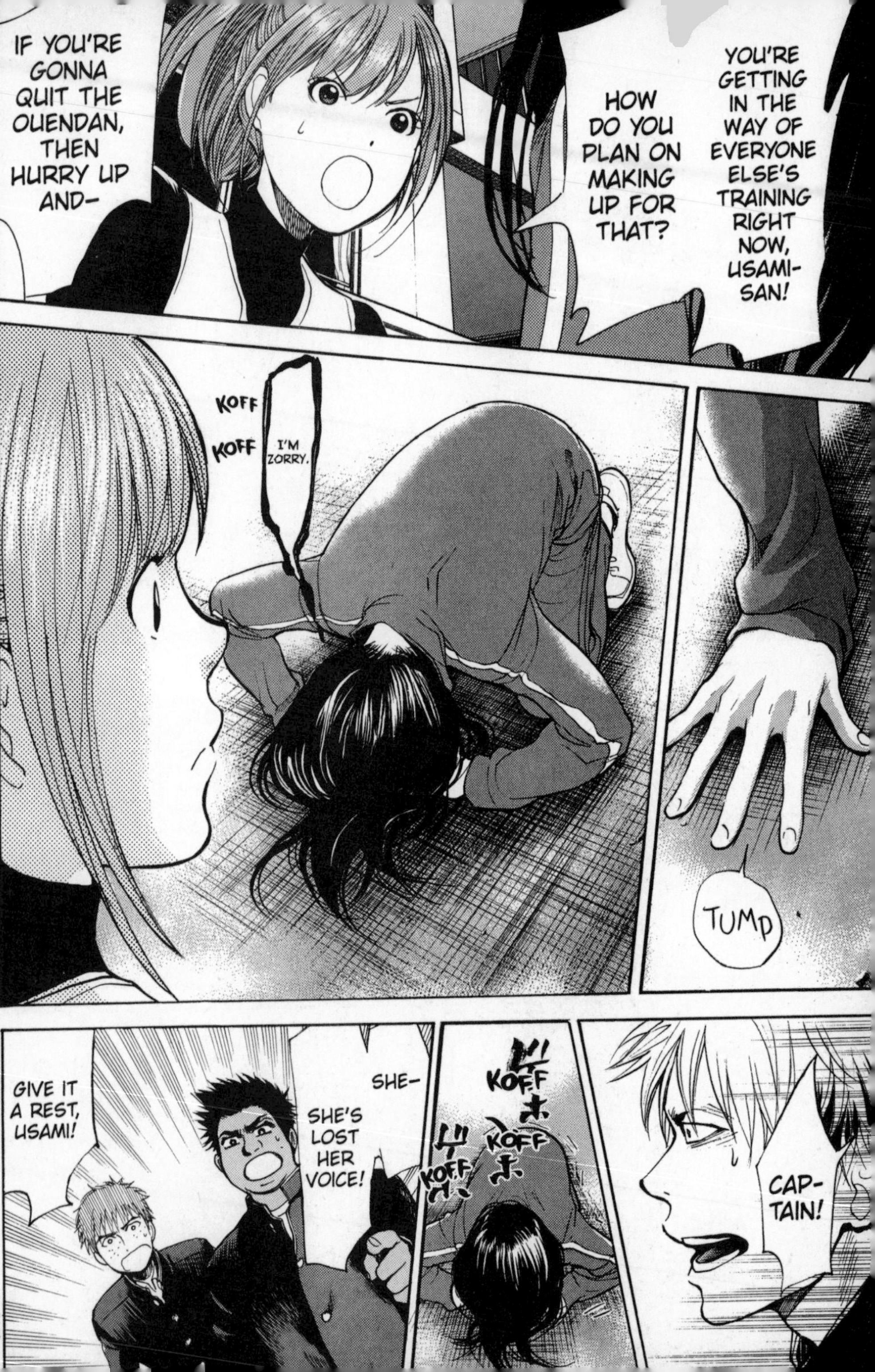
YOU'RE GETTING IN THE WAY OF EVERYONE ELSE'S TRAINING RIGHT NOW, USAMI-SAN!
HOW DO YOU PLAN ON MAKING UP FOR THAT?
IF YOU'RE GONNA QUIT THE OUENDAN, THEN HURRY UP AND-
TUMP
KOFF
KOFF
I'M ZORRY.
CAP-TAIN!
KOFF
KOFF
KOFF
SHE-
SHE'S LOST HER VOICE!
GIVE IT A REST, USAMI!

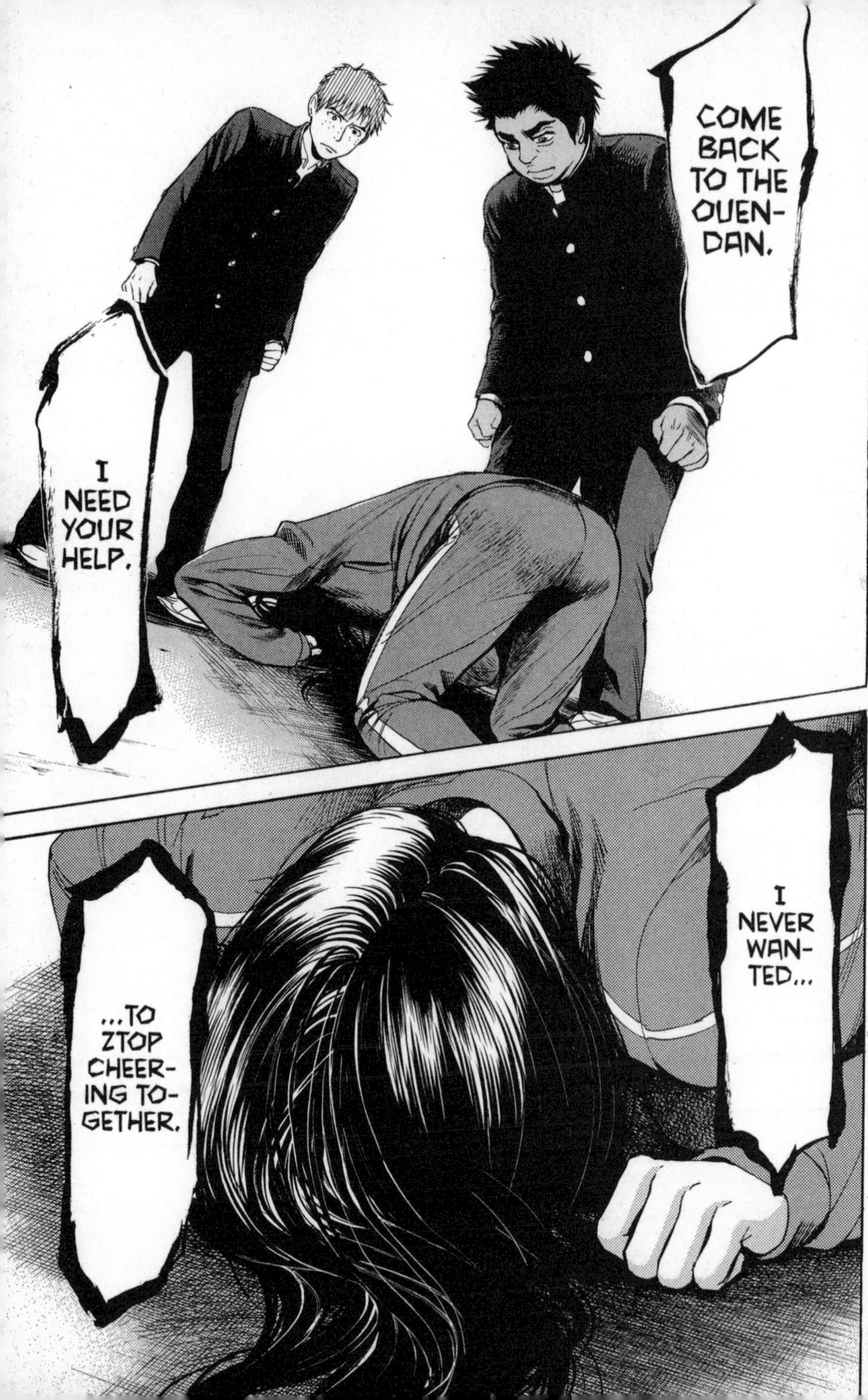
COME BACK TO THE OUEN-DAN.
I NEED YOUR HELP.
I NEVER WANTED...
...TO ZTOP CHEERING TOGETHER.

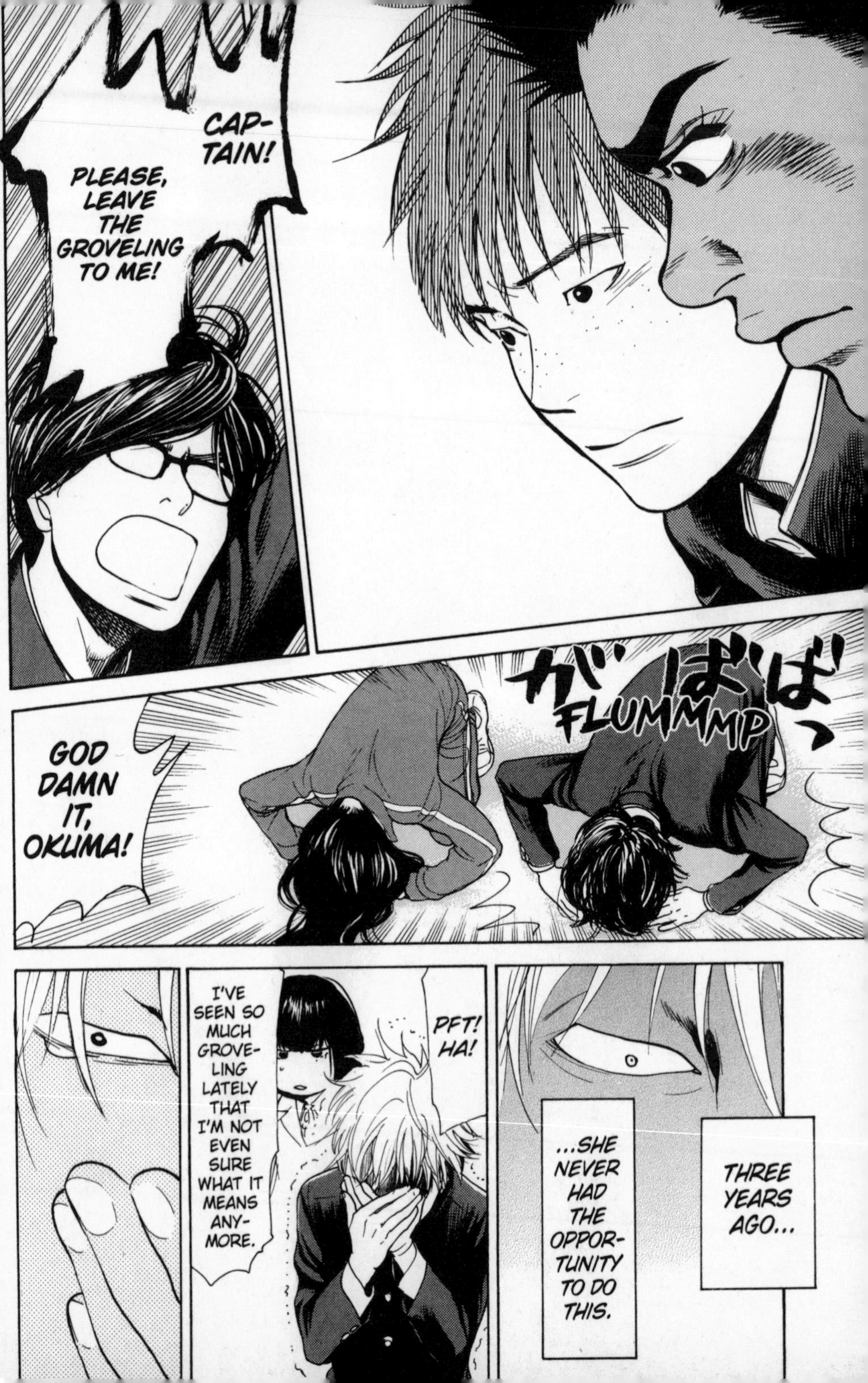
CAP-TAIN!
PLEASE, LEAVE THE GROVELING TO ME!
がばっ
FLUMMMP
GOD DAMN IT, OKUMA!
THREE YEARS AGO...
...SHE NEVER HAD THE OPPOR-TUNITY TO DO THIS.
PFT! HA!
I'VE SEEN SO MUCH GROVE-LING LATELY THAT I'M NOT EVEN SURE WHAT IT MEANS ANY-MORE.

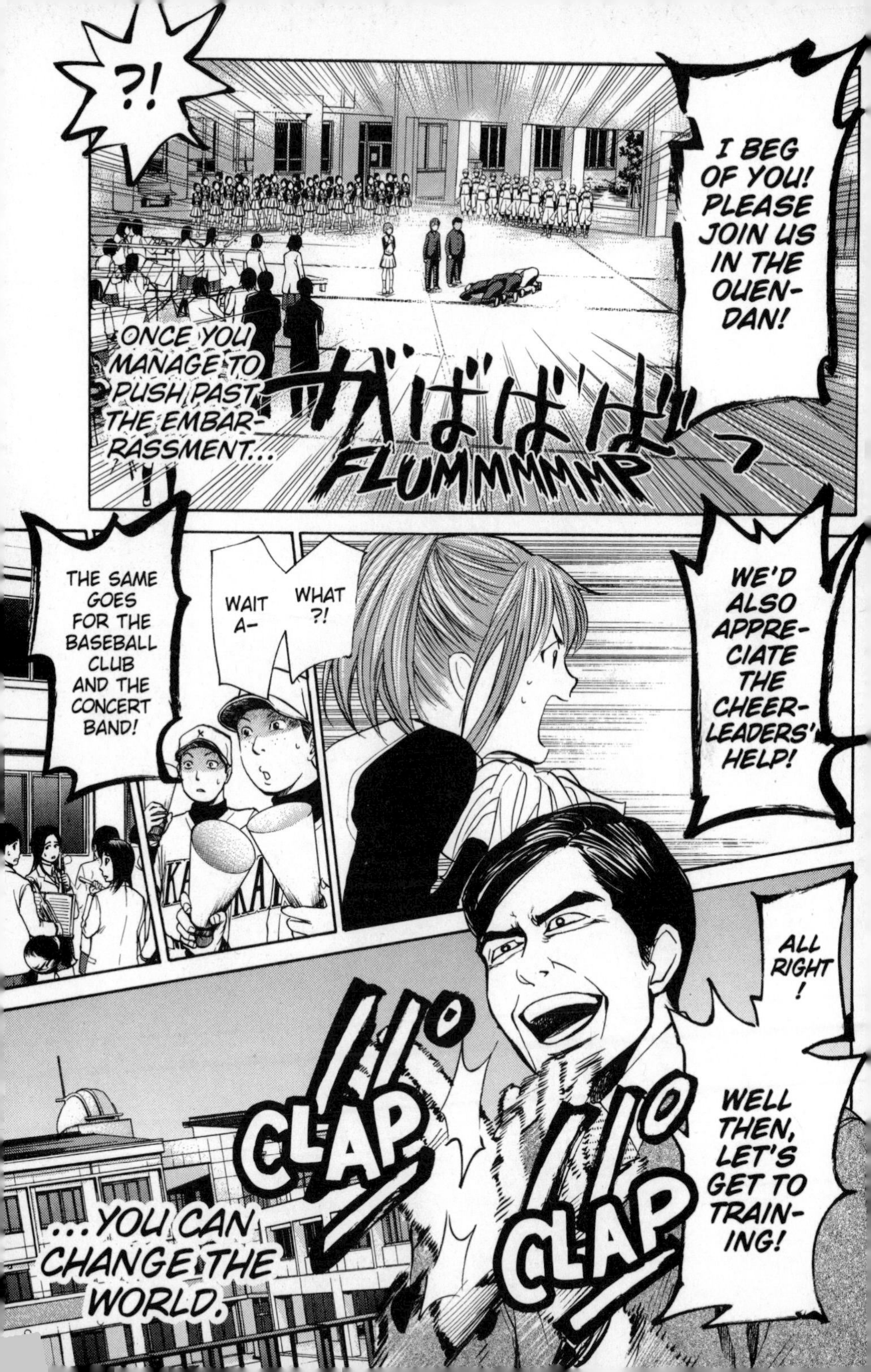
I BEG OF YOU! PLEASE JOIN US IN THE OUEN-DAN!
?!
ONCE YOU MANAGE TO PUSH PAST THE EMBAR-RASSMENT...
がばばばっ
FLUMMMMMP
WE'D ALSO APPRE-CIATE THE CHEER-LEADERS' HELP!
WHAT ?!
WAIT A-
THE SAME GOES FOR THE BASEBALL CLUB AND THE CONCERT BAND!
ALL RIGHT!
WELL THEN, LET'S GET TO TRAIN-ING!
CLAP
CLAP
...YOU CAN CHANGE THE WORLD.

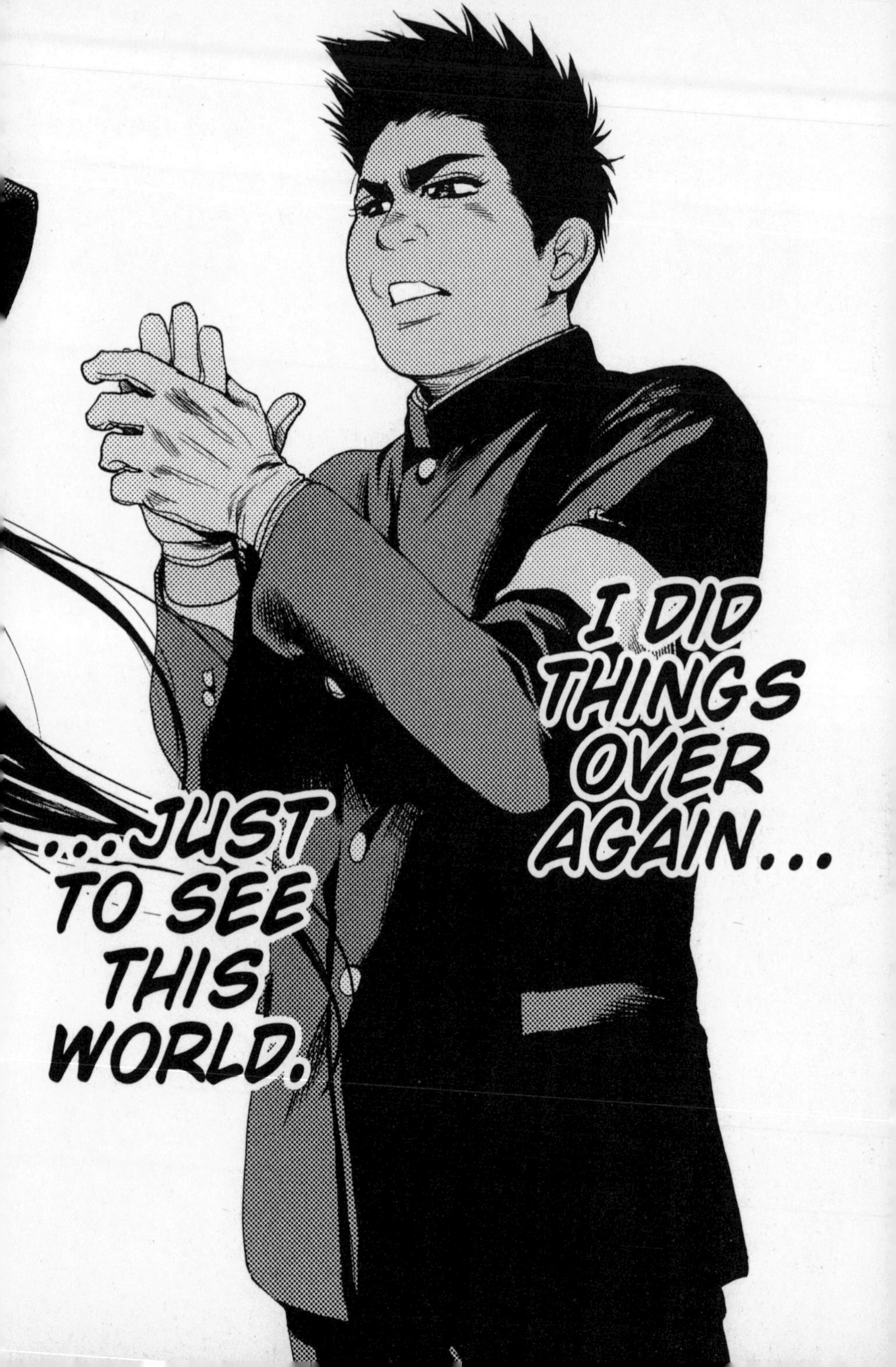
I DID THINGS OVER AGAIN...
...JUST TO SEE THIS WORLD.

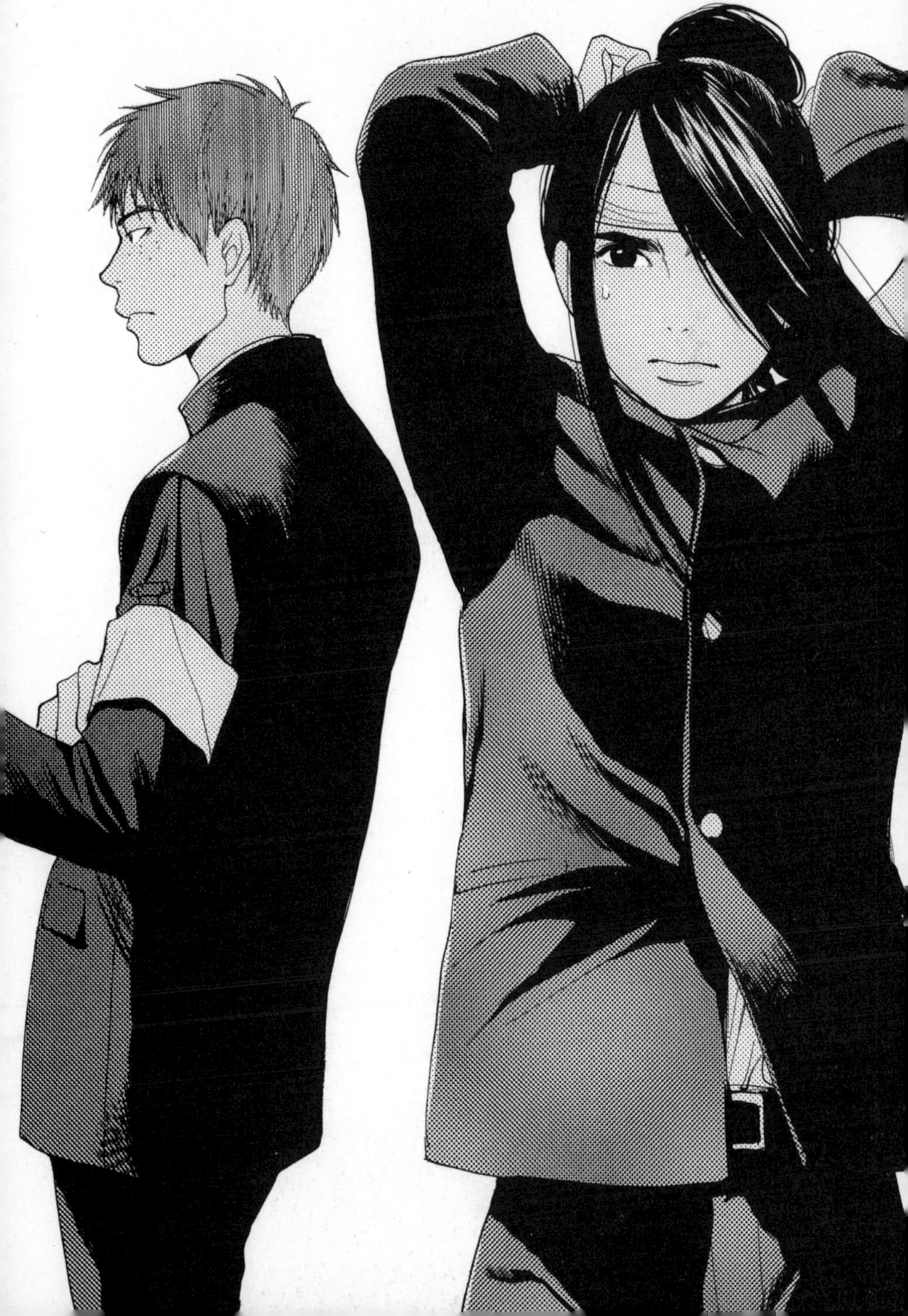

Again!!
アゲイン!!

17. CHEER!!!

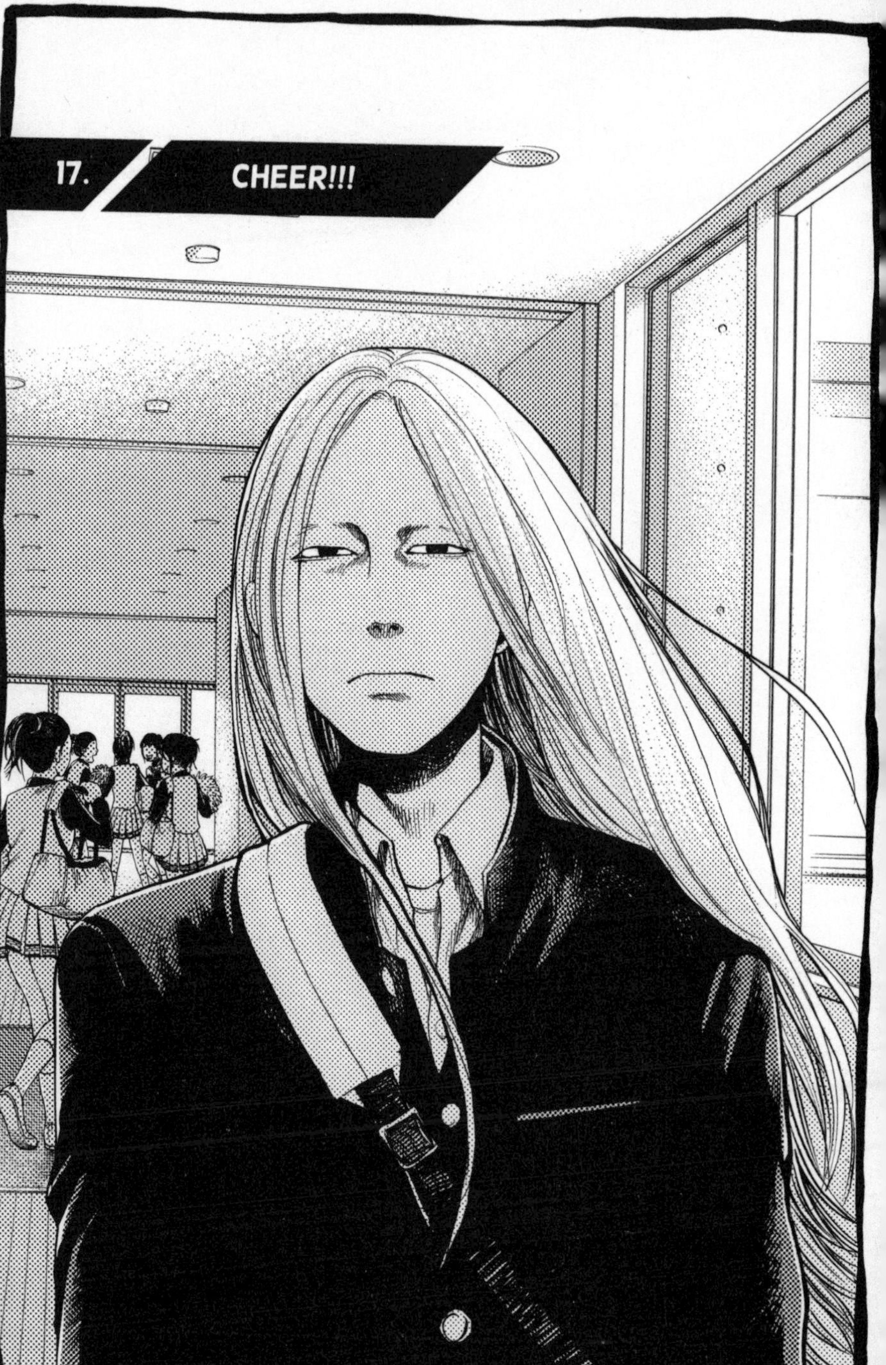

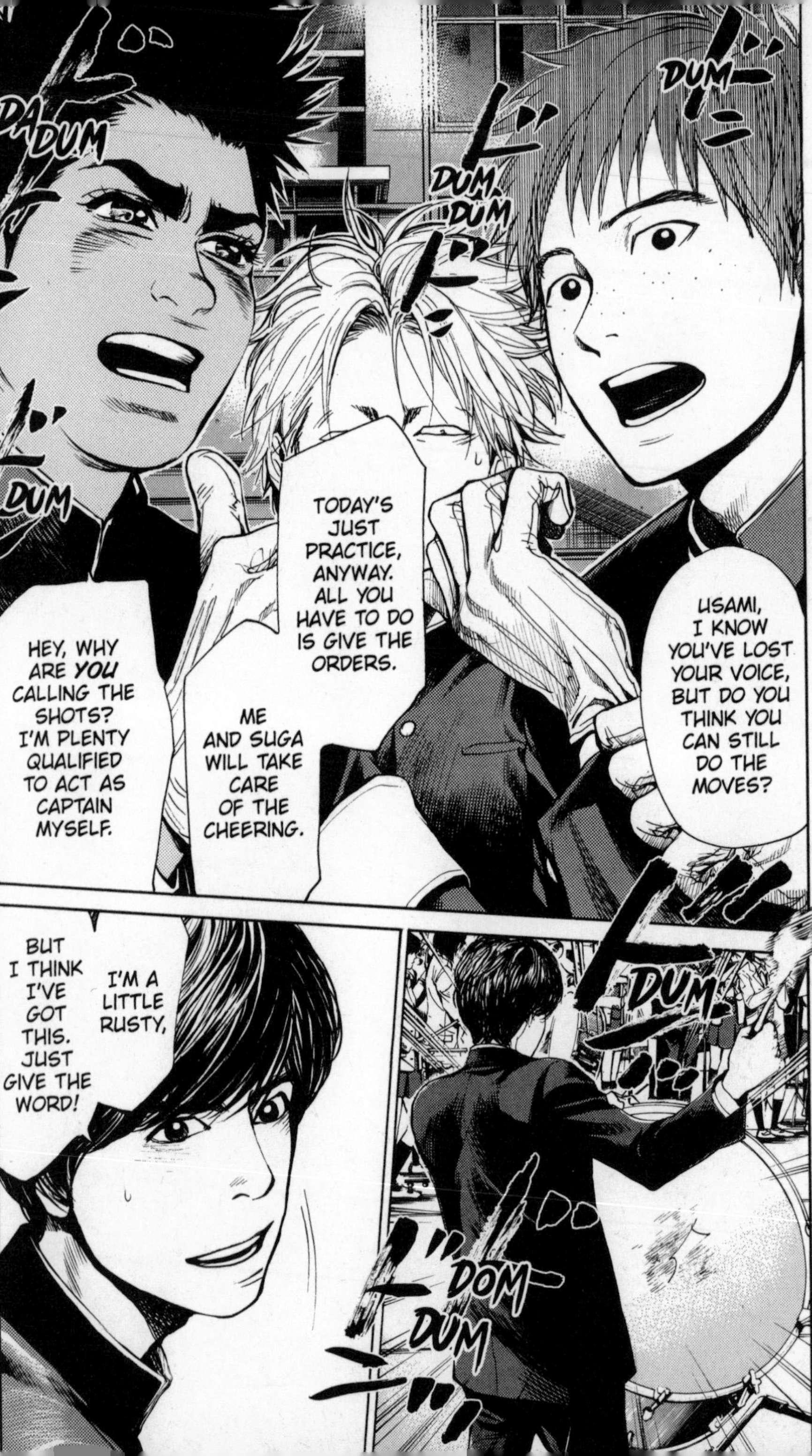
DUM
DUM DUM
DA DUM
DUM
USAMI, I KNOW YOU'VE LOST YOUR VOICE, BUT DO YOU THINK YOU CAN STILL DO THE MOVES?
TODAY'S JUST PRACTICE, ANYWAY. ALL YOU HAVE TO DO IS GIVE THE ORDERS.
ME AND SUGA WILL TAKE CARE OF THE CHEERING.
HEY, WHY ARE *YOU* CALLING THE SHOTS? I'M PLENTY QUALIFIED TO ACT AS CAPTAIN MYSELF.
DUM
DOM DUM
I'M A LITTLE RUSTY,
BUT I THINK I'VE GOT THIS. JUST GIVE THE WORD!

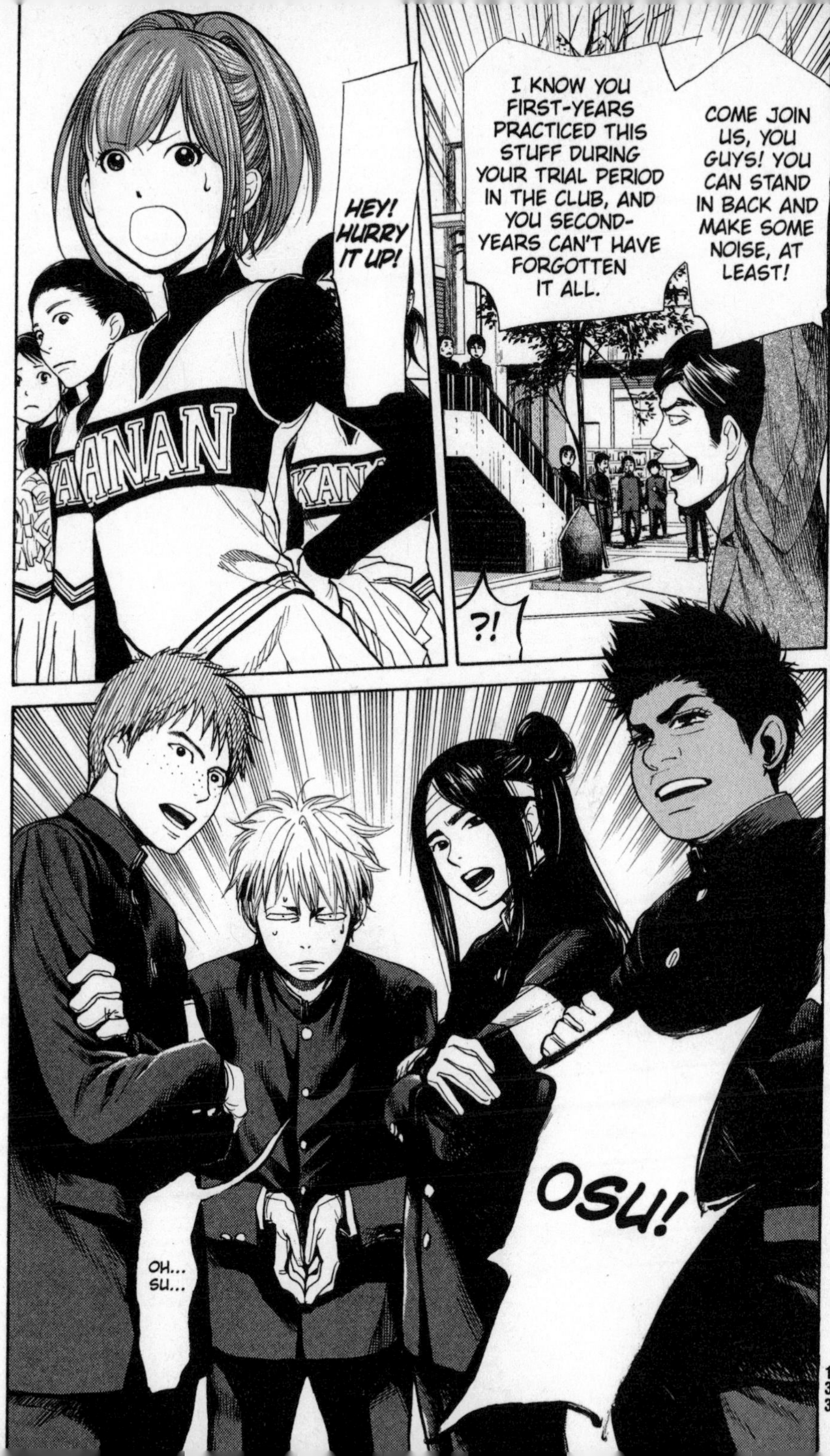
COME JOIN US, YOU GUYS! YOU CAN STAND IN BACK AND MAKE SOME NOISE, AT LEAST!
I KNOW YOU FIRST-YEARS PRACTICED THIS STUFF DURING YOUR TRIAL PERIOD IN THE CLUB, AND YOU SECOND-YEARS CAN'T HAVE FORGOTTEN IT ALL.
?!
HEY! HURRY IT UP!
KANAN
OSU!
OH... SU...

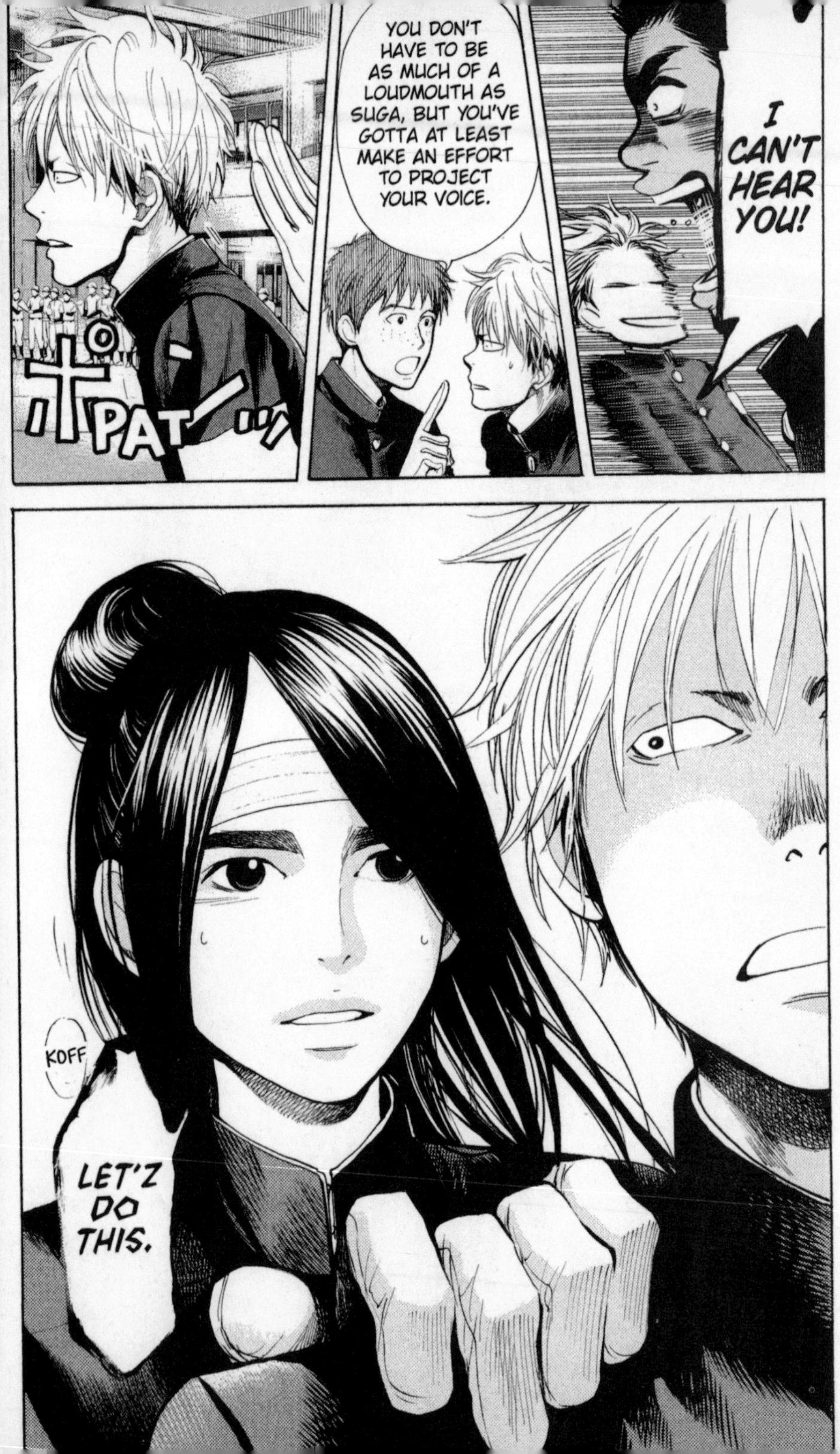
I CAN'T HEAR YOU!
YOU DON'T HAVE TO BE AS MUCH OF A LOUDMOUTH AS SUGA, BUT YOU'VE GOTTA AT LEAST MAKE AN EFFORT TO PROJECT YOUR VOICE.
PAT
KOFF
LET'Z DO THIS.

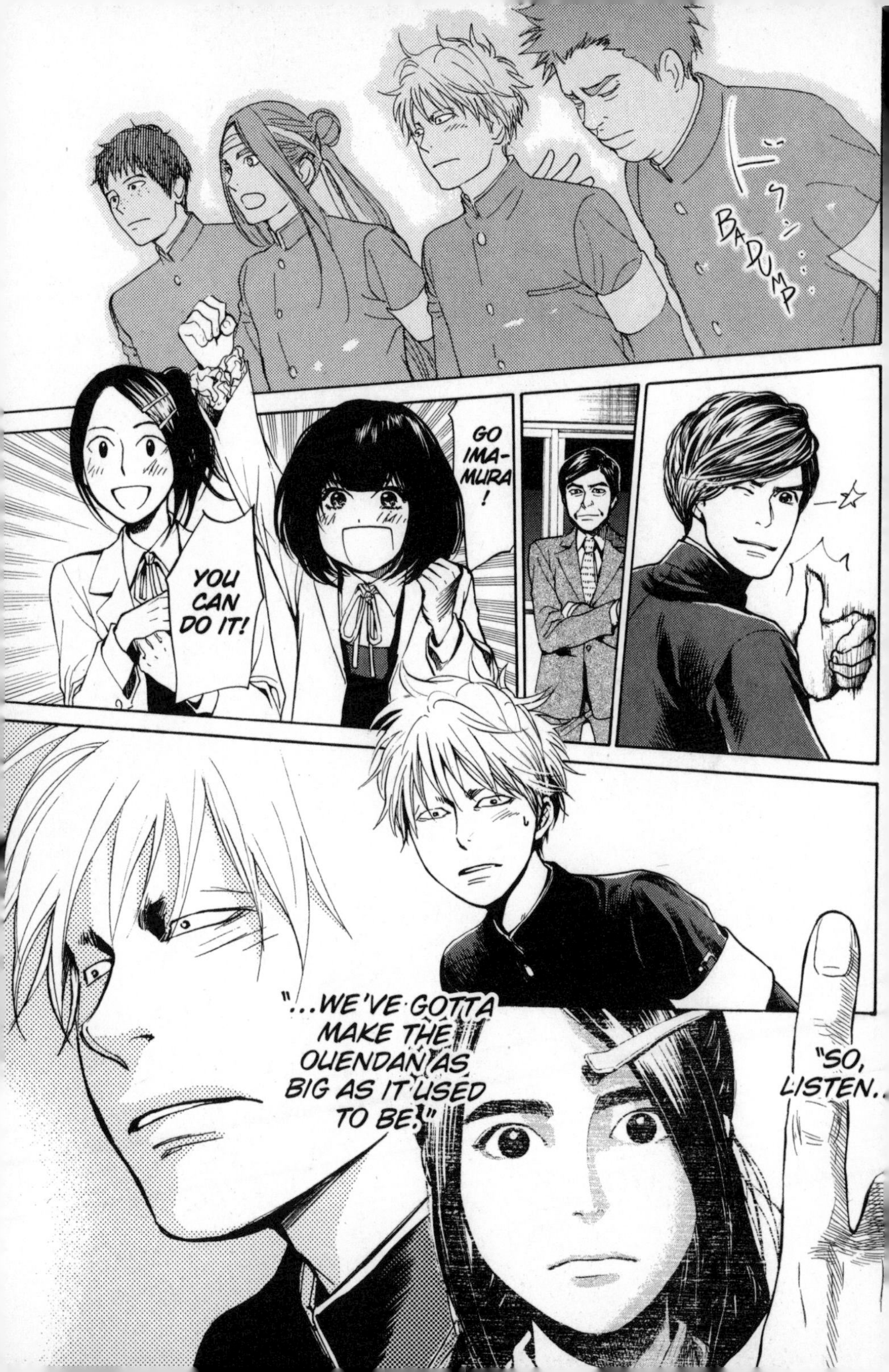

ドクン
BADUMP
GO IMAMURA!
YOU CAN DO IT!
"SO, LISTEN...
"...WE'VE GOTTA MAKE THE OUENDAN AS BIG AS IT USED TO BE."

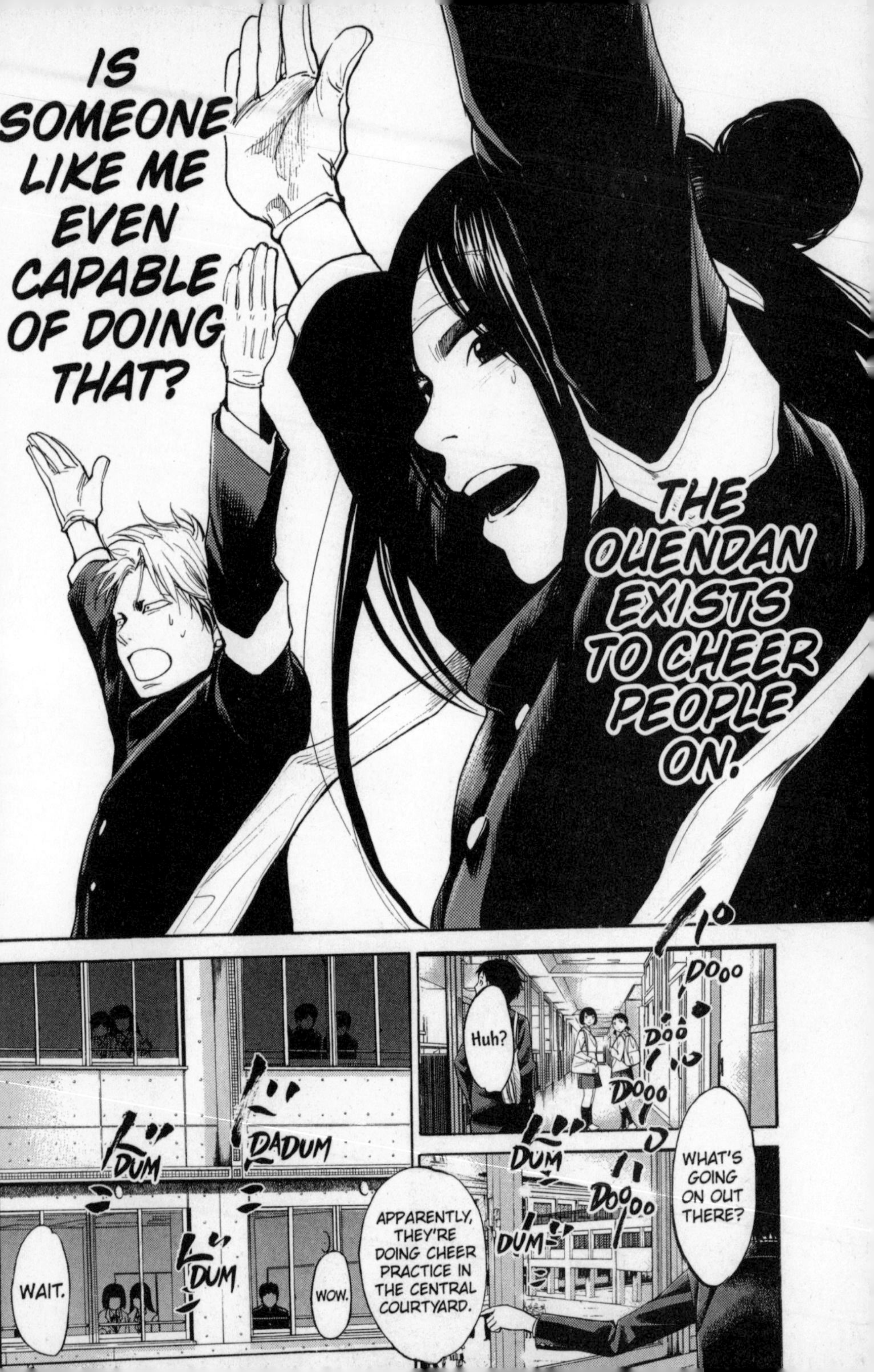
THE OUENDAN EXISTS TO CHEER PEOPLE ON.
IS SOMEONE LIKE ME EVEN CAPABLE OF DOING THAT?
DOOO
DOOO
DOOO
Huh?
DOOOOO
DUM
DUM
WHAT'S GOING ON OUT THERE?
APPARENTLY, THEY'RE DOING CHEER PRACTICE IN THE CENTRAL COURTYARD.
DADUM
DUM
DUM
WOW.
WAIT.

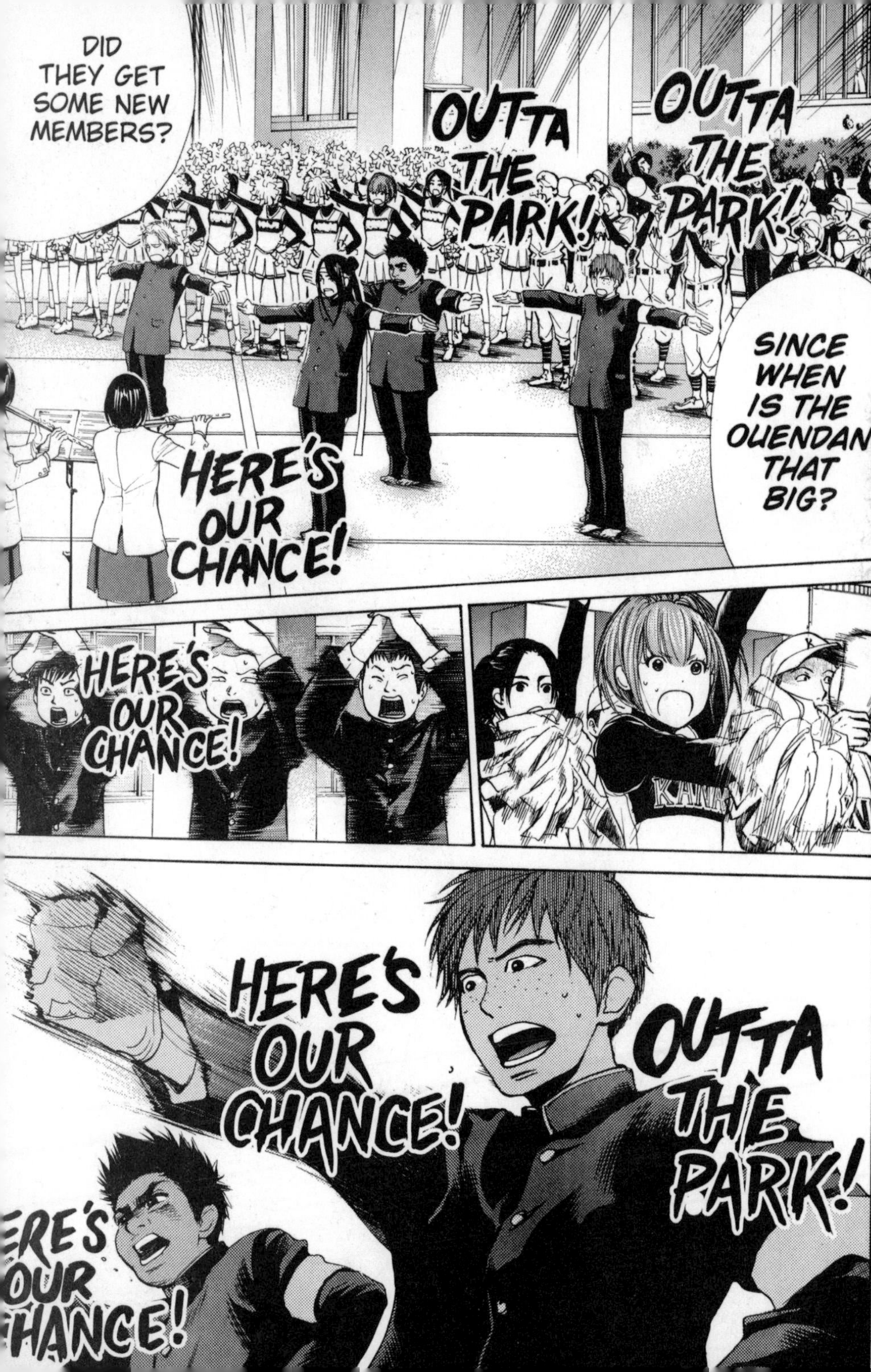
OUTTA THE PARK!
OUTTA THE PARK!
DID THEY GET SOME NEW MEMBERS?
SINCE WHEN IS THE OUENDAN THAT BIG?
HERE'S OUR CHANCE!
HERE'S OUR CHANCE!
OUTTA THE PARK!
HERE'S OUR CHANCE!
ERE'S OUR HANCE!

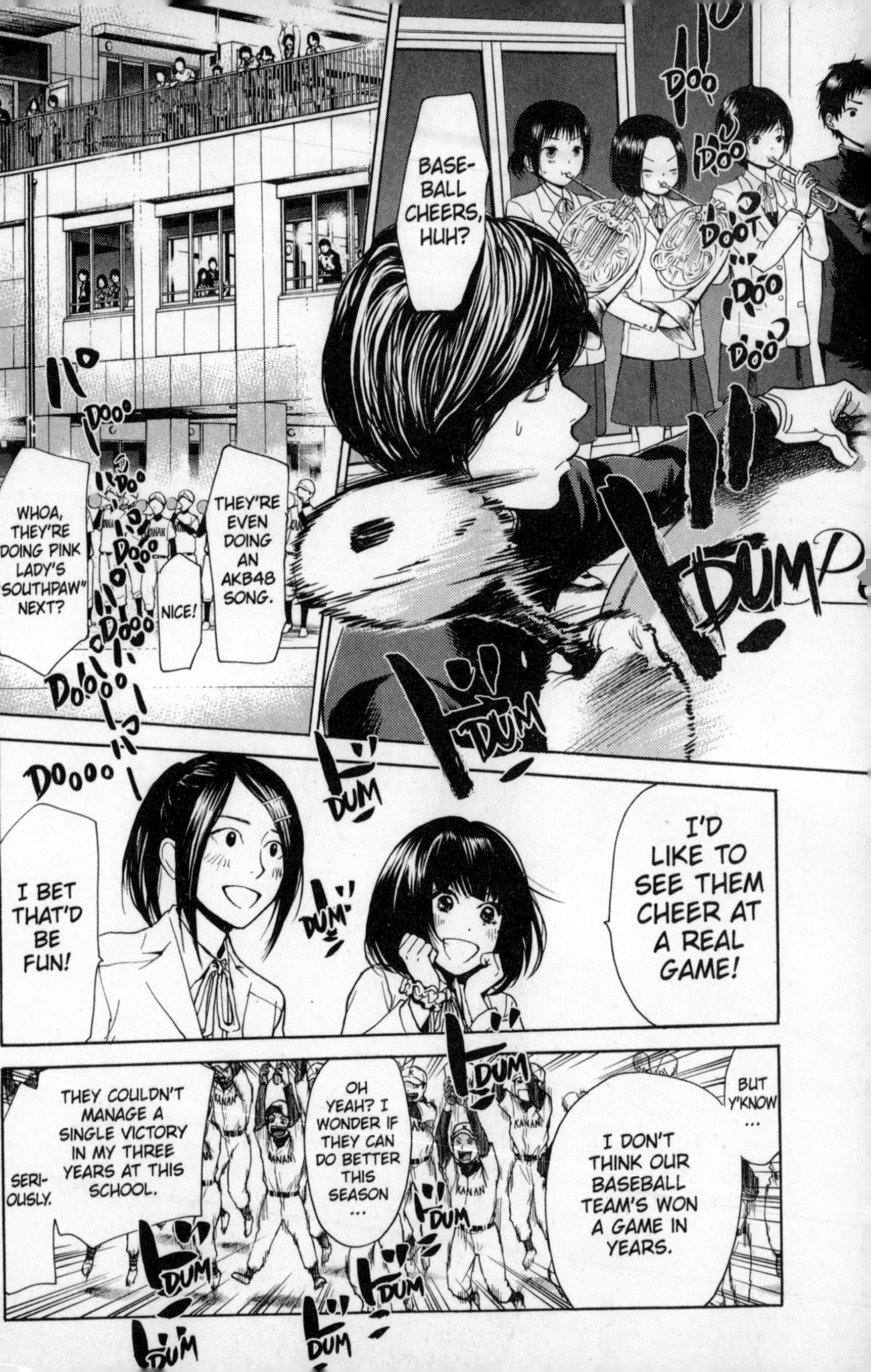
DOO
DOO
DOOT
DOO
DOO
BASE-BALL CHEERS, HUH?
DUM
DUM
DOOO
DOO
DOOO
DOOOO
DOOOO
THEY'RE EVEN DOING AN AKB48 SONG.
NICE!
WHOA, THEY'RE DOING PINK LADY'S "SOUTHPAW" NEXT?
DOOOO
DUM
I'D LIKE TO SEE THEM CHEER AT A REAL GAME!
DUM
I BET THAT'D BE FUN!
DUM
BUT Y'KNOW...
I DON'T THINK OUR BASEBALL TEAM'S WON A GAME IN YEARS.
OH YEAH? I WONDER IF THEY CAN DO BETTER THIS SEASON...
THEY COULDN'T MANAGE A SINGLE VICTORY IN MY THREE YEARS AT THIS SCHOOL.
SERI-OUSLY.
DUM
DUM
DUM
DUM
DUM

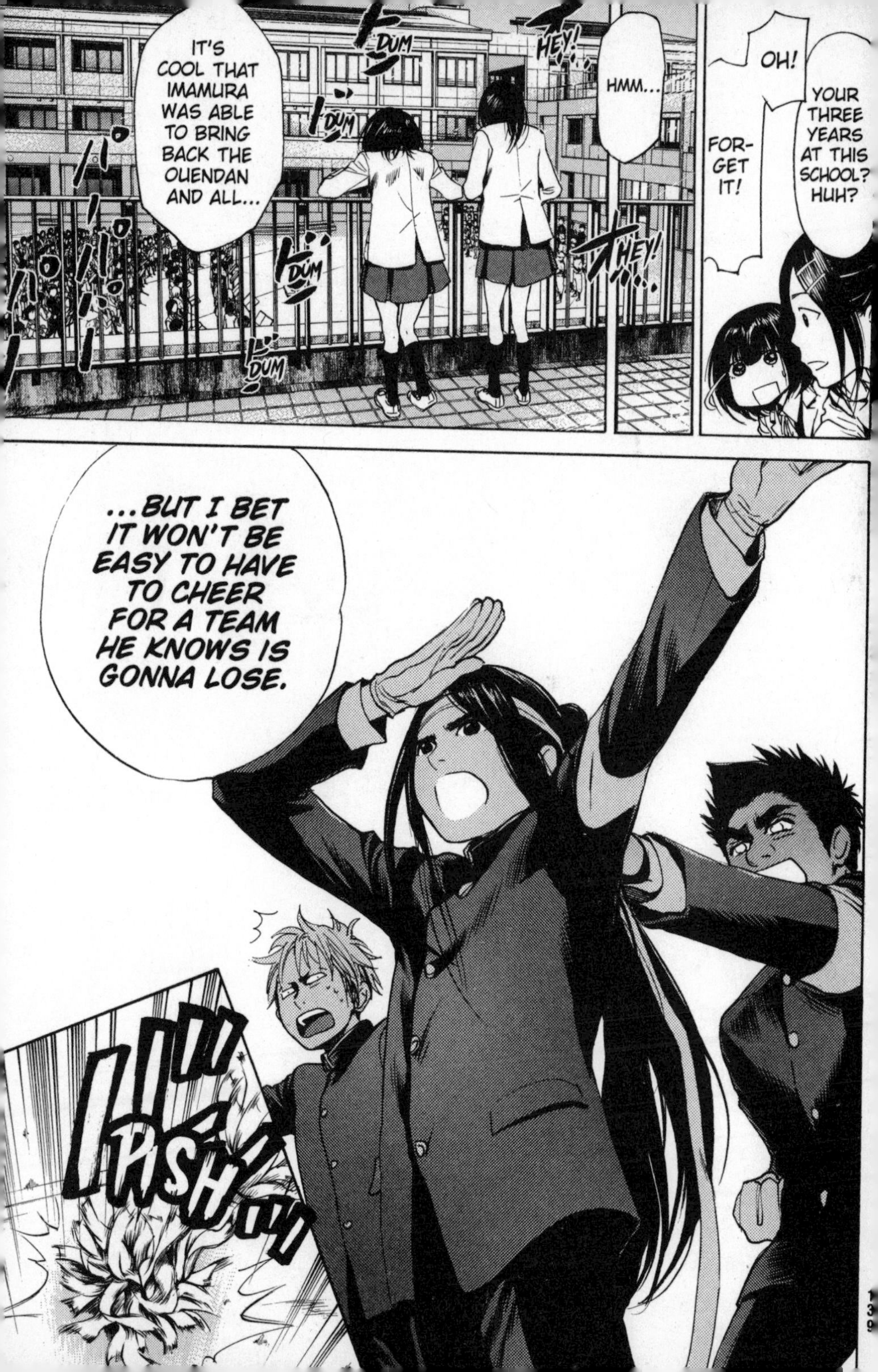
OH!
YOUR THREE YEARS AT THIS SCHOOL? HUH?
FOR-GET IT!
HEY!
HMM...
HEY!
IT'S COOL THAT IMAMURA WAS ABLE TO BRING BACK THE OUENDAN AND ALL...
DUM
DUM
DUM
DUM
...BUT I BET IT WON'T BE EASY TO HAVE TO CHEER FOR A TEAM HE KNOWS IS GONNA LOSE.
PSH

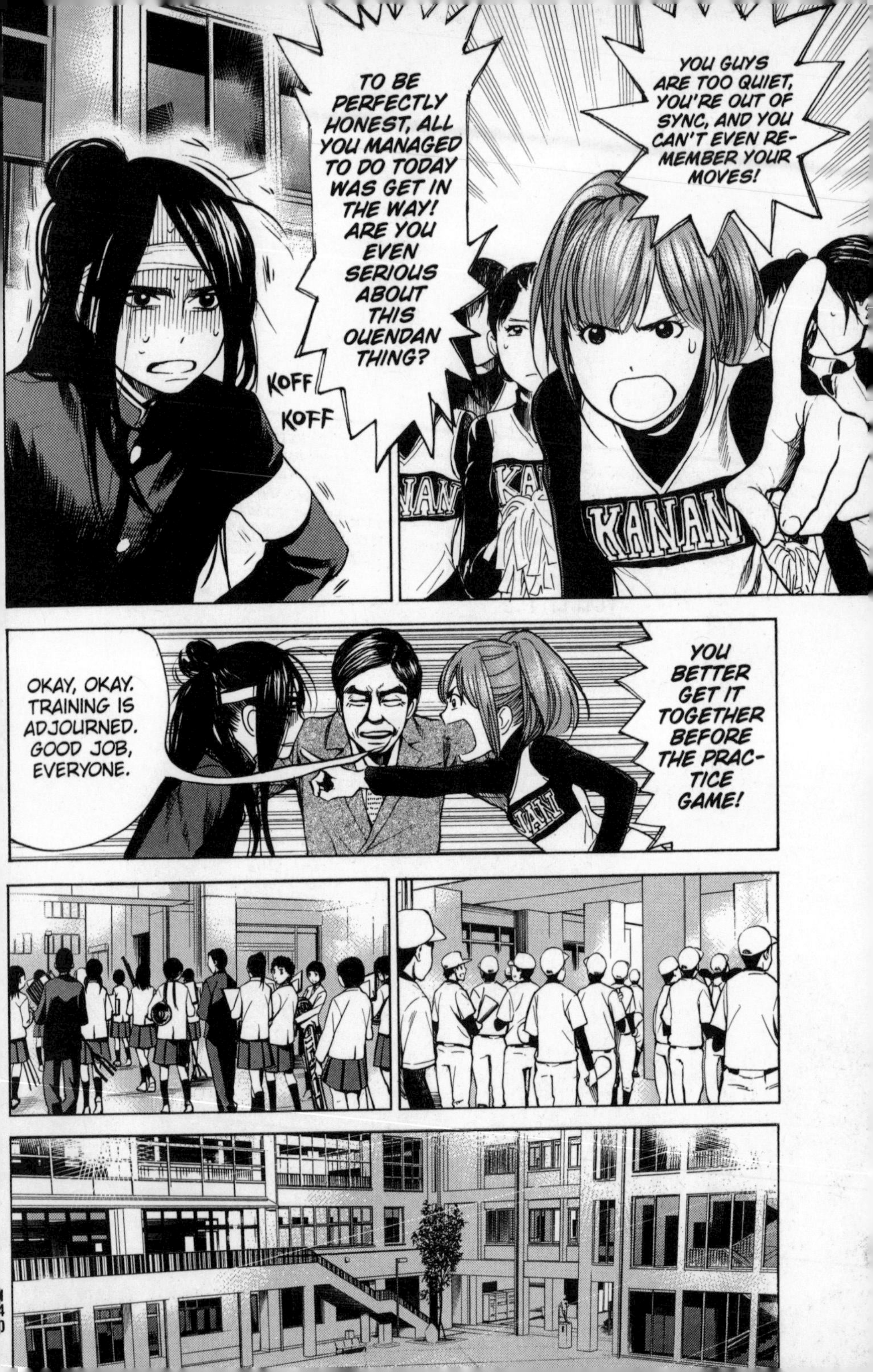
YOU GUYS ARE TOO QUIET, YOU'RE OUT OF SYNC, AND YOU CAN'T EVEN RE-MEMBER YOUR MOVES!
TO BE PERFECTLY HONEST, ALL YOU MANAGED TO DO TODAY WAS GET IN THE WAY! ARE YOU EVEN SERIOUS ABOUT THIS OUENDAN THING?
KOFF
KOFF
KANAN
YOU BETTER GET IT TOGETHER BEFORE THE PRAC-TICE GAME!
OKAY, OKAY. TRAINING IS ADJOURNED. GOOD JOB, EVERYONE.

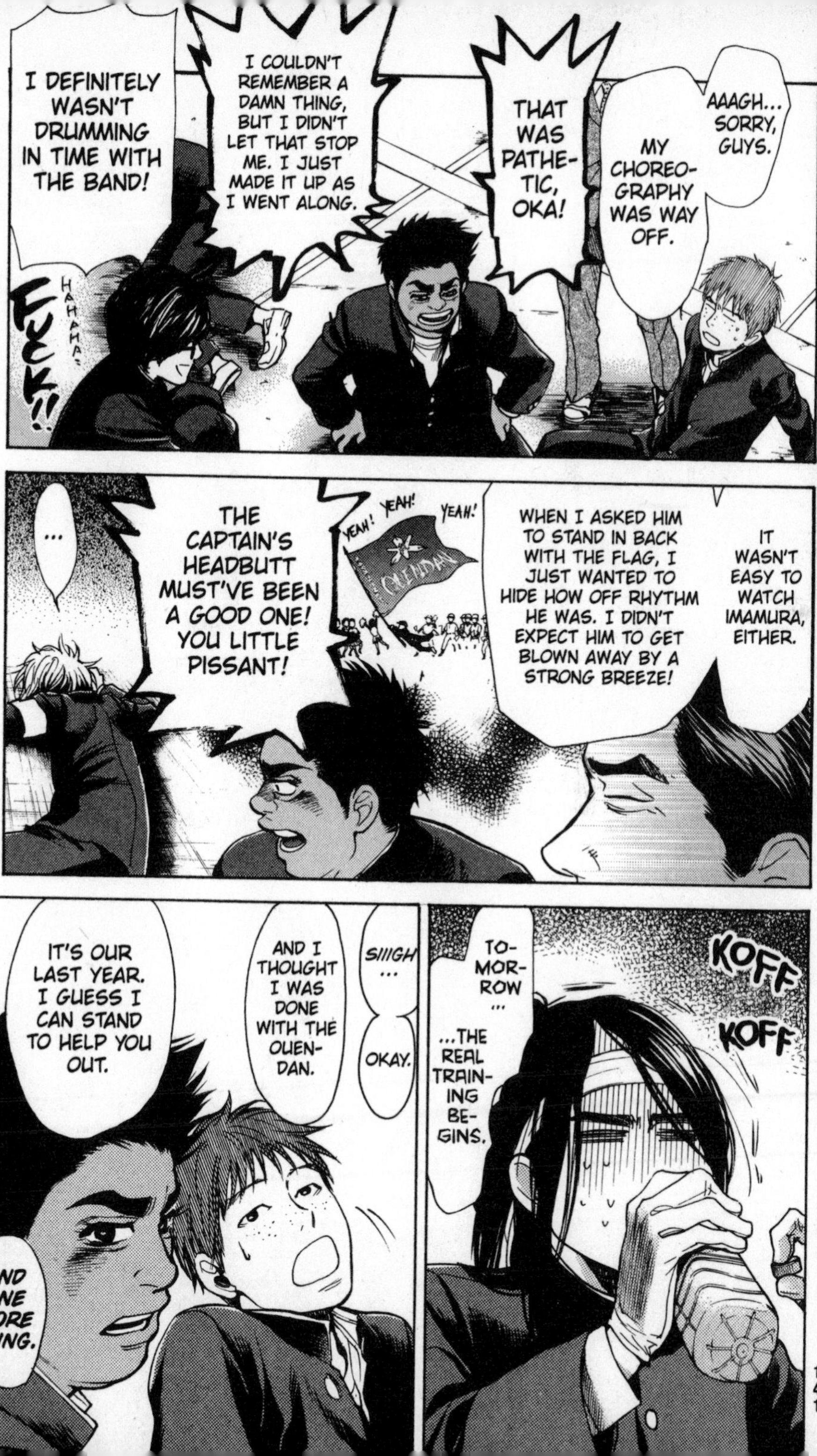
AAAGH... SORRY, GUYS.
MY CHOREOGRAPHY WAS WAY OFF.
THAT WAS PATHETIC, OKA!
I COULDN'T REMEMBER A DAMN THING, BUT I DIDN'T LET THAT STOP ME. I JUST MADE IT UP AS I WENT ALONG.
I DEFINITELY WASN'T DRUMMING IN TIME WITH THE BAND!
HAHAHA
FUCK!!
IT WASN'T EASY TO WATCH IMAMURA, EITHER.
WHEN I ASKED HIM TO STAND IN BACK WITH THE FLAG, I JUST WANTED TO HIDE HOW OFF RHYTHM HE WAS. I DIDN'T EXPECT HIM TO GET BLOWN AWAY BY A STRONG BREEZE!
YEAH! YEAH! YEAH!
THE CAPTAIN'S HEADBUTT MUST'VE BEEN A GOOD ONE! YOU LITTLE PISSANT!
...
KOFF
KOFF
TOMORROW...
...THE REAL TRAINING BEGINS.
SIIIGH...
OKAY.
AND I THOUGHT I WAS DONE WITH THE OUEN-DAN.
IT'S OUR LAST YEAR. I GUESS I CAN STAND TO HELP YOU OUT.
AND ONE MORE THING.

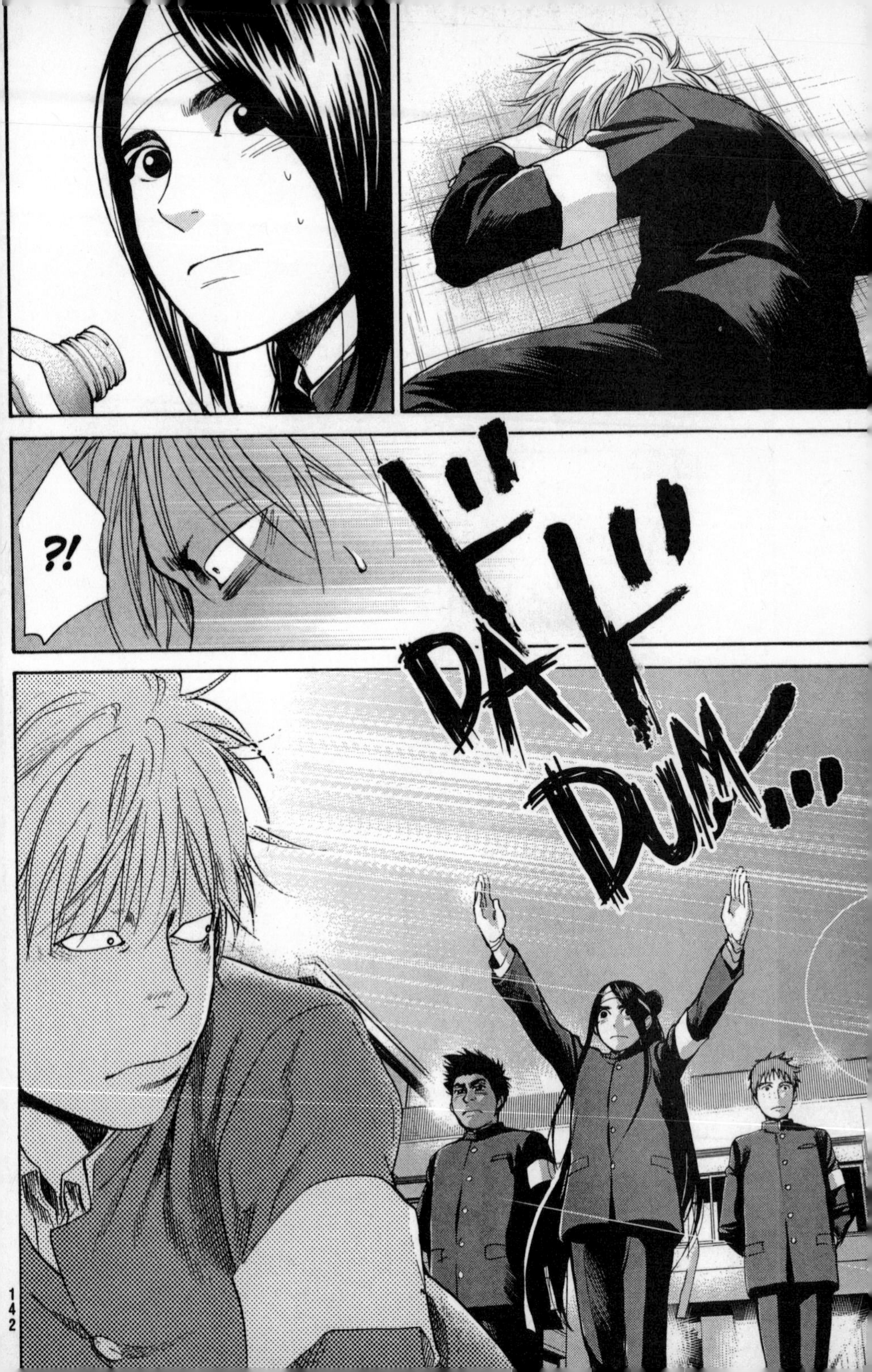
?!
DA DUM...

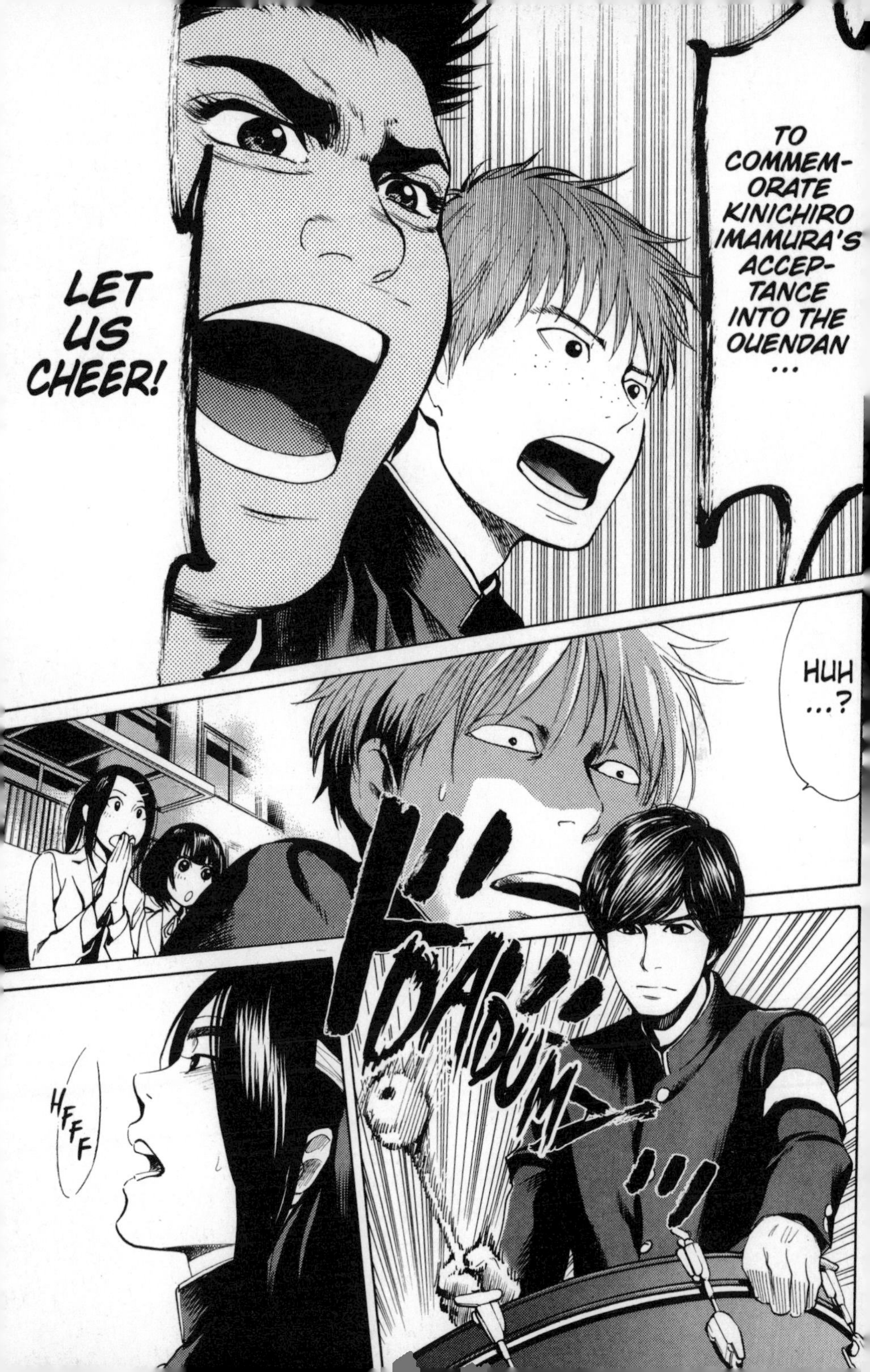
TO COMMEM-ORATE KINICHIRO IMAMURA'S ACCEP-TANCE INTO THE OUENDAN ...
LET US CHEER!
HUH ...?
DADUM
HFFF

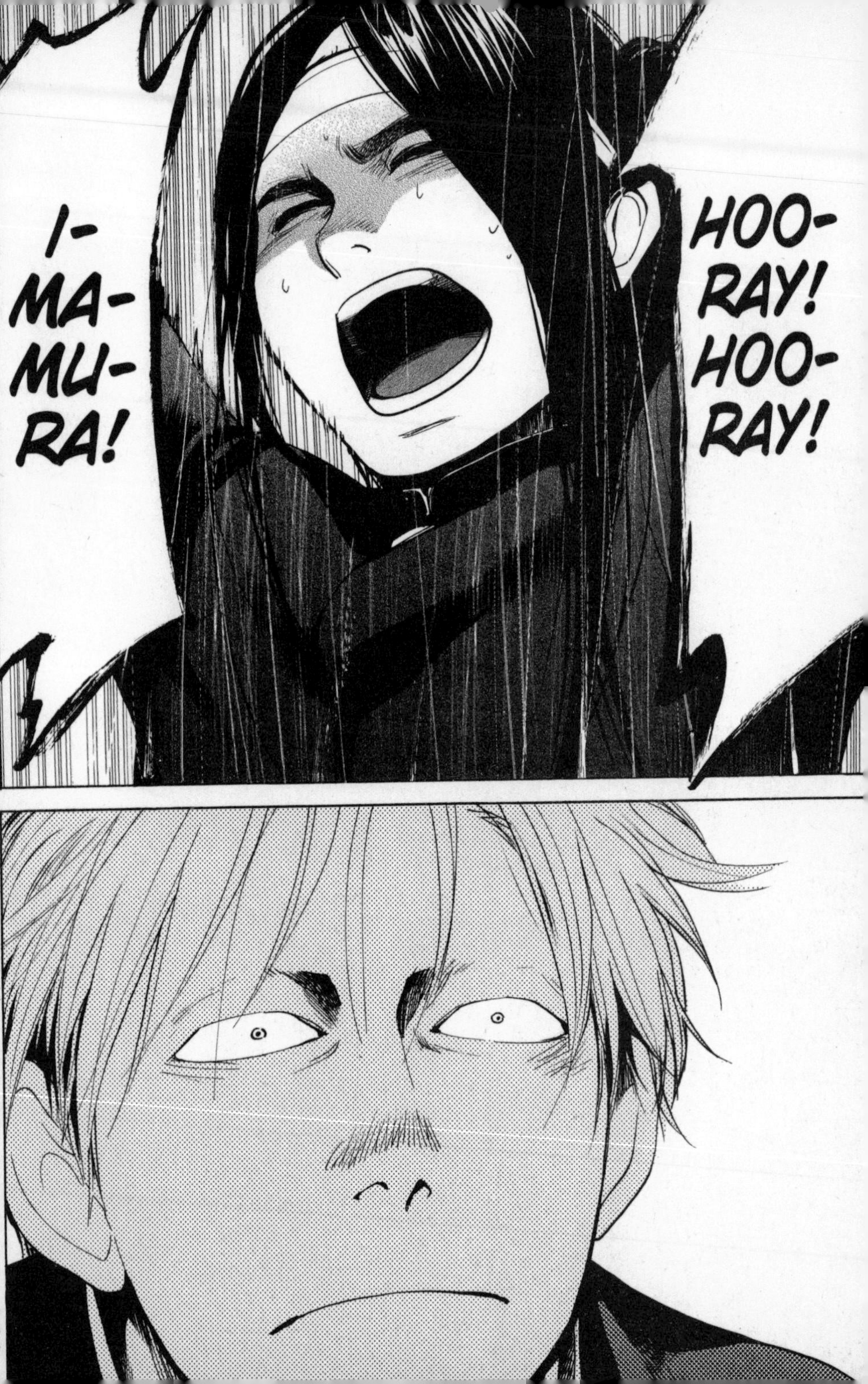
HOO-RAY! HOO-RAY!
I-MAMURA!

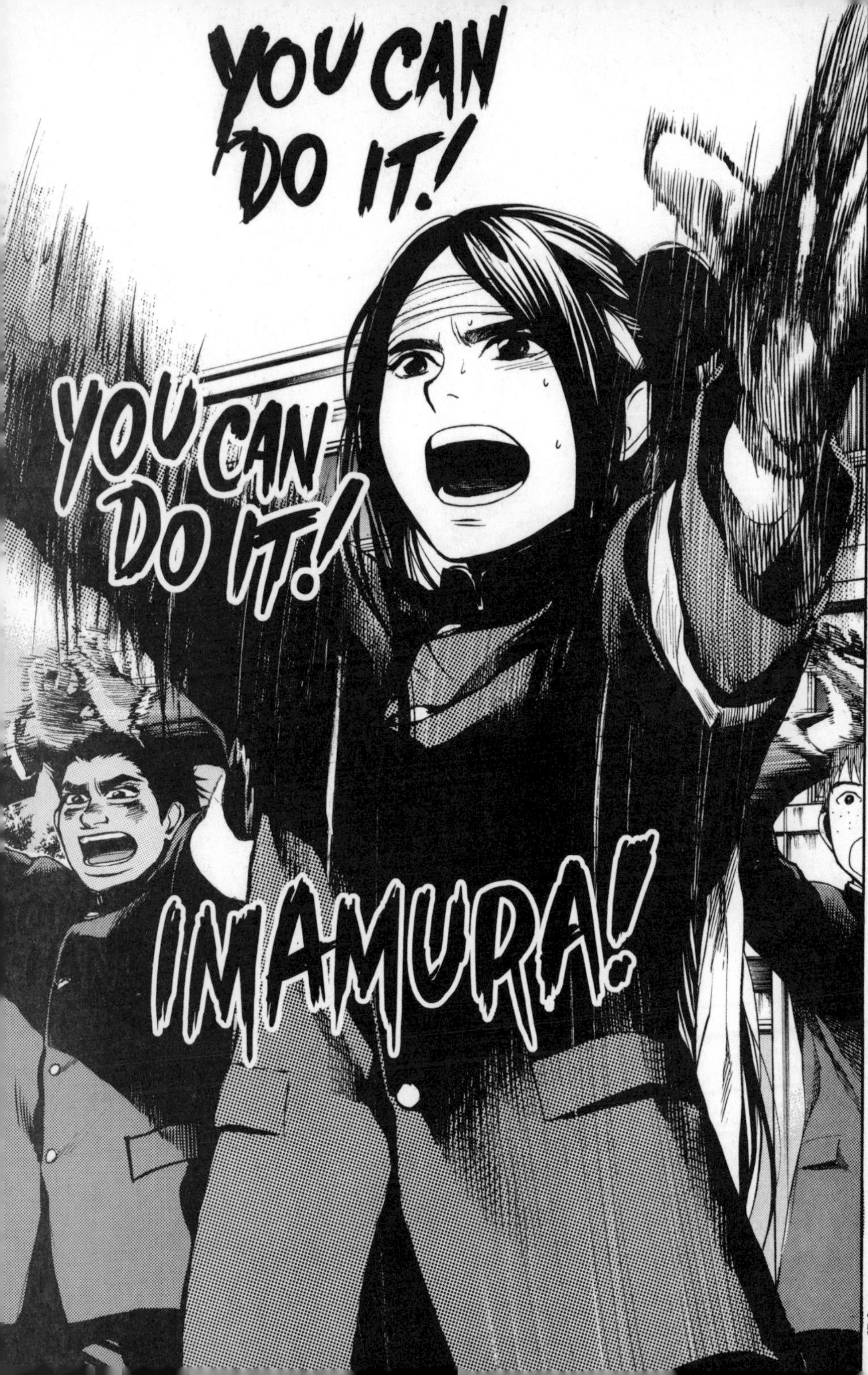
YOU CAN DO IT!
YOU CAN DO IT!
IMAMURA!

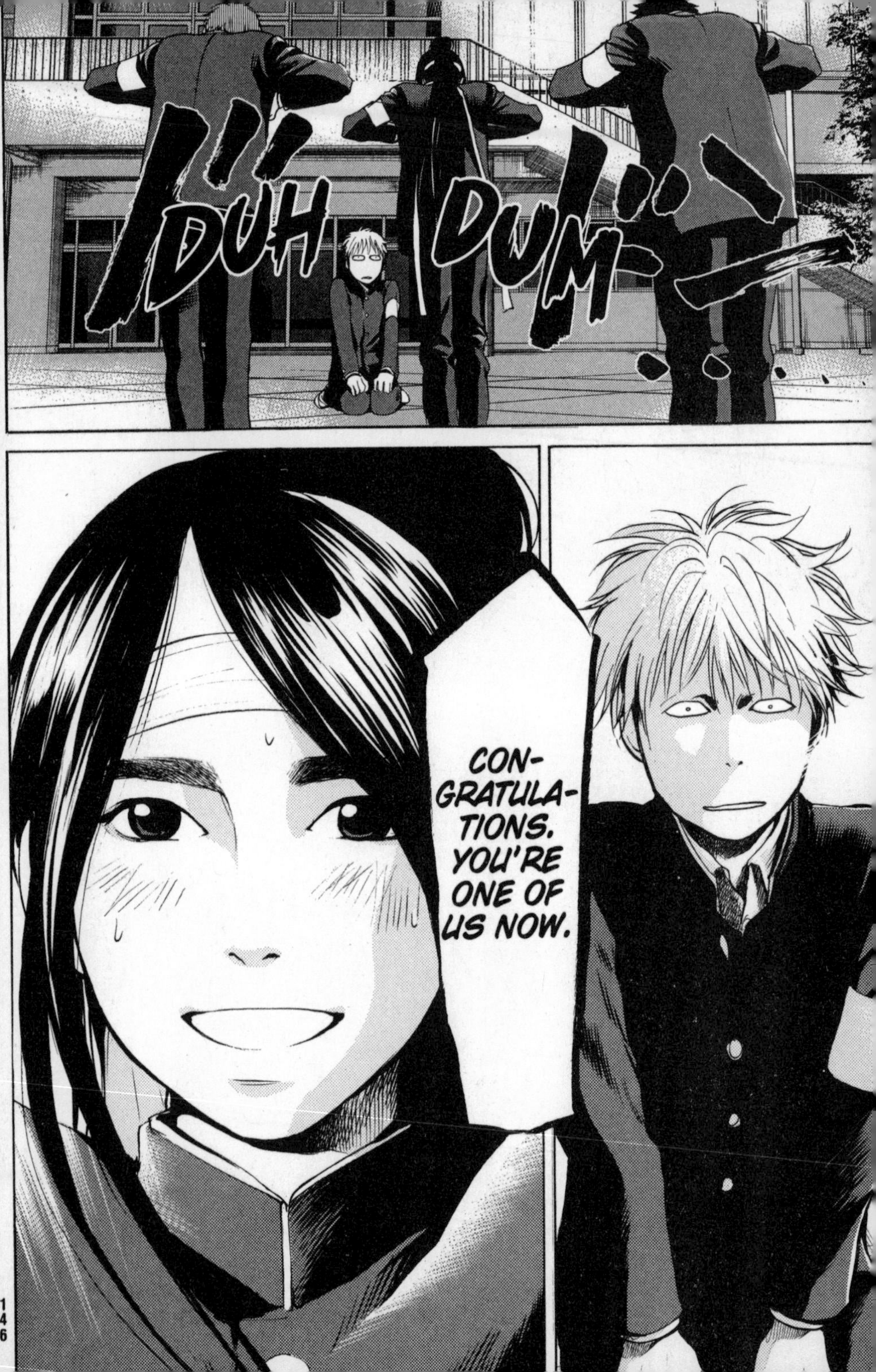
DUH DUM--
CON-GRATULA-TIONS. YOU'RE ONE OF US NOW.

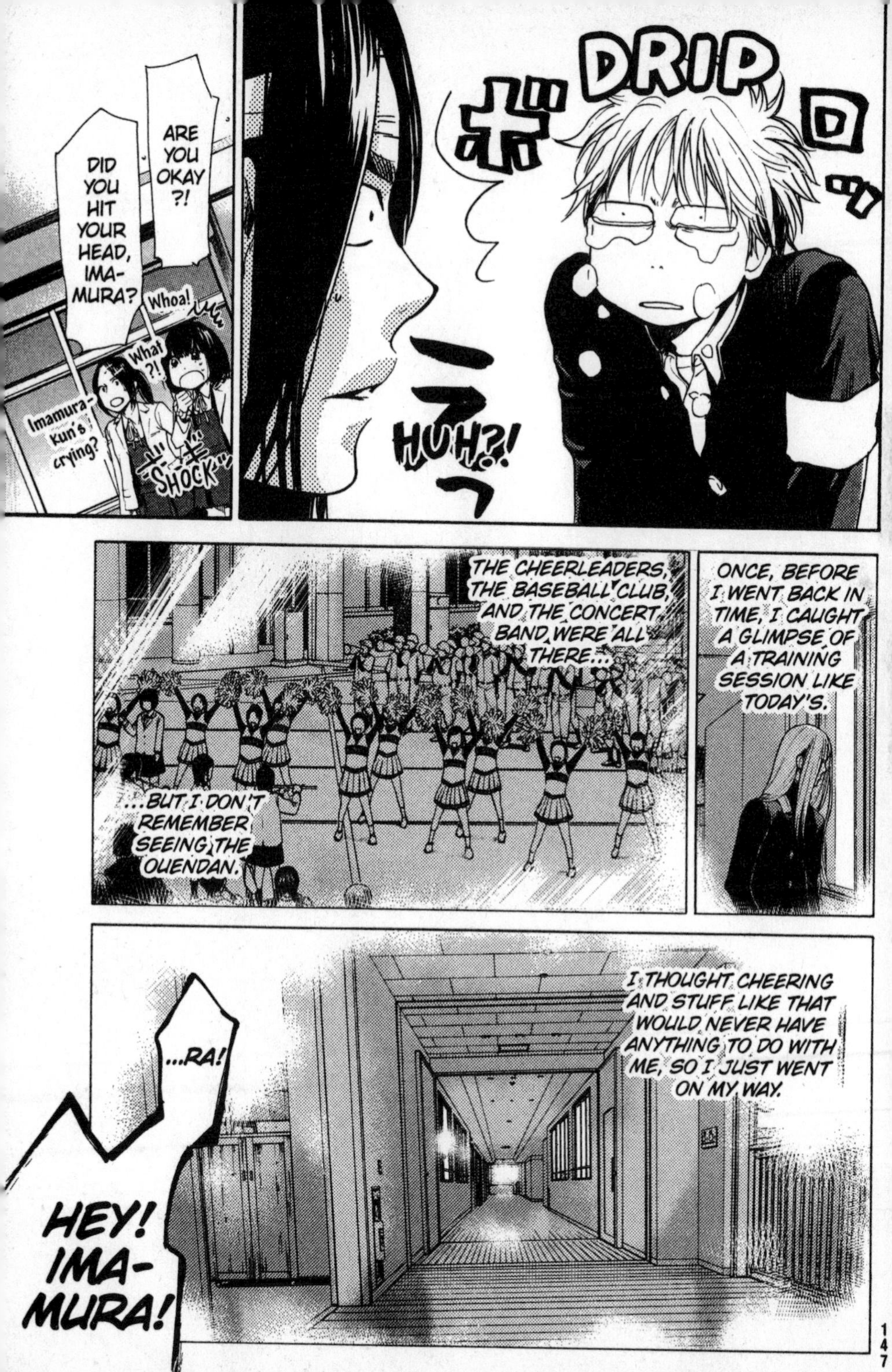

DRIP
HUH?!
ARE YOU OKAY?!
DID YOU HIT YOUR HEAD, IMA-MURA?
Whoa!
What?!
Imamura-kun's crying?
SHOCK
ONCE, BEFORE I WENT BACK IN TIME, I CAUGHT A GLIMPSE OF A TRAINING SESSION LIKE TODAY'S.
THE CHEERLEADERS, THE BASEBALL CLUB, AND THE CONCERT BAND WERE ALL THERE...
...BUT I DON'T REMEMBER SEEING THE OUENDAN.
I THOUGHT CHEERING AND STUFF LIKE THAT WOULD NEVER HAVE ANYTHING TO DO WITH ME, SO I JUST WENT ON MY WAY.
...RA!
HEY! IMA-MURA!

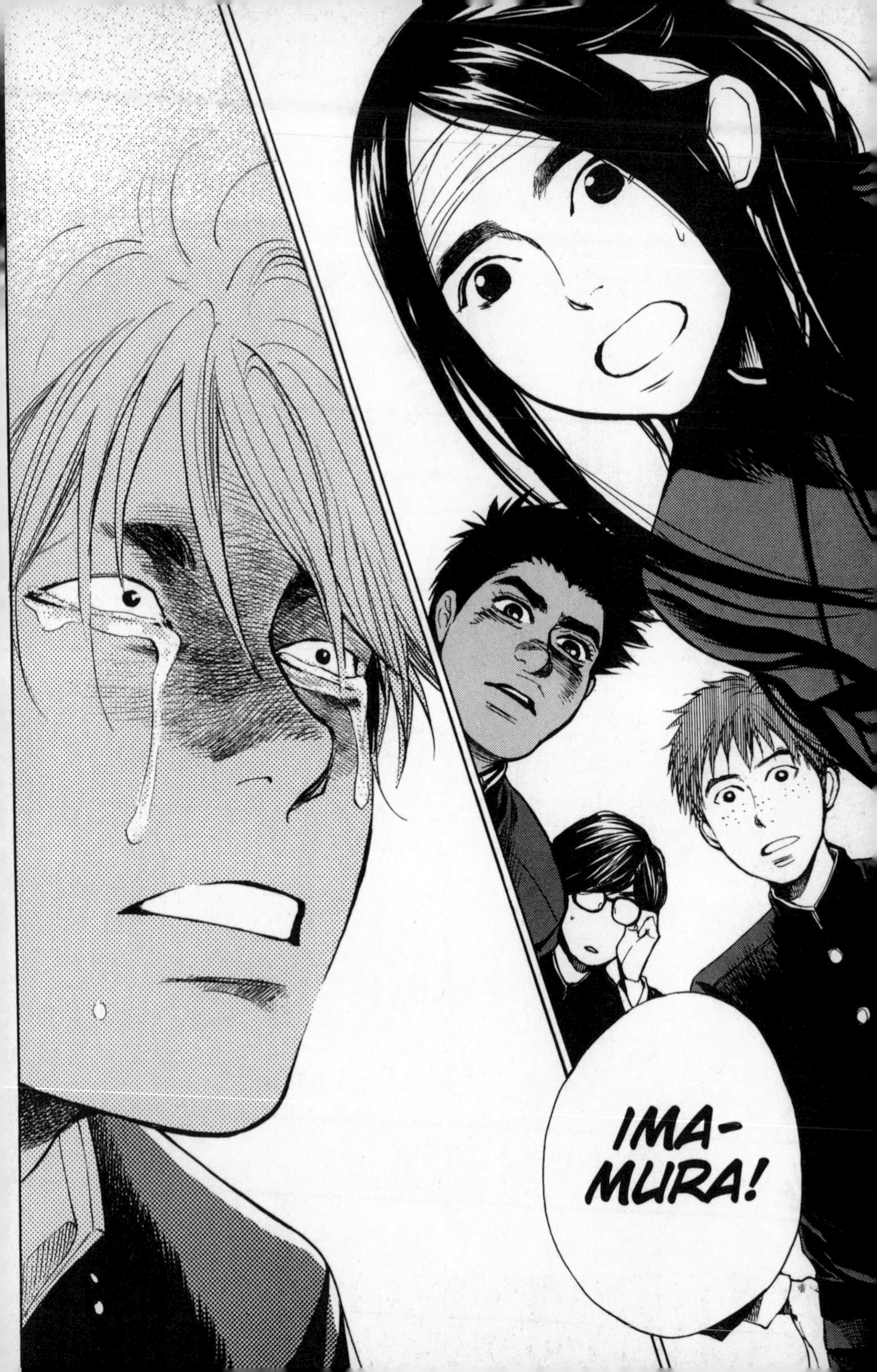
IMA-
MURA!

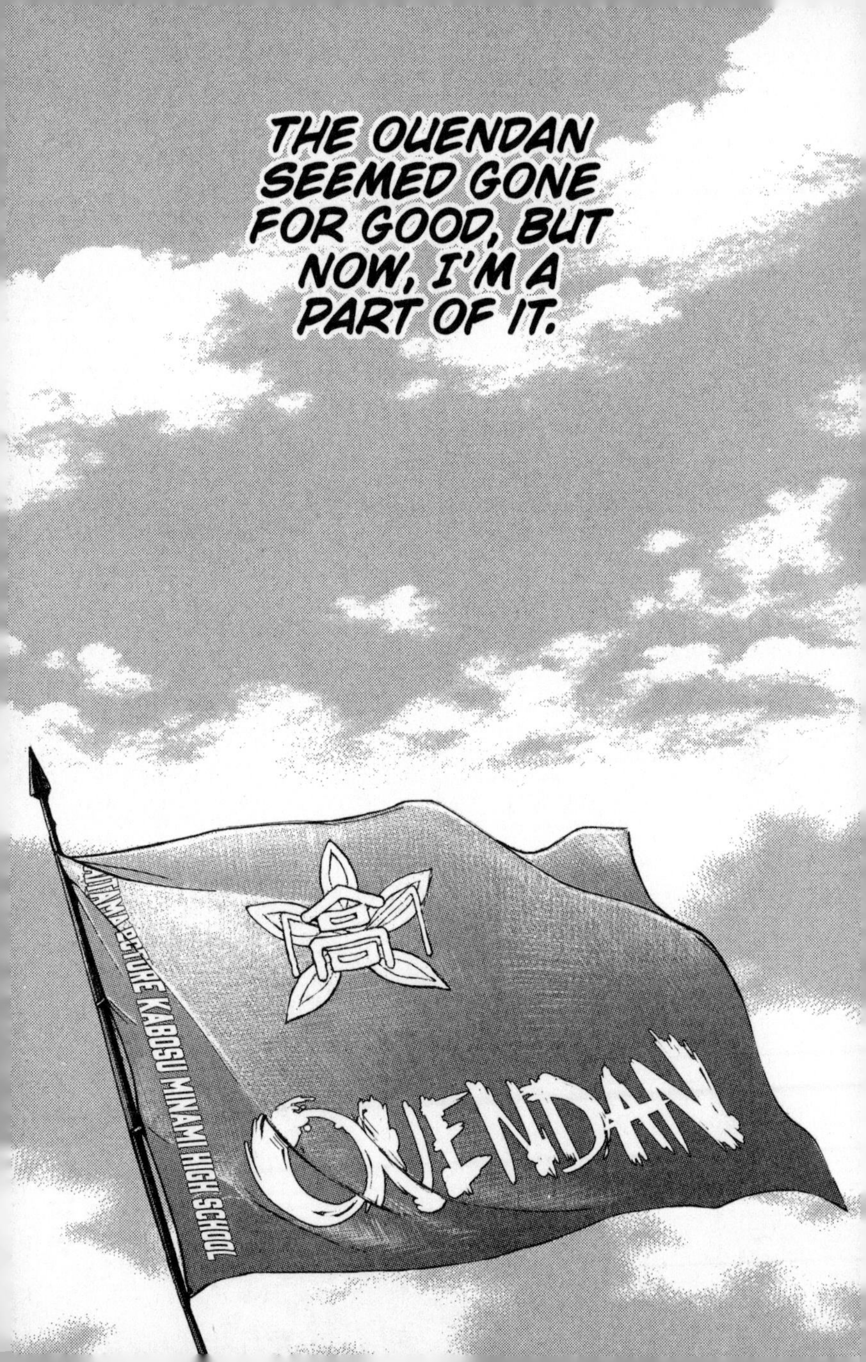
THE OUENDAN SEEMED GONE FOR GOOD, BUT NOW, I'M A PART OF IT.
KABOSU MINAMI HIGH SCHOOL
OUENDAN

Again!!
アゲイン!!

18. THE GIRL WHO DIDN'T WANT TO LEAP THROUGH TIME

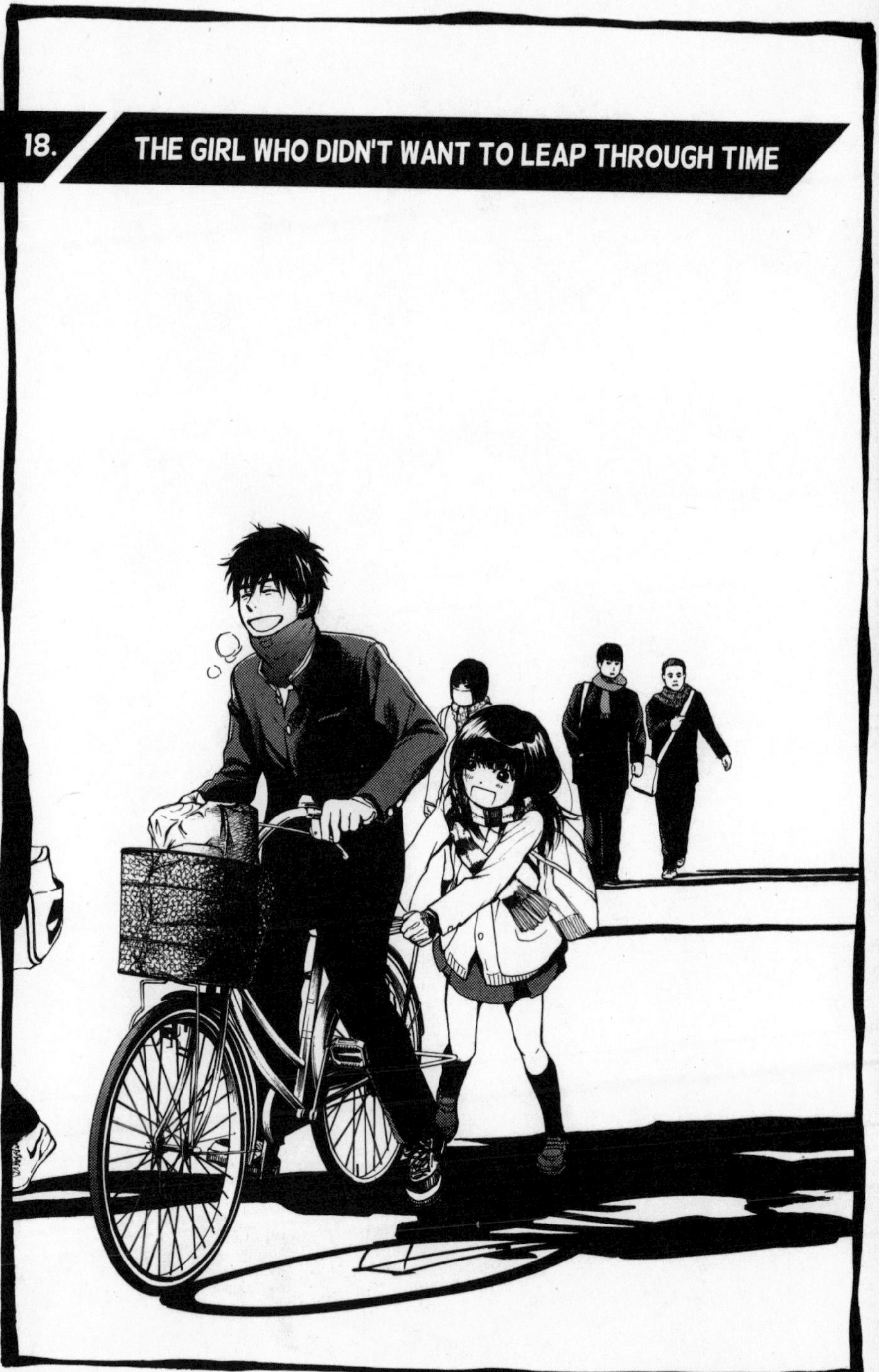

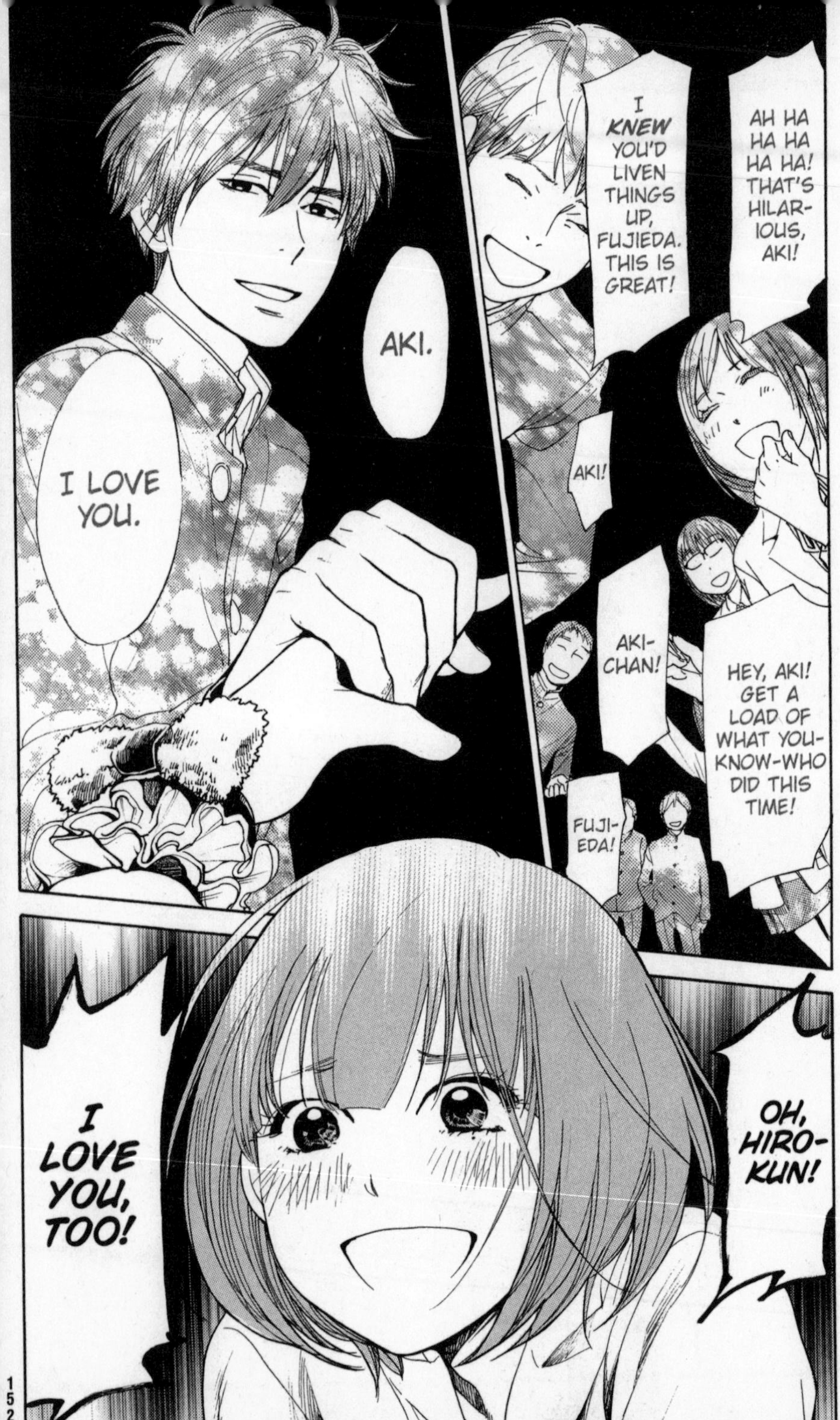
AH HA HA HA HA HA! THAT'S HILAR-IOUS, AKI!
I *KNEW* YOU'D LIVEN THINGS UP, FUJIEDA. THIS IS GREAT!
AKI!
HEY, AKI! GET A LOAD OF WHAT YOU-KNOW-WHO DID THIS TIME!
AKI-CHAN!
FUJI-EDA!
AKI.
I LOVE YOU.
OH, HIRO-KUN!
I LOVE YOU, TOO!

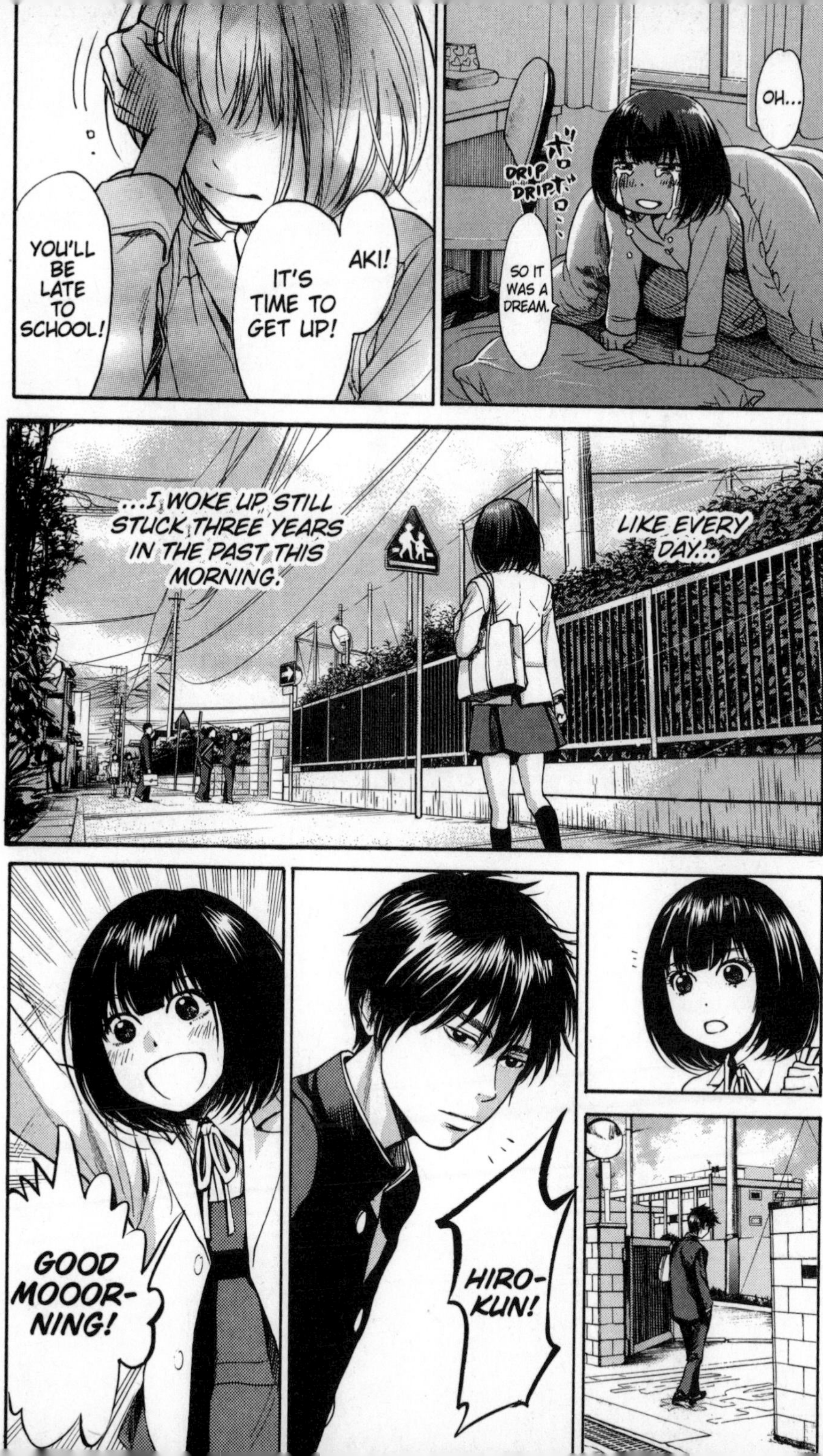
OH...
DRIP DRIP
SO IT WAS A DREAM.
AKI! IT'S TIME TO GET UP!
YOU'LL BE LATE TO SCHOOL!
LIKE EVERY DAY...
...I WOKE UP STILL STUCK THREE YEARS IN THE PAST THIS MORNING.
HIRO-KUN!
GOOD MOOOR-NING!

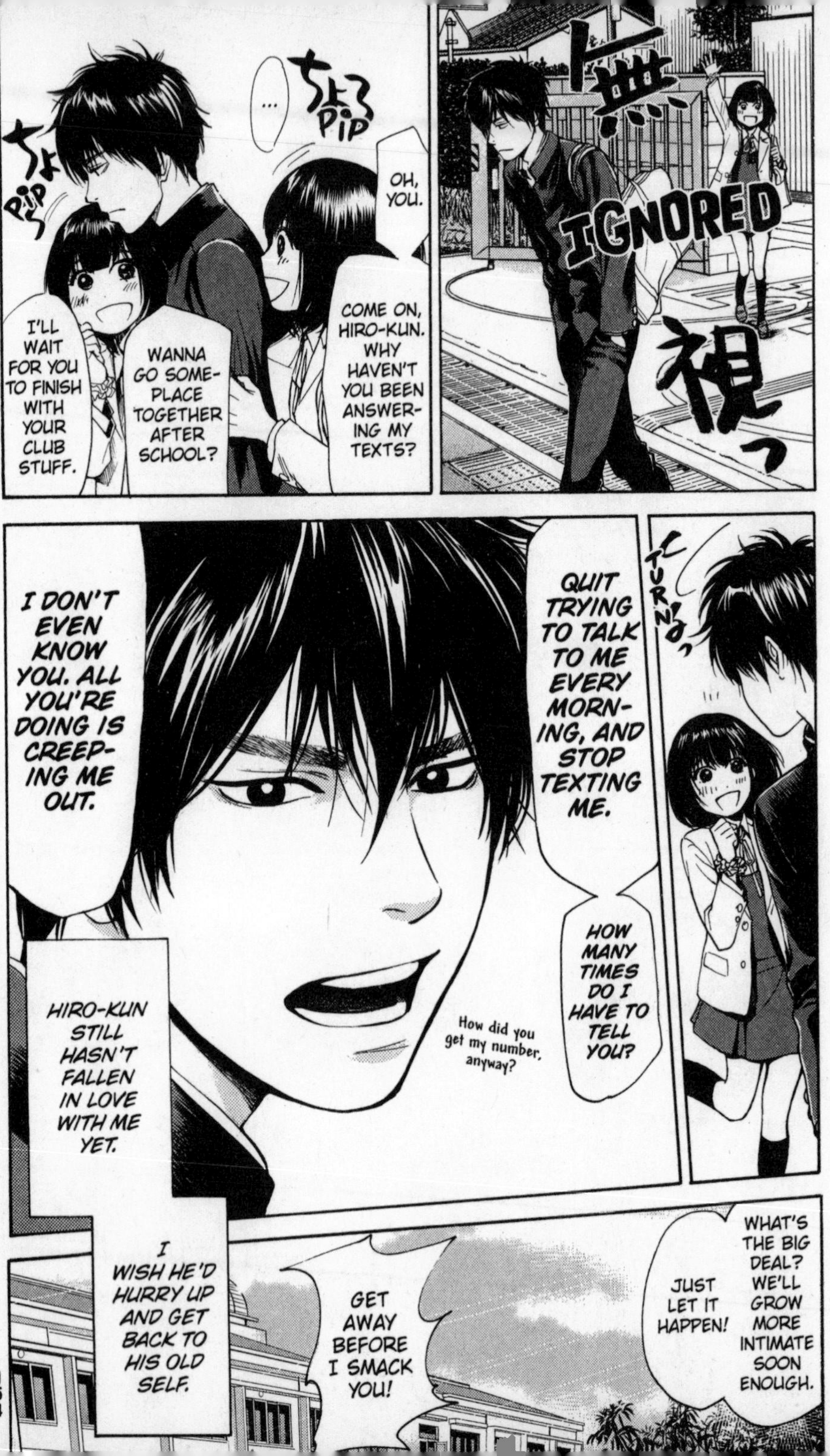

無視っ
IGNORED
...
ちょろ PIP
OH, YOU.
COME ON, HIRO-KUN. WHY HAVEN'T YOU BEEN ANSWERING MY TEXTS?
WANNA GO SOMEPLACE TOGETHER AFTER SCHOOL?
ちょ PIP
I'LL WAIT FOR YOU TO FINISH WITH YOUR CLUB STUFF.
TURN
QUIT TRYING TO TALK TO ME EVERY MORNING, AND STOP TEXTING ME.
HOW MANY TIMES DO I HAVE TO TELL YOU?
How did you get my number, anyway?
I DON'T EVEN KNOW YOU. ALL YOU'RE DOING IS CREEPING ME OUT.
HIRO-KUN STILL HASN'T FALLEN IN LOVE WITH ME YET.
WHAT'S THE BIG DEAL? WE'LL GROW MORE INTIMATE SOON ENOUGH.
JUST LET IT HAPPEN!
GET AWAY BEFORE I SMACK YOU!
I WISH HE'D HURRY UP AND GET BACK TO HIS OLD SELF.

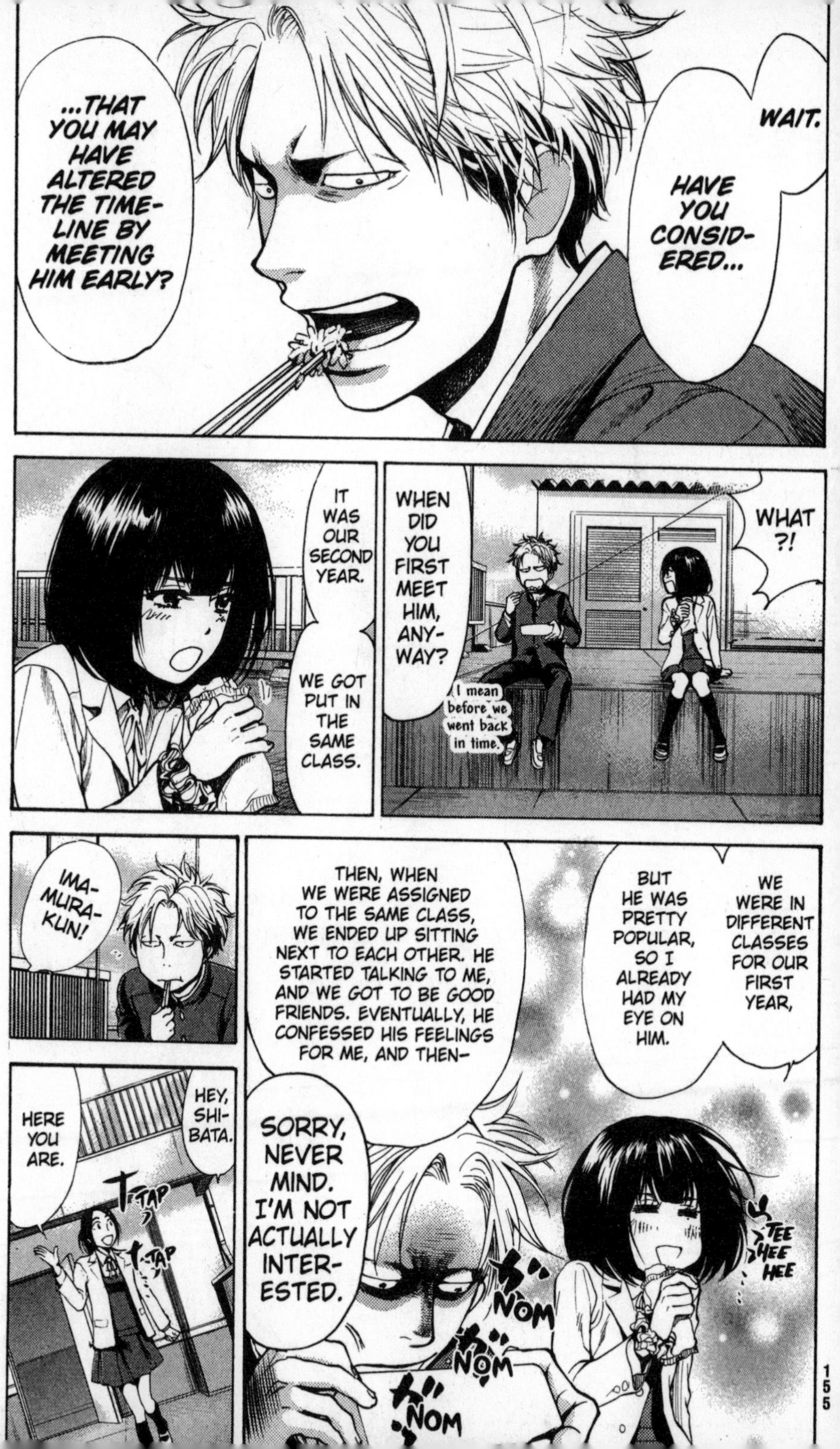
WAIT.
HAVE YOU CONSIDERED...
...THAT YOU MAY HAVE ALTERED THE TIMELINE BY MEETING HIM EARLY?
WHAT?!
WHEN DID YOU FIRST MEET HIM, ANYWAY?
I mean before we went back in time.
IT WAS OUR SECOND YEAR.
WE GOT PUT IN THE SAME CLASS.
WE WERE IN DIFFERENT CLASSES FOR OUR FIRST YEAR,
BUT HE WAS PRETTY POPULAR, SO I ALREADY HAD MY EYE ON HIM.
THEN, WHEN WE WERE ASSIGNED TO THE SAME CLASS, WE ENDED UP SITTING NEXT TO EACH OTHER. HE STARTED TALKING TO ME, AND WE GOT TO BE GOOD FRIENDS. EVENTUALLY, HE CONFESSED HIS FEELINGS FOR ME, AND THEN–
TEE HEE HEE
SORRY, NEVER MIND. I'M NOT ACTUALLY INTERESTED.
NOM
NOM
NOM
IMAMURA-KUN!
HEY, SHIBATA.
HERE YOU ARE.
TAP
TAP

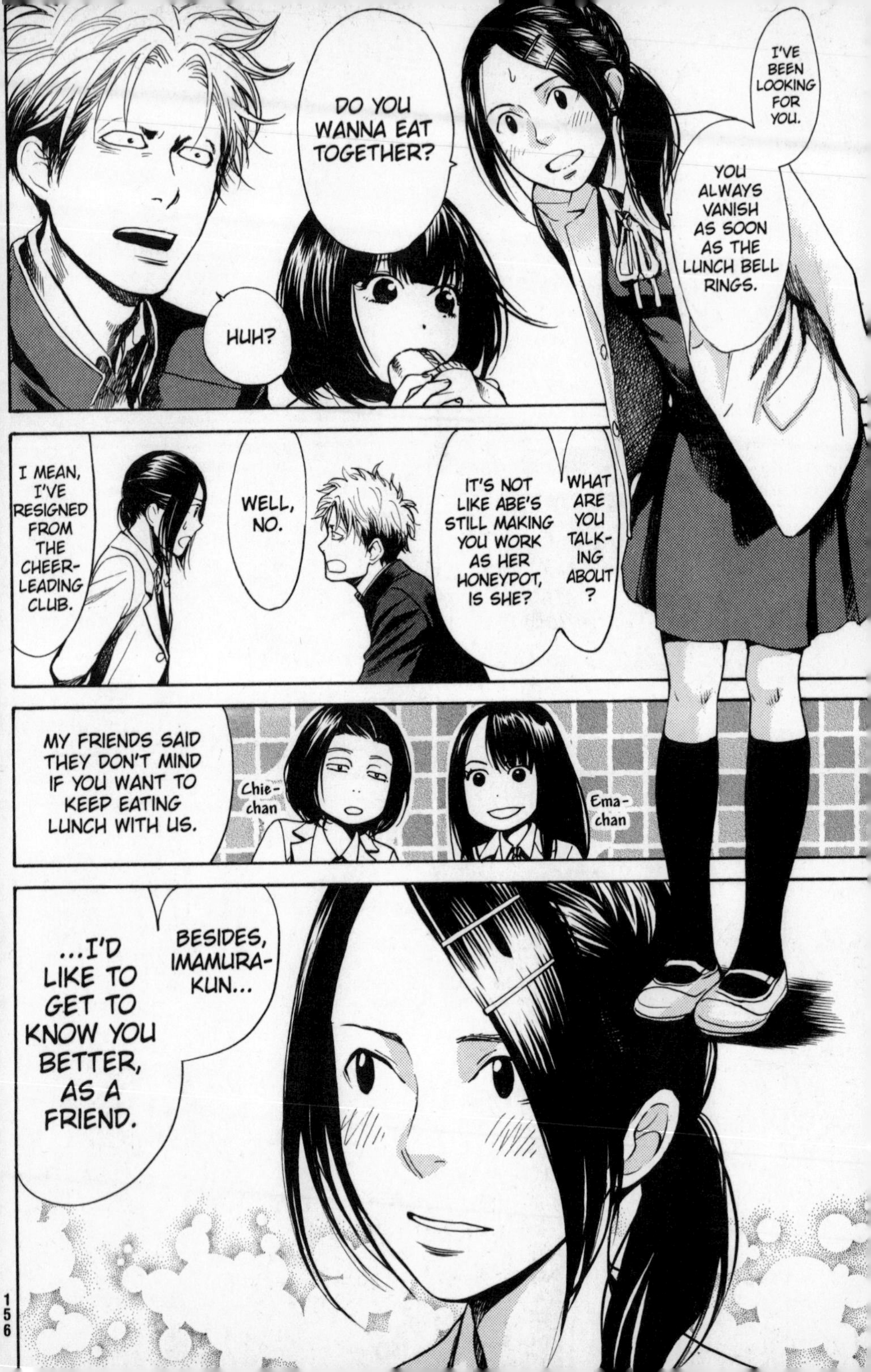
I'VE BEEN LOOKING FOR YOU.
YOU ALWAYS VANISH AS SOON AS THE LUNCH BELL RINGS.
DO YOU WANNA EAT TOGETHER?
HUH?
WHAT ARE YOU TALKING ABOUT?
IT'S NOT LIKE ABE'S STILL MAKING YOU WORK AS HER HONEYPOT, IS SHE?
WELL, NO.
I MEAN, I'VE RESIGNED FROM THE CHEER-LEADING CLUB.
MY FRIENDS SAID THEY DON'T MIND IF YOU WANT TO KEEP EATING LUNCH WITH US.
Ema-chan
Chie-chan
BESIDES, IMAMURA-KUN...
...I'D LIKE TO GET TO KNOW YOU BETTER, AS A FRIEND.

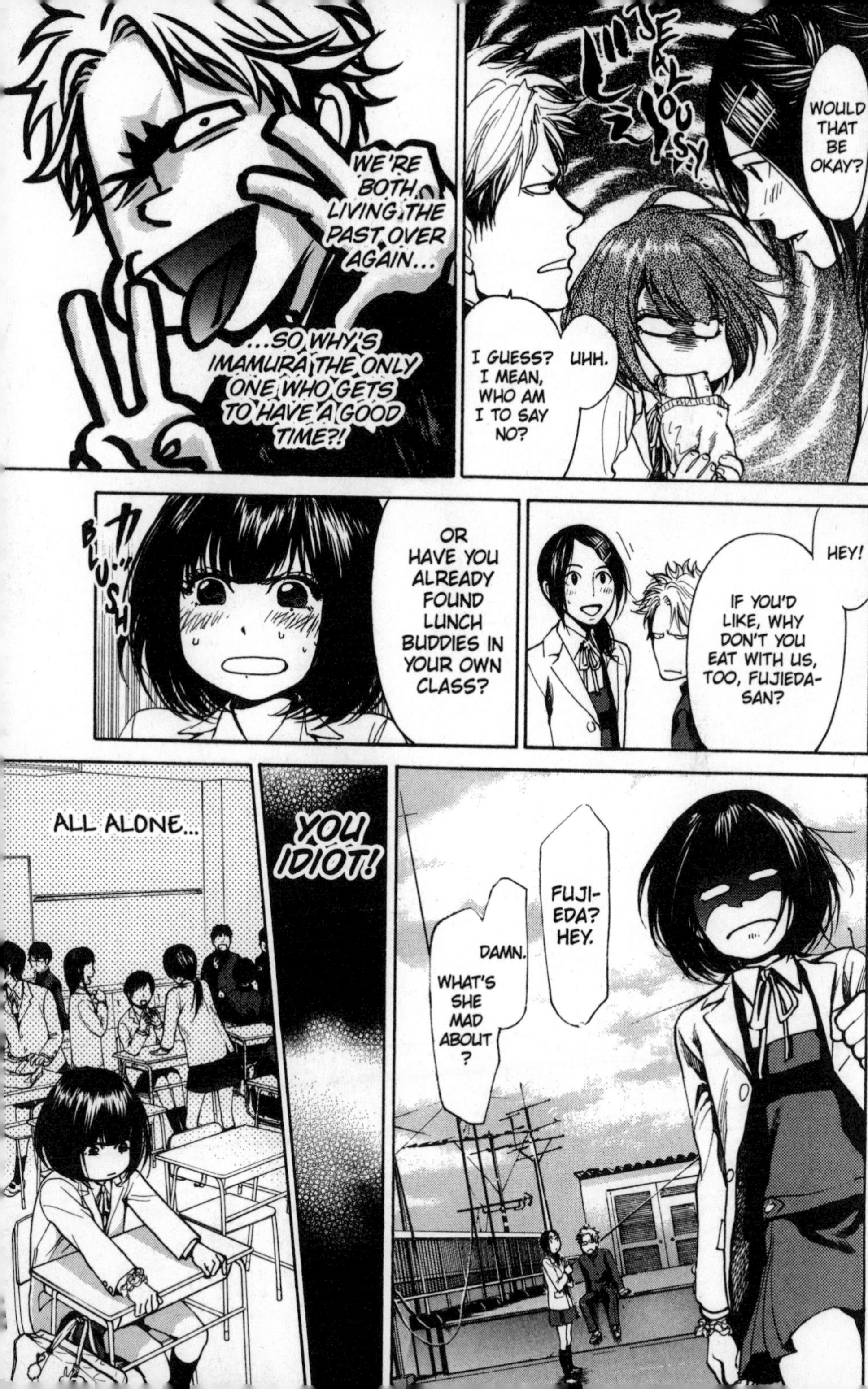
JEALOUSY
WOULD THAT BE OKAY?
UHH.
I GUESS? I MEAN, WHO AM I TO SAY NO?
WE'RE BOTH LIVING THE PAST OVER AGAIN...
...SO WHY'S IMAMURA THE ONLY ONE WHO GETS TO HAVE A GOOD TIME?!
HEY!
IF YOU'D LIKE, WHY DON'T YOU EAT WITH US, TOO, FUJIEDA-SAN?
OR HAVE YOU ALREADY FOUND LUNCH BUDDIES IN YOUR OWN CLASS?
BLUSH
FUJI-EDA? HEY.
DAMN. WHAT'S SHE MAD ABOUT?
YOU IDIOT!
ALL ALONE...

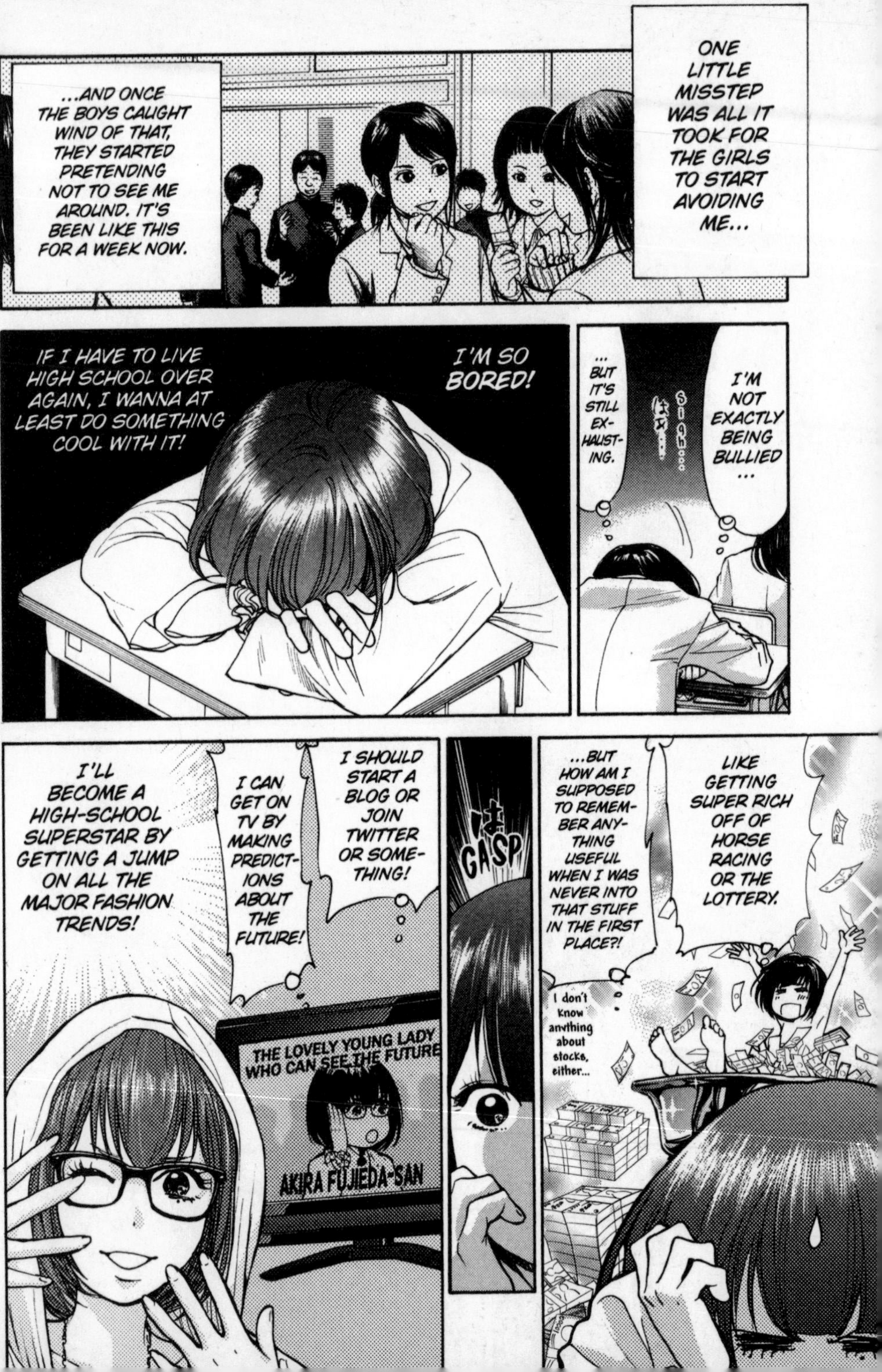
ONE LITTLE MISSTEP WAS ALL IT TOOK FOR THE GIRLS TO START AVOIDING ME...
...AND ONCE THE BOYS CAUGHT WIND OF THAT, THEY STARTED PRETENDING NOT TO SEE ME AROUND. IT'S BEEN LIKE THIS FOR A WEEK NOW.
I'M NOT EXACTLY BEING BULLIED...
Sigh...
...BUT IT'S STILL EX-HAUST-ING.
I'M SO BORED!
IF I HAVE TO LIVE HIGH SCHOOL OVER AGAIN, I WANNA AT LEAST DO SOMETHING COOL WITH IT!
LIKE GETTING SUPER RICH OFF OF HORSE RACING OR THE LOTTERY.
...BUT HOW AM I SUPPOSED TO REMEM-BER ANY-THING USEFUL WHEN I WAS NEVER INTO THAT STUFF IN THE FIRST PLACE?!
I don't know anything about stocks, either...
GASP
I SHOULD START A BLOG OR JOIN TWITTER OR SOME-THING!
I CAN GET ON TV BY MAKING PREDICT-IONS ABOUT THE FUTURE!
THE LOVELY YOUNG LADY WHO CAN SEE THE FUTURE
AKIRA FUJIEDA-SAN
I'LL BECOME A HIGH-SCHOOL SUPERSTAR BY GETTING A JUMP ON ALL THE MAJOR FASHION TRENDS!

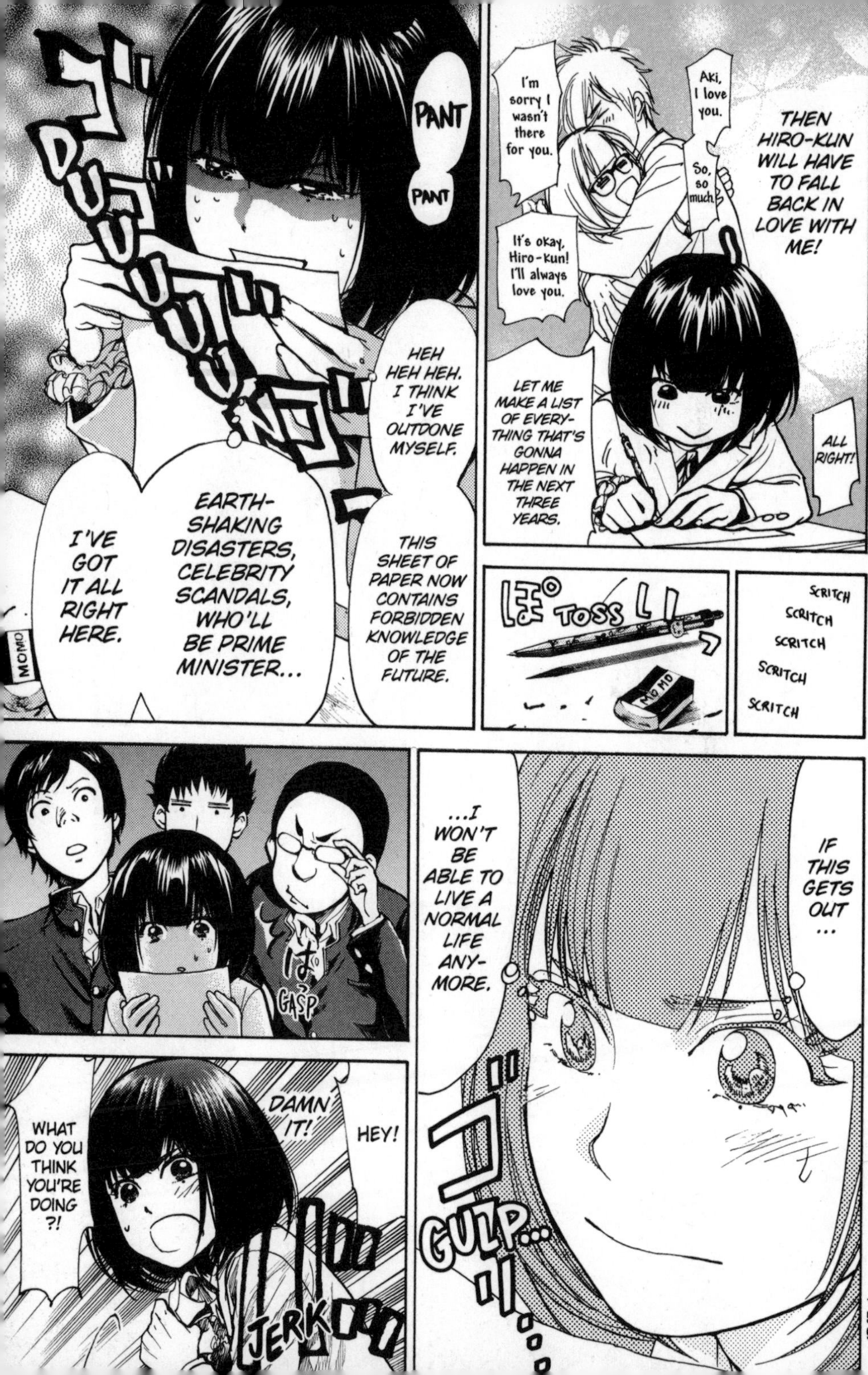
THEN HIRO-KUN WILL HAVE TO FALL BACK IN LOVE WITH ME!
Aki, I love you.
So, so much.
I'm sorry I wasn't there for you.
It's okay, Hiro-kun! I'll always love you.
ALL RIGHT!
LET ME MAKE A LIST OF EVERYTHING THAT'S GONNA HAPPEN IN THE NEXT THREE YEARS.
SCRITCH
SCRITCH
SCRITCH
SCRITCH
SCRITCH
TOSS
MOMO
PANT
PANT
DUUUUUN
HEH HEH HEH. I THINK I'VE OUTDONE MYSELF.
THIS SHEET OF PAPER NOW CONTAINS FORBIDDEN KNOWLEDGE OF THE FUTURE.
EARTH-SHAKING DISASTERS, CELEBRITY SCANDALS, WHO'LL BE PRIME MINISTER...
I'VE GOT IT ALL RIGHT HERE.
MOMO
IF THIS GETS OUT...
...I WON'T BE ABLE TO LIVE A NORMAL LIFE ANYMORE.
GULP...
GASP
HEY!
DAMN IT!
WHAT DO YOU THINK YOU'RE DOING?!
JERK

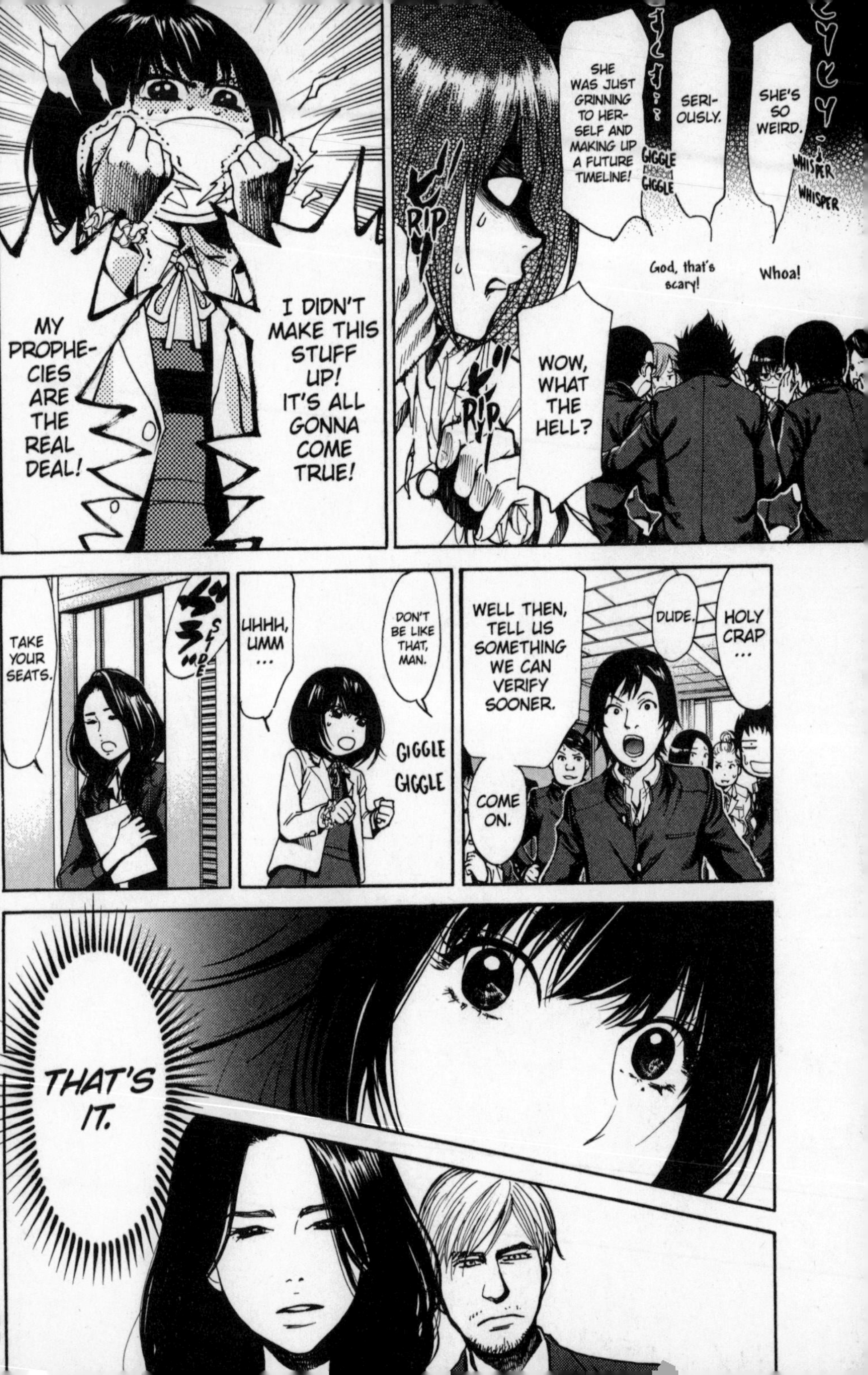
SHE'S SO WEIRD.
WHISPER WHISPER
SERI-OUSLY.
SHE WAS JUST GRINNING TO HER-SELF AND MAKING UP A FUTURE TIMELINE!
GIGGLE GIGGLE
Whoa!
God, that's scary!
RIP
RIP
WOW, WHAT THE HELL?
I DIDN'T MAKE THIS STUFF UP! IT'S ALL GONNA COME TRUE!
MY PROPHE-CIES ARE THE REAL DEAL!
HOLY CRAP...
DUDE.
WELL THEN, TELL US SOMETHING WE CAN VERIFY SOONER.
COME ON.
DON'T BE LIKE THAT, MAN.
UHHH, UMM...
GIGGLE
GIGGLE
SLIDE
TAKE YOUR SEATS.
THAT'S IT.

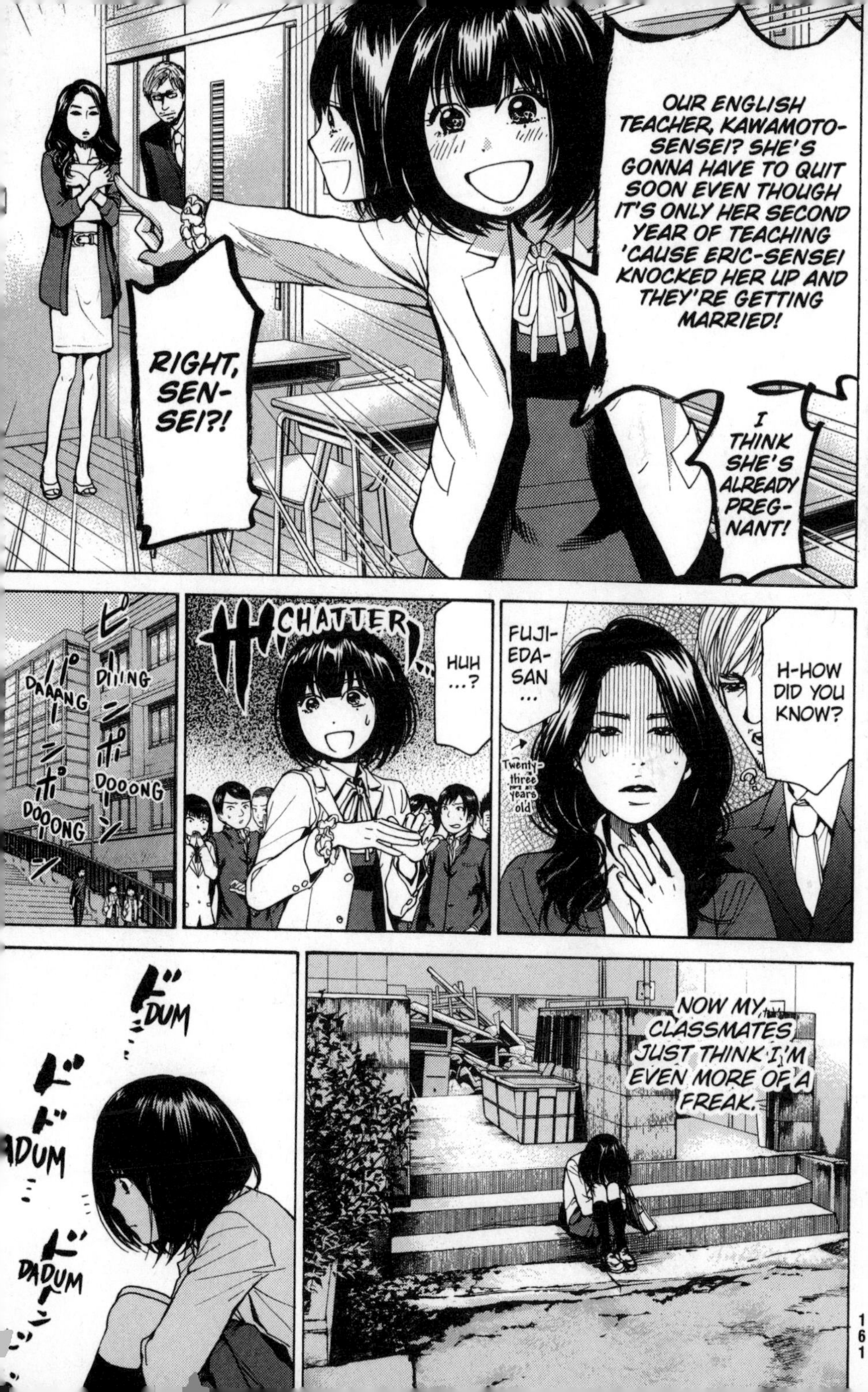
OUR ENGLISH TEACHER, KAWAMOTO-SENSEI? SHE'S GONNA HAVE TO QUIT SOON EVEN THOUGH IT'S ONLY HER SECOND YEAR OF TEACHING 'CAUSE ERIC-SENSEI KNOCKED HER UP AND THEY'RE GETTING MARRIED!
I THINK SHE'S ALREADY PREG-NANT!
RIGHT, SEN-SEI?!
H-HOW DID YOU KNOW?
FUJI-EDA-SAN ...
Twenty-three years old
HUH ...?
CHATTER
DIIING
DAAANG
DOOONG
DOOONG
NOW MY CLASSMATES JUST THINK I'M EVEN MORE OF A FREAK.
DUM
DADUM
DADUM

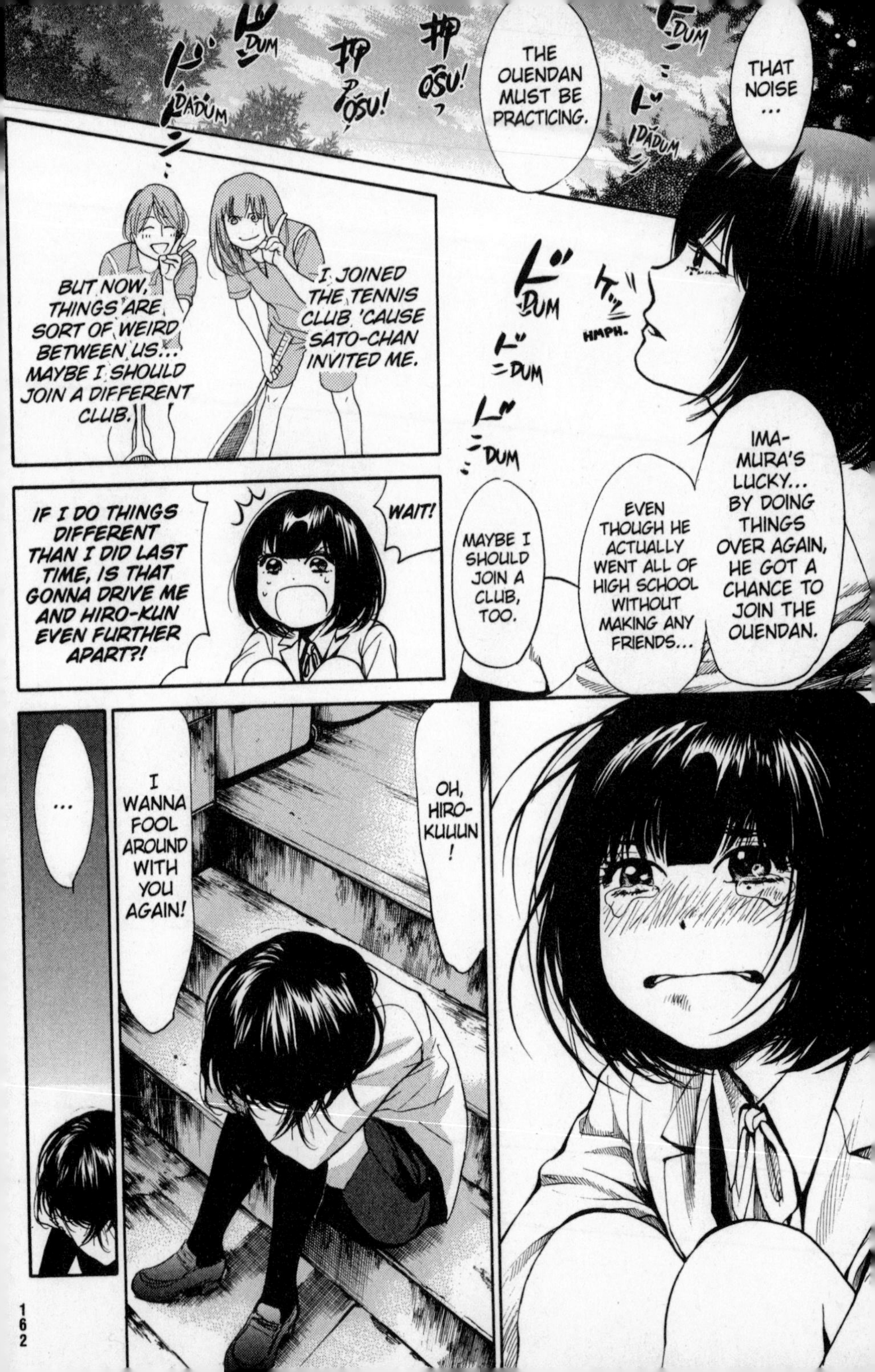
DUM
DADUM
THAT NOISE...
THE OUENDAN MUST BE PRACTICING.
OSU!
OSU!
DUM
DADUM
HMPH.
DUM
DUM
DUM
IMA-MURA'S LUCKY... BY DOING THINGS OVER AGAIN, HE GOT A CHANCE TO JOIN THE OUENDAN.
EVEN THOUGH HE ACTUALLY WENT ALL OF HIGH SCHOOL WITHOUT MAKING ANY FRIENDS...
MAYBE I SHOULD JOIN A CLUB, TOO.
I JOINED THE TENNIS CLUB 'CAUSE SATO-CHAN INVITED ME.
BUT NOW, THINGS ARE SORT OF WEIRD BETWEEN US... MAYBE I SHOULD JOIN A DIFFERENT CLUB.
WAIT!
IF I DO THINGS DIFFERENT THAN I DID LAST TIME, IS THAT GONNA DRIVE ME AND HIRO-KUN EVEN FURTHER APART?!
OH, HIRO-KUUUN!
I WANNA FOOL AROUND WITH YOU AGAIN!
...

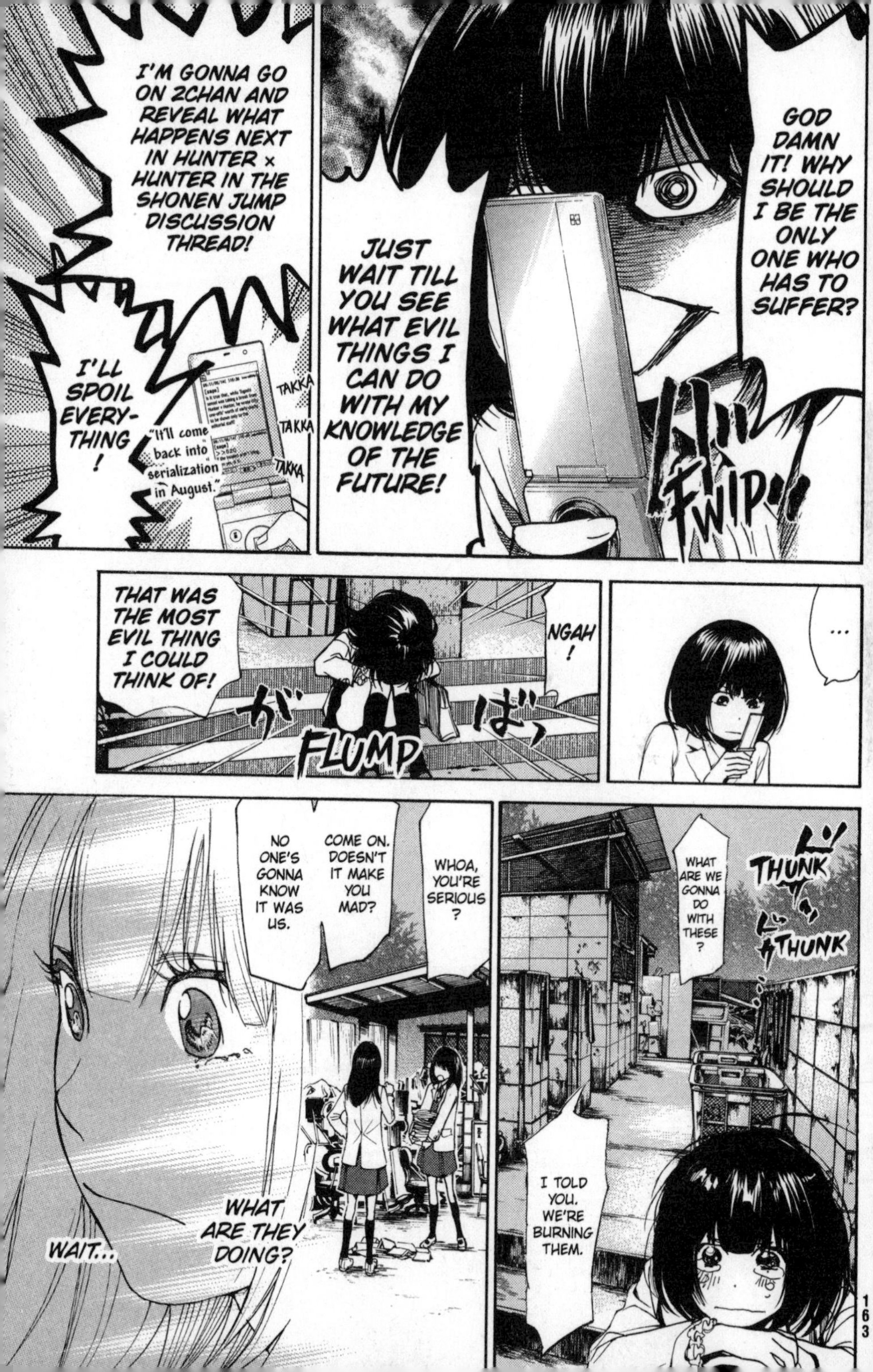
GOD DAMN IT! WHY SHOULD I BE THE ONLY ONE WHO HAS TO SUFFER?
JUST WAIT TILL YOU SEE WHAT EVIL THINGS I CAN DO WITH MY KNOWLEDGE OF THE FUTURE!
FWIP
I'M GONNA GO ON 2CHAN AND REVEAL WHAT HAPPENS NEXT IN HUNTER × HUNTER IN THE SHONEN JUMP DISCUSSION THREAD!
TAKKA
TAKKA
TAKKA
"It'll come back into serialization in August."
I'LL SPOIL EVERYTHING!
...
NGAH!
THAT WAS THE MOST EVIL THING I COULD THINK OF!
FLUMP
THUNK
THUNK
WHAT ARE WE GONNA DO WITH THESE?
I TOLD YOU. WE'RE BURNING THEM.
WHOA, YOU'RE SERIOUS?
COME ON. DOESN'T IT MAKE YOU MAD?
NO ONE'S GONNA KNOW IT WAS US.
WHAT ARE THEY DOING?
WAIT...

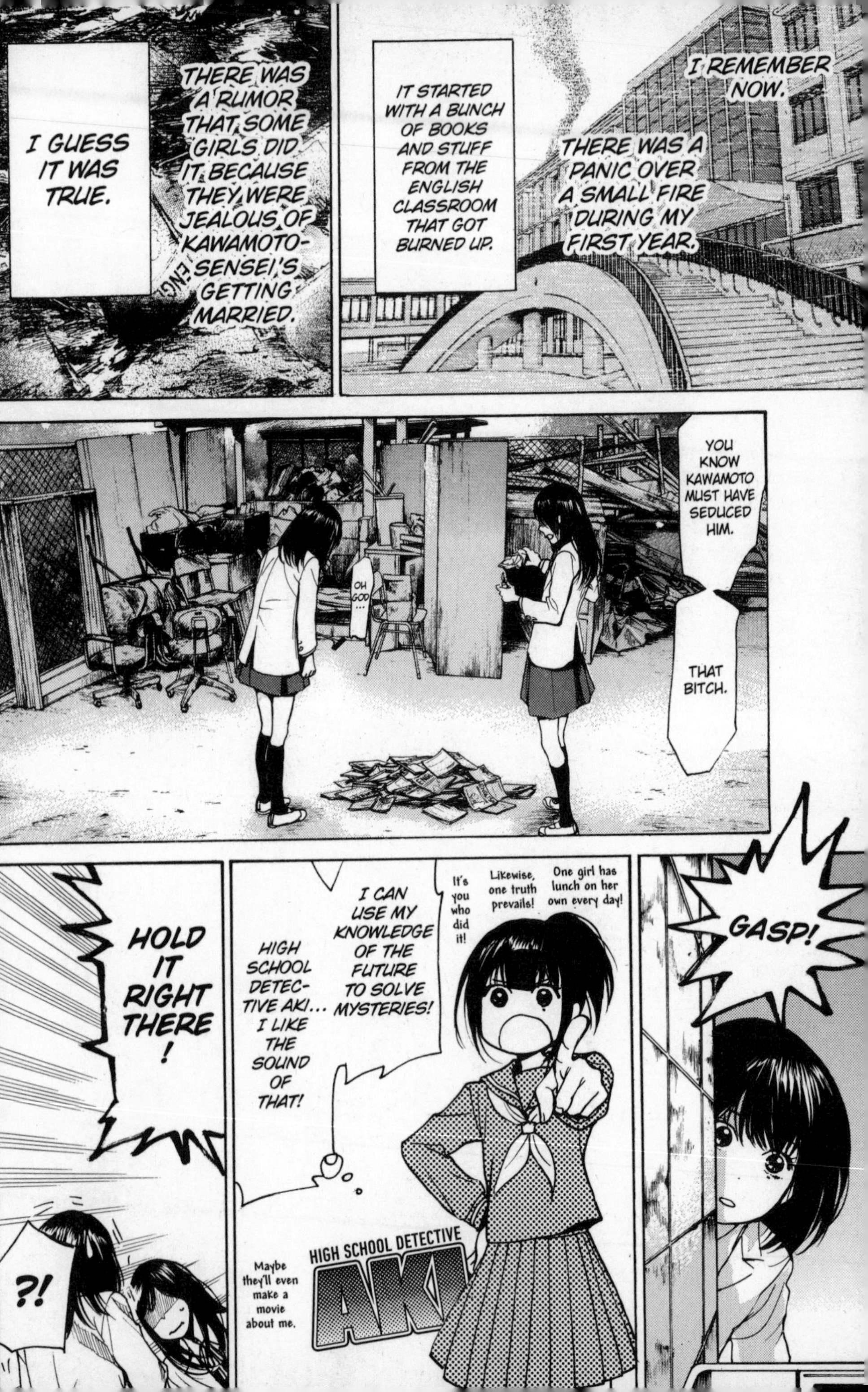
I REMEMBER NOW.
THERE WAS A PANIC OVER A SMALL FIRE DURING MY FIRST YEAR.
IT STARTED WITH A BUNCH OF BOOKS AND STUFF FROM THE ENGLISH CLASSROOM THAT GOT BURNED UP.
THERE WAS A RUMOR THAT SOME GIRLS DID IT BECAUSE THEY WERE JEALOUS OF KAWAMOTO-SENSEI'S GETTING MARRIED.
ENG
I GUESS IT WAS TRUE.
YOU KNOW KAWAMOTO MUST HAVE SEDUCED HIM.
THAT BITCH.
OH GOD...
GASP!
One girl has lunch on her own every day!
Likewise, one truth prevails!
It's you who did it!
I CAN USE MY KNOWLEDGE OF THE FUTURE TO SOLVE MYSTERIES!
HIGH SCHOOL DETECTIVE AKI... I LIKE THE SOUND OF THAT!
HIGH SCHOOL DETECTIVE AKI
Maybe they'll even make a movie about me.
HOLD IT RIGHT THERE!
?!

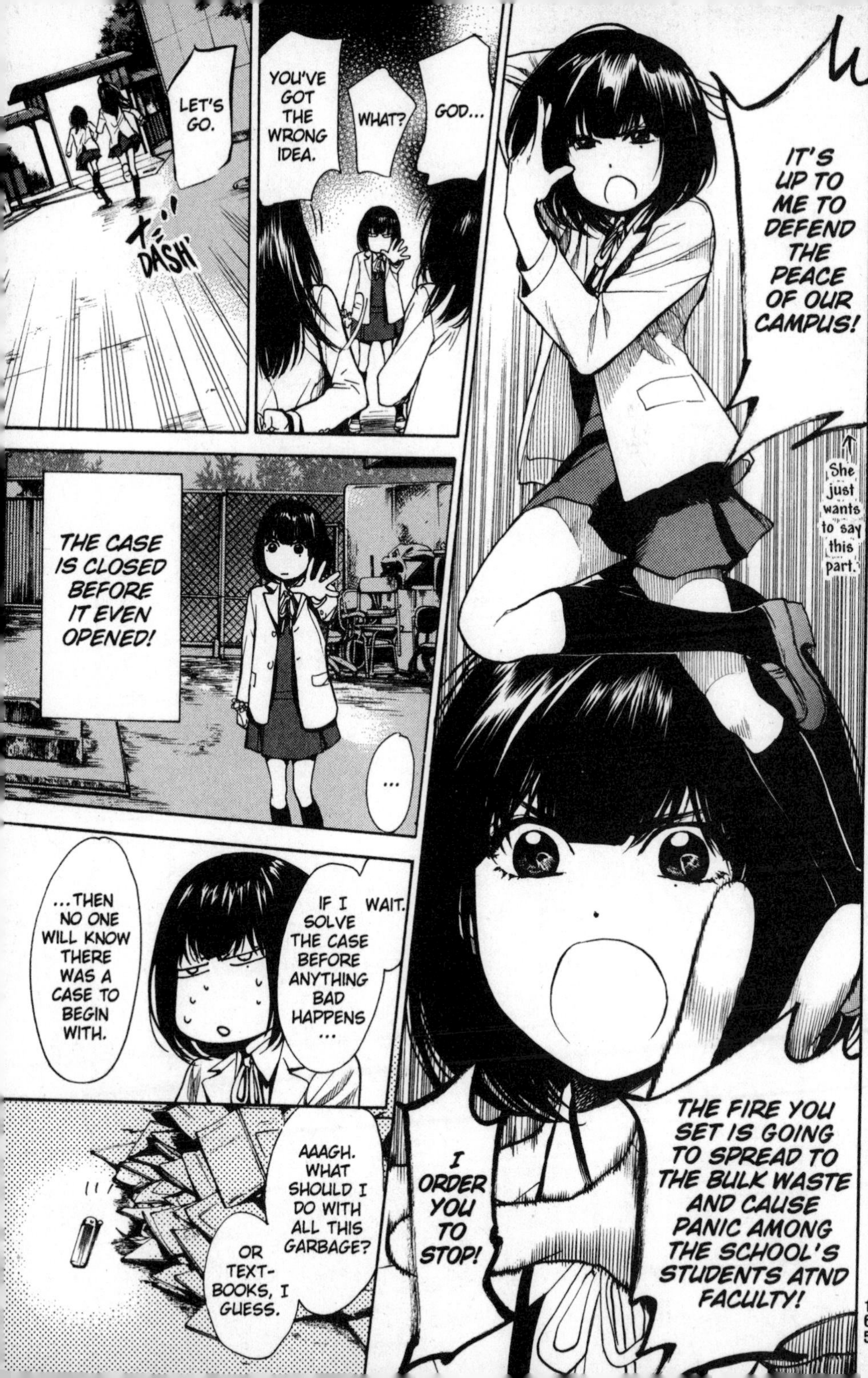

IT'S UP TO ME TO DEFEND THE PEACE OF OUR CAMPUS!
She just wants to say this part.
THE FIRE YOU SET IS GOING TO SPREAD TO THE BULK WASTE AND CAUSE PANIC AMONG THE SCHOOL'S STUDENTS ATND FACULTY!
I ORDER YOU TO STOP!
GOD...
WHAT?
YOU'VE GOT THE WRONG IDEA.
LET'S GO.
DASH
THE CASE IS CLOSED BEFORE IT EVEN OPENED!
...
WAIT.
IF I SOLVE THE CASE BEFORE ANYTHING BAD HAPPENS...
...THEN NO ONE WILL KNOW THERE WAS A CASE TO BEGIN WITH.
AAAGH. WHAT SHOULD I DO WITH ALL THIS GARBAGE?
OR TEXT-BOOKS, I GUESS.

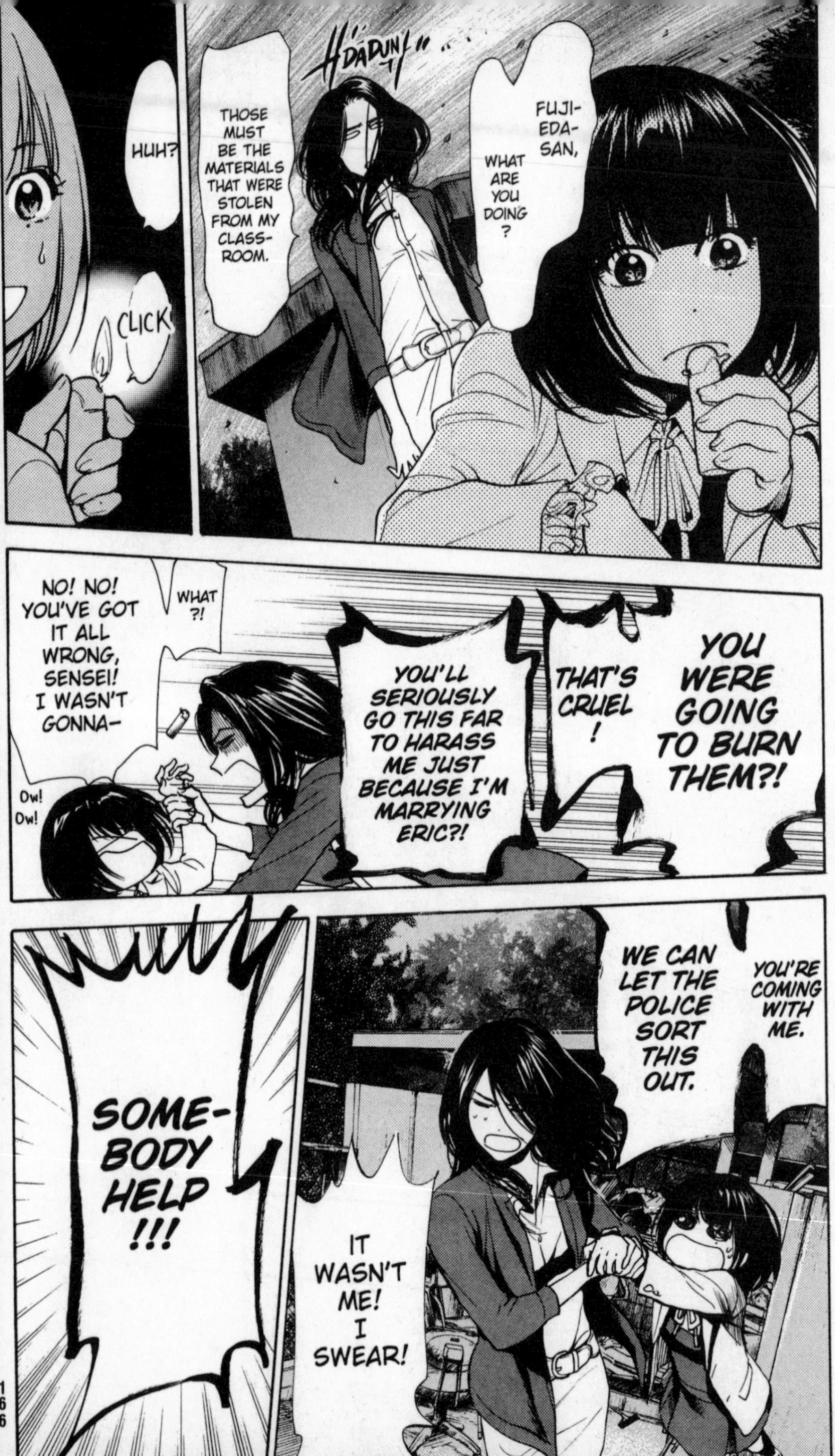
FUJI-EDA-SAN,
WHAT ARE YOU DOING?
DADUN
THOSE MUST BE THE MATERIALS THAT WERE STOLEN FROM MY CLASS-ROOM.
HUH?
CLICK
YOU WERE GOING TO BURN THEM?!
THAT'S CRUEL!
YOU'LL SERIOUSLY GO THIS FAR TO HARASS ME JUST BECAUSE I'M MARRYING ERIC?!
WHAT?!
NO! NO! YOU'VE GOT IT ALL WRONG, SENSEI! I WASN'T GONNA-
Ow! Ow!
YOU'RE COMING WITH ME.
WE CAN LET THE POLICE SORT THIS OUT.
IT WASN'T ME! I SWEAR!
SOME-BODY HELP!!!

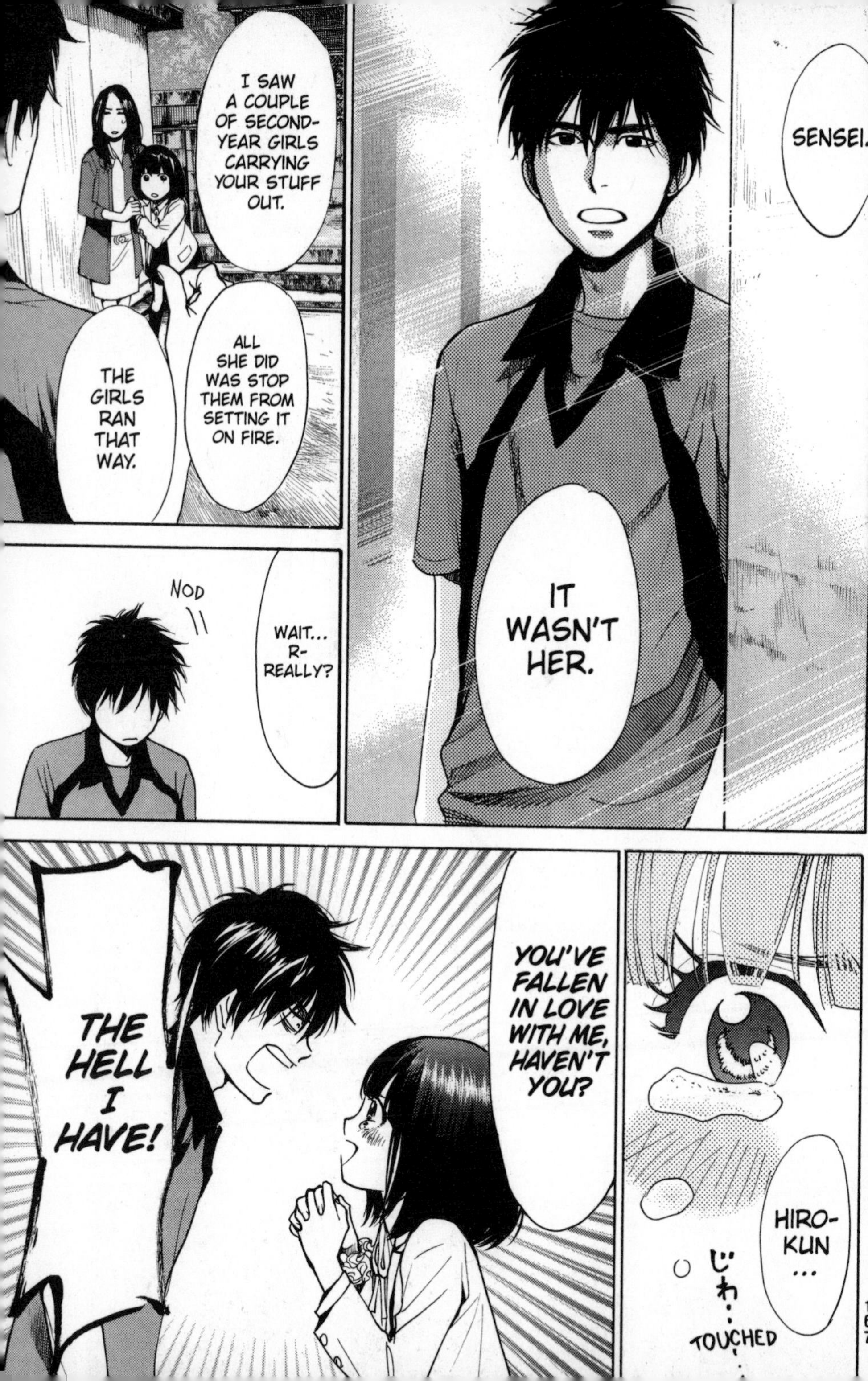
SENSEI.
IT WASN'T HER.
I SAW A COUPLE OF SECOND-YEAR GIRLS CARRYING YOUR STUFF OUT.
ALL SHE DID WAS STOP THEM FROM SETTING IT ON FIRE.
THE GIRLS RAN THAT WAY.
WAIT... R-REALLY?
NOD
HIRO-KUN...
じわ・・
TOUCHED
YOU'VE FALLEN IN LOVE WITH ME, HAVEN'T YOU?
THE HELL I HAVE!

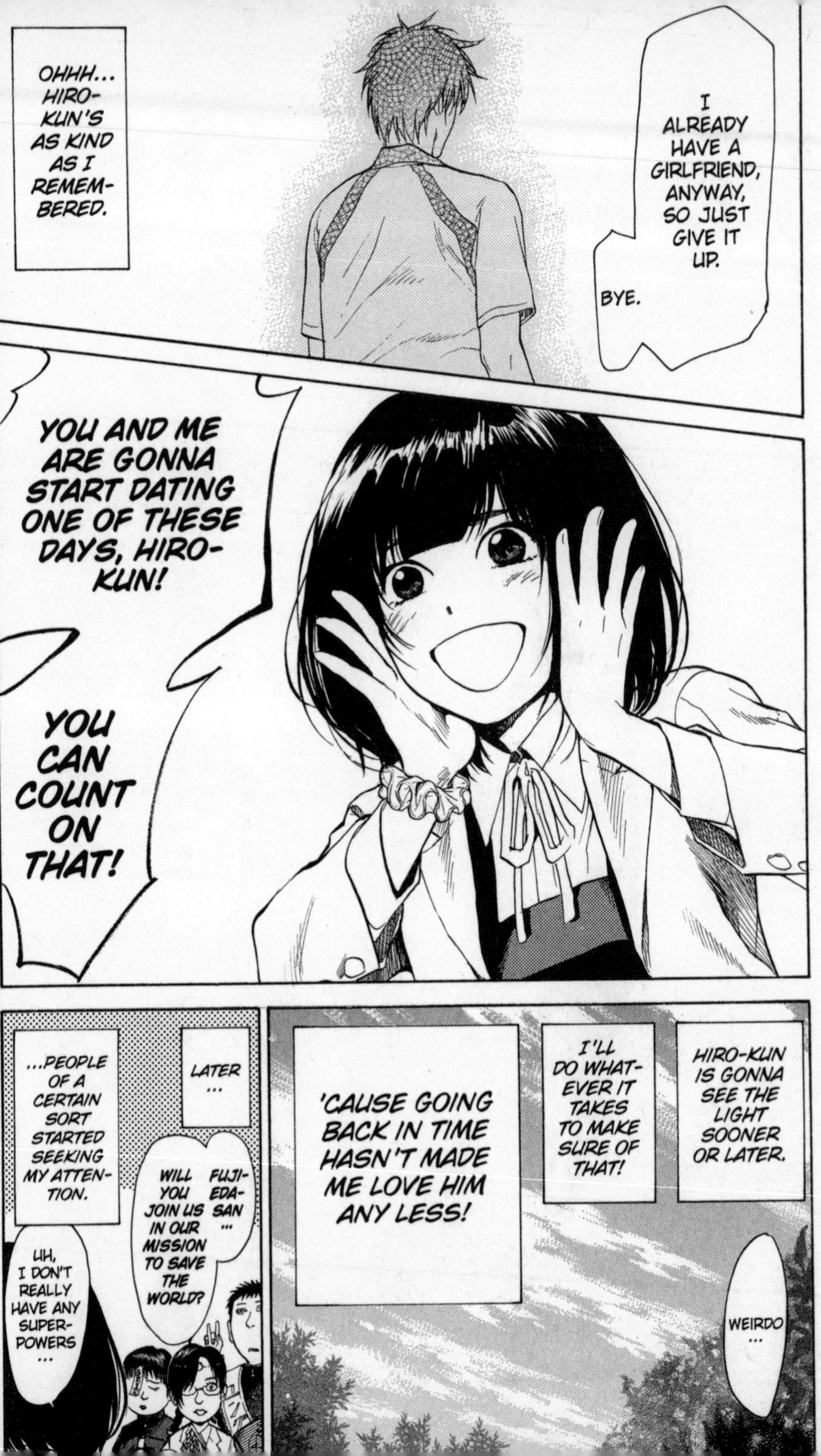
I ALREADY HAVE A GIRLFRIEND, ANYWAY, SO JUST GIVE IT UP.
BYE.
OHHH... HIRO-KUN'S AS KIND AS I REMEMBERED.
YOU AND ME ARE GONNA START DATING ONE OF THESE DAYS, HIRO-KUN!
YOU CAN COUNT ON THAT!
HIRO-KUN IS GONNA SEE THE LIGHT SOONER OR LATER.
I'LL DO WHATEVER IT TAKES TO MAKE SURE OF THAT!
'CAUSE GOING BACK IN TIME HASN'T MADE ME LOVE HIM ANY LESS!
WEIRDO...
LATER...
...PEOPLE OF A CERTAIN SORT STARTED SEEKING MY ATTENTION.
FUJIEDA-SAN...
WILL YOU JOIN US IN OUR MISSION TO SAVE THE WORLD?
UH, I DON'T REALLY HAVE ANY SUPERPOWERS...

19. DESTINED FOR DEFEAT

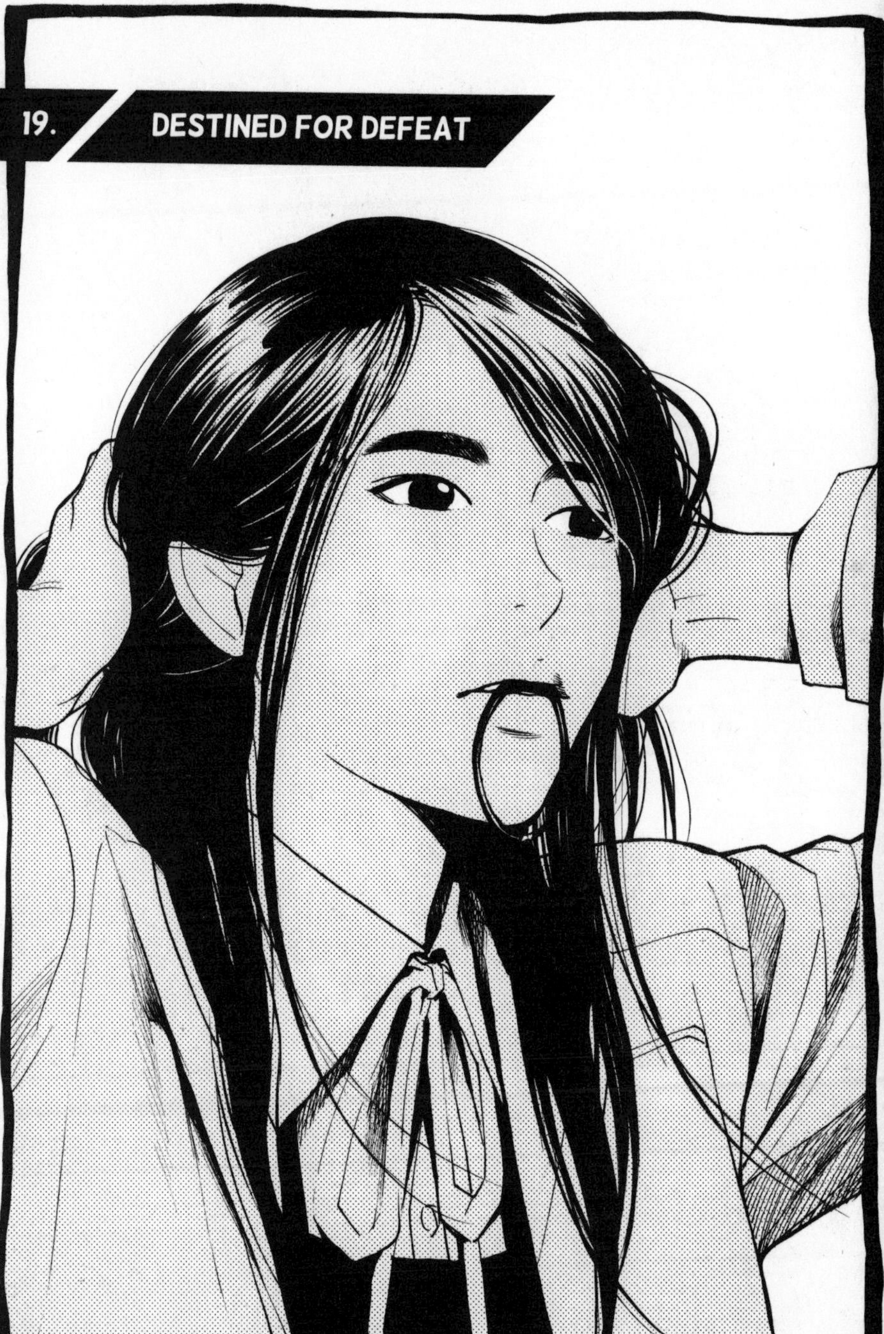

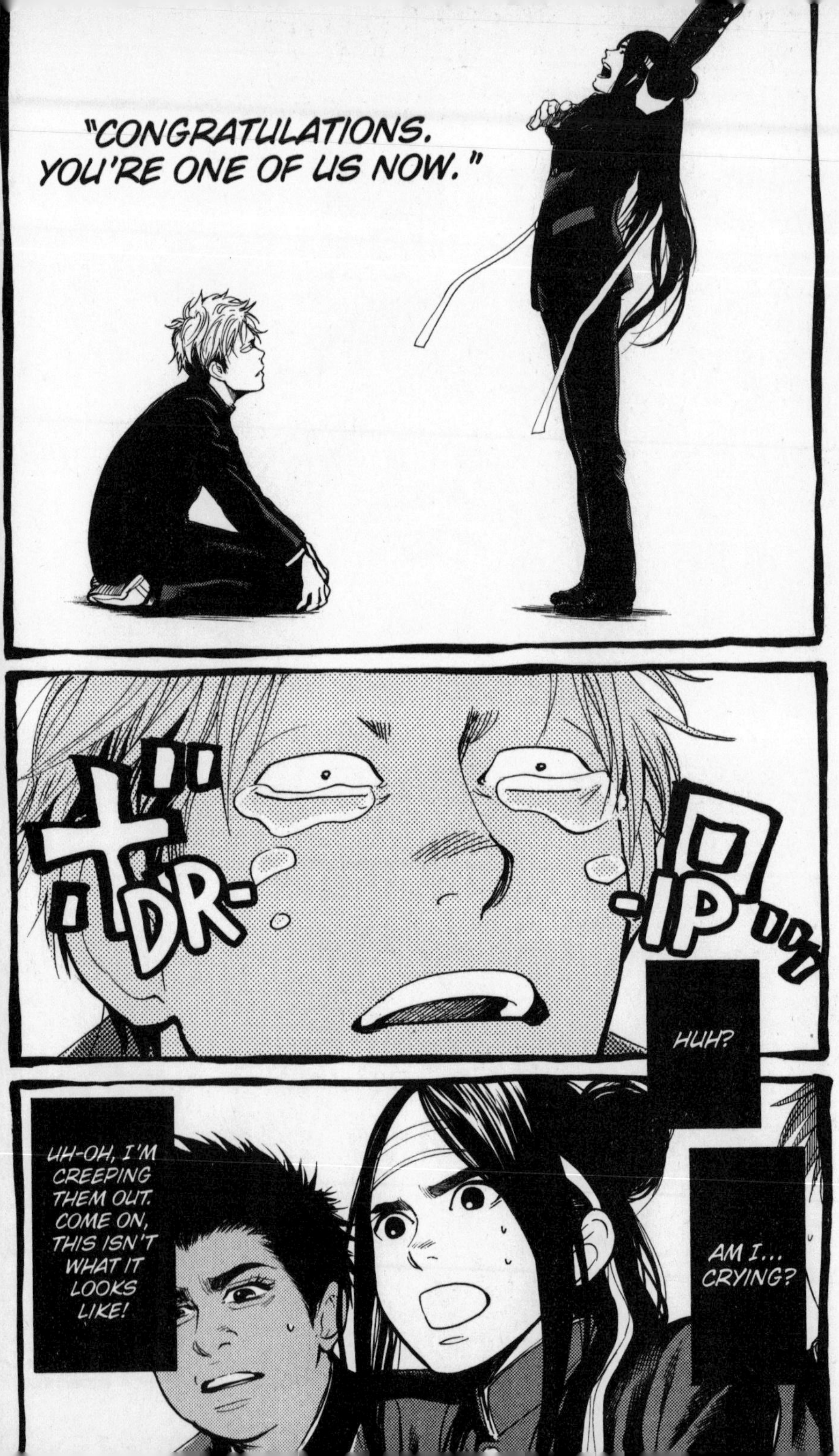
"CONGRATULATIONS. YOU'RE ONE OF US NOW."
DR- -IP
HUH?
AM I... CRYING?
UH-OH, I'M CREEPING THEM OUT. COME ON, THIS ISN'T WHAT IT LOOKS LIKE!

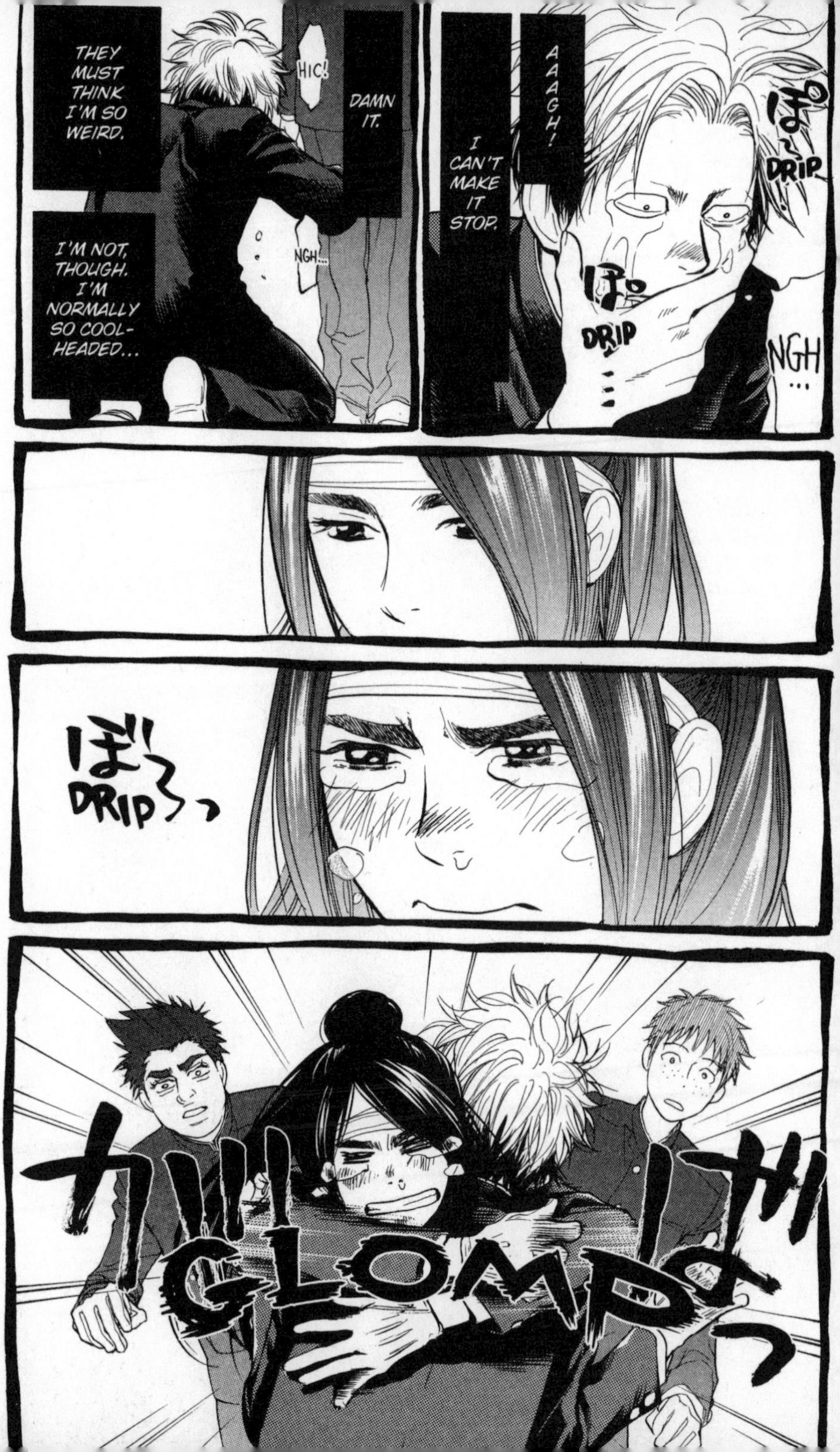
AAAAGH!
I CAN'T MAKE IT STOP.
DRIP
DRIP
NGH...
DAMN IT.
HIC!
THEY MUST THINK I'M SO WEIRD.
I'M NOT, THOUGH. I'M NORMALLY SO COOL-HEADED...
NGH...
DRIP
GLOMP

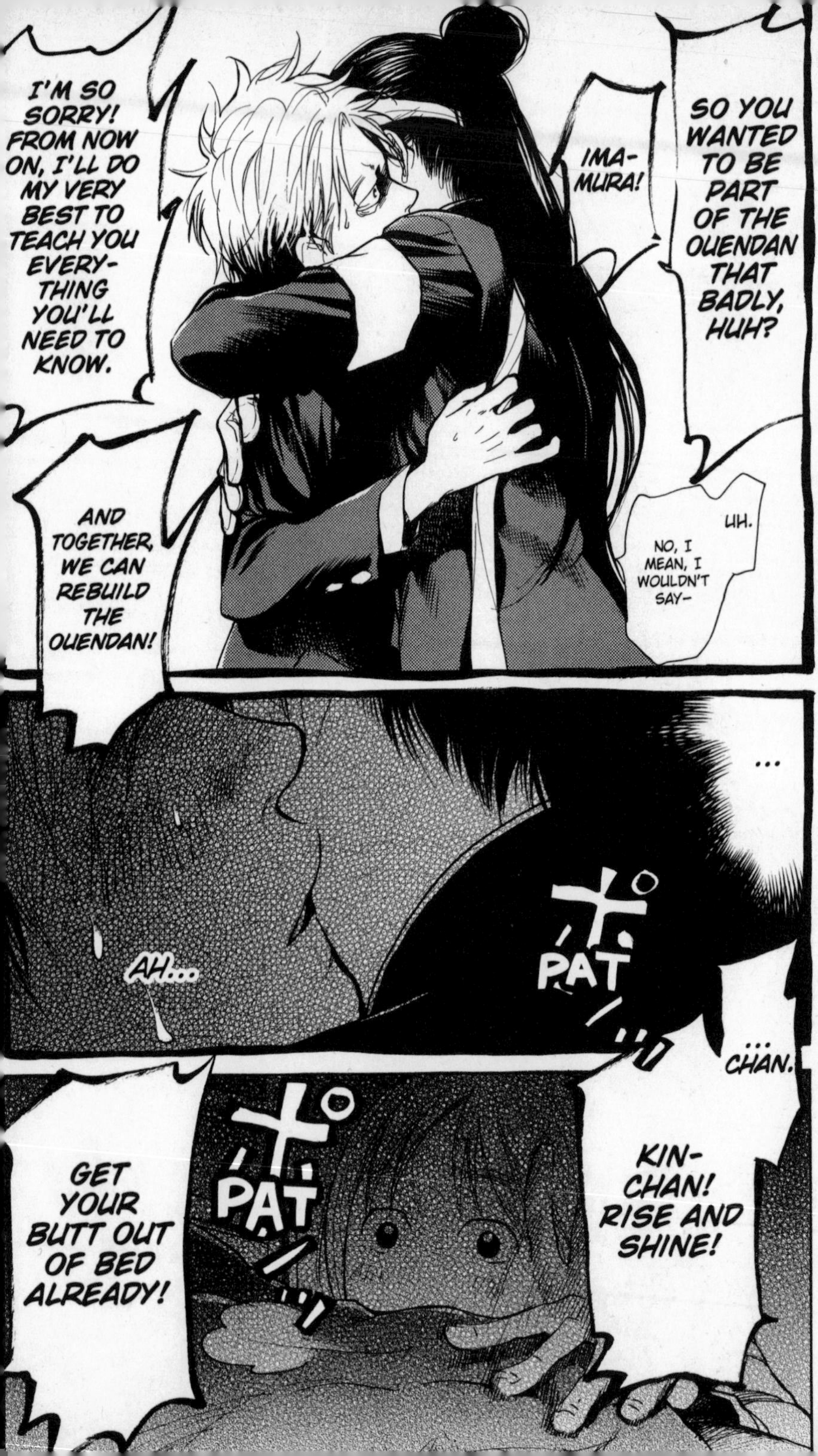
SO YOU WANTED TO BE PART OF THE OUENDAN THAT BADLY, HUH?
IMA-MURA!
I'M SO SORRY! FROM NOW ON, I'LL DO MY VERY BEST TO TEACH YOU EVERY-THING YOU'LL NEED TO KNOW.
UH.
NO, I MEAN, I WOULDN'T SAY–
AND TOGETHER, WE CAN REBUILD THE OUENDAN!
...
PAT
AH...
...CHAN.
KIN-CHAN! RISE AND SHINE!
PAT
GET YOUR BUTT OUT OF BED ALREADY!

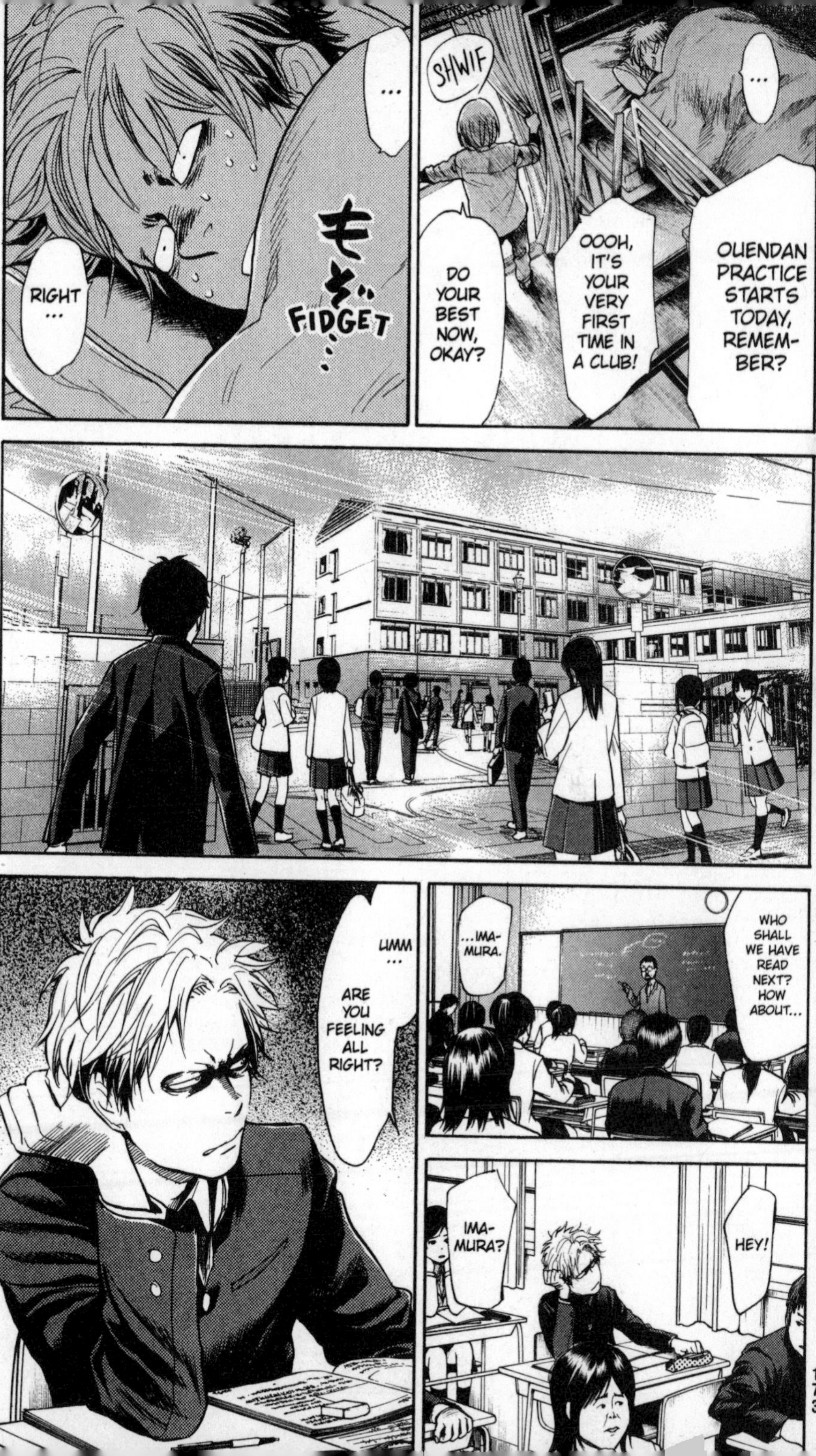
...
SHWIF
OUENDAN PRACTICE STARTS TODAY, REMEMBER?
OOOH, IT'S YOUR VERY FIRST TIME IN A CLUB!
DO YOUR BEST NOW, OKAY?
...
もぞ
FIDGET
RIGHT ...
WHO SHALL WE HAVE READ NEXT? HOW ABOUT...
...IMAMURA.
HEY!
IMAMURA?
UMM ...
ARE YOU FEELING ALL RIGHT?

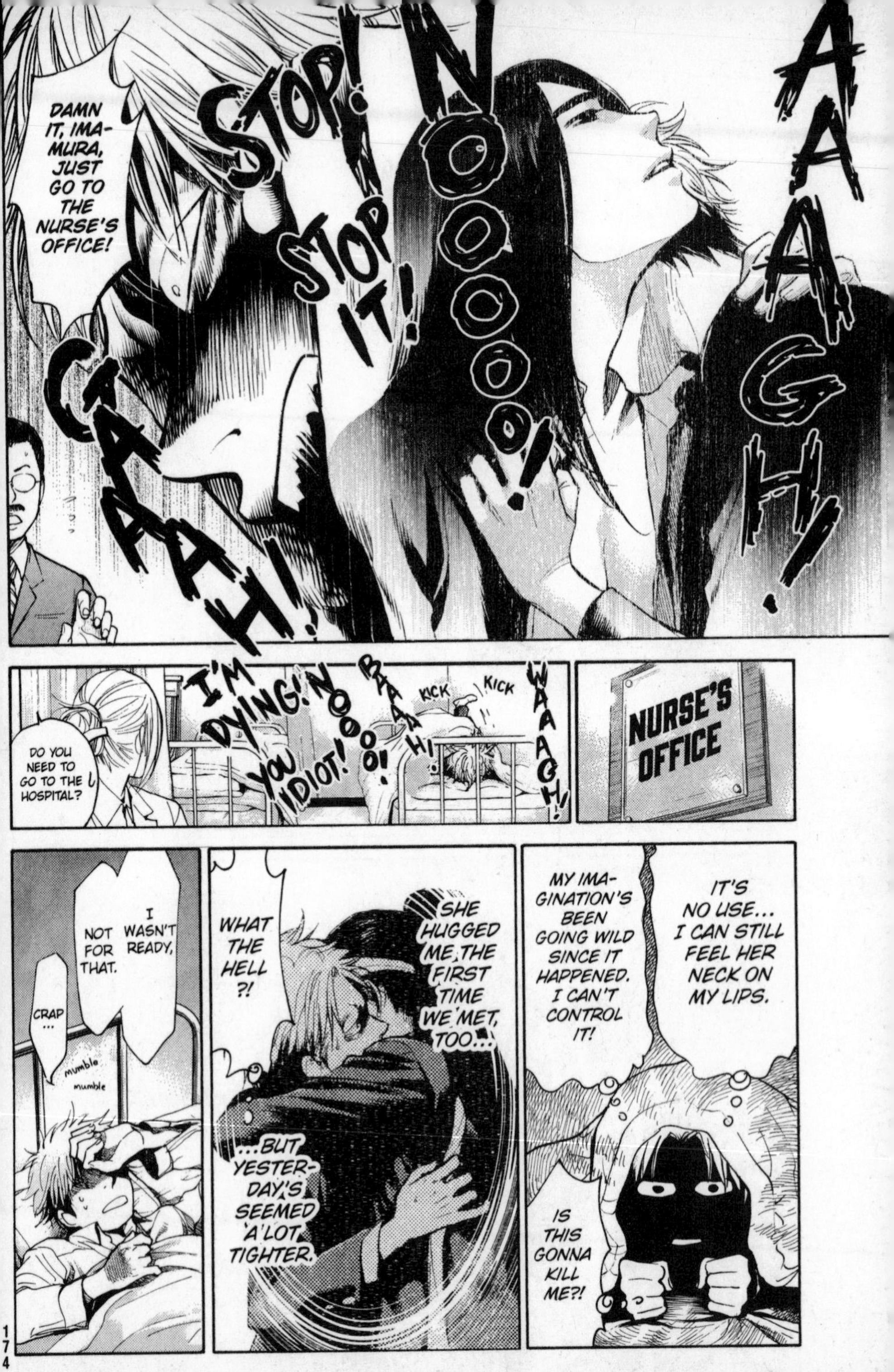

AAAGH!
NOOOOOOO!
STOP! STOP IT!
CAAAH!
DAMN IT, IMAMURA, JUST GO TO THE NURSE'S OFFICE!
NURSE'S OFFICE
WAAAGH!
KICK KICK
BRAAAAH!
NOOOOO!
I'M DYING! YOU IDIOT!
DO YOU NEED TO GO TO THE HOSPITAL?
IT'S NO USE... I CAN STILL FEEL HER NECK ON MY LIPS.
MY IMAGINATION'S BEEN GOING WILD SINCE IT HAPPENED. I CAN'T CONTROL IT!
IS THIS GONNA KILL ME?!
SHE HUGGED ME THE FIRST TIME WE MET, TOO...
WHAT THE HELL?!
...BUT YESTERDAY'S SEEMED A LOT TIGHTER.
I WASN'T READY,
NOT FOR THAT.
CRAP...
mumble mumble

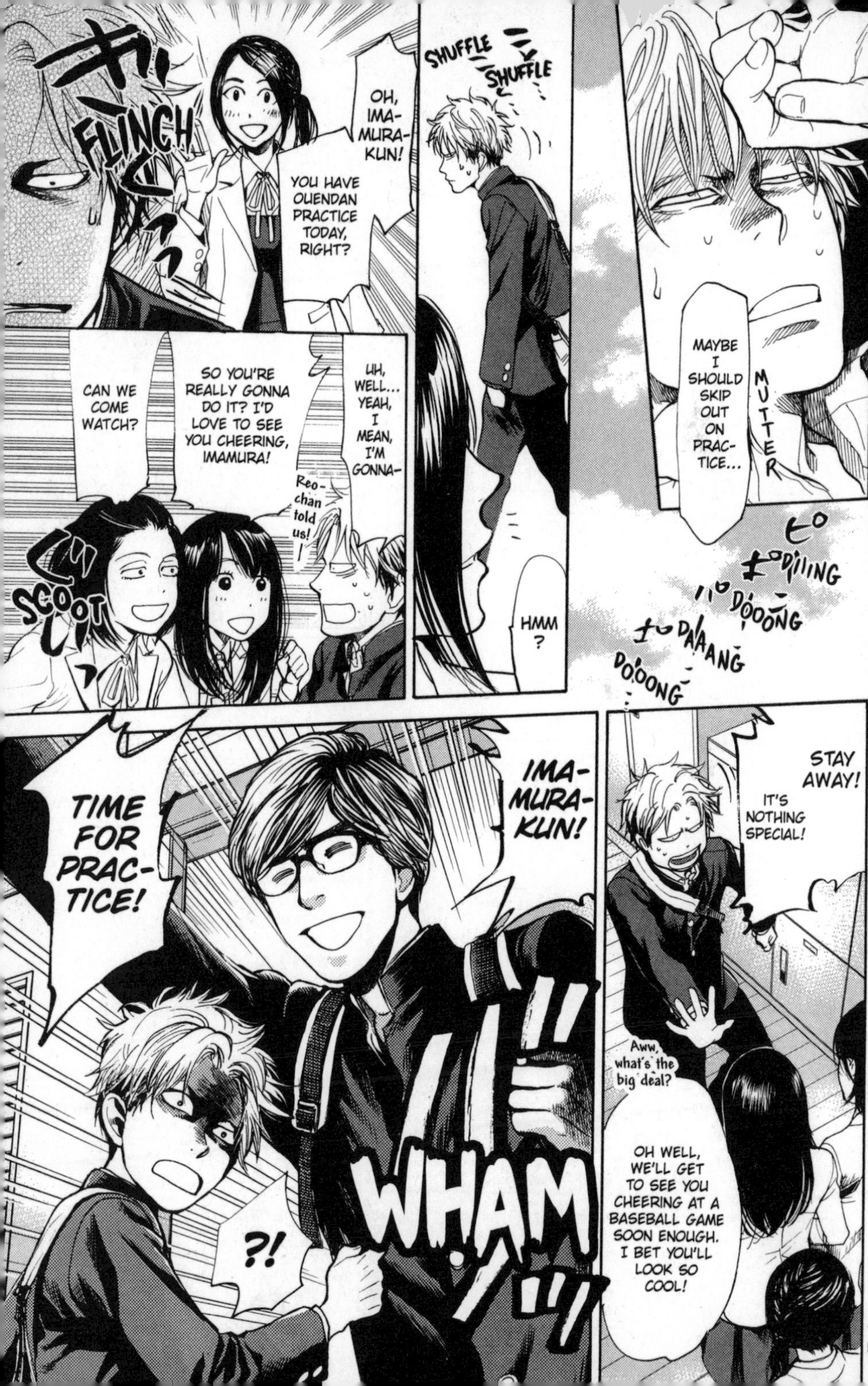
MAYBE I SHOULD SKIP OUT ON PRACTICE...
MUTTER
DIIING
DOOONG
DAAANG
DOOONG
SHUFFLE SHUFFLE
HMM?
FLINCH
OH, IMAMURA-KUN!
YOU HAVE OUENDAN PRACTICE TODAY, RIGHT?
UH, WELL... YEAH, I MEAN, I'M GONNA-
Reo-chan told us!
SO YOU'RE REALLY GONNA DO IT? I'D LOVE TO SEE YOU CHEERING, IMAMURA!
CAN WE COME WATCH?
SCOOT
STAY AWAY!
IT'S NOTHING SPECIAL!
Aww, what's the big deal?
OH WELL, WE'LL GET TO SEE YOU CHEERING AT A BASEBALL GAME SOON ENOUGH. I BET YOU'LL LOOK SO COOL!
IMA-MURA-KUN!
TIME FOR PRAC-TICE!
WHAM
?!

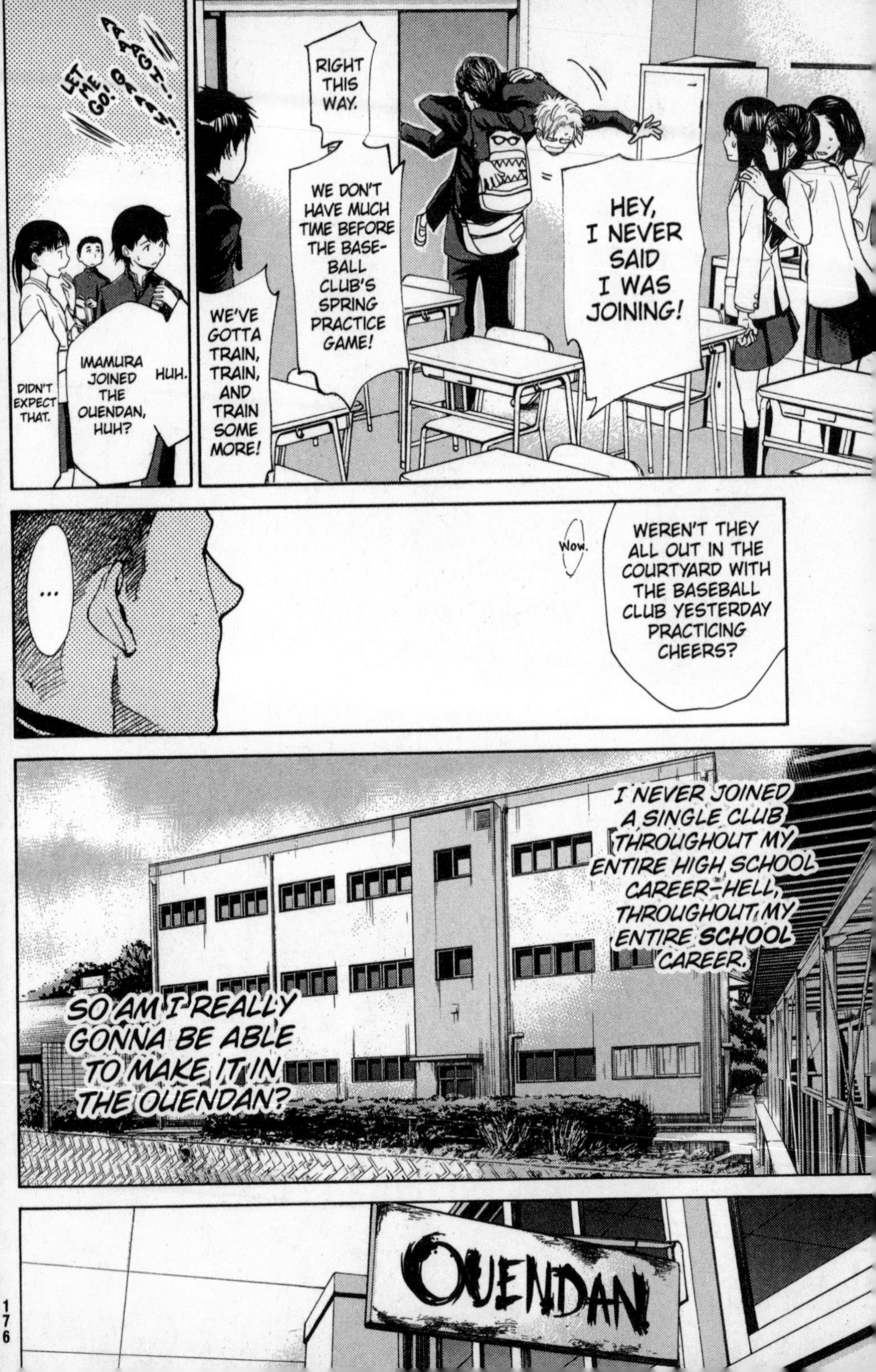
RIGHT THIS WAY.
HEY, I NEVER SAID I WAS JOINING!
WE DON'T HAVE MUCH TIME BEFORE THE BASE-BALL CLUB'S SPRING PRACTICE GAME!
WE'VE GOTTA TRAIN, TRAIN, AND TRAIN SOME MORE!
AAAGH!! OKAAAY!
LET ME GO!
HUH.
IMAMURA JOINED THE OUENDAN, HUH?
DIDN'T EXPECT THAT.
WEREN'T THEY ALL OUT IN THE COURTYARD WITH THE BASEBALL CLUB YESTERDAY PRACTICING CHEERS?
Wow.
...
I NEVER JOINED A SINGLE CLUB THROUGHOUT MY ENTIRE HIGH SCHOOL CAREER—HELL, THROUGHOUT MY ENTIRE SCHOOL CAREER.
SO AM I REALLY GONNA BE ABLE TO MAKE IT IN THE OUENDAN?
OUENDAN

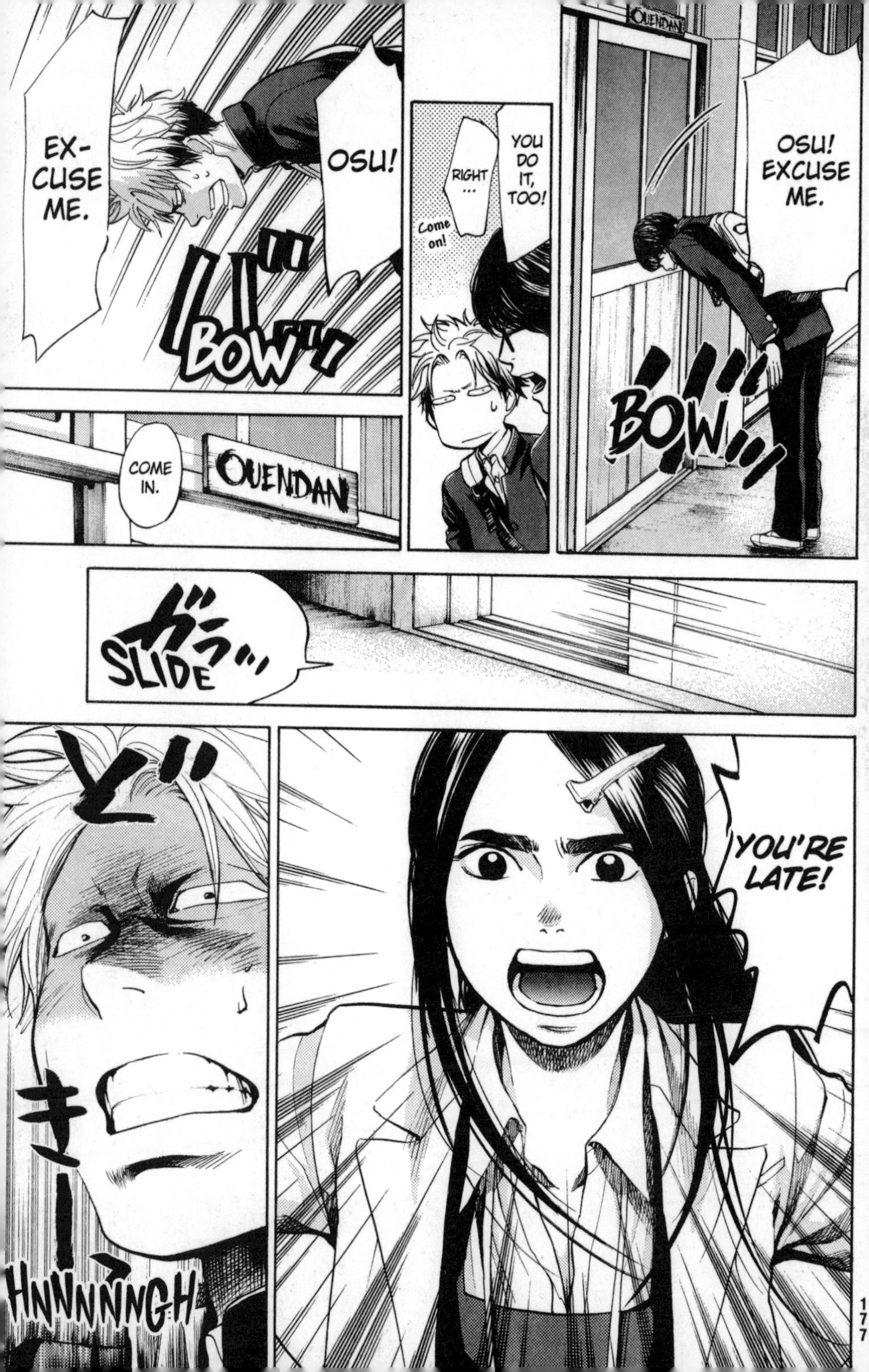
OUENDAN
OSU! EXCUSE ME.
BOW
YOU DO IT, TOO!
RIGHT...
Come on!
OSU!
EX-CUSE ME.
BOW
COME IN.
OUENDAN
SLIDE
YOU'RE LATE!
HNNNNNGH

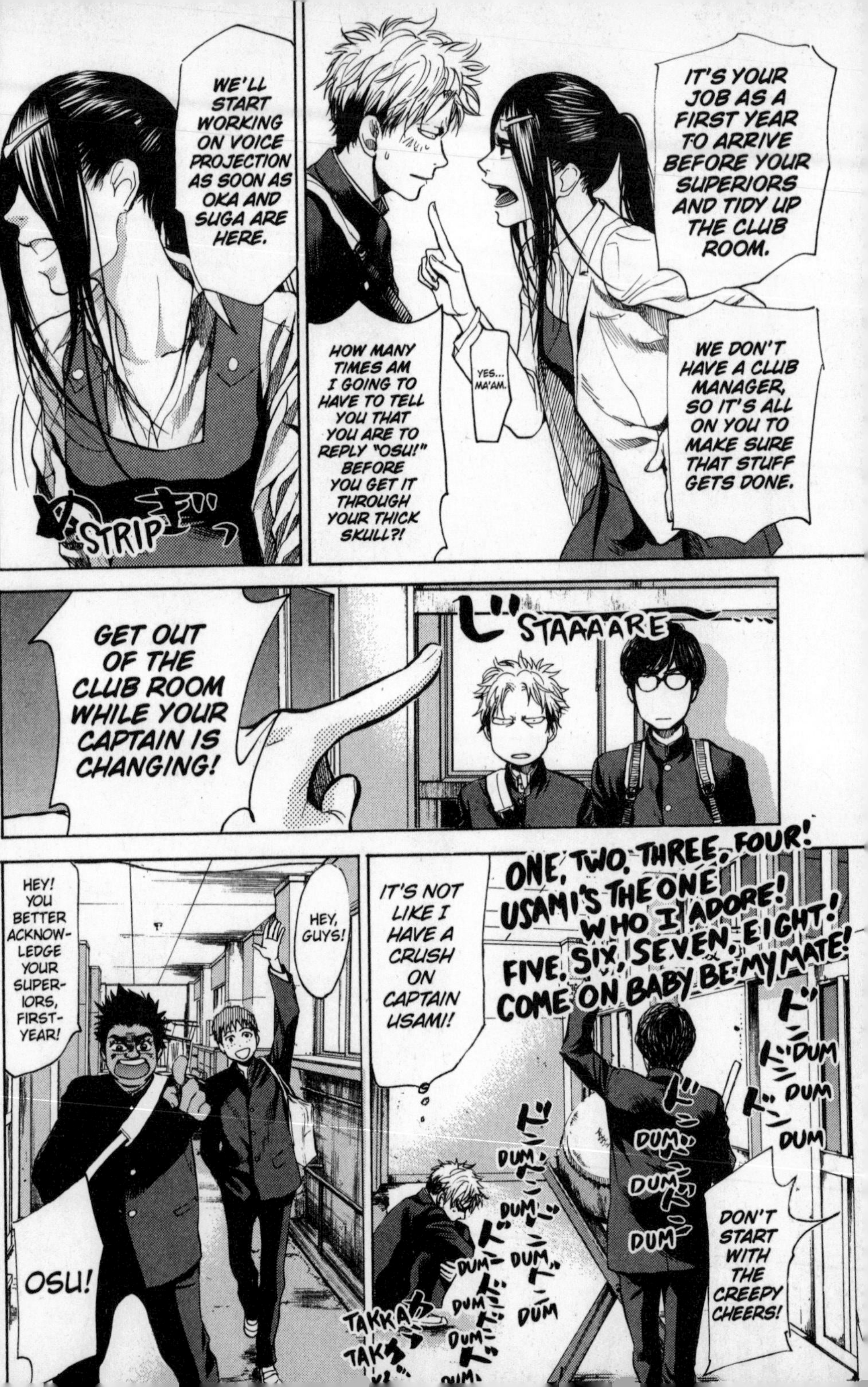
IT'S YOUR JOB AS A FIRST YEAR TO ARRIVE BEFORE YOUR SUPERIORS AND TIDY UP THE CLUB ROOM.
WE DON'T HAVE A CLUB MANAGER, SO IT'S ALL ON YOU TO MAKE SURE THAT STUFF GETS DONE.
YES... MA'AM.
HOW MANY TIMES AM I GOING TO HAVE TO TELL YOU THAT YOU ARE TO REPLY "OSU!" BEFORE YOU GET IT THROUGH YOUR THICK SKULL?!
WE'LL START WORKING ON VOICE PROJECTION AS SOON AS OKA AND SUGA ARE HERE.
STRIP
STAAAARE
GET OUT OF THE CLUB ROOM WHILE YOUR CAPTAIN IS CHANGING!
ONE, TWO, THREE, FOUR! USAMI'S THE ONE WHO I ADORE!
FIVE, SIX, SEVEN, EIGHT! COME ON BABY BE MY MATE!
DUM DUM DUM
DUM DUM DUM
DUM DUM DUM DUM DUM DUM DUM
TAKKA TAKKA
IT'S NOT LIKE I HAVE A CRUSH ON CAPTAIN USAMI!
DON'T START WITH THE CREEPY CHEERS!
HEY, GUYS!
HEY! YOU BETTER ACKNOW-LEDGE YOUR SUPER-IORS, FIRST-YEAR!
OSU!

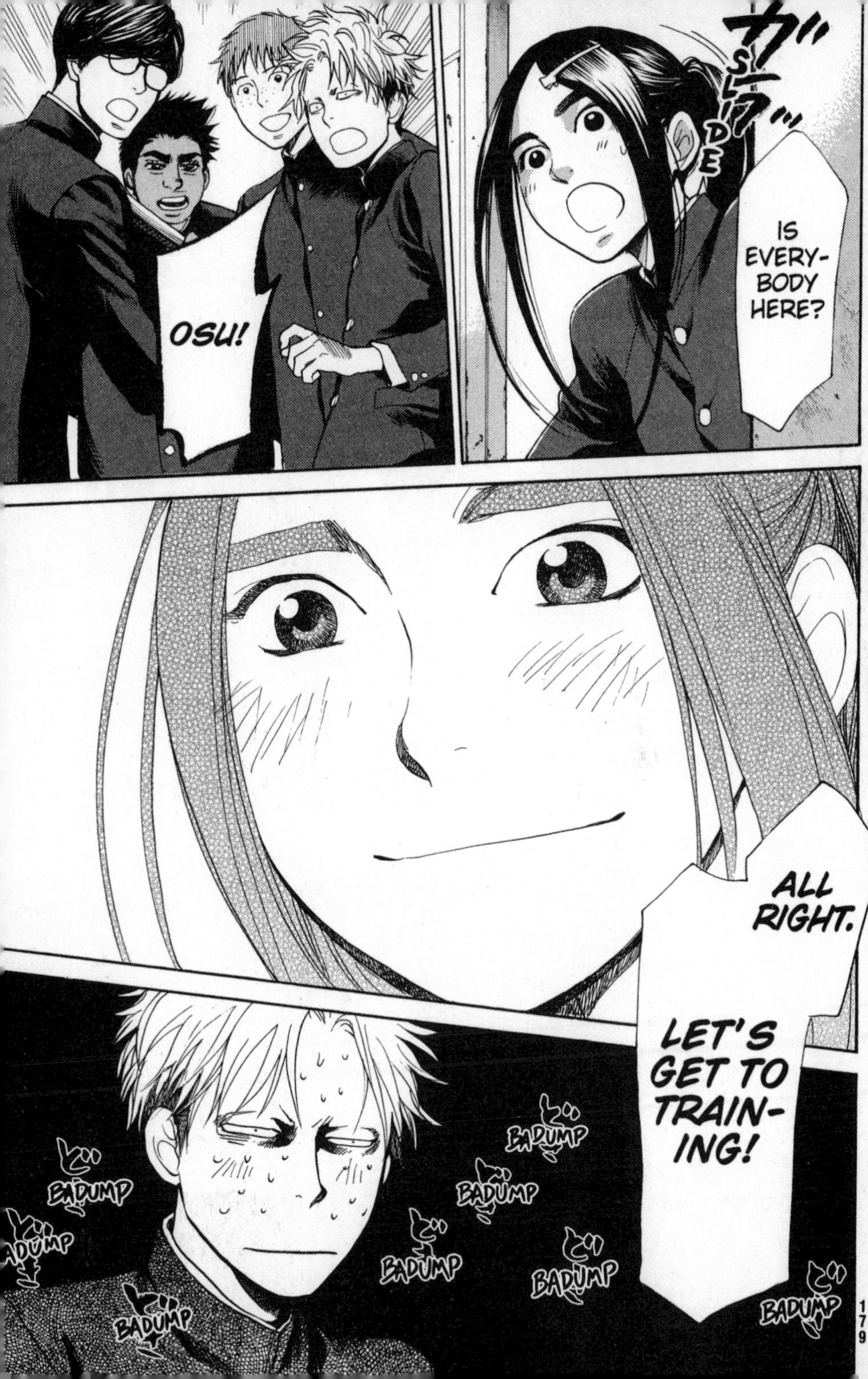
SLIDE
IS EVERY-BODY HERE?
OSU!
ALL RIGHT.
LET'S GET TO TRAIN-ING!
BADUMP
BADUMP
BADUMP
BADUMP
BADUMP
BADUMP
BADUMP
BADUMP

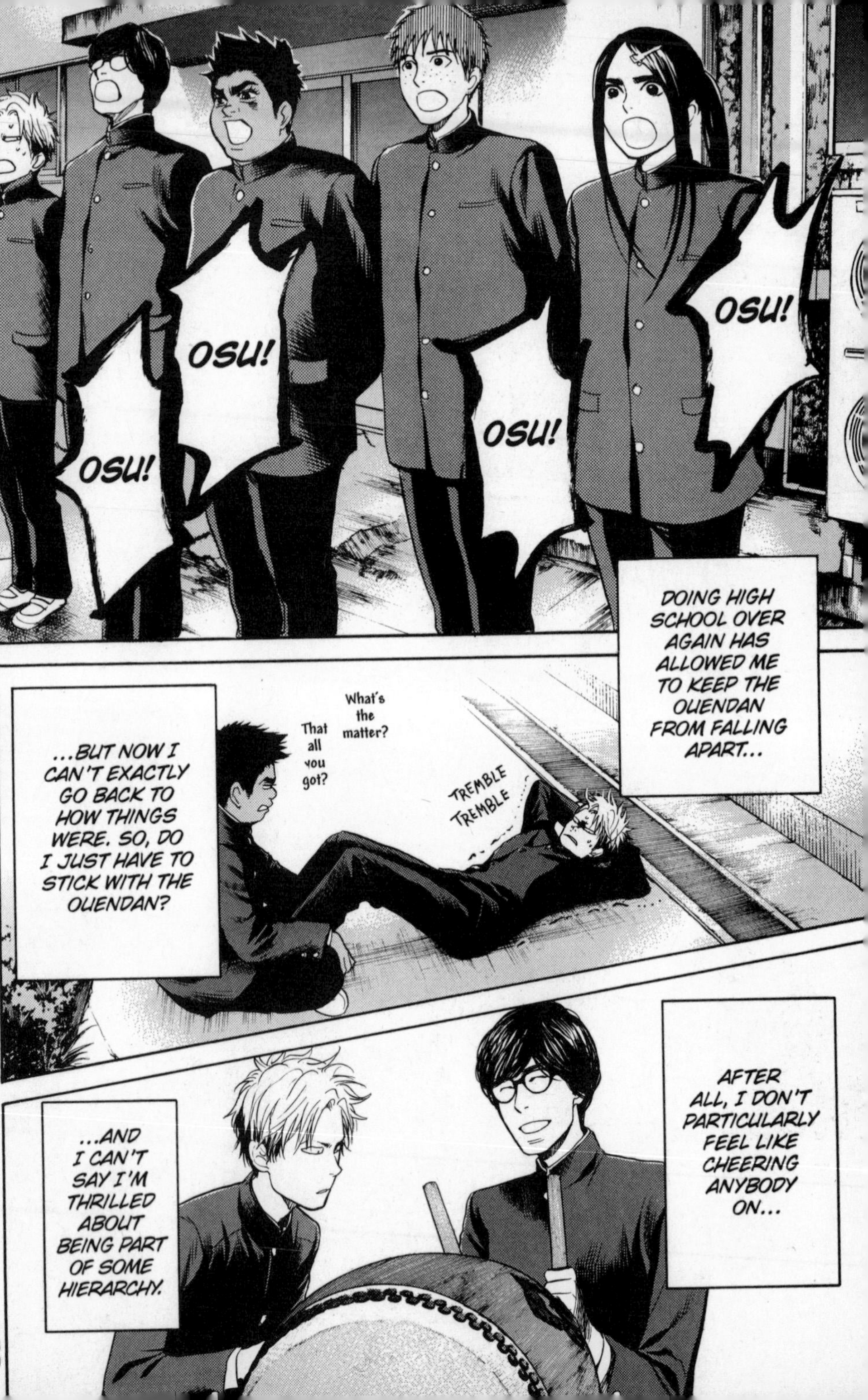

OSU!
OSU!
OSU!
OSU!
DOING HIGH SCHOOL OVER AGAIN HAS ALLOWED ME TO KEEP THE OUENDAN FROM FALLING APART...
What's the matter?
That all you got?
TREMBLE TREMBLE
...BUT NOW I CAN'T EXACTLY GO BACK TO HOW THINGS WERE. SO, DO I JUST HAVE TO STICK WITH THE OUENDAN?
AFTER ALL, I DON'T PARTICULARLY FEEL LIKE CHEERING ANYBODY ON...
...AND I CAN'T SAY I'M THRILLED ABOUT BEING PART OF SOME HIERARCHY.

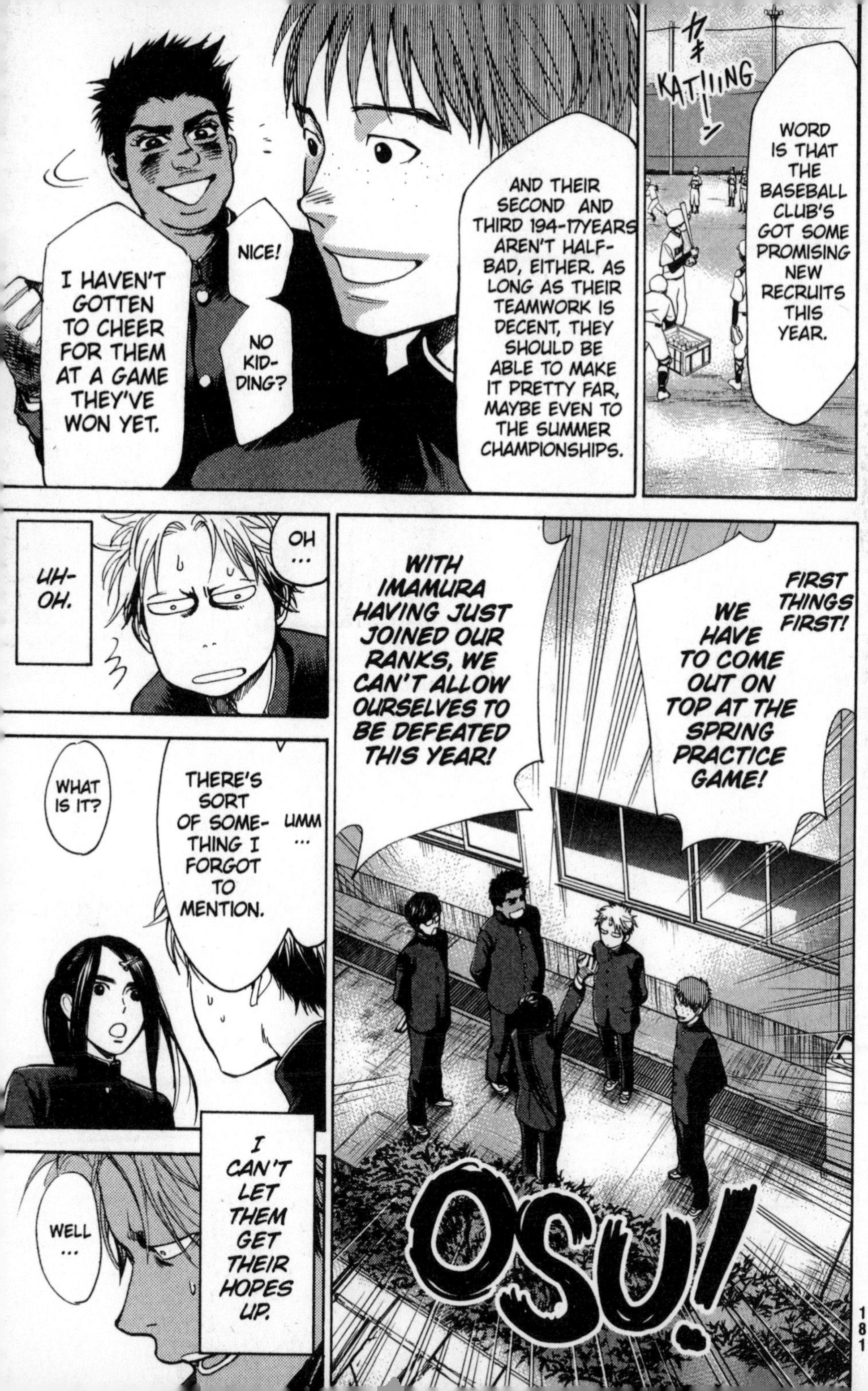
KATIIING
WORD IS THAT THE BASEBALL CLUB'S GOT SOME PROMISING NEW RECRUITS THIS YEAR.
AND THEIR SECOND AND THIRD 194-17YEARS AREN'T HALF-BAD, EITHER. AS LONG AS THEIR TEAMWORK IS DECENT, THEY SHOULD BE ABLE TO MAKE IT PRETTY FAR, MAYBE EVEN TO THE SUMMER CHAMPIONSHIPS.
NICE!
NO KIDDING?
I HAVEN'T GOTTEN TO CHEER FOR THEM AT A GAME THEY'VE WON YET.
FIRST THINGS FIRST!
WE HAVE TO COME OUT ON TOP AT THE SPRING PRACTICE GAME!
WITH IMAMURA HAVING JUST JOINED OUR RANKS, WE CAN'T ALLOW OURSELVES TO BE DEFEATED THIS YEAR!
OSU!
OH ...
UH-OH.
UMM ...
THERE'S SORT OF SOME-THING I FORGOT TO MENTION.
WHAT IS IT?
I CAN'T LET THEM GET THEIR HOPES UP.
WELL ...

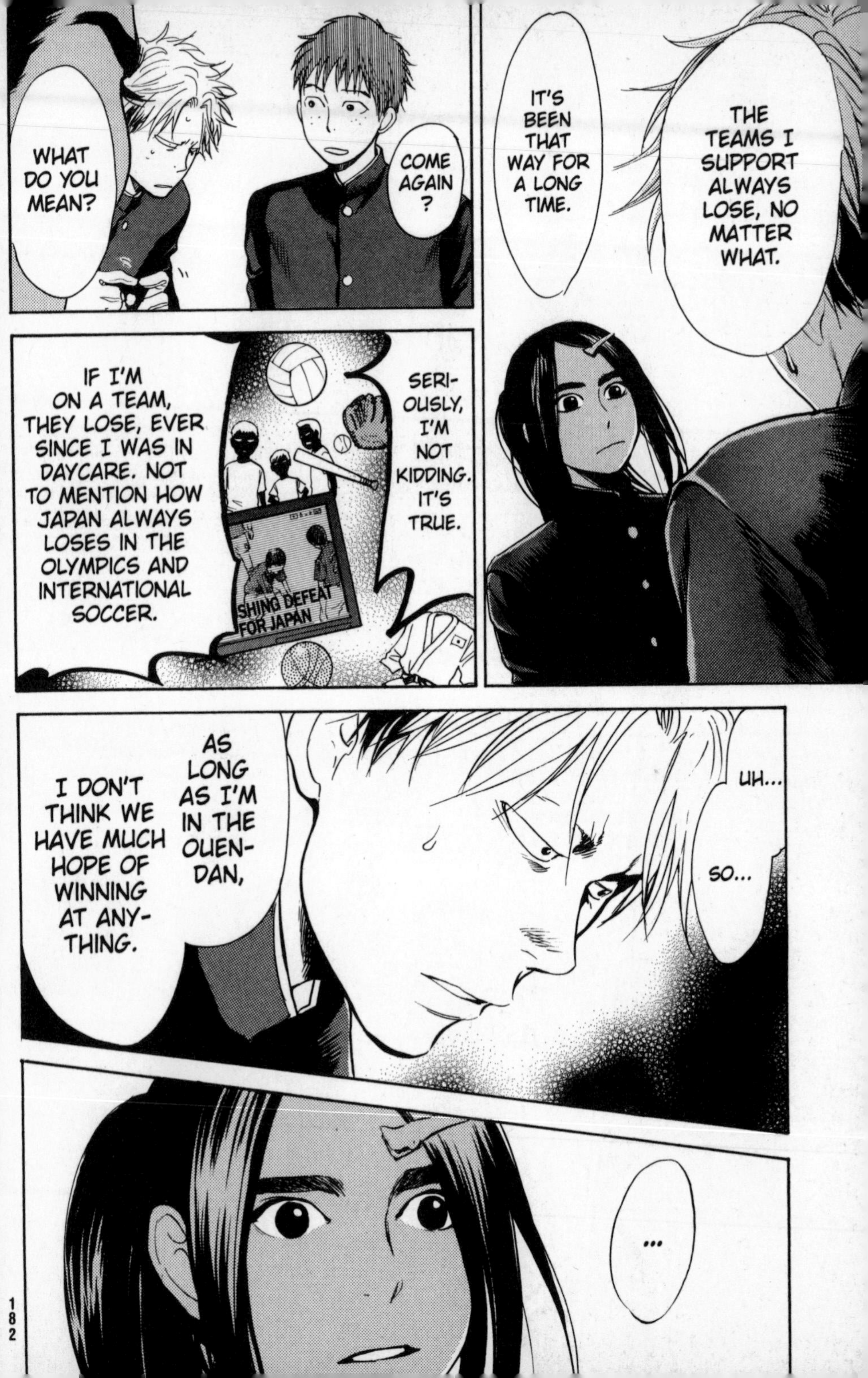
THE TEAMS I SUPPORT ALWAYS LOSE, NO MATTER WHAT.
IT'S BEEN THAT WAY FOR A LONG TIME.
COME AGAIN ?
WHAT DO YOU MEAN?
SERIOUSLY, I'M NOT KIDDING. IT'S TRUE.
IF I'M ON A TEAM, THEY LOSE, EVER SINCE I WAS IN DAYCARE. NOT TO MENTION HOW JAPAN ALWAYS LOSES IN THE OLYMPICS AND INTERNATIONAL SOCCER.
SHING DEFEAT FOR JAPAN
UH...
SO...
AS LONG AS I'M IN THE OUEN-DAN,
I DON'T THINK WE HAVE MUCH HOPE OF WINNING AT ANY-THING.
...

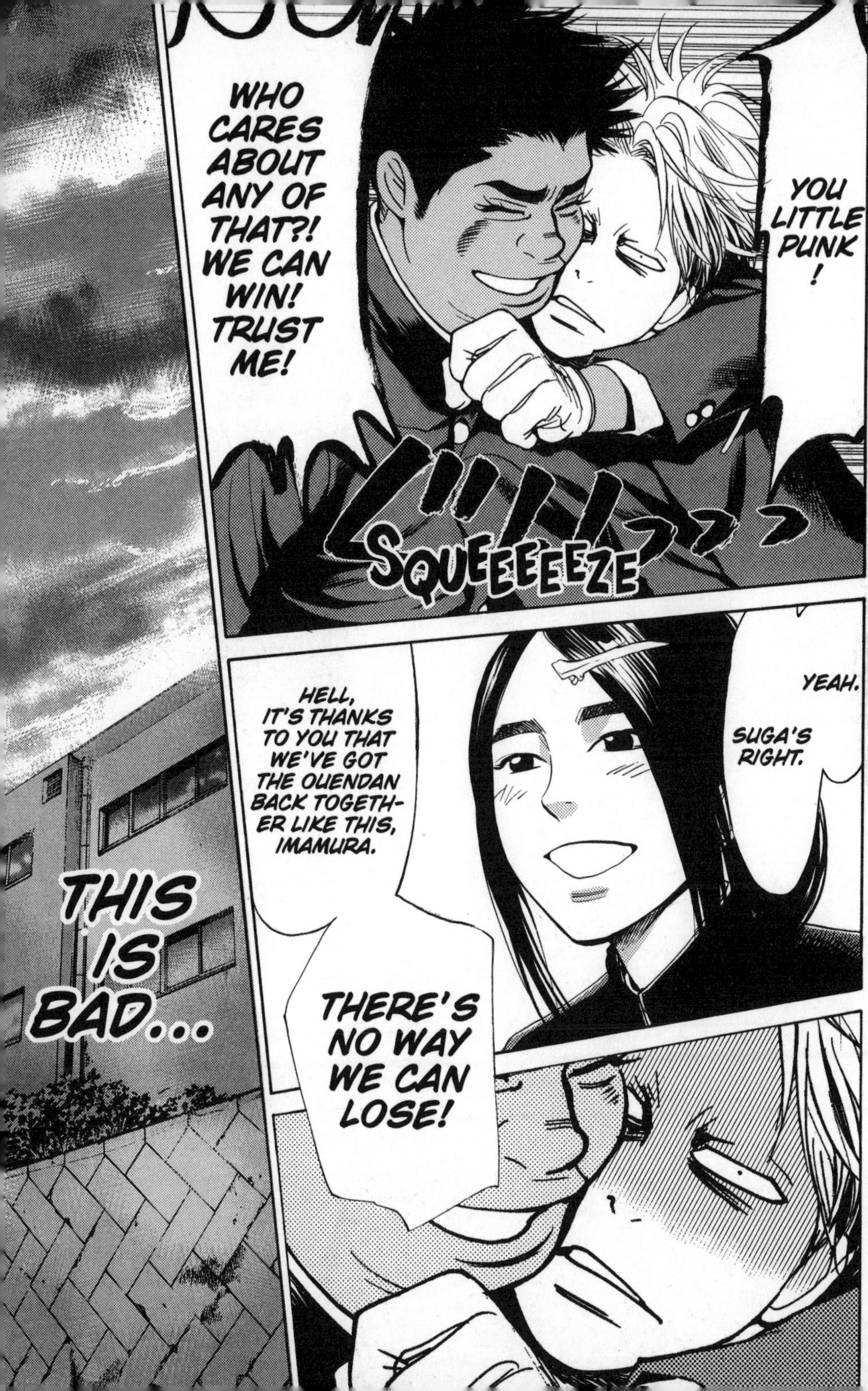
YOU LITTLE PUNK!
WHO CARES ABOUT ANY OF THAT?! WE CAN WIN! TRUST ME!
SQUEEEEEEZE
YEAH.
SUGA'S RIGHT.
HELL, IT'S THANKS TO YOU THAT WE'VE GOT THE OUENDAN BACK TOGETHER LIKE THIS, IMAMURA.
THERE'S NO WAY WE CAN LOSE!
THIS IS BAD...

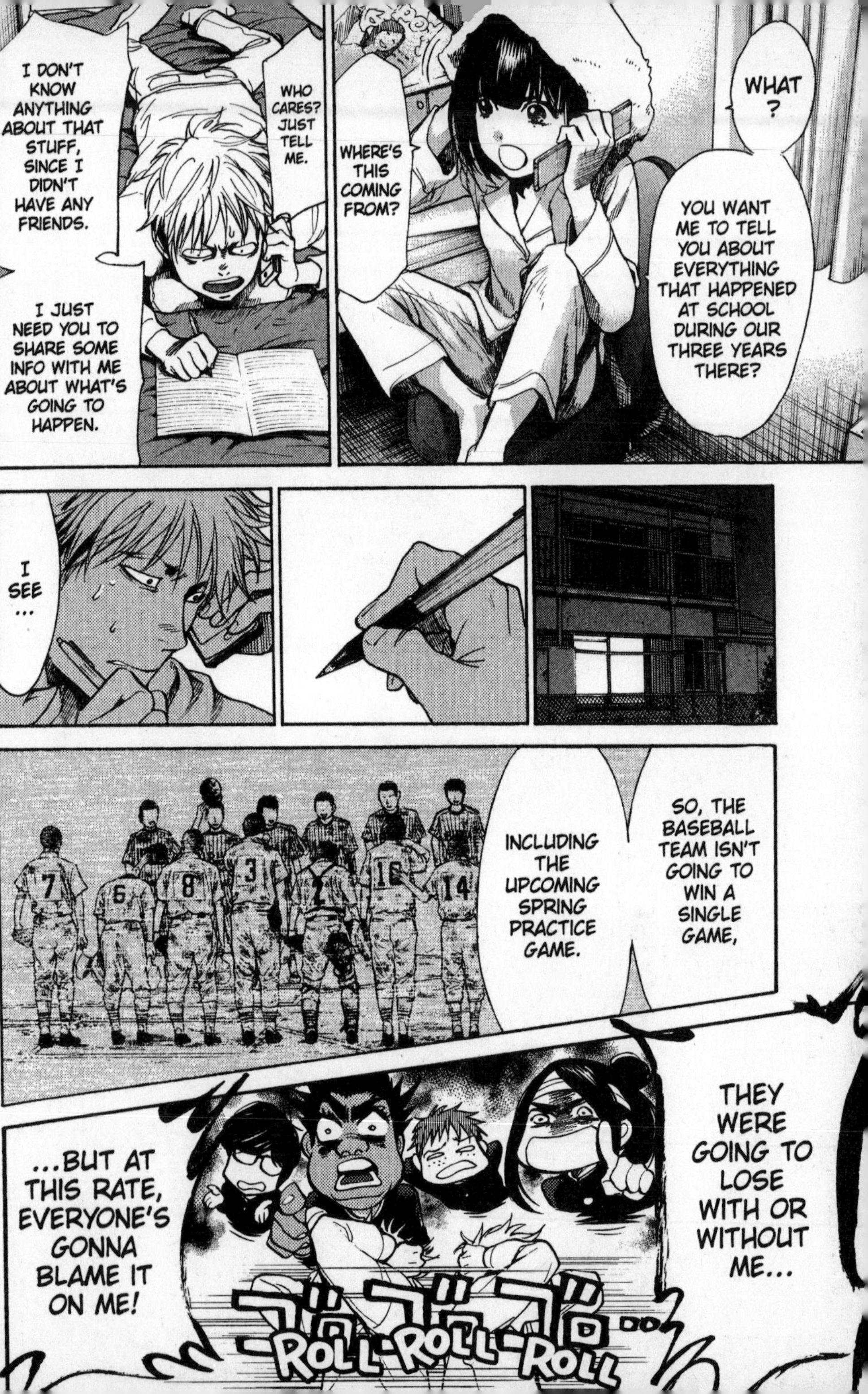
WHAT?
YOU WANT ME TO TELL YOU ABOUT EVERYTHING THAT HAPPENED AT SCHOOL DURING OUR THREE YEARS THERE?
WHERE'S THIS COMING FROM?
WHO CARES? JUST TELL ME.
I DON'T KNOW ANYTHING ABOUT THAT STUFF, SINCE I DIDN'T HAVE ANY FRIENDS.
I JUST NEED YOU TO SHARE SOME INFO WITH ME ABOUT WHAT'S GOING TO HAPPEN.
I SEE...
SO, THE BASEBALL TEAM ISN'T GOING TO WIN A SINGLE GAME,
INCLUDING THE UPCOMING SPRING PRACTICE GAME.
THEY WERE GOING TO LOSE WITH OR WITHOUT ME...
...BUT AT THIS RATE, EVERYONE'S GONNA BLAME IT ON ME!
ROLL-ROLL-ROLL

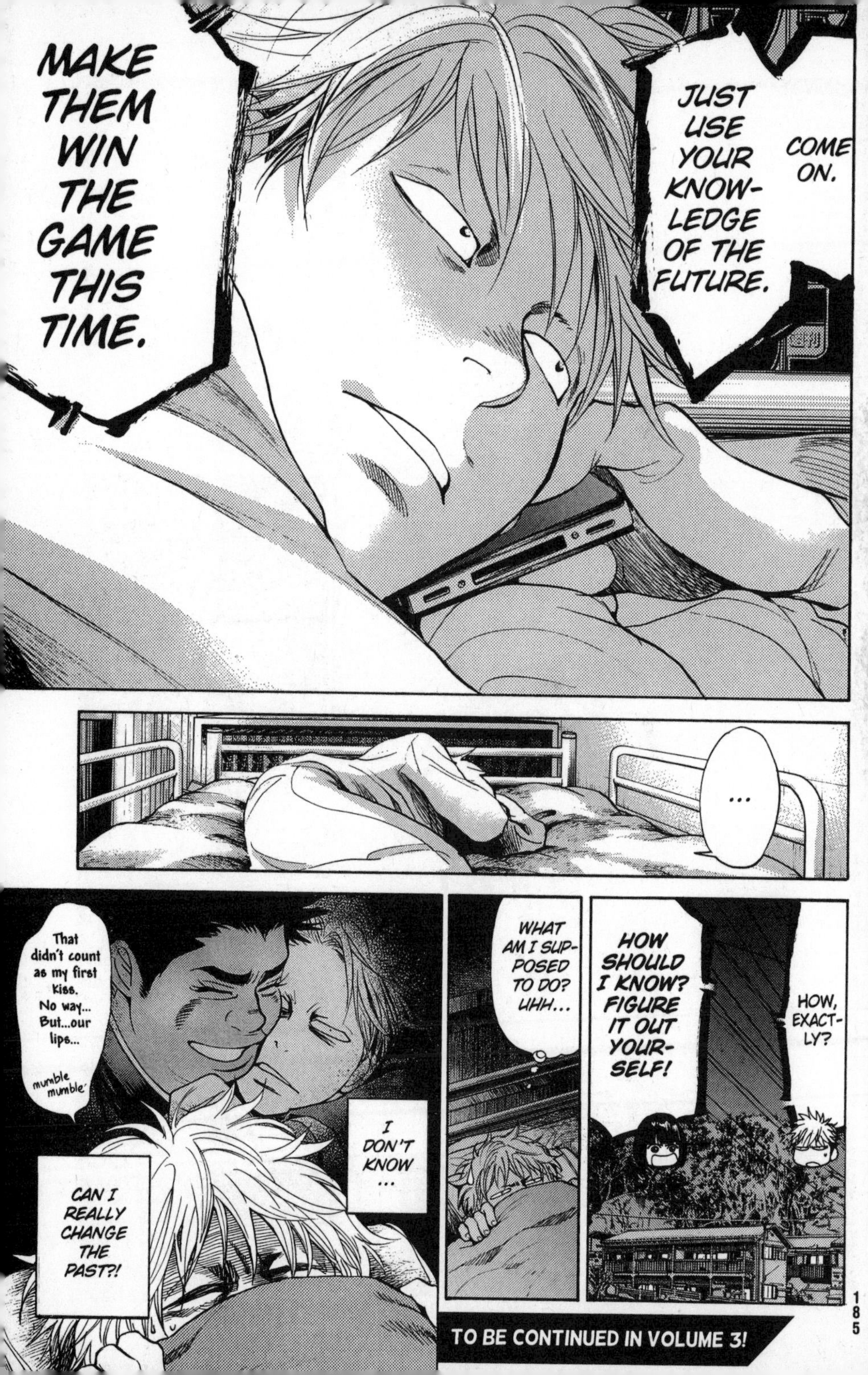
COME ON.
JUST USE YOUR KNOW-LEDGE OF THE FUTURE.
MAKE THEM WIN THE GAME THIS TIME.
...
HOW, EXACTLY?
HOW SHOULD I KNOW? FIGURE IT OUT YOUR-SELF!
WHAT AM I SUP-POSED TO DO? UHH...
That didn't count as my first kiss. No way... But...our lips...
mumble mumble
I DON'T KNOW...
CAN I REALLY CHANGE THE PAST?!
TO BE CONTINUED IN VOLUME 3!

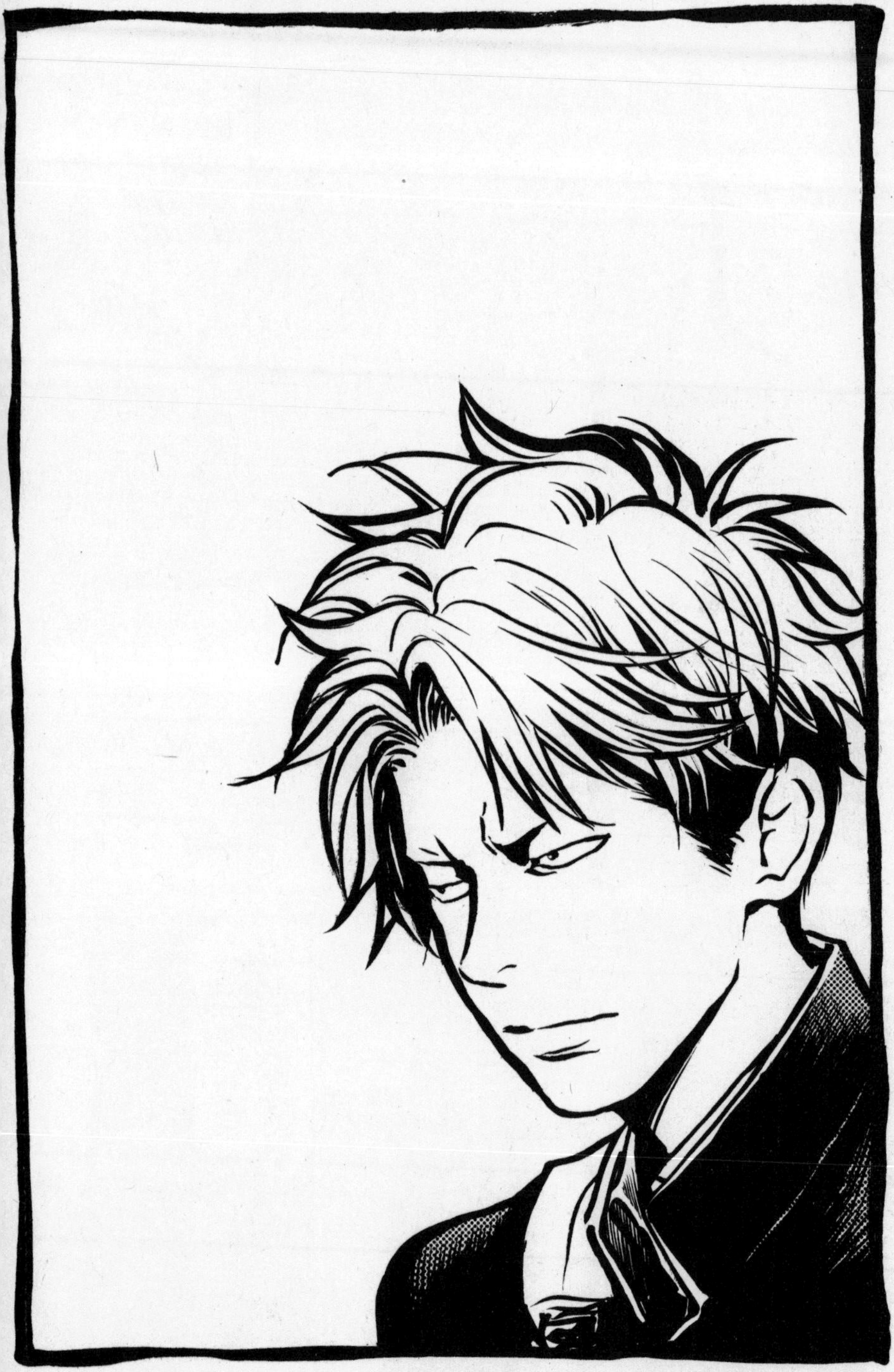

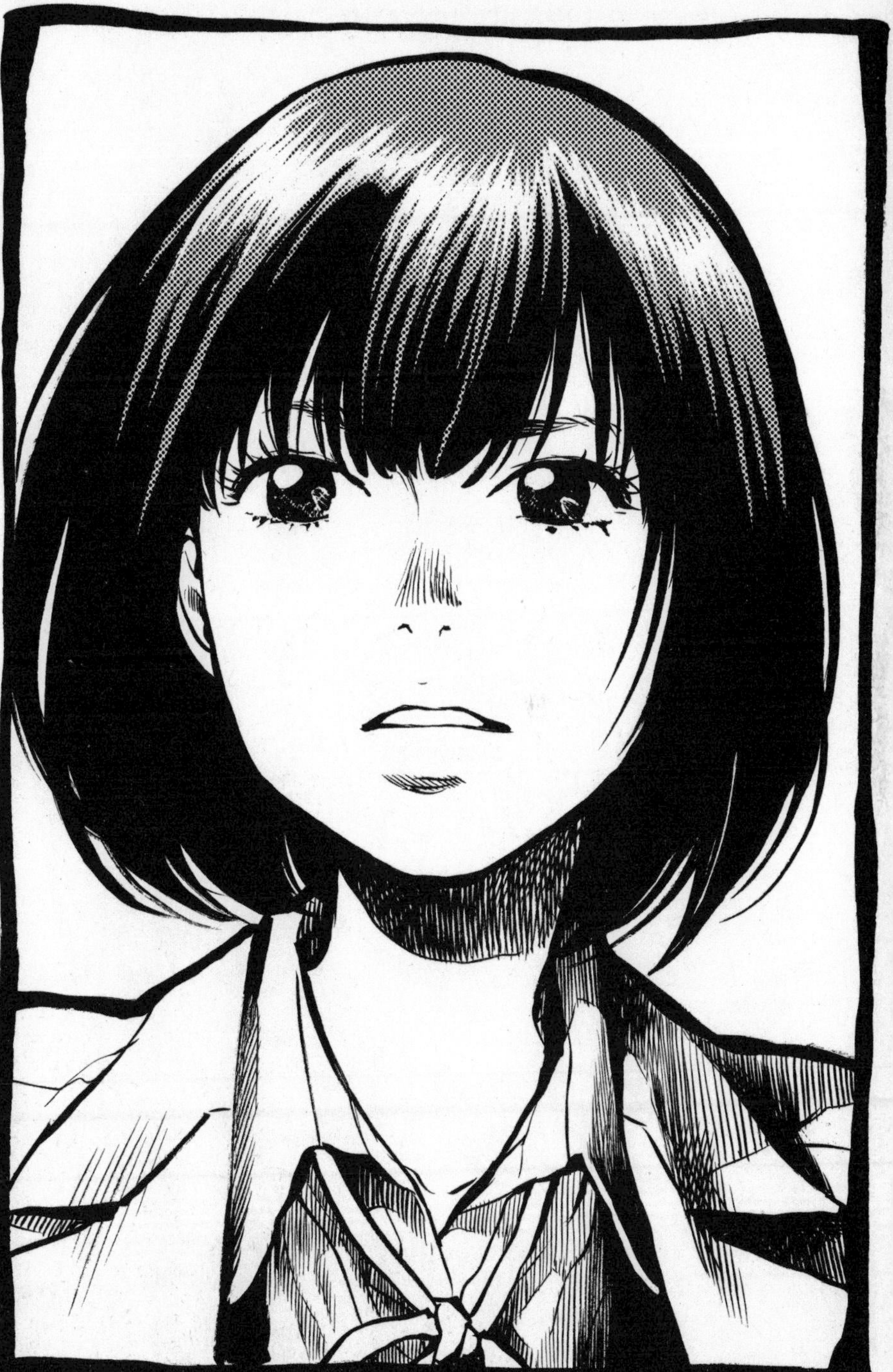

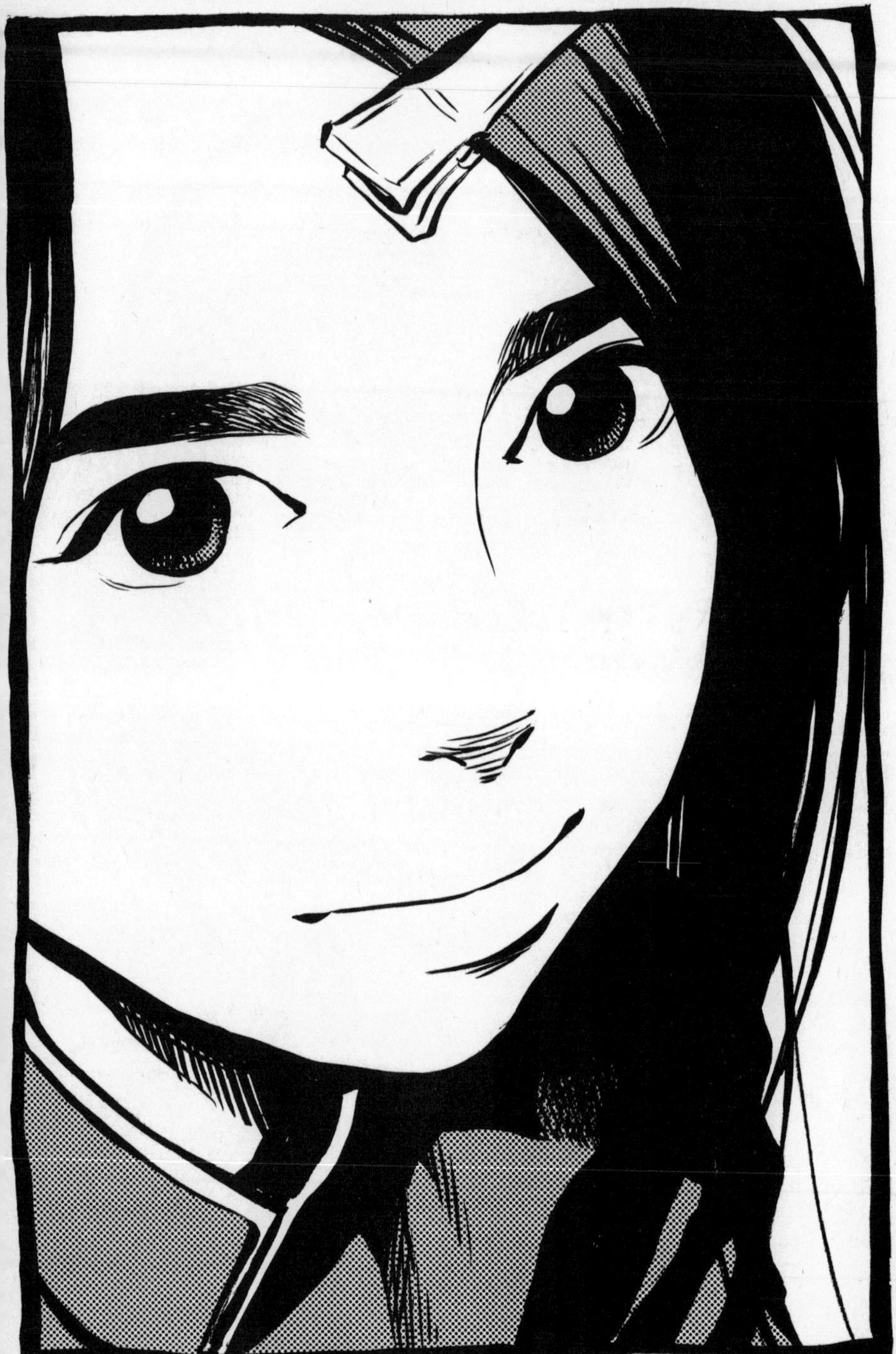

This is the AFTERWORD!

On this page, I thought I'd include a sketch or two that I drew as concept art for this series when I was getting ready for it to begin serialization. But once I'd dug them up, I was shocked at how much Captain Usami's face has changed since then.

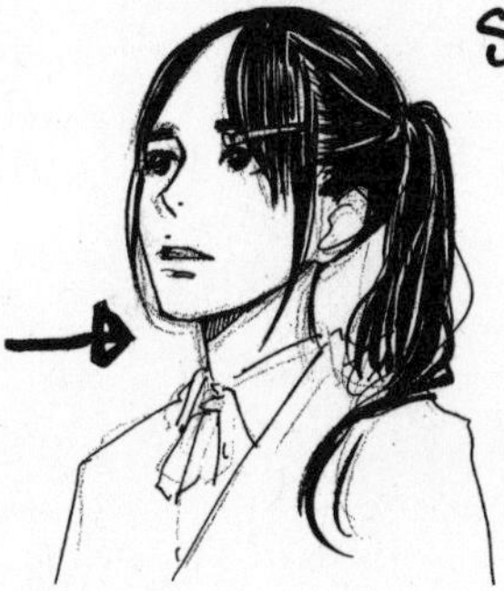
See?

Maybe I was thinking about making her a frailer character with some sort of not-all-there vibe... I can't remember.

I get the feeling I ended up making her more of a strong character because I started work on the final draft of chapter one right around when the big earthquake hit.

Although, I guess I never have been one to draw princesses who just expect people to protect them for no reason!

2011.10. 久保ミツロウ☆

Mitsurou Kubo, October 2011

☆ My Agent: Hiromi Sakitani

☆ My Assistants: Shunsuke Ono, Hiromu Sugawara, Yousuke Takahashi, Yukinori Tateda, Shiori Mizoguchi, and Youko Mikuni

Translation Notes

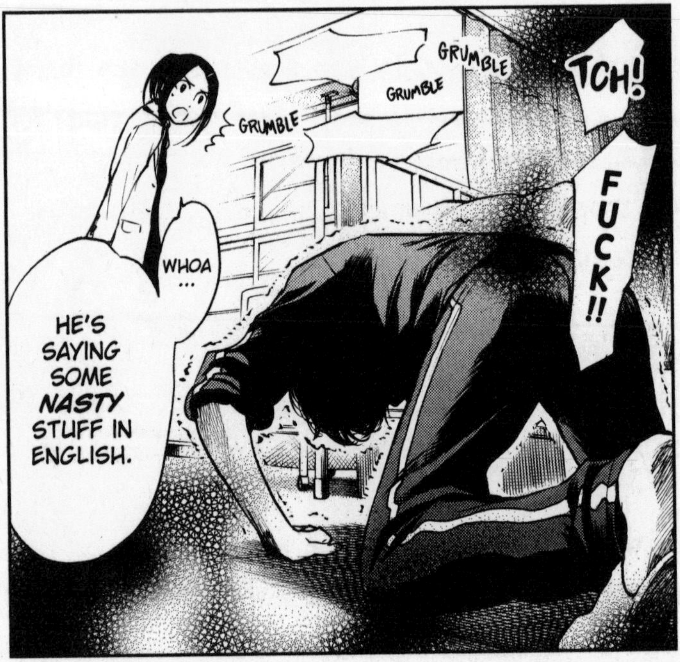
TCH!
FUCK!!
GRUMBLE
GRUMBLE
GRUMBLE
WHOA ...
HE'S SAYING SOME NASTY STUFF IN ENGLISH.

Okuma's English
Page 13

Okuma, having grown up partially overseas, frequently inserts English words into his speech. He seems to be particularly fond of profanity. Sometimes he speaks to himself in more elaborate English, which is indicated using angle brackets as below.

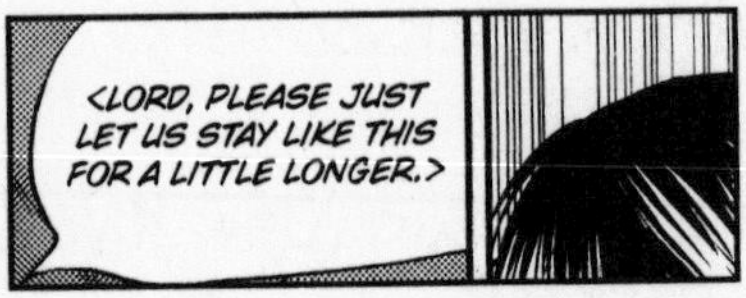
<LORD, PLEASE JUST LET US STAY LIKE THIS FOR A LITTLE LONGER.>

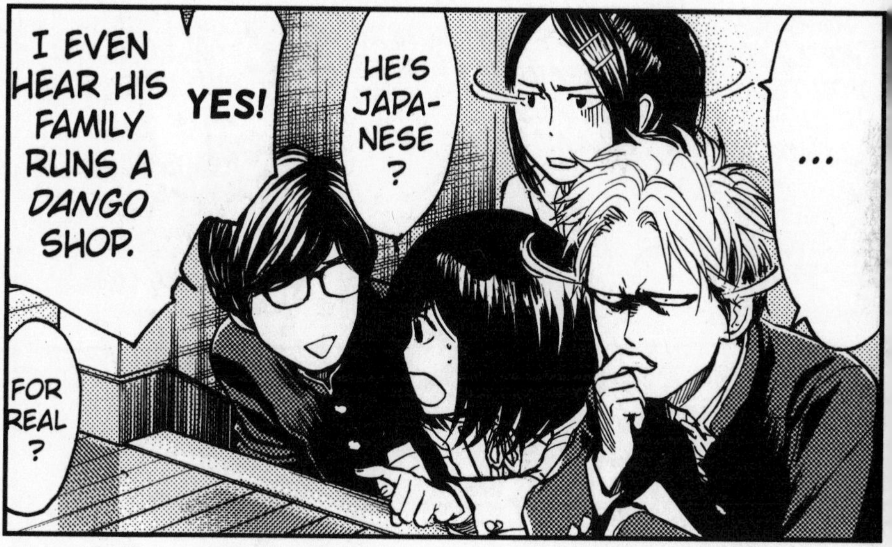
...
HE'S JAPA-NESE?
YES!
I EVEN HEAR HIS FAMILY RUNS A DANGO SHOP.
FOR REAL?

Dango Shop
Page 23

Dango are sweet Japanese dumplings made from rice flour and typically served on a skewer. Suga's family running one is so comically, wholesomely Japanese, that Okuma's statement here is akin to calling him "as American as apple pie."

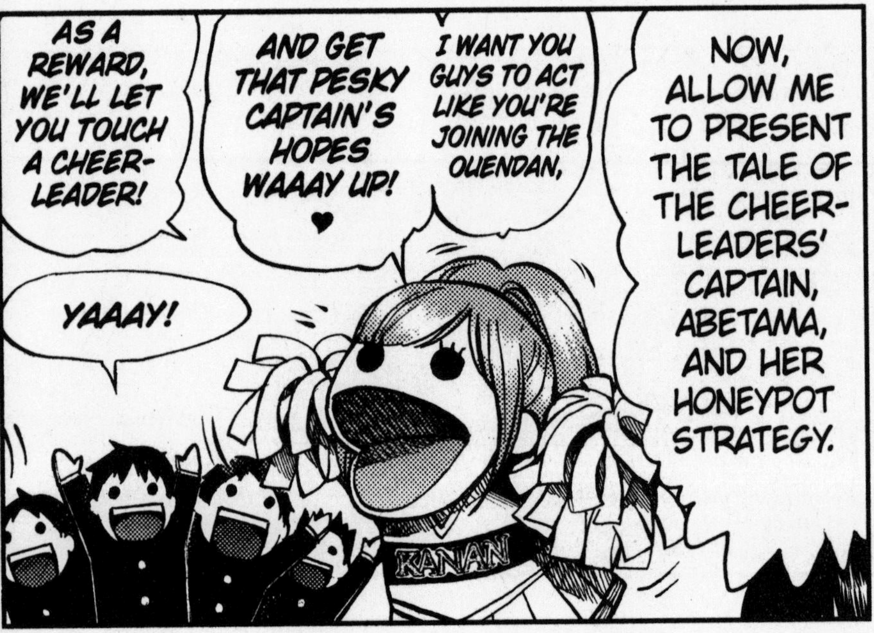
NOW, ALLOW ME TO PRESENT THE TALE OF THE CHEER-LEADERS' CAPTAIN, ABETAMA, AND HER HONEYPOT STRATEGY.
I WANT YOU GUYS TO ACT LIKE YOU'RE JOINING THE OUENDAN,
AND GET THAT PESKY CAPTAIN'S HOPES WAAAY UP! ♥
AS A REWARD, WE'LL LET YOU TOUCH A CHEER-LEADER!
YAAAY!
KANAN

Abetama
Page 23

This is a portmanteau of Tamaki Abe's first and last names. Calling her this comes across as somewhat denigrating.

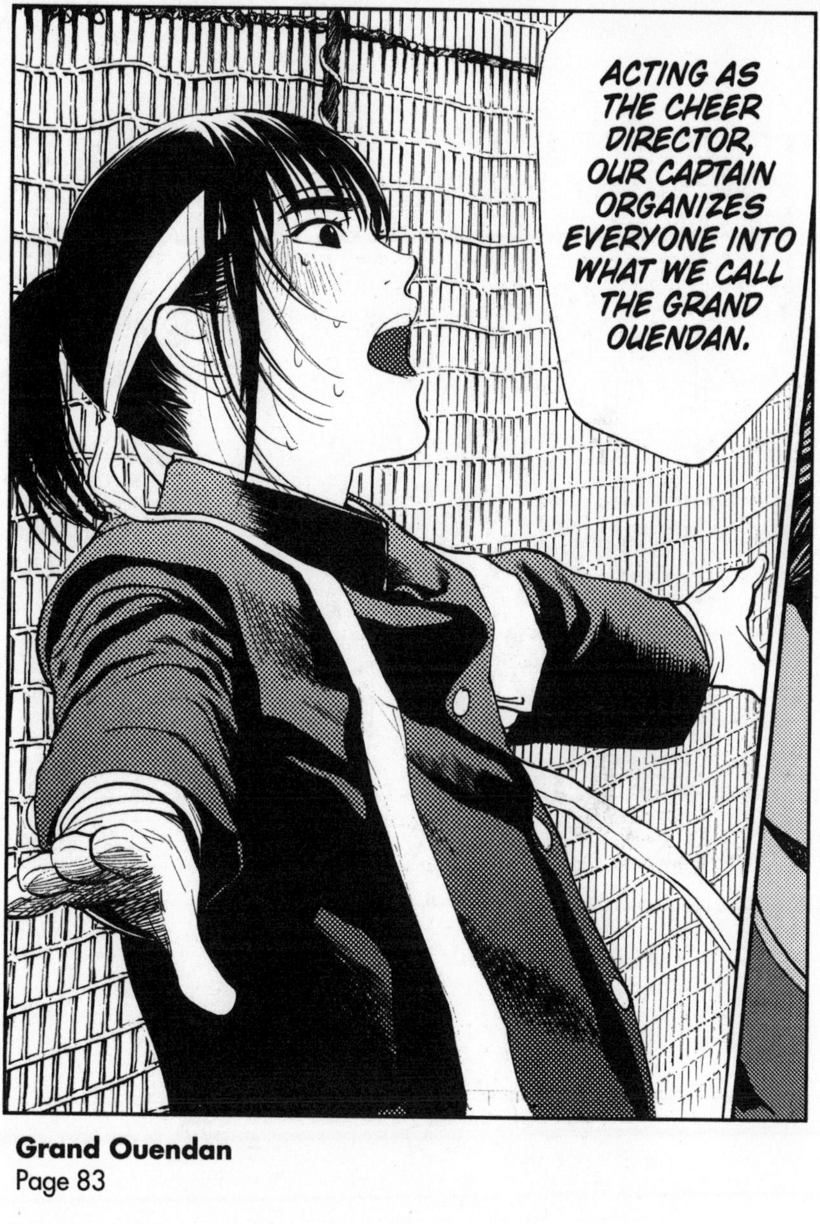
ACTING AS THE CHEER DIRECTOR, OUR CAPTAIN ORGANIZES EVERYONE INTO WHAT WE CALL THE GRAND OUENDAN.

Grand Ouendan
Page 83

Rendered literally, ouendan translates as "cheering group," or depending on the context, one might even translate it as "support group." When Okuma says that the cheer director organizes everyone into the "grand ouendan," he's not referring to a specific club called the ouendan, but something larger than the club itself that serves the same purpose on a greater scale.

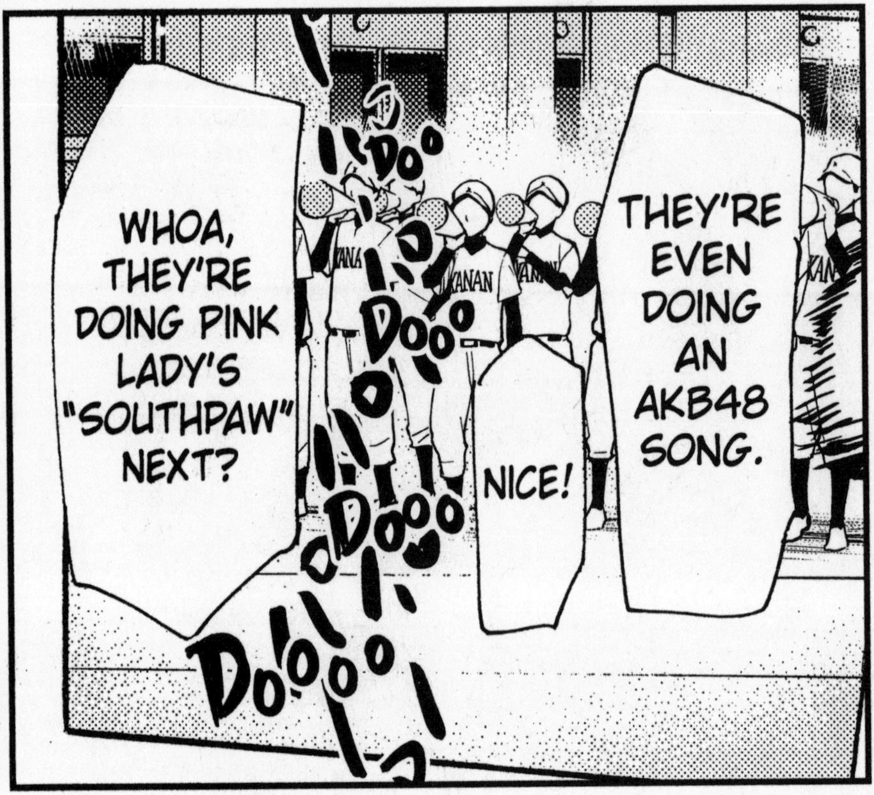
THEY'RE EVEN DOING AN AKB48 SONG.
NICE!
WHOA, THEY'RE DOING PINK LADY'S "SOUTHPAW" NEXT?
DOO
DOOO
DOOOO
DOOOO

AKB48 and Pink Lady
Page 138

AKB48 is a 48-member pop ensemble based in the Akihabara district of Tokyo, whose die-hard fans have helped it dominate the pop charts in the 2010s. Pink Lady, meanwhile, was a pop duo whose heydey was the late '70s and early '80s, and whose style and presentation was partially responsible for defining the "idol" style of pop star, of which AKB48 is only the latest incarnation.

I'M GONNA GO ON 2CHAN AND REVEAL WHAT HAPPENS NEXT IN HUNTER × HUNTER IN THE SHONEN JUMP DISCUSSION THREAD!
I'LL SPOIL EVERY-THING!
575:11/05/14( )15:38
[sage]
Is it true that, while Togashi sensei was taking a break from Hunter × Hunter, he wrote fifty one-offs' worth of early drafts to be shown only to the editorial staff?
576:11/05/14( )15:45
[sage]
>>520
"It'll come back into serialization in August."
TAK
TAK
TAKK

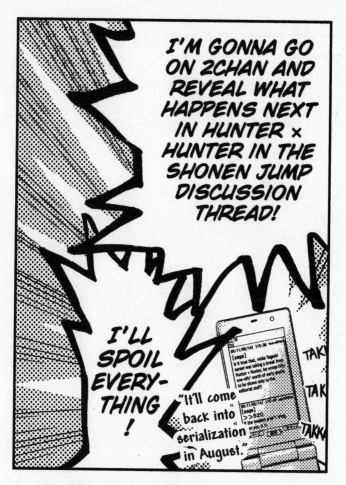

2chan, Hunter x Hunter
Page 163

2chan is a huge discussion forum that's central to Japanese internet culture. *Hunter x Hunter*, meanwhile, is Yoshihiro Togashi's long-running, critically acclaimed shonen manga. If you wanted to post spoilers to make a bunch of fans on the internet very angry, this would be a good way to do it.

you enjoyed Mitsurou Kubo's *AGAIN!!*, then you'll like...
MOTEKI
Love Strikes!
Yukiyo Fujimoto's life has been in a rut. He is about to turn 30 and has never held a steady job or had a girlfriend. When the prospects for hope seem to be at their lowest, out of the blue he is contacted by several women from his past! Yukiyo may seem to have more romantic options than he can handle, but is he ready for love? The stage for love might be set, but the time might only be ripe for him to finally grow up!
Volume 1 available from
Vertical Comics in April 2018!
438 pages | $18.95 U.S./ 19.95 CAN | ISBN 9781945054808
Mitsurou Kubo/Kodansha, Ltd.
www.vertical-comics.com

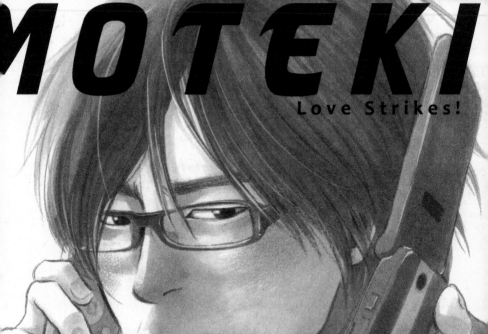

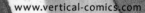

Aho-Girl

\\'ahôˌg rl\\ *Japanese, noun.*
A clueless girl.

**Anime now
available on
Crunchyroll!**

   **AHO-
GIRL**

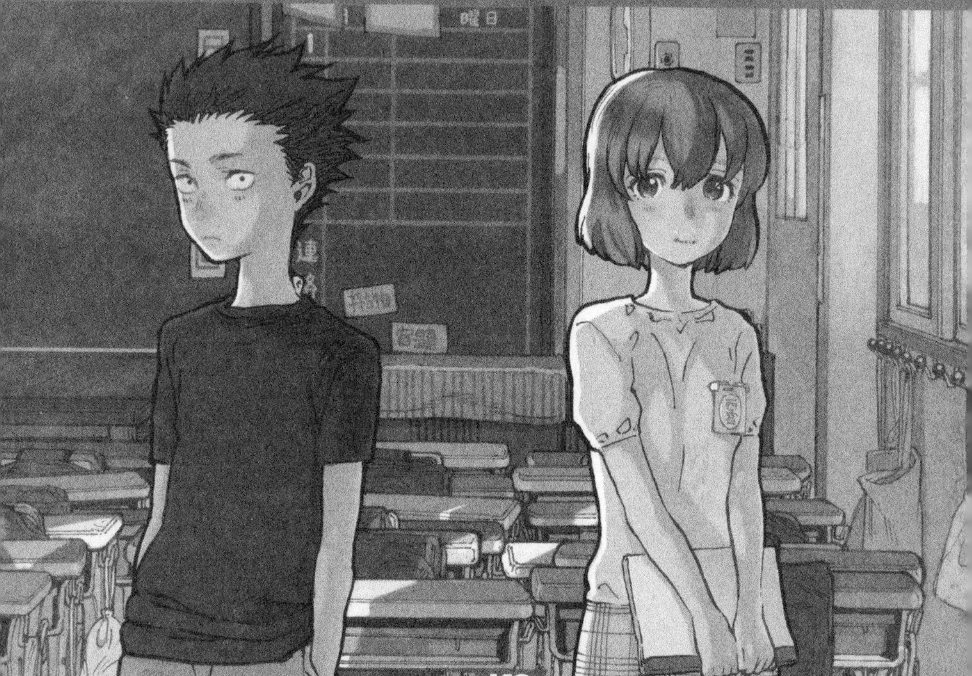

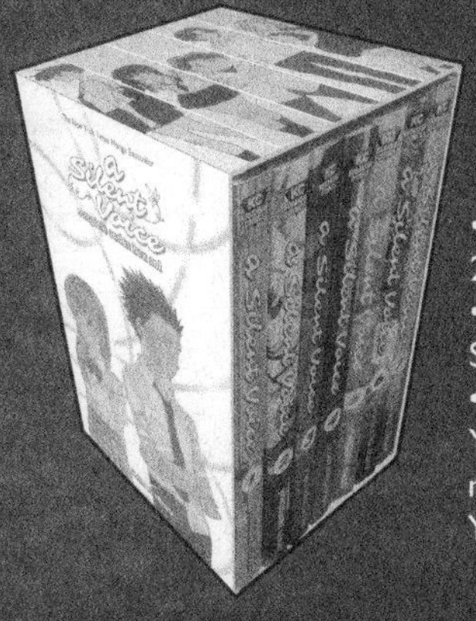

17 years after the original *Cardcaptor Sakura* manga ended, CLAMP returns with more magical adventures from a beloved manga classic!

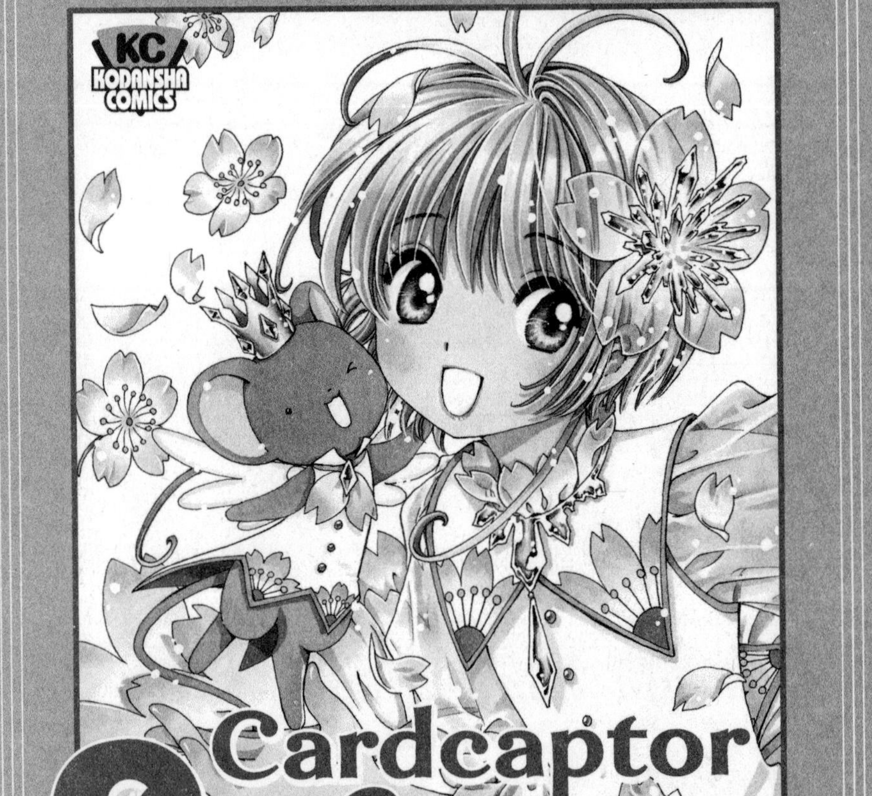
KC
KODANSHA COMICS
Cardcaptor
Sakura
CLEAR CARD

Sakura Kinomoto's about to start middle school, and everything's coming up cherry blossoms. Not only has she managed to recapture the scattered Clow Cards and make them her own Sakura Cards, but her sweetheart Syaoran Li has moved from Hong Kong to Tokyo and is going to be in her class! But her joy is interrupted by a troubling dream in which the cards turn transparent, and when Sakura awakens to discover her dream has become reality, it's clear that her magical adventures are far from over...

DELUXE EDITION

BATTLE ANGEL ALITA

After more than a decade out of print, the original cyberpunk action classic returns in glorious 400-page hardcover deluxe editions, featuring an all-new translation, color pages, and new cover designs!

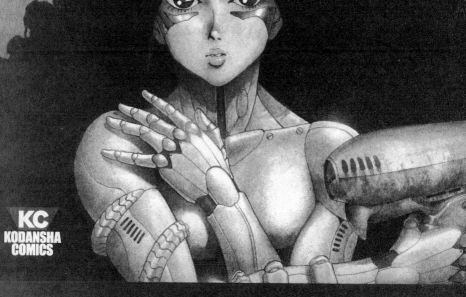

KC
KODANSHA
COMICS

Far beneath the shimmering space-city of Zalem lie the trash-heaps of The Scrapyard... Here, cyber-doctor and bounty hunter Daisuke Ido finds the head and torso of an amnesiac cyborg girl. He names her Alita and vows to fill her life with beauty, but in a moment of desperation, a fragment of Alita's mysterious past awakens in her. She discovers that she possesses uncanny prowess in the legendary martial art known as panzerkunst. With her newfound skills, Alita decides to become a hunter-warrior - tracking down and taking out those who prey on the weak. But can she hold onto her humanity in the dark and gritty world of The Scrapyard?

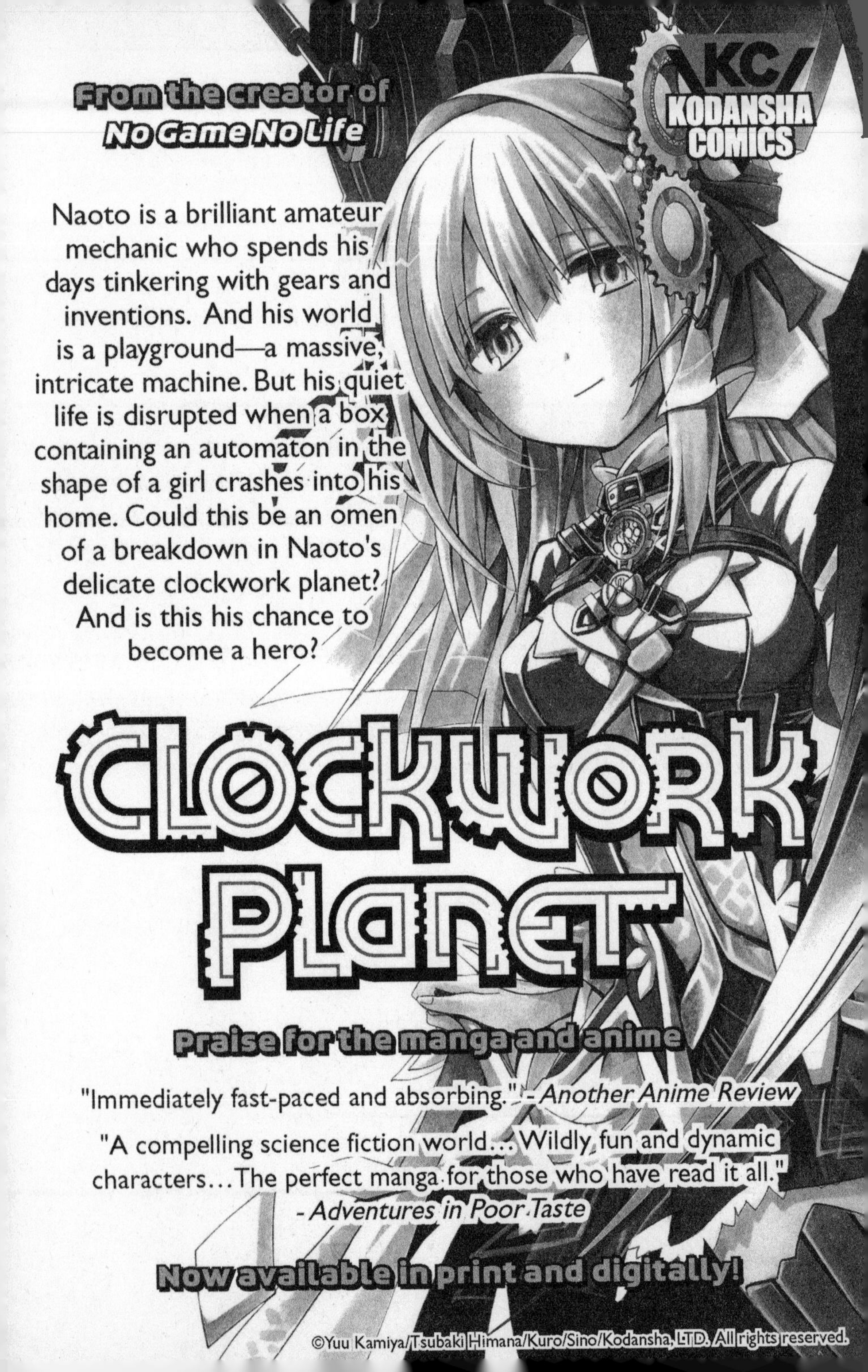
KC KODANSHA COMICS
From the creator of
No Game No Life
Naoto is a brilliant amateur mechanic who spends his days tinkering with gears and inventions. And his world is a playground—a massive, intricate machine. But his quiet life is disrupted when a box containing an automaton in the shape of a girl crashes into his home. Could this be an omen of a breakdown in Naoto's delicate clockwork planet? And is this his chance to become a hero?
CLOCKWORK PLANET
Praise for the manga and anime
"Immediately fast-paced and absorbing." - Another Anime Review
"A compelling science fiction world... Wildly fun and dynamic characters...The perfect manga for those who have read it all." - Adventures in Poor Taste
Now available in print and digitally!
©Yuu Kamiya/Tsubaki Himana/Kuro/Sino/Kodansha, LTD. All rights reserved.

The award-winning manga about what happens inside you!

"Far more entertaining than it ought to be... wha
kid doesn't want to think that every time they
sneeze a torpedo shoots out their nose?"
—Anime News Network

Strep throat! Hay fever! Influenza
The world is a dangerous place for
a red blood cell just trying to get her
deliveries finished. Fortunately,
she's not alone...she's got a
whole human body's worth of
cells ready to help out! The
mysterious white blood
cells, the buff and brash
killer T cells, even the
cute little platelets—
everyone's got to
come together if
they want to keep you
healthy!

Cells at Work!

はたらく細胞

By Akane Shimizu

The Black Museum: The Ghost and the Lady

By Kazuhiro Fujita

Deep in Scotland Yard in London sits an evidence room dedicated to the greatest mysteries of British history. In this "Black Museum" sits a misshapen hunk of lead—two bullets fused together—the key to a wartime encounter between Florence Nightingale, the mother of modern nursing, and a supernatural Man in Grey. This story is unknown to most scholars of history, but a special guest of the museum will tell the tale of The Ghost and the Lady...

Praise for Kazuhiro Fujita's *Ushio and Tora*

"A charming revival that combines a classic look with modern depth and pacing... **Essential viewing both for curmudgeons and new fans alike.**" — Anime News Network

"GREAT! The first episode of Ushio and Tora captures the essence of '90s anime." — IGN

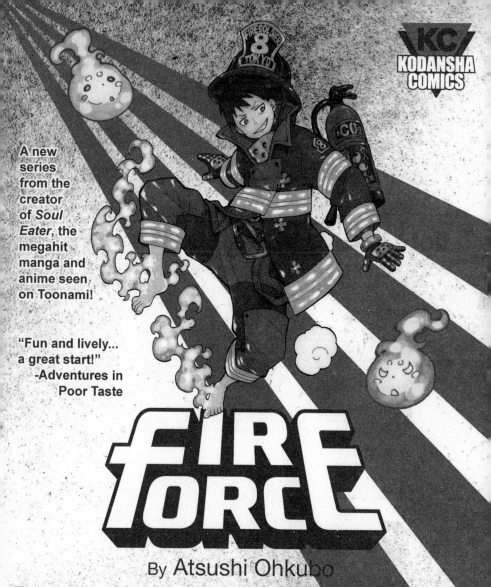

A new series from the creator of *Soul Eater*, the megahit manga and anime seen on Toonami!

"Fun and lively... a great start!"
-Adventures in Poor Taste

FIRE FORCE

By Atsushi Ohkubo

The city of Tokyo is plagued by a deadly phenomenon: spontaneous human combustion! Luckily, a special team is there to quench the inferno: The Fire Force! The fire soldiers at Special Fire Cathedral 8 are about to get a unique addition. Enter Shinra, a boy who possesses the power to run at the speed of a rocket, leaving behind the famous "devil's footprints" (and destroying his shoes in the process). Can Shinra and his colleagues discover the source of this strange epidemic before the city burns to ashes?

Japan's most powerful spirit medium delves into the ghost world's greatest mysteries!

Story by Kyo Shirodaira, famed author of mystery fiction and creator of *Spiral*, *Blast of Tempest*, and *The Record of a Fallen Vampire*.

Both touched by spirits called yôkai, Kotoko and Kurô have gained unique superhuman powers. But to gain her powers Kotoko has given up an eye and a leg, and Kurô's personal life is in shambles. So when Kotoko suggests they team up to deal with renegades from the spirit world, Kurô doesn't have many other choices, but Kotoko might just have a few ulterior motives...

IN/SPECTRE

STORY BY **KYO SHIRODAIRA**
ART BY **CHASHIBA KATASE**

HAPPINESS

ハピネス

By Shuzo Oshimi

From the creator of *The Flowers of Evil*

Nothing interesting is happening in Makoto Ozaki's first year of high school. His life is a series of quiet humiliations: low-grade bullies, unreliable friends, and the constant frustration of his adolescent lust. But one night, a pale, thin girl knocks him to the ground in an alley and offers him a choice. Now everything is different. Daylight is searingly bright. Food tastes awful. And worse than anything is the terrible, consuming thirst...

Praise for Shuzo Oshimi's *The Flowers of Evil*

"A shockingly readable story that vividly—one might even say queasily—evokes the fear and confusion of discovering one's own sexuality. Recommended." —The Manga Critic

"A page-turning tale of sordid middle school blackmail." —Otaku USA Magazine

"A stunning new horror manga." —Third Eye Comics

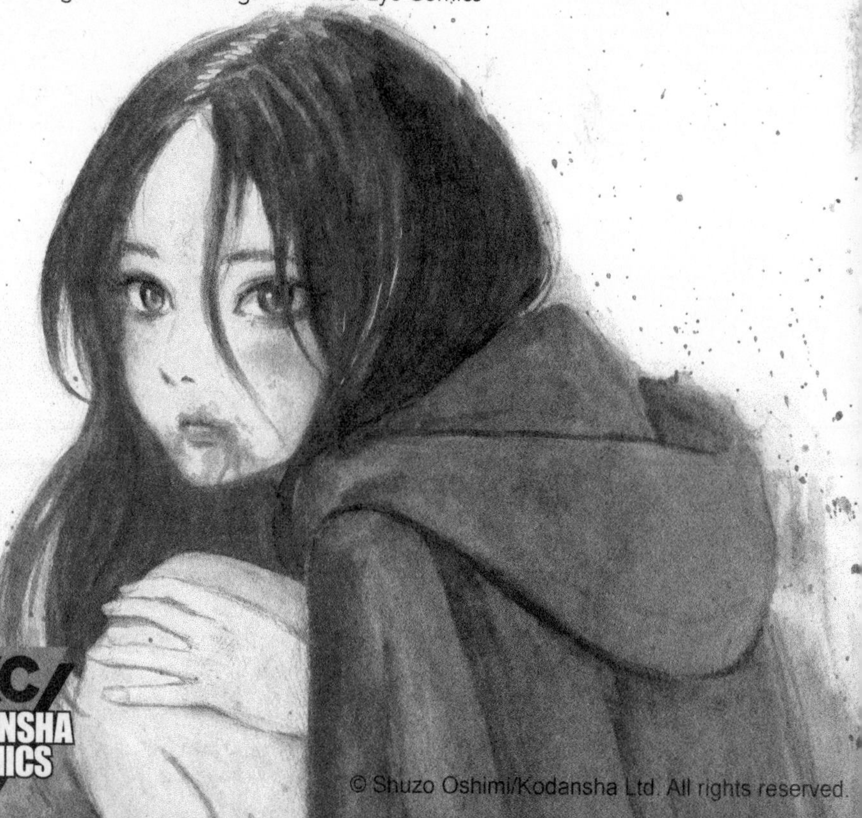

KC KODANSHA COMICS

Based on the critically acclaimed classic horror manga

The first new *Parasyte* manga in over 20 years!

NEO PARASYTE *f*

BY ASUMIKO NAKAMURA, EMA TOYAMA, MIKI RINNO, LALAKO KOJIMA, KAORI YUKI, BANKO KUZE, YUUKI OBATA, KASHIO, YUI KUROE, ASIA WATANABE, MIKIMAKI, HIKARU SURUGA, HAJIME SHINJO, RENJURO KINDAICHI, AND YURI NARUSHIMA

A collection of chilling new *Parasyte* stories from Japan's top shojo artists!

Parasites: shape-shifting aliens whose only purpose is to assimilate with and consume the human race... but do these monsters have a different side? A parasite becomes a prince to save his romance-obsessed female host from a dangerous stalker. Another hosts a cooking show, in which the real monsters are revealed. These and 13 more stories, from some of the greatest shojo manga artists alive today, together make up a chilling, funny, and entertaining tribute to one of manga's horror classics!

KC
KODANSHA
COMICS

New action series from Hiroyuki Takei, creator of the classic shonen franchise Shaman King!

In medieval Japan, a bell hanging on the collar is a sign that a cat has a master. Norachiyo's bell hangs from his katana sheath, but he is nonetheless a stray — a ronin. This one-eyed cat samurai travels across a dishonest world, cutting through pretense and deception with his blade.

Nekogahara
STRAY CAT SAMURAI

By
Hiroyuki Takei

A Kodansha Comics Trade Paperback Original.

Published in the United States by Kodansha Comics, an imprint of Kodansha USA Publishing, LLC, New York.

Publication rights for this English edition arranged through Kodansha Ltd., Tokyo.

First published in Japan in 2011 by Kodansha Ltd., Tokyo, as *Agein!!* volume 2.

ISBN 978-1-63236-646-7

Printed in the United States of America.

www.kodanshacomics.com

9 8 7 6 5 4 3 2 1

Translator: Rose Padgett
Lettering: E. K. Weaver
Editing: Paul Starr
Editorial Assistance: Tiff Ferentini
Kodansha Comics edition cover design by Phil Balsman